PELICAN BOOKS

SERMONS AND SOCIETY

Advisory Editor: Professor D. Nineham

Paul A. Welsby was born in 1920. He graduated from University College, Durham, in 1942, and was awarded a Ph.D. from Sheffield University in 1958. He attended Lincoln Theological College and was ordained in 1944, after which he was curate of Boxley, Kent, for three years. He then became curate of St Mary-le-Tower, Ipswich (1947–52). From 1952 until 1966 he was Rector of three country parishes in Suffolk. He has been a Proctor of Convocation since 1964, and Canon Residentiary of Rochester Cathedral, Examining Chaplain to the Bishop of Rochester, and Director of Post Ordination Training in the Diocese of Rochester since 1966. For the last fourteen years he has lectured on historical and theological subjects for the Workers' Educational Association and for Adult Education, both in Suffolk and Kent. He has been involved in journalistic work over the past ten years, and is the author of the following books: *Lancelot Andrewes, 1555–1626* (1958); *George Abbot: The Unwanted Archbishop, 1562–1633* (1962); *How the Church of England Works* (1960); *The Bond of Church and State* (1962); *History of the National Society, 1870–1961* (1961).

SERMONS AND SOCIETY

An Anglican Anthology

EDITED BY
PAUL A. WELSBY

PENGUIN BOOKS

Penguin Books Ltd, Harmondsworth, Middlesex, England
Penguin Books Inc., 7110 Ambassodor Road, Baltimore, Maryland 21207, U.S.A.
Penguin Books Australia Ltd, Ringwood, Victoria, Australia

—

First published 1970

—

Copyright © Paul A. Welsby, 1970

—

Made and printed in Great Britain by
Cox & Wyman Ltd, London, Reading and Fakenham
Set in Monotype Plantin

TO
THE DEAN AND CHAPTER OF ROCHESTER

CONTENTS

CONTENTS

PREFACE

THE object of this anthology is to illustrate the attitude of Anglican preachers, from the Reformation onwards, towards social conditions in this country. In the process of reading their sermons we can also see, through the eyes of the preacher, what life in England was like at the time the sermon was preached. In other words, this selection of passages is both descriptive of what the social, economic or educational system was like and also a witness to the attitude of the Established Church towards that situation – whether it accepted the *status quo*, whether it approved of reform, whether it was active in promoting reform. There are, however, two limiting factors which must be taken into account. First, the selection is confined to preachers of the Established Church and thus no account is taken of the social consciousness of dissenting preachers and their Churches. This can be justified by the requirements of space and also – more importantly – by the fact that the Church of England throughout this period was the largest Christian body and the National Church. The second limitation is that, the selection being confined to sermons, it would be unfair to judge the Church of England's social consciousness, or lack of it, from this alone, for many Anglicans proclaimed their views in pamphlets, in books, and in lectures, rather than in the pulpit.

I would like to thank the following for allowing me to remove from the institutions under their care a large number of volumes in order that extracts might be photographed: the President and Court of Governors of Sion College, the Trustees of Dr Williams's Library, the Dean and Chapter of Rochester Cathedral, and the Warden of Rochester Theological College.

I would also like to record my indebtedness for assistance of various kinds to the following: Mr Patrick Collinson, Miss M. Hammond, Professor D. E. Nineham, the Rev. H. D. Rack and the Venerable C. J. Stranks. I am grateful to the publishers for their help and courtesy, both in the preparation and the publishing of the work. Above all, I acknowledge my greatest debt – to my wife, for her invaluable help in correlating material and in the production of the final manuscript.

PAUL A. WELSBY

Rochester
May 1970

INTRODUCTION

WHEN a man is ordained to the priesthood in the Church of England he is charged to be 'a faithful dispenser of the Word of God' and is given authority 'to preach the Word of God'. This makes explicit what is implicit in the whole conception of the Christian ministry – that it is a ministry of the Word as well as a ministry of the Sacraments. From the time of Jesus Christ himself the Church has been a preaching Church and this function has been based upon certain theological convictions which, although they stem primarily from Jesus Christ, are linked with certain pre-Christian, Old Testament, insights. The Old Testament conviction was that God had a Word to communicate to his People and that through this Word he revealed his mind, will, and purpose to them. This Word, moreover, was not an abstraction or a body of teaching but was declared in the events of history. Because this was so, his Word required interpretation. In the Old Testament the 'mighty acts of God' in history were interpreted by the prophets, whose mission was to tell forth God's Word as it was revealed in the historical events of their day.

When 'the fulness of time' came, God no longer spoke his word to men, as in times past, through the prophets, but through his Son. 'The Word became flesh and dwelt among us' (John i, 14). All that the Word of God had been *saying* in the Old Testament was now *seen in action* in a Person. Jesus, the Word of God, moved among men, revealing to them God, in his own Person, in his actions and in his words. Since the Ascension, the Word of the Lord, 'the Word made flesh', has been proclaimed by the Church. In each age the Church proclaims the Word of God in terms intelligible to that generation, but it is the same Word of God as was disclosed in his mighty acts, interpreted by the prophets and focused in the Person of Jesus Christ. Preaching, in the words of Herbert Farmer, is ' God's great activity of redemption in history, in the world of persons, focusing itself in challenge and succour on "these persons here present"".*

This is the theology underlying all preaching. Because of this, Christian preaching must declare certain truths concerning the events and circumstances of history contemporaneous with the preacher, for it must look at history and society as they exist at a particular time and in a particular place and declare whatever within them bears witness to the will and purpose of God and whatever within them is contrary to the will and purpose of God. In this respect the Christian preacher is the direct heir of the Hebrew prophet, for the latter, when he declared the Word of God as revealed in the events of his day, passed judgement upon contemporary society. God, proclaimed Amos, Hosea, Micah, Isaiah and the rest, is righteous and faithful and just. Therefore, they continued, God requires righteousness, faithfulness and justice from his worshippers, not only in their personal relationships, but also in political, economic and social life. Consequently, social injustice, economic oppression, judicial perversion are some of the targets for prophetic attack. The Christian preacher has certain specific Christian insights which add edge to *his* attack upon such social injustices. He worships a Lord who, in his days on earth, was concerned with healing the bodies of those who were sick and with feeding those who were hungry. Indeed, the fact that, according to Christian belief, God in Christ took a human body, walked this earth and shared in human relationships, was sufficient to inspire Christians with a concern for the material situations in which men live on this earth. Moreover, it is quite clear that Christ's command, 'Thou shalt love thy neighbour as thyself', has implications in the social, political, and economic fields. If we take with all this the fact that a central feature of Christ's teaching was the conception of the Kingdom of God as the sphere where men allow God to rule, and that the kingdom consists of those who acknowledge and accept God's claim upon their lives and who try to do his will in the world – then a Christian who prays, 'Thy kingdom come', is committed to do all he can to make that kingdom more of a reality in social, political and economic life. Finally, Christians hold certain views about the

* Herbert Farmer, *The Servant of the Word*, Nisbet, 1941, p. 29.

nature of the world and the nature of man which have serious implications in the realms of social, political and economic affairs.

Those are some of the Christian convictions which contribute to 'the social gospel' which each Christian preacher in every age has a duty to proclaim. Consequently, if we examine the extant sermons of preachers in other ages we can learn much about the social habits, the economic circumstances and the sociological outlook pertaining to the age in which they preached. In the process we also obtain an insight into the preacher's own attitude, and thus into that of the Church (or the group within the Church), which he represents, towards these phenomena. Such a study also reveals how often the judgement of preachers and of a whole Church may be prejudiced by contemporary social and economic values and presuppositions and how, as a result, the just proportion of the Gospel which they are committed to preach becomes warped and misdirected by sociological factors. What many of them said in judgement upon the society of their day becomes in turn a judgement upon themselves and the Church of which they are the mouthpieces.

For most of the period covered by this anthology church-going was part of the social life of the nation. Consequently, as W. K. Jordan points out, the sermon 'was without doubt the most important single instrumentality for the moulding of thought, the forming of resolution'.* This had an effect upon the individual which was greater than can be measured. As Professor Butterfield has written:

The ordinary historian, when he comes, shall we say, to the year 1800 does not think to point out to his readers that in this year, still, as in so many previous years, thousands and thousands of priests and ministers were preaching the Gospel week in and week out, constantly reminding the farmer and the shopkeeper of charity and humility, persuading them to think for a moment about the great issues of life, and inducing them to confess their sins. Yet this was a phenomenon calculated greatly to alter the quality of life and the very texture of human history.†

* W. K. Jordan, *Philanthropy in England, 1480-1660*, Allen & Unwin, 1959, p. 156.

† H. Butterfield, *Christianity and History*, Bell, 1949, p. 131.

There can be little doubt that in the sixteenth and seventeenth centuries the effectiveness of preaching bore fruit in shaping the social vision which directed the responsibility and generosity of men of influence towards the relief of those whom we today would regard as the victims of the social and economic system. It also inculcated in the minds of men the dogma that duly-constituted kings and governments were of divine appointment and that rebellion was a deadly sin against God; that the division of society into classes was a blessing of Providence and that to attack or to attempt to change the order of society was blasphemous; that wealth was a privilege and a responsibility and that poverty could be a blessing. Consequently, control of the pulpit was of considerable political and social importance, comparable with control of press and radio today. 'Those who hold the helm of the pulpit,' said Thomas Fuller, 'always steer the people's hearts as they please.' Francis Bacon declared that there would be 'a perpetual disaffection except you keep men in by preaching as well as the law doth by punishing.'* For the majority of Englishmen the sermon was the main source of political information and political ideas and of guidance on political, social and economic conduct. Thus, Cromwell's Injunctions of 1536 instructed the clergy to preach on the royal supremacy twice a year, and the Visitation Articles of 1559 ask whether ministers 'have exhorted the people to obedience to the Queen's majesty and ministers'. James I instructed preachers in London to point their sermons at certain social evils, such as 'the insolency of our women' and their 'undesirable attire', with the result that John Chamberlain wrote in a letter that 'our pulpits ring continually of the insolence and impudence of women' so that they 'can come nowhere but their ears tingle'.† The sermons at Paul's Cross, the most notable preaching platform in London and the resort (in the words of one contemporary) 'of every orator under heaven', were almost official government pronouncements, for the preacher was appointed by the Bishop of London or by some government official. The Paul's Cross sermons had become an institution by 1316

* Quoted in C. Hill, *Reformation to Industrial Revolution*, Weidenfeld & Nicolson, 1967, p. 88.
† *Letters*, edited J. E. McClure, 1939, II, p. 289.

and were a gathering-place, not only for Londoners, but for visitors 'up from the country'. These sermons, together with the Spittal Sermons,* most of which were published, are a window through which we glimpse a picture of social conditions in the sixteenth and seventeenth centuries and of the Church's attitude towards them.†

The early post-Reformation preachers were concerned about the administration of justice and they castigate those magistrates who take bribes and favour the rich. Women with a taste for fine clothes, cosmetics and extravagant hair styles arouse disapproval. Public officials are charged with lack of upright conduct. The preachers detect the root sin of covetousness lying behind these evils, which also manifests itself in the practice of usury and in the extortions of landlords, who enclose, engross and shamefully rack-rent their tenants. Theatres are condemned, not only because they are the resort of immoral persons and breeding places for the plague, but also because more people are attracted by them than by sermons! Gluttony and drunkenness, brothels and gaming, the breaking of the Sabbath and indifference to church-going – these were perennial themes. Indeed, portraits of blasphemers, vain women, usurers and corrupt judges became almost a convention for Paul's Cross preachers. Not even the congregation was spared. Civic dignitaries, as they sat in their galleries around the pulpit, were at times rebuked for their 'costly robes and golden chains'.

Although these social judgements were made in the name of the Christian Gospel, much of what was said was influenced by sociological and political, rather than theological, factors. This remained a characteristic of Anglican preaching for three centuries, for there is little evidence that Christian preachers passed judgement upon the actual framework of society. The Hammonds were justified in saying that 'Christianity was not a standard by which to

---

* Preached from the pulpit cross in the courtyard of St Mary's Hospital, without Bishopsgate, on Easter Monday, Tuesday and Wednesday, and attended by the Mayor and Corporation of London.

† See M. Maclure, *The Paul's Cross Sermons 1534-1642*, Oxford University Press, 1958, and H. Gareth Owen, 'Paul's Cross; The Broadcasting House of Elizabethan London', in *History Today*, December 1942.

judge the institutions of society, but a reason for accepting them.'
Preachers were but children of their age, and for most of our period
the prevailing view was that one might as well try to stop the wind
as to try to change economic laws. Those few who thought otherwise had to persuade the Church itself that economic laws were
not immutable before they could proclaim this gospel to society
with conviction.

It was this situation which led R. H. Tawney to make his well-
known comment that from the sixteenth century 'the social
teaching of the Church had ceased to count, because the Church
itself had ceased to think'.* Before the rise of capitalism and
modern industry, the Church, possessed of a gospel which had
implications for the *whole* life of man, political, economic and
social as well as personal, had certain criteria which it used to commend or judge those areas of human life. In the Middle Ages, for
example, society was regarded as an organism and religion embraced all aspects of human activity within the organism. The
organism was composed of different groups of people, each with
its own function – prayer, defence, trade, tilling the soil. Within
classes there must be equality but between classes there must be
inequality. It is true that in practice this did not work out quite
as idyllically, for exploitation was common under the feudal
system and the Church itself was part of the system. The secular
class structure, the inequalities of wealth and status, and the
hierarchical outlook were reproduced within the Church itself.

Nevertheless, medieval religious thought was adamant on
certain aspects of social and economic life. It affirmed strongly the
Doctrine of the Just Price and the Prohibition of Usury. According
to the first, the price of an article should be fixed on moral grounds,
with due regard to the cost of materials and labour and to reasonable profit; the seller was not entitled merely to ask the utmost
that the purchaser would pay; in particular he must never charge
more because the buyer's need was great. According to the second,
'to take usury is contrary to Scripture; it is contrary to Aristotle;
it is contrary to nature, for it is to live without labour.'† Both these

* R. H. Tawney, *Religion and the Rise of Capitalism*, Pelican edition, 1938,
p. 171.
   † ibid., p. 55.

conceptions well fitted an age when buying and selling were local transactions and when loans were not required for capital transactions.

The latter part of the Middle Ages saw the beginning of the process which, in the seventeenth century, led to a far more complex economic system and one in which neither the Just Price nor the Prohibition of Usury were easily applicable. Thus, the economic and commercial classes became impatient with the medieval ecclesiastical restrictions on their activities. When goods came from the ends of the earth, who could fix the Just Price ? How was the Prohibition of Usury applicable when it was no longer a case of the wealthy making cruel use of the necessities of an impoverished neighbour who required a loan, but a well-to-do man making use of his surplus wealth to finance a commercial enterprise which could bring about the economic well-being of society as a whole. If a man was prepared to risk his money in such an enterprise, was he not entitled to some return ?

Unfortunately, religious opinion remained conservative and made no real attempt to face the new situation. The Church was preoccupied with its own doctrinal and ecclesiastical struggles and was left floundering in a backward-looking, medieval outlook which became more and more irrelevant to society. Because it failed to translate the traditional social teaching into terms applicable to an age of capitalism, world markets and impersonal finance, the Church, officially, had little to contribute to social thinking for two hundred and fifty years. That is not to say that during this period it possessed no social gospel, but that the implications of that gospel for society were unacknowledged. Nor does it imply that the Christian thinking of groups and individuals within the Church had no influence upon society. On the whole, however, it was not until the beginning of the present century that the Church once again began to make a positive contribution to social thinking.

One of the economic problems upon which the post-Reformation preachers were vocal was the agrarian problem, or 'the Land Question', as it was called. Landlord and tenant farmer were enclosing the commons and converting arable to pasture, thus de-populating the villages and causing great hardship to evicted tenants. Coupled with this was the fact that when Henry VIII dissolved the monasteries, he failed to use the vast wealth that came to him as a result to assist education and to promote social justice, but squandered it on continental wars. It was from the pulpit that many of the complaints and challenges were made about the land question and the wasteful policy of King Henry. The most vocal were the so-called 'commonwealth men' – men like Hugh Latimer (I–V) and John Hales.

As these men flailed the ungodliness and inhumanity of their fellow-men, trouncing every iniquity, from merciless landlordism which oppressed the poor with fines, rack-rents, evictions and enclosures, to the tyranny of bishops and the bizarre, costly mysteries of the law (and much in between), so did they indignantly lament the betrayal of the Reformation from which they hoped so much.*

Some of these men had denounced the social abuses of the old order – the 'abbey lubbers' and the worldly prelates. Now they laid about the new with even greater violence. So, for example, Thomas Lever attacked the recipients of the monastic wealth (see X).

How much of this, however, reveals any attempt on the part of the preacher to understand the complexities of the changing economic order? As J. J. Scarisbrick has pointed out, 'what they denounced as mere greed and heartlessness was probably more often than not a legitimate desire of landlords struggling to hold their own against inflation, to improve their circumstances by raising rents, enclosing etc.'† The problem was that the Church, through her preachers, still treated every commercial transaction and every economic situation as a case of personal conduct involving personal responsibility. In an age of impersonal finance this was too simple a diagnosis of a complex situation and the traditional social doctrines, which were expressed in terms of an individualist ethic, needed re-thinking on new lines. This the Church failed to do (see XV).

The result of this failure was that such judgements as the Church passed on social affairs really dealt with the by-products

*J. J. Scarisbrick, *Henry VIII*, Eyre & Spottiswoode, 1968, p. 523.
† ibid., p. 524.

and the results of economic and social developments rather than with the developments themselves. The old medieval doctrines were quietly dropped and Churchmen came to assume that economic affairs operated according to their own independent principles, and that riches and poverty were part of the divine plan. There was genuine solicitude for the poor, particularly for their spiritual welfare, and there was condemnation for some of the more extreme cruelties of the system – but the system itself was unchallenged. Indeed, success in business became a mark of divine approval and the very qualities which were most conducive to commercial success – thrift, moderation, diligence, sobriety – were the ones most extolled by Christian preachers. Idleness was the greatest of evils and often the really poor were regarded as the victims, not of circumstances or of the system, but of their own shiftlessness and dishonesty. The 'needy poor' should be helped only with great discrimination, for indiscriminate charity was a sin which undermined character, condoned idleness and encouraged wickedness. Moreover, higher wages would lead only to more idleness and wilfulness. Vagrants and beggars should be dealt with as harshly as possible by correction and by stern laws. Society had no responsibility for the causes of distress, for a man's situation in life was due to his own virtue or lack of it. The kind of thinking which emerges from a study of sermons from the sixteenth to the nineteenth century is that the poor are part of God's ordering of the world and the presence of the poor is necessary in order to remind the rich to be thankful for their wealth and to give them the opportunity of bestowing alms. The latter is a duty highly acceptable to God and the rich derive spiritual advantage from its exercise, for it cleanses their souls. In addition to being given the opportunity of showing the Christian spirit of love, the charitable man will still have enough and his charity will never bring him into want. Again, if all men were equal, there could be no government in the world; equality would breed confusion because no one would be prepared to obey an equal. Inequality is necessary for trade and industry, for the majority of men will not work unless compelled. This insistence 'on the virtues of contentedness and resignation, from a political point of view, was of great service to those men who wanted to see labourers ruthlessly exploited for the benefit of the national wealth, which was for the most part the wealth of the rich.'*

It is against this background that we must see the activities of those Puritans who led and inspired the positive and sustained attack upon the national problem of poverty. As W. K. Jordan has fully demonstrated, it was from the new commercial classes – merchants and middling gentry – that the inspiration arose.† In the words of Charles Smyth, 'from the Reformation onward the care of the poor – not merely the relief of poverty, but social rehabilitation, the provision of educational opportunities, apprenticeships and training in useful skills – became the central social preoccupation of the English middle classes.'‡ Much of the impetus for this philanthropy came from preachers and, as a result, household relief, almshouses, social rehabilitation of prisoners, hospitals for the sick and education of the poor were undertaken on a considerable scale.

It was in the field of education that the Church made its greatest contribution. Under its auspices charity schools were founded by the hundred all over England in the eighteenth century to educate the children of the poor in reading, writing, moral discipline and the principles of the Church of England. If today we criticize these early efforts because of the narrowness of the curriculum and because their protagonists saw their purpose as one of educating the poor to be docile and submissive, we must remember that there were at the time a large number of people who contended that education should not be offered to the poor lest it should give them better opportunities in life, thus making them discontented with their lot, which in turn might induce them to resort to revolutionary methods to overthrow the order of society. To this fear the advocates of the schools replied that the aim of education was to teach children to be 'industrious and frugal, sober and moderate, faithful and obedient', fitting them to be-

---

* R. B. Schlatter, *Social Ideas of Religious Leaders, 1660–1688*, Oxford University Press, 1940, p. 82.

† W. K. Jordan, *Philanthropy in England, 1480–1660*, Allen & Unwin, 1959, p. 156.

‡ Charles Smyth, *The Church and the Nation*, Hodder & Stoughton, 1962, p. 87.

come 'useful servants, good husbands and careful masters of a family'.* This is a constant theme of preachers at the large charity services held annually in the London churches. To this early charity school movement we must add the work done from 1811 onwards by the 'National Society for Educating the Poor according to the principles of the Church of England'. Thus, in spite of the absence of a satisfactory theological critique of society, the Church was responsible for the education of thousands of children at a time when the state did nothing.

Another field of Christian social action was the provision of hospitals for the sick. At the opening of the sixteenth century there was practically no organized system of help available for the treatment of sickness. This shocking situation was eloquently denounced by the preachers to such effect that the civic authorities of London began to organize and endow hospitals. W. K. Jordan points out that from 1560 onwards the tradition was well established that every London merchant of substance left at least something to one or more of the London hospitals. Not only were the physically ill cared for, but also the elderly and the mentally sick. The condition of the prisons and the treatment of discharged prisoners were other outlets for philanthropic benevolence.

The eighteenth century was the great era for founding 'religious societies' to care for the less fortunate members of society. Ford K. Brown has listed no less than some eighty hospitals, infirmaries, religious, moral, educational institutions and societies founded between 1700 and 1800.† They include hospitals for the physically and mentally ill, societies for the observance of the Lord's day, for the care of abandoned children, for the education of the poor, for the reception of penitent prostitutes, for widows, for the abolition of vice and immorality, etc. etc. Most of these societies held annual services at which a sermon was preached emphasizing the divine foundation of the work and appealing to the wealthy for funds. During the sermon the annual report of the society was read, and many of these sermons have given future

* Quoted in Michael Hennell, *John Venn and the Clapham Sect*, Lutterworth Press, 1958, p. 138.

† Ford K. Brown, *Fathers of the Victorians*, Cambridge University Press, 1961, pp. 329 ff.

generations an idea of the nature of the work undertaken by the societies, an insight into the motives behind their activities and a picture of the conditions they sought to relieve (see XXXII, XXXIII, XXXVIII, XLIV, LVIII).

With the coming of the Industrial Revolution, from the middle of the eighteenth century, accompanied by the rise of large and overcrowded towns and a factory system with appalling conditions and hours of work, reform was seriously impeded because of the unwillingness to attack where attack alone would be successful – the system itself. To this unwillingness the Church gave its blessing.

> The rich man in his castle,
> The poor man at his gate,
> God made them high and lowly,
> And ordered their estate.

Mrs C. F. Alexander was merely echoing in extreme form the words of the Prayer Book Catechism that it was a Christian's duty to 'order myself lowly and reverently to all my betters'. That was what every parish priest in England taught the children of his parish to repeat after him. Thus they learnt what it meant to be a Christian. Society being thus arranged by God, it was blasphemous to alter it. E. R. Wickham tells of Mr William Ibbotson, the owner of a Sheffield steel works, who, after a dispute in 1836, told his workmen:

'While the foreman gets his 30s. or 40s. the striker whose labour is more severe only receives his 20s. or 30s.; while he that has served apprenticeship obtains his 20s. to 30s., the learner and the mere labourer gets his 10s. to 18s. In all these cases the God of nature has established a just and equitable Law which man has no right to disturb. When he ventures to do so, it is always certain that he sooner or later meets with a corresponding punishment.'*

Even Thomas Arnold, who considered it intolerable that so little was done to relieve poverty and misery, saw the existing stratification of society as the only just and practical one. The aristocracy might at the moment be failing in their duty, but they

* E. R. Wickham, *Church and People in an Industrial City*, Lutterworth Press, 1957, p. 106.

were the cream of society and any change in the condition of the lower orders must come from above. 'I say quite plainly,' he wrote 'that the great means of blessing are the Aristocracy and the Christian Church.' He admitted that the lower classes had just cause for complaint, but he advised them to shun violence, to respect property, to beware of agitators and to refrain from forming trade unions.* Like most of his contemporaries, Arnold failed completely to see that moral and intellectual enlightenment would solve no problems unless there was a change in the actual economic arrangements of society.

There were two consequences of this outlook. First, because of its view of the divine stratification of society, the Church tended to patronize the workers in the new industrial towns rather than to regard them as fully responsible adults. Churchmen would do a great deal *for* the poor, but they were not prepared to work *with* the poor or to encourage them to produce their own leadership. This reluctance was ministered to, after 1789, by the pathological fear of violence and atheism which, as a result of the French Revolution, was associated in men's minds with any granting of concessions to working-class aspirations. Secondly, the attitude encouraged Christian Churchmen to oppose all radical sentiments:

A preacher could spend his life surrounded by the squalor of a manufacturing town without feeling any twinge of socially radical sentiment, when he believed that many poor people were suffering for their own sins, and that the plight of the rest was the result of spiritual ordinances which it would be impious to question and of economic laws which it was foolish to resist.†

The nineteenth century witnessed two movements of spiritual revival in the Church of England. The first of these was the second flowering of the eighteenth-century Evangelical movement. Not only were the Evangelicals enthusiastic supporters of the many 'societies' for the alleviation of the lot of the poor, but they were in the forefront of the campaign to extend education, while many

* T. W. Bamford, *Thomas Arnold*, Cresset Press, 1960, pp. 44f.
† K. S. Inglis, *Churches and the Working Classes in Victorian England*, Routledge & Kegan Paul, 1963, p. 251.

of them participated in the movements for the reduction of the hours of labour in the factories which crystallized in the agitation for the Ten Hours Bill, presented to the Commons in 1832. This Bill was ultimately sponsored by Anthony Ashley Cooper, later Seventh Earl of Shaftesbury. Shaftesbury was an Evangelical whose work for reform emerged out of an intense religious conviction that he was called to this task by God. The most famous group of Evangelicals was the Clapham Sect, which included William Wilberforce, who used their money, influence and ability to support all kinds of philanthropic enterprise. Nevertheless, it is a fact, illustrated by many a sermon, that, eager though the Evangelicals were to relieve distress and even to press for legislation in parliament, they were fundamentally conservative in their attitude to the workers themselves and to the social order in which they lived. They showed a keen sense of moral responsibility, they believed that true religion must manifest itself in good works, but they continued to accept the basic assumption that the structure of society was divinely appointed and they were averse to the working classes taking any action on their own behalf.

The same outlook is found among those who were influenced by the second movement of spiritual revival. The main concerns of the leading Tractarians were theological and ecclesiastical and their utterances reveal the conservatism of their politics. Hurrell Froude was 'a Tory of the old Cavalier stamp',* Keble was 'a Tory of the Old School'† and John Tulloch reminds us that Revolutionary Paris was such anathema to Newman that he kept indoors when he stopped at Algiers, so as not to see the Tricolour.‡ The Tractarians saw the poor as individual souls to be saved and not as members of a society to be transformed. Their aim was essentially religious and in their teaching of the duties of rich and poor their purpose was to develop holiness and spiritual perfection. They did not consider possible readjustments of the social system and their efforts rarely extended beyond private charity.

* J. H. Newman, *Apologia pro Vita Sua*, Everyman edition, p. 48.
† J. Tulloch, *Movement of Religious Thought in Britain during the Nineteenth Century*, 1885, p. 87.
‡ ibid.

It is significant that the Tractarian leaders were themselves members of the landed class. John Henry Newman did not question the social order. He accepted the fact that riches could produce injustice, but to be discontented with injustice was sin (see LVIII). Pusey took the Gospel more seriously and expressed social judgements. Nevertheless, 'his idea of social justice was essentially the restoration of the hierarchy of classes, in which each man knew his place and possessed both rights and duties belonging to it'* (see LIII). Even John Keble, who had great sympathy with the working class and their hardship, never sought to identify himself with the efforts to improve social conditions as a whole. 'God has divided the world into rich and poor,' he proclaimed in a sermon, 'that there might be more exercise of charity and patience.'† His biographer says bluntly that 'his blindness in this respect must be accounted one of Keble's greatest limitations.'‡ G. K. Gloyn has posed a question to the Tractarians and all who held their approach to social problems – 'if the purpose of difference of rank in society was to develop holiness', why were 'the harsher duties of the poor' obligatory, 'while those of the rich were voluntary'? Why did the Tractarians teach 'that God *demanded* obedience of the poor but only *asked* for self-denial of the rich'?§ On the other hand, their sermons reveal that the Tractarians repudiated irresponsible individualism, which was one of the characteristics of *laissez-faire* industrial economy. The mere possession of property was not a sign of righteousness, and their teaching and their lives encouraged a sense of responsibility among those of the landed classes who listened to them. Their ideal was a society of mutual relationships and responsibilities, centred upon the Church, the symbol of order and the guide to holiness. As the *British Critic*‖ expressed it, 'they longed for Christian fellowship which is best cemented as it is best exhibited, by united adoration in the same temple of the Lord by which the

* Stephen Mayor, *The Churches and the Labour Movement*, Independent Press, 1967, p. 12.

† John Keble, *Sermons: Occasional and Parochial*, 1868, p. 174.

‡ Georgina Battiscombe, *John Keble*, Constable, 1963, p. 134.

§ G. K. Gloyn, *The Church in the Social Order*, Pacific University Press, Oregon, 1942, p. 81.

‖ No. XXI, 1837, p. 329.

poor are elevated without being made turbulent, and the rich are humbled without being degraded'.

It is not surprising that in the 1830s and 40s the Chartists did not look to the Church for encouragement. The Church of England was identified by them with the Establishment which sought to preserve the *status quo*. During the prosecution of Chartists in 1839, when they found their right of public meeting curtailed, they adopted the method of assembling on Sunday, forming a procession and marching to Church. They attempted to fill the seats before the regular congregation arrived, although they usually gave warning to the incumbent of their intention. They also requested him to preach on such texts as, 'Go to now, ye rich men, weep and howl for your miseries are coming upon you', or, 'The husbandman that laboureth shall be the first partaker of the fruits'. In this way they demonstrated at such places as Newcastle-on-Tyne, Stockport, or Blackburn. Sometimes the demonstration was small, sometimes the church was packed. There were only occasional irreverences. The clergy, having received the chosen text, were loth to make use of it and many preferred to preach on passive resistance and the folly of placing one's trust in the things of this life. One preacher, who refused to have anything to do with the chosen text, preached on, 'My house shall be called a house of prayer, but ye have made it a den of thieves'! The Chartists left in a body! At Blackburn, John Whittaker, who had been asked to preach on, 'Go to now, ye rich . . .', complied with the request, but told his congregation that it was the height of injustice to apply such words to England with its just and equal laws. He went further and had the temerity to tell the crowd of four thousand that there were no more than a hundred real Chartists among them and that the rest were there for notoriety (see XLVI). The aim of this church-going was to display the strength of Chartism and to register a dissatisfaction at the attitude of the Church towards Chartist aspirations. There was no uncertainty about the latter. H. L. Faulkener has gone so far as to assert that 'the Chartists recognized in the clergymen of the Church of England their bitterest enemies',* as almost to a man they opposed further extension of the suffrage and preached innumerable

* H. L. Faulkener, *Chartism and the Churches*, New York, 1916, p. 59.

sermons on passive obedience, the sacredness of the *status quo*, and respect for lawful authority.

Nevertheless, there was at this time the sprouting of a seed which was to bear much fruit in time to come. A group of 'Christian Socialists' came into being in the 1840s, largely through the efforts of the brilliant young lawyer, J. E. Ludlow. Two other names associated with this movement were Frederick Denison Maurice and Charles Kingsley. The former was primarily a theologian and the brains behind the movement; the latter was 'the impatient parson', full of boundless energy and dynamic enthusiasm. Maurice was insistent that Christianity should penetrate and reform the competitive system rather than merely mitigate the social results of the system. He challenged the system and thus challenged the Church itself to turn its attention away from the question of how to fulfil a Christian vocation within a competitive economy towards the task of asking how the economy itself could be remodelled on a Christian basis (see XLVII). To further this, Maurice was prepared to support the organized protests of the men most oppressed by the industrial system. Thus, he and his fellows were prepared to identify themselves with the Chartist cause, although at the same time they urged the Chartists not to hope that Chartism alone would set all things right.

In 1851 Charles Kingsley preached his famous sermon on 'The Message of the Church to the Labouring Man' (see XLIX), which was one in a series arranged by G. S. Drew, incumbent of St John's, Fitzroy Square, London. So strongly did the sermon give Christian support to the socialist cause that at the end of the service the incumbent declared it to be his painful duty to make a public protest. 'Some things which the preacher said may be very useful,' declared Mr Drew, 'much that he has said I think very imprudent.' This caused a near-riot in the church as people began to surge forward, hissing the incumbent. Kingsley, however, with head bowed, came down from the pulpit and walked to the vestry. The Bishop of London expressed his displeasure and forbade Kingsley to preach in his diocese. On the other hand, at a meeting of working men on Kennington Common, a vote of sympathy was passed with acclamation. Shortly afterwards the Bishop of

London read Kingsley's sermon and interviewed the preacher. As a result, the prohibition to preach was withdrawn and a fortnight later Kingsley preached the same sermon at St Luke's, Chelsea.* Professor Owen Chadwick has pointed out with an optimism which contains some element of truth, that this sermon 'was important to the Christian Socialists. They could no longer be dismissed by the workers as parsonical amateurs and by the Tories as silly and harmless sentimentalists. To be denounced by a parson for equating Christianity with socialism was the quickest route to the confidence of the Chartist labourer.'†

Chadwick also makes the point that 'the Christian Socialists achieved among working men an influence astonishing in so small a group'. Yet the identification which they made between Christianity and socialism was not an absolute one. Most of them had certain doubts about Chartism because of their innate belief that men's hearts could never be changed by Act of Parliament. What they really desired was to show the necessity of socializing Christianity and of Christianizing socialism. Somehow the Christian dynamic must be infused into socialism; somehow the Christian Church must be infused with a concern with the social system and with a readiness to encourage the aspirations of the workers. Moreover, even the Christian Socialists were not free from paternalism. This emerges in their criticism that the Chartists were too narrowly political and failed to appeal to the higher creative and spiritual faculties of the nation. Maurice, Kingsley and Ludlow themselves were 'soaked through with middle-class self-consciousness and irrepressible condescension'.‡ It must also be remembered that 'socialism' meant something different in that age from what it does now. It was rarely, if ever, used to mean state ownership of the means of production, distribution and exchange. 'Socialism' merely meant, in the words of Maurice Reckitt, 'that the working class, or some association thereof, should undertake something for themselves.'§

* Una Pope-Hennessy, *Canon Charles Kingsley*, Chatto & Windus, 1948, pp. 107 ff.

† Owen Chadwick, *The Victorian Church*, I, Black, 1966, pp. 359 f.

‡ Peter d'A. Jones, *The Christian Socialist Revival, 1877–1914*, Oxford University Press, 1968, p. 24.

§ Maurice Reckitt, *Maurice to Temple*, Faber & Faber, 1947, p. 87.

In the middle of the nineteenth century even that was regarded as dangerous.

A more militant approach came from the Guild of St Matthew, founded by Stewart Headlam, a curate at Bethnal Green. The first object of the Guild was 'to justify God to the People', but in order to do this it felt bound to support the socialist aims of the workers. The Guild was aggressive both in its activities and its preaching. One of its best-known preachers was Thomas Hancock (see LXII, LXIII).

In 1889 the Christian Social Union had been founded, with the main object of the peaceful persuasion of the man-in-the-pew. Henry Scott Holland, a Canon of St Paul's, was one of its founders and among other distinguished members were B. F. Westcott, E. S. Talbot and Charles Gore. By Christian socialism they meant the application of 'the moral truths and principles of Christianity to the social and economic difficulties of the present time', but they did not subscribe to the political activism of the Guild of St Matthew. One of their activities was the organization of courses of sermons in London for businessmen, proclaiming the implications of Christianity for social questions (see LIX, LXIV, LXV, LXXI).

The Christian Social Union was a highly distinguished and respectable institution. The background of the leaders of the movement shut them off from real contact with the mass of the people. Working-class people did not belong to the C.S.U. and the Union failed utterly to attract to itself a sufficient body of trade unionists to make any effective impact on the Labour movement. It was primarily an Anglican Church Society, concerned with propaganda among Church people. As such it served a most useful purpose and its achievements were seen in the growing awareness of social problems shown by successive Church Congresses. There can be no doubt that the leading members of the C.S.U. helped to change the *official* attitude of the Established Church to social and economic questions.

Another movement was begun in 1906 when the Christian Socialist League was founded, among the members of which were Lewis Donaldson, P. T. Widdrington and Conrad Noel. In that year the Parliamentary Labour Party had been founded and the

Christian Socialist League saw itself as the infant Party's 'soul', taking as its slogan, 'Christianity is the religion of which socialism is the practice'.*

These various movements, guilds and societies did much to change the outlook of the Church of England, which gradually began to acknowledge its responsibility towards the social and economic system. Indeed, it is surprising how speedily, in the end of the day, the Church did swing away from its old paternalistic attitude and begin to concern itself with the system as well as with its victims. For example, the Report of the Committee of the 1897 Lambeth Conference contained these words:

> Christian opinion . . . ought to condemn the belief that economic conditions are to be left to the action of material causes and mechanical laws, uncontrolled by any moral responsibility. . . . It can insist that the employer's personal responsibility, as such, is not lost by his membership of a commercial or industrial Company. . . . It can speak plainly of evils which attach to the economic system under which we live, such as . . . the dishonesties of trade into which men are driven by feverish competition, and the violence and reprisals of industrial warfare.†

In 1918 one of the Committees which was set up as a result of the National Mission of Repentance and Hope, showed a similar concern that Christianity should be binding upon men 'in their economic activity and industrial organization'. In 1924 there was the famous Conference on Politics, Economics and Citizenship (C.O.P.E.C.) at Birmingham, which, in its resolutions, called upon Christian people to do all in their power to discover a remedy for unemployment, to launch effective housing schemes and to extend educational facilities. The chairman of this Conference was William Temple, future Archbishop of Canterbury, who was to do more than any other person to shape the Church of England's concern for the social order.

Thus, in the early part of this century a profound change was coming over the Church of England. It was no longer concerned merely with ambulance work, but with the system itself. It was

* It was F. L. Donaldson who gave the Christian Socialist League this slogan. See Peter d'A. Jones, op. cit., p. 258.

† *The Six Lambeth Conferences, 1867–1920,* 1929, pp. 207, 267f.

no longer an attitude of paternalism, but an identification with the needs of the workers. It is true that this is an over-simplification, for there were still very many who preserved the old outlook. Nevertheless, the Church was beginning to think again and to emancipate herself from the constricting theology of the past three hundred years. Thus, all through the inter-war years we see the Church greatly concerned with the problems of the social and economic order. In 1941 there came the Malvern Conference, probably the most powerful representation of the Church of England ever gathered to consider such a subject, which was (in the words of William Temple) to ask 'what are the fundamental facts which are directly relevant to the ordering of the new society that is quite evidently emerging?' The findings of the Conference had much to say about a system which produced unemployment, low wages, malnutrition, bad housing and lack of educational opportunity. The problem which the Church failed to solve during these years was whether the existing structure of society was sufficiently sound, so that all that was required was the elimination of abuses, or whether it was in itself basically un-Christian and therefore should give way to something different.

Here we must leave the subject. So much of what the Church ignored until the close of the nineteenth century has been rectified; so much for which she struggled in the first half of this century has been achieved under successive post-war Education, National Insurance and National Health Acts. The social and economic picture of England today is far better than it was before 1939. Most men are paid decent wages, there is social security for all save a small minority, the educational system gives a reasonably fair opportunity for all, and conditions of work and housing bear little resemblance to the disgraceful situation between the wars. This by no means implies that all is well. The Church can, and should, point to glaring gaps and gross abuses in all these fields. Nevertheless, in the achievement of such improvements as have taken place, the Church, having sided with the forces of reaction for so long and having been paralysed by a false theology, has turned about and played some part in creating a climate of opinion which now regards these provisions as part of the elementary rights of men.

This anthology does not extend beyond 1920. There are reasons for this. Of course, sermons continued to be preached and still are preached, setting forth the Christian social gospel and denouncing evils in the social system. Nowadays, however, the sermon no longer has the unique place it once had. Books and pamphlets, the press and other mass media, coinciding with universal education and with the paucity of church-going, have eclipsed the pulpit in news value and as a forum for social and economic debate. Moreover, the power of preaching itself has regrettably declined: clergymen question the place of the sermon in regular worship; the day of great preachers, with a few notable exceptions, seems to be over. Will it ever return? Or have preachers lost for ever the fire of conviction which must communicate itself to others in this way?

NOTE: Quotations from the Bible are from the Authorized Version of 1611. Spelling and punctuation of contemporary sources have been modernized.

I

HUGH LATIMER (*c.* 1485–1555)

HUGH LATIMER, son of a yeoman farmer, was appointed Bishop of Winchester in 1535 and was a staunch supporter of the Reformation. In 1539 he resigned his See because his Protestant beliefs displeased Henry VIII, and was imprisoned. He was released when Edward VI became king in 1547. He became popular as a court preacher. Throughout his career he denounced social injustices and ecclesiastical abuses. In 1554, after Mary I had succeeded, he was excommunicated and in the following year he was burnt at the stake at Oxford, along with Bishop Nicholas Ridley. His sermons were racy, vivid, simple and direct. They were outspoken and utterly fearless.

I

From the 'Sermon on the Plough', preached at the Shrouds* at St Paul's on 18 January 1548, on the text: 'Whatsoever things were written, were written for our learning' (*Rom. xv, 4*). *It is a lament on the wickedness of London.*

Now what shall we say of these rich citizens of London? What shall I say of them? Shall I call them proud men of London, malicious men of London, merciless men of London? No, no, I may not say so; they will be offended with me then. Yet must I speak. For is there not reigning in London as much pride, as much covetousness, as much cruelty, as much oppression, and as much superstition, as was in Nebo? Yes, I think, and much more too. Therefore I say, repent, O London; repent, repent. Thou hearest thy faults told thee, amend them, amend them. I think, if

---

* When the weather was inclement the St Paul's Cross Sermons were preached in a place called 'The Shrouds', apparently the side of the Cathedral Church, where there was cover and shelter.

Nebo had had the preaching that thou hast, they would have converted. And, you rulers and officers, be wise and circumspect, look to your charge, and see you do your duties; and rather be glad to amend your ill living than to be angry when you are warned or told of your fault. What ado was there made in London at a certain man, because he said (and indeed at that time on a just cause), 'Burgesses!' quoth he, 'nay, butterflies.' Lord, what ado there was for that word! And yet would God they were no worse than butterflies! Butterflies do but their nature: the butterfly is not covetous, is not greedy, of other men's goods; is not full of envy and hatred, is not malicious, is not cruel, is not merciless. The butterfly glorieth not in her own deeds, nor preferreth the traditions of men before God's word; it committeth not idolatry, nor worshippeth false gods. But London cannot abide to be rebuked; such is the nature of man. If they be pricked, they will kick; if they be rubbed on the gall, they will wince; but yet they will not amend their faults, they will not be ill spoken of. But how shall I speak well of them? If you could be content to receive and follow the word of God, and favour good preachers, if you could bear to be told of your faults, if you could amend when you hear of them, if you would be glad to reform that is amiss; if I might see any such inclination in you, that you would leave to be merciless, and begin to be charitable, I would then hope well of you, I would then speak well of you. But London was never so ill as it is now. In times past men were full of pity and compassion, but now there is no pity; for in London their brother shall die in the streets for cold, he shall lie sick at the door between stock and stock, I cannot tell what to call it, and perish there for hunger: was there ever more unmercifulness in Nebo? I think not. In times past, when any rich man died in London, they were wont to help the poor scholars of the Universities with exhibition. When any man died, they would bequeath great sums of money towards the relief of the poor. When I was a scholar in Cambridge myself, I heard very good report of London, and knew many that had relief of the rich men of London: but now I can hear no such good report, and yet I inquire of it, and hearken for it; but now charity is waxen cold, none helpeth the scholar, nor yet the poor. And in those days, what did they when they helped the scholars? Marry, they maintained and gave them livings that were very papists, and professed the pope's doctrine: and now that the knowledge of God's word is brought to light, and many earnestly study and labour to set it forth, now almost no man helpeth to maintain them.

Oh London, London! repent, repent; for I think God is more displeased with London than ever he was with the city of Nebo. Repent therefore, repent, London, and remember that the same God liveth now that punished Nebo, even the same God, and none other; and he will punish sin as well now as he did then: and he will punish the iniquity of London, as well as he did then of Nebo. Amend therefore. And ye that be prelates, look well to your office; for right prelating is busy labouring, and not lording. Therefore preach and teach, and let your plough be doing. Ye lords, I say, that live like loiterers, look well to your office; the plough is your office and charge. If you live idle and loiter, you do not your duty, you follow not your vocation: let your plough therefore be going, and not cease, that the ground may bring forth fruit.

II

From the 'First Sermon preached before King Edward the Sixth', 8 March 1549, on the text: 'Whatsoever things were written, were written for our learning' *(Rom. xv, 4). A condemnation of extortion and enclosures.**

Well, then, if God will not allow a king too much, whether will he allow a subject too much? No, that he will not. Whether have any man here in England too much? I doubt most rich men have too much; for without too much we can get nothing. As for example, the physician: if the poor man be diseased, he can have no help without too much. And of the lawyer, the poor man can get no

* According to modern historians the process of enclosures was largely over by 1517. Latimer and other preachers were expressing the fears and sufferings of a generation which was in fact passed. The ill-estate of England in 1549 was due to many and complex causes – e.g. debasement of the coinage, inflation, the collapse of the cloth and wool markets. 'It is not too much to say that the rich and eloquent body of protest which we find classically expressed in this period bore little relation to the economic realities.' (W. K. Jordan, *Edward VI: The Young King*, 1968, p. 415.)

counsel, expedition, nor help in his matter, except he give him too much. At merchants' hands no kind of ware can be had, except we give for it too much. You landlords, you rent-raisers, I may say you step-lords, you unnatural lords, you have for your possessions yearly too much. For that here before went for twenty or forty pound by year (which is an honest portion to be had gratis in one lordship of another man's sweat and labour) now is let for fifty or an hundred pound by year. Of this 'too much' cometh this monstrous and portentous dearth made by man, notwithstanding God doth send us plentifully the fruits of the earth, mercifully, contrary unto our deserts: notwithstanding, too much, which these rich men have, causeth such dearth, that poor men, which live of their labour, cannot with the sweat of their face have a living, all kind of victuals is so dear: pigs, geese, capons, chickens, eggs, etc. These things with other are so unreasonably enhanced; and I think verily that if it thus continue, we shall at length be constrained to pay for a pig a pound.

I will tell you, my lords and masters, this is not for the King's honour. Yet some will say, Knowest thou what belongeth unto the King's honour better than we? I answer, that the true honour of a king is most perfectly mentioned and painted forth in the Scriptures, of which if ye be ignorant, for lack of time that ye cannot read it; albeit that your counsel be never so politic, yet is it not for the King's honour. What his honour meaneth, ye cannot tell. It is the King's honour that his subjects be led in the true religion; that all his prelates and clergy be set about their work in preaching and studying, and not to be interrupted from their charge. Also it is the King's honour that the commonwealth be advanced; that the dearth of these foresaid things be provided for, and the commodities of this realm so employed, as it may be to the setting of his subjects on work, and keeping them from idleness. And herein resteth the King's honour and his office. So doing, his account before God shall be allowed and rewarded. Furthermore, if the King's honour, as some men say, standeth in the great multitude of people, then these graziers, inclosers, and rent-rearers, are hinderers of the King's honour. For where as have been a great many householders and inhabitants, there is now but a shepherd and his dog: so they hinder the King's honour most of all. My lords and masters, I say also, that all such proceedings which are against the King's honour (as I have a part declared before, and as far as I can perceive) do intend plainly to make the yeomanry slavery, and the clergy slavery. For such works are all singular, private wealth and commodity. We of the clergy had too much; but that is taken away, and now we have too little. But for mine own part I have no cause to complain, for, I thank God and the King, I have sufficient; and God is my judge, I came not to crave of any man any thing: but I know them that have too little. There lieth a great matter by these appropriations:* great reformation is to be had in them. I know where is a great market town, with divers hamlets and inhabitants, where do rise yearly of their labours to the value of fifty pound, and the vicar that serveth, being so great a cure, hath but twelve or fourteen marks by year; so that of this pension he is not able to buy him books, nor give his neighbour drink; all the great gain goeth another way.

My father was a yeoman, and had no lands of his own, only he had a farm of three or four pound by year at the uttermost, and hereupon he tilled so much as kept half a dozen men. He had walk for a hundred sheep; and my mother milked thirty kine. He was able, and did find the King a harness, with himself and his horse, while he came to the place that he should receive the King's wages. I can remember that I buckled his harness when he went unto Blackheath field.† He kept me to school, or else I had not been able to have preached before the King's Majesty now. He married my sisters with five pound, or twenty nobles apiece; so that he brought them up in godliness and fear of God. He kept hospitality for his poor neighbours, and some alms he gave to the poor. And all this he did of the said farm, where he that now hath it payeth sixteen pound by year, or more, and is not able to do anything for his prince, for himself, nor for his children, or give a cup of drink to the poor.

* 'Appropriation' was the arrangement whereby tithes, etc., of benefices had been annexed to monasteries. At the dissolution of the monasteries these tithes, etc., instead of being returned to the parish clergy, were made over to the Crown, from which they passed into various hands.

† Where the Cornish rebels were defeated in 1497. Presumably Latimer's father was summoned to the King's army.

Thus all the enhancing and rearing goeth to your private commodity and wealth. So that where ye had a single too much, you have that; and since the same, ye have enhanced the rent, and so have increased another too much: so now ye have double too much, which is too too much. But let the preacher preach till his tongue be worn to the stumps, nothing is amended. We have good statutes made for the commonwealth, as touching commoners and inclosers; many meetings and sessions; but in the end of the matter there cometh nothing forth.* Well, well, this is one thing I will say unto you: from whence it cometh I know, even from the devil. I know his intent in it. For if ye bring it to pass that the yeomanry be not able to put their sons to school (as indeed universities do wonderously decay already) and that they be not able to marry their daughters to the avoiding of whoredom; I say, ye pluck salvation from the people, and utterly destroy the realm. For by yeomen's sons the faith of Christ is and hath been maintained chiefly. Is this realm taught by rich men's sons? No, no; read the chronicles: ye shall find sometime noblemen's sons which have been unpreaching bishops and prelates, but ye shall find none of them learned men. But verily they that should look to the redress of these things be the greatest against them. In this realm are a great many folk, and amongst many I know but one of tender zeal, who at the motion of his poor tenants hath let down his lands to the old rents for their relief. For God's love let not him be a phoenix, let him not be alone, let him not be an hermit closed in a wall; some good man follow him, and do as he giveth example.

Surveyors there be, that greedily gorge up their covetous goods; hand-makers,† I mean: honest men I touch not; but all such as survey, they make up their mouths, but the commons be utterly undone by them; whose bitter cry ascending up to the ears of the God of Sabaoth, the greedy pit of hell-burning fire, without great

* Five statutes, the last two in 1534 and 1536, had been passed to protect tillage and to prohibit depopulation. A Royal Commission had been issued and acted upon in 1548. The Tudors, however, did not dare to enforce these laws rigorously because to have done so would have required the full support of the gentry, as Justices of the Peace, and the latter were the worst offenders! (See W. K. Jordan, *Edward VI: The Young King*, 1968, p. 410.)

† 'profiteers'

repentance, doth tarry and look for them. A redress God grant! For surely, surely, but that two things do comfort me, I would despair of redress in these matters. One is, that the King's Majesty, when he cometh to age, will see a redress of these things so out of frame; giving example by letting down his own lands first, and then enjoin his subjects to follow him. The second hope I have, is, I believe that the general accounting day is at hand, the dreadful Day of Judgement, I mean, which shall make an end of all these calamities and miseries.

III

From the 'Fifth Sermon preached before King Edward the Sixth', 5 April 1549, on the text: 'Whatsoever things were written, were written for our learning' (Rom. xv, 4). *A vivid picture of the mal-administration of justice.*

I heard of late of a notable bloodshed: '*Audio*,' saith St Paul; and so do I: I know it not, but I hear of it. There was a searcher in London which, executing his office, displeased a merchantman, in so much that when he was doing his office they were at words: the merchantman threatened him; the searcher said the king should not lose his custom. The merchant goes me home, and sharpens his wood-knife, and comes again and knocks him on the head, and kills him. They that told me the tale say it is winked at; they look through their fingers, and will not see it. Whether it be taken up with a pardon, or no, I cannot tell; but this I am sure, and if ye bear with such matters, the devil shall bear you away to hell. Bloodshed and murder would have no bearing. It is a heinous thing bloodshedding, and especially voluntary murder and prepensed* murder. For in Numbers God saith, it polluteth the whole realm: *Polluitur illa terra, &c., et non potest expiari sine sanguine;* 'The land cannot be purified nor cleansed again, till his blood be shed that shed it.' It is the office of a king to see such murderers punished with death; for *non frustra gestat gladium.* What will you make of a king? He beareth a sword before him,

* 'deliberate'

not a peacock's feather. I go not about to stir you now to cruelty; but I speak against the bearing of bloodshed: this bearing must be looked upon. In certain causes of murder such great circumstances may be, that the king may pardon a murder. But if I were worthy to be of counsel, or if I were asked mine advice, I would not have the king to pardon a voluntary murder, a prepensed murder.

I can tell where one man slew another in a township, and was attached upon the same: twelve men were impanelled: the man had friends: the sheriff laboured the bench: the twelve men stuck at it, and said, 'Except he would disburse twelve crowns, they would find him guilty.' Means were found that the twelve crowns were paid. The quest* comes in, and says 'Not guilty.' Here was 'not guilty' for twelve crowns. This is a bearing, and if some of the bench were hanged, they were well served. This makes men bold to do murder and slaughter. We should reserve murdering till we come to our enemies, and the king bid us fight: he that would bestir him then were a pretty fellow indeed. Crowns! if their crowns were shaven to the shoulders, they were served well enough.

I know where a woman was got with child, and was ashamed at the matter, and went into a secret place, where she had no woman at her travail, and was delivered of three children at a birth. She wrung their necks, and cast them into a water, and so killed her children: suddenly she was gaunt† again; and her neighbours, suspecting the matter, caused her to be examined, and she granted all. Afterwards she was arraigned at the bar for it, and dispatched and found not guilty, through bearing of friends, and bribing of the judge: where, at the same sessions, another poor woman was hanged for stealing a few rags off a hedge that were not worth a crown.

There was a certain gentleman, a professor of the word of God (he sped never the better for that, ye may be sure), who was accused for murdering of a man, whereupon he was cast into prison; and by chance, as he was in prison, one of his friends came unto him for to visit him; and he declared to his friend that he was never guilty in the murdering of the man: so he went his ways.

* 'jury' † 'slim'

The gentleman was arraigned and condemned; and as he went to his execution, he saw his friend's servant, and said unto him, 'Commend me to thy master, and I pray thee tell him, I am the same man still I was when he was with me; and if thou tarry awhile, thou shalt see me die.' There was suit made for this man's pardon, but it could not be gotten. Belike the sheriffs or some other bare him no good will: but he died for it. And afterward, I being in the Tower, having leave to come to the lieutenant's table, I heard him say, that there was a man hanged afterward that killed the same man for whom this gentleman was put to death. O Lord, what bearing, what bolstering of naughty matters is this in a Christian realm! I desire your Majesty to remedy the matter, and God grant you to see redress in this realm in your own person. Although my lord Protector,* I doubt not, and the rest of the council do, in the meanwhile, all that lieth in them to redress things; I would such as be rulers, noblemen, and masters, should be at this point with their servants, to certify them on this sort: if any man go about to do you wrong, I will do my best to help you in your right; but if ye break the law, ye shall have justice.

IV

From the 'Last Sermon preached before King Edward the Sixth', in Lent, 1550, on the text: 'Take heed and beware of covetousness' (Luke xii, 15). All men are equal in Christ and even the poorest in the land have certain needs. He discusses the proper place of women (with a note on current fashions), the dissolute life of the nobles and the sharp practices of men of business.

They in Christ are equal with you. Peers of the realm must needs be. The poorest ploughman is in Christ equal with the greatest prince that is. Let them, therefore, have sufficient to maintain them, and to find them their necessaries. A plough-land must have sheep; yea, they must have sheep to dung their ground for bearing of corn; for if they have no sheep to help to fat the ground they shall have but bare corn and thin. They must have swine for their food, to make their veneries† or bacon of: their bacon is their

* The Duke of Somerset.   † 'game'

venison, for they shall now have *hangum tuum*,* if they get any other venison; so that bacon is their necessary meat to feed on, which they may not lack. They must have other cattle: as horses to draw their plough, and for carriage of things to the markets; and kine for their milk and cheese, which they must live upon and pay their rents. These cattle must have pasture, which pasture if they lack, the rest must needs fail them: and pasture they cannot have, if the land be taken in, and enclosed from them. . . . Achab was a king, but Jezebel, Jezebel, she was the perilous woman. She would rule her husband, the king; she would bear a stroke in all things, and she would order matters as pleased her. And so will many women do; they will rule their husbands, and do all things after their own minds. They do therein against the order by God appointed them: they break their injunction that God gave unto them. Yea, it is now come to the lower sort, to mean men's wives; they will rule and apparel themselves gorgeously, and some of them far above their degrees, whether their husbands will or no. But they break their injunction, and do therein contrary to God's ordinance. God saith, *Subdita eris sub potestate viri*, 'Thou shalt be subject under the power of thy husband.' Thou shalt be subject. Women are subjects; ye be subjects to your husbands. At the first, the man and the woman were equal. But after that she had given credit to the serpent, then she had an injunction set upon her: *Subdita eris sub potestate viri*, 'Thou shalt be subject under the power of thy husband.' . . . It is a part of your penance to be subjects unto your husbands: ye are underlings, underlings, and must be obedient. But this is now made a trifle and a small matter: and yet it is a sad matter, a godly matter, a ghostly matter, a matter of damnation and salvation. And Paul saith, that 'a woman ought to have a power on her head'. What is this, 'to have a power on her head' ? It is a manner of speaking of the Scripture; and to have her power on her head, is to have a sign and token of power, which is by covering of her head, declaring that she hath a superior above her, by whom she ought to be ruled and ordered: for she is not immediately under God, but mediately. For by their injunction, the husband is their head under God, and they subjects unto their

* A phrase indicating 'a hanging matter', i.e. it will be 'a hanging matter' if 'they get any other venison'.

husbands. But this 'power' that some of them have is disguised gear and strange fashions. They must wear French hoods, and I cannot tell you, I, what to call it. And when they make them ready, and come to the covering of their head, they will call and say, 'Give me my French hood, and give me my bonnet, or my cap'; and so forth. I would wish that the women would call the covering of their heads by the terms of the Scripture: as when she would have her cap, I would she would say, 'Give me my power.' I would they would learn to speak as the Holy Ghost speaketh, and call it by such a name as St Paul doth. I would they would (as they have much pricking*), when they put on their cap, I would they would have this meditation: 'I am now putting on my power upon my head.' If they had this thought in their minds, they would not make so much pricking-up of themselves as they do nowadays. But now here is a vengeance devil: we must have our power from Turkey, of velvet, and gay it must be; far-fetched, dear-bought; and when it cometh, it is a false sign. I had rather have a true English sign, than a false sign from Turkey. It is a false sign when it covereth not their heads as it should do. For if they would keep it under the power as they ought to do, there should not any such tussocks nor tufts be seen as there be; nor such laying out of the hair, nor braiding to have it open. I would marvel of it, how it should come to be so abused, and so far out of order; saving that I know by experience that many will not be ruled by their husbands, as they ought to be. I have been desired to exhort some, and with some I could do little in that matter. But there be now many Adams that will not displease their wives, but will in this behalf let them have all their own minds, and do as them listeth. And some others again there be nowadays that will defend it, and say it may be suffered well enough, because it is not expressed in Scripture, nor spoken of by name. Though we have not express mention in Scripture against such laying of the hair in tussocks and tufts, yet we have in Scripture express mention *de tortis crinibus*, of wreathen hair; that is, for the nonce forced to curl. But of these tussocks that are laid out nowadays there is no mention made in Scriptures, because they were not used in Scripture-time. They were not yet come to be so far out of order as

* 'dressing for show'

to lay out such tussocks and tufts. But I will tell thee, if thou wilt needs lay it out, or if thou wilt needs shew thy hair, and have it seen, go and poll thy head, or round it, as men do; for to what purpose is it to pull it out so, and to lay it out? Some do it, say they, of a simplicity: some do it of a pride; and some of other causes. But they do it because they will be quarter-master with their husbands. Quarter-masters? Nay, half-masters; yea, some of them will be whole masters, and rule the roost as they list themselves.

But these defenders of it will not have it evil, because it is not spoken of in Scripture. But there be other things as evil as this, which are not spoken of in Scripture expressly; but they are implied in Scripture, as well as though they were expressly spoken of. For the prophet Isaiah saith: *Vae qui consurgitis mane ad comessandum, ad ebrietatem sectandam et potando usque ad vesperam, ut vino aestuetis.* 'Wo unto you that arise early in the morning, and go to drinking until night, that ye may swim in wine.' This is the Scripture against banqueting and drunkenness. But now they banquet all night, and lie abed in the day time till noon, and the Scripture speaketh nothing of that. But what then? The devil hath his purpose this way, as well as the other: he hath his purpose as well by revelling and keeping ill rule all night, as by rising early in the morning and banqueting all day. So the devil hath his purpose both ways. Ye noblemen, ye great men, I wot not what rule ye keep. For God's sake, hear the complaints and suits of the poor. Many complain against you, that ye lie abed till eight, or nine, or ten of the clock. I cannot tell what revel ye have overnight; whether in banqueting, or dicing, or carding, or how it is; but in the morning, when poor suitors come to your house, ye cannot be spoken withal: they are kept sometimes without your gates, or if they be let into the hall, or some outer chamber, out cometh one or other, 'Sir, ye cannot speak with my lord yet; my lord is asleep; or he hath had business of the King's all night,' etc. And thus poor suitors are driven off from day to day, that they cannot speak with you in three, or four days, yea, a whole month: what shall I say more? yea, a whole year sometimes, ere they can come to your speech, to be heard of you. For God's love look better to it. Speak with poor men when they come to your houses; and dispatch poor suitors, as indeed some noblemen do; and would Christ that all noblemen would so do! But some do. I went one day myself betime in the morning to a great man's house to speak with him in business that I had of mine own. And methought I was up betimes; but when I came thither, the great man was gone forth about such affairs as behoved him, or I came. Well: yet, thought I, this is well, I like this well: this man doth somewhat regard and consider his office and duty. I came too late for mine own matter, and lost my journey, and my early rising too: and yet I was glad that I had been so beguiled. For God's love follow this example, ye great men, and arise in the mornings, and be ready for men to speak with them, and to dispatch suitors that resort unto you. But all these I bring to disprove them that defend evil things, because they be not expressly spoken against in the Scripture. But what forceth that, when the devil hath his purpose, and is served as well one way as another way? Though it be not expressly spoken against in Scripture, yet I reckon it plainly enough implied in the Scripture. . .

And here one suit more to Your Highness: there lacketh one thing in this realm, that it hath need of; for God's sake make some promoters.* There lack promoters, such as were in King Henry the Seventh's days, your grandfather. There lack men to promote the King's officers when they do amiss, and to promote all offenders. I think there is great need of such men of godly discretion, wisdom, and conscience, to promote transgressors, as rent-raisers, oppressors of the poor, extortioners, bribers, usurers. I hear there be usurers in England, that will take forty in the hundred†, but I hear of no promoters to put them up. We read not, this covetous farmer or landed man of the gospel bought corn in the markets to lay it up in store, and then sell it again. But, and if it please Your Highness, I hear say that in England we have landlords, nay, step-lords I might say, that are become graziers; and burgesses are become regraters‡: and some farmers will regrate and buy up all the corn that cometh to the markets, and lay

* Informers who prosecuted offenders against the law and received part of the fine imposed.

† By an Act of 1545 it was illegal to charge men more than 'ten in the hundred'.

‡ Those who bought up goods, especially victuals, with a view to selling at a profit.

it up in store, and sell it again at a higher price, when they see their time. I heard a merchantman say, that he had travailed all the days of his life in the trade of merchandise, and had gotten three or four thousand pounds by buying and selling; but in case he might be licensed or suffered so to do, he would get a thousand pound a year by only buying and selling of grain here within this realm. Yea, and (as I hear say) aldermen nowadays are become colliers: they be both woodmongers and makers of coals. I would wish he might eat nothing but coals for awhile, till he had amended it. There cannot a poor body buy a sack of coals, but it must come through their hands.

V

From 'The Fifth Sermon on the Lord's Prayer' (no date). It deals with the inequalities of wealth, the responsibility of the rich to the poor, and the wickedness of usury.

But here I must ask you rich men a question. How chanceth it you have your riches? 'We have them of God,' you will say. But by what means have you them? 'By prayer,' you will say. 'We pray for them unto God, and he giveth us the same.' Very well. But I pray you tell me, what do other men which are not rich? Pray they not as well as you do? 'Yes,' you must say; for you cannot deny it. Then it appeareth that you have your riches not through your own prayers only, but other men help you to pray for them: for they say as well, 'Our Father, give us this day our daily bread', as you do; and peradventure they be better than you be, and God heareth their prayer sooner than yours. And so it appeareth most manifestly, that you obtain your riches of God, not only through your own prayer, but through other men's too: other men help you to get them at God's hand. Then it followeth, that seeing you get not your riches alone through your own prayer, but through the poor man's prayer, it is meet that the poor man should have part of them; and you ought to relieve his necessity and poverty. But what meaneth God by this inequality, that he giveth to some an hundred pound; unto this man five thousand pound; unto this man in a manner nothing at all? What meaneth he by this inequality? Here he meaneth, that the rich ought to distribute his riches abroad amongst the poor: for the rich man is but God's officer, God's treasurer: he ought to distribute them according unto his Lord God's commandment. If every man were rich, then no man would do anything: therefore God maketh some rich and some poor. Again; that the rich may have where to exercise his charity, God made some rich and some poor: the poor he sendeth unto the rich to desire of him in God's name help and aid. Therefore, you rich men, when there cometh a poor man unto you, desiring your help, think none otherwise but that God hath sent him unto you; and remember that thy riches be not thy own but thou art but a steward over them . . .

Certain it is, that usury was allowed by the laws of this realm yet it followed not that usury was godly, nor allowed before God. For it is not a good argument, to say, 'It is forbidden to take ten pounds of the hundred, *ergo*, I may take five'; like as a thief cannot say, 'It is forbidden in the law to steal thirteen-pence halfpenny; *ergo*, I may steal sixpence, or three-pence, or two-pence.' No, no; this reasoning will not serve afore God: for though the law of this realm hangeth him not, if he steal four-pence, yet for all that he is a thief before God, and shall be hanged on the fiery gallows in hell. So he that occupieth usury, though by the laws of this realm he might do it without punishment (for the laws are not so precise), yet for all that he doth wickedly in the sight of God. For usury is wicked before God, be it small or great; like as theft is wicked. But I will tell you how you shall be usurers to get much gain. Give it unto the poor; then God will give it to thee with gain. Give twenty-pence, and thou shalt have forty-pence. It shall come again, thou shalt not lose it; or else God is not God. What needeth it to use such deceitfulness and falsehood to get riches? Take a lawful way to get them; that is, to scatter this abroad that thou hast, and then thou shalt have it again with great gain: *quadruplum*, 'four times', saith Scripture. Now God's word saith, that I shall have again that which I laid out with usury, with gain. Is it true that God saith? Yes: then let me not think, that giving unto the poor doth diminish my stock, when God saith the contrary, namely, that it shall increase; or else we make God a liar. For if I believe not his sayings, then by mine infidelity I make him a liar, as much as is in me. Therefore learn here to commit usury: and specially you rich men, you must learn this lesson well; for of you it is written, 'Whosoever hath much, must make account for much.' And you have much, not to that end, to do with it what you lust; but you must spend it as God appointeth you in his word to do: for no rich man can say before God, 'This is my own.' No, he is but an officer over it, an almoner, God's treasurer. Our Saviour saith, *Omnis qui reliquerit agrum, &c., centuplum accipiet*. 'Whosoever shall leave his field, shall receive it again an hundred fold.'

2

ROGER EDGEWORTH (d. 1560)

ROGER EDGEWORTH was born at Holt Castle, Denbigh. He was elected Fellow of Oriel College, Oxford, in 1508, and after ordination he became a noted preacher in the University and elsewhere. In 1542 he became Prebendary of Bristol Cathedral and Canon of both Salisbury and Wells. He was zealous for the Catholic cause and tells us that he abstained from preaching during the reign of Edward VI.

VI

The sermon from which the following extracts are taken was preached during the reign of Henry VIII and illustrates the attitude of preachers towards the Tudor woman's use of cosmetics.

Because Saint Peter had bidden all wives to please their husbands with obedience and due subjection, lest they should think this subjection and pleasing of their husbands to stand in trimming and dressing their bodies curiously and wantonly for their husband's pleasure, he declareth that he meaneth nothing less, and biddeth them that they are not to make their hair for the nonce, setting it abroad smoothly sleeked, to make it shine in men's eyes, or curiously plaited in traces, or, as gentlewomen do nowadays, purposely neglected hanging about their eyes, as it were saying: I care not how my hair lie, and yet while they do so, they most care how to pull abroad their locks to be seen. And so when they take upon them to care least, then they care most for their hair. Some there be that cannot be content with their hair as God made it, but do paint it and set in it another hue, as when it was white, they dye it fair and yellow, or if it be black as a crow, it must be set in some lighter colour, as brown, or auburn, or red: and so must their brows and their eyelids be painted proportionably.

All this disguising of women's hair Saint Peter calleth by one name, *Capillatura*, making their hair, or curiously dressing their hair, which he dissuadeth and counselleth to the contrary. And St Paul, 1 Timothy ii, biddeth all women apparel and array themselves in comely raiment with bashfulness and shamefacedness, and with sobriety. . . . So let the dressing of your heads, and the appareling of your bodies be chaste, clean, and after a sober fashion, not like players disguised after any wanton manner, lest the lightness of your dressing show the lightness of your conditions. . . . Their trimmed shoes, their nouches,* brooches, and rings, their chains, and pendents, their costly edges and precious habiliments shall come to naught. And then their pleasant odours of musk, civet, and of all perfumes, shall be turned into stench. . . . And for joy and mirth, shall come sorrow and mourning, for their pride and exaltation, shall come lowliness and dejection. . . . This adulteration and changing of God's handiwork by painting women's hair to make it seem fair and yellow, or of their cheeks to make them look ruddy, or of their forehead to hide the wrinkles and to make them look smooth, is of the devil's invention and never of God's teaching. Therefore I must exhort all women to beware of counterfeiting, adulterating, or changing the fashion and form of God's work, either by yellow colour, black or red powder, or by any other medicine corrupting or changing the natural lineaments of favour of man or woman, because they that use that manner of doing seemeth to go about to correct or amend the thing that God hath made, and striveth against God, violently setting hand upon his work. If there were an excellent painter or a carver that had made a goodly image of the best fashion that he could, if a busybody would take a tool, and take upon him to amend the image so made, should he not do injury to the said gay workman, and also despite unto him ? Yes surely, for he should seem to count the workman but a fool, and nothing cunning. Then consider Almighty God, the workman of all workmen. He made the face and the body of man and woman as he thought best; then I pray you what arrogance and presumption is it for man or woman to set to the pencil or tool to make it better ? Thinkest thou that God will not take vengeance on thee for thy

* 'Projections' or 'projecting parts'.

striving with him to amend: yea, rather to mar that he hath made. Therefore in that thou thinkest thyself that thou art made fairer, thou art made fouler indeed, begging of colours made with powder of stones, with rhinds of trees or with juice of herbs the thing which thou hast not of thyself. Moreover Christ saith . . . 'Thou canst not make one hair of thy head white or black.' And yet thou by thy pride wilt prove him a liar, and make thyself a better workman than he, painting thy hair or thy face not only black or white (for women set little by such colours) but also yellow or red. . . . Now I pray thee that so paintest thyself, art thou not afraid, lest when thou shalt appear afore the Judge at the General Judgement, he will not know thee, but will put thee away from the reward that is provided for all good people in Heaven, saying: what have we here? The figure of her face is stained or polluted into a strange countenance. How canst thou see God with such eyes as he made not, but as the devil's craft hath dyed and stained like the fiery glistering eyes of the serpent, with whom thou shalt burn for evermore? The first that I read of, that thus painted her physiognomy, was the naughty Queen Jezebel, the common butcher and murderer of all the preachers and prophets of Almighty God. . . . But now married women will pretend, and make an excuse by their husbands, saying that they take all the labours in painting and trimming themselves to please their husbands; and so doing, they make their husbands partakers of their offence, and consequently of their damnation for company sake. And I shall advertise all married men, and all them that have daughters to keep, that whether the tiring or trimming of your wives and daughters be so to please you as they say, or to please themselves as you say, that you suffer them not to use it, because it is not godly (as I have told you) and also because of the peril that may come of it. For when they set themselves forth so curiously, and goeth abroad in the streets, or sitteth in their shop windows, or else peradventure at feasts and banquets with vicious company, it is not you alone that would have to look upon them, it is not you alone that is pleased with the sight of them, it is not you alone that casteth their eyes after them, or that draweth long sighs of carnal love after them, this is not the way to keep them for your-selves. Beware, therefore, good husbands that you set not your wives or daughters so to sale, for fear lest harm come of it. And you good wives beware to the danger and peril of your honesty, and specially beware of the peril of your souls.

3

BOOK OF HOMILIES (1547–63)

IN 1547 the government issued a book of twelve prescribed
homilies for the use of illiterate clergy. In 1563 a second book,
with twenty-one more homilies, was completed, although it was
not published until 1571.

VII

*From 'The Third Part of the Homily against Disobedience and
Wilful Rebellion'.*

What an abominable sin against God and man rebellion is, and
how dreadfully the wrath of God is kindled and inflamed against
all rebels, and what horrible plagues, punishments, and deaths,
and finally, eternal damnation, doth hang over their heads: as
how, on the contrary part, good and obedient subjects are in God's
favour, and be partakers of peace, quietness, and security, with
other God's manifold blessings in this world, and by his mercies
through our Saviour Christ, of life everlasting also in the world to
come. How horrible a sin against God and man rebellion is,
cannot possibly be expressed according unto the greatness thereof. For he that nameth rebellion, nameth not a singular or one
only sin, as is theft, robbery, murder, and such like; but he
nameth the whole puddle and sink of all sins against God and
man, against his prince, his country, his countrymen, his parents,
his children, his kinsfolks, his friends, and against all men universally; all sins, I say, against God and all men heaped together,
nameth he, that nameth rebellion. For concerning the offence of
God's majesty, who seeth not that rebellion riseth first by contempt of God and of his holy ordinances and laws, wherein he so
straitly commandeth obedience, forbiddeth disobedience and
rebellion ? And besides the dishonour done by rebels unto God's

holy name, by their breaking of the oath made to their prince, with the attestation of God's name, and calling of his Majesty to witness, who heareth not the horrible oaths and blasphemies of God's holy name, that are used daily amongst rebels, that is either amongst them, or heareth the truth of their behaviour? Who knoweth not that rebels do not only themselves leave all works necessary to be done upon work days undone, whiles they accomplish their abominable work of rebellion, and to compel others that would gladly be well occupied, to do the same; but also how rebels do not only leave the Sabbath day of the Lord unsanctified, the temple and church of the Lord unresorted unto, but also do by their works of wickedness most horribly profane and pollute the Sabbath day, serving Satan, and, by doing of his work, making it the devil's day instead of the Lord's day? Besides that, they compel good men, that would gladly serve the Lord, assembling in his temple and church upon his day, as becometh the Lord's servants, to assemble and meet armed in the field, to resist the fury of such rebels. Yea, and many rebels, lest they should leave any part of God's commandments in the first table of his law unbroken, or any sin against God undone, do make rebellion for the maintenance of their images, and idols, and of their idolatry committed, or to be committed by them; and, in despite of God, cut and tear in sunder his holy word, and tread it under their feet, as of late ye know was done.... The rebels do not only dishonour their prince, the parent of their country, but also do dishonour and shame their natural parents, if they have any, do shame their kindred and friends, do disherit and undo for ever their children and heirs. Thefts, robberies, and murders, which of all sins are most loathed of most men, are in no men so much, nor so perniciously and mischievously, as in rebels. For the most arrant thieves, and cruellest murderers that ever were, so long as they refrain from rebellion, as they are not many in number, so spreadeth their wickedness and damnation unto a few, they spoil but a few, they shed the blood but of few in comparison. But rebels are the cause of infinite robberies, and murders of great multitudes, and of those also whom they should defend from the spoil and violence of other: and as rebels are many in number, so doth their wickedness and damnation spread itself unto many...

Thus you see that all God's laws are by rebels violated and broken, and that all sins possible to be committed against God or man be contained in rebellion: which sins if a man list to name by the accustomed names of the seven capital or deadly sins, as pride, envy, wrath, covetousness, sloth, gluttony, and lechery, he shall find them all in rebellion, and amongst rebels. For first, as ambition and desire to be aloft, which is the property of pride, stirreth up many men's minds to rebellion, so cometh it of a Luciferian pride and presumption, that a few rebellious subjects should set themselves up against the majesty of their prince, against the wisdom of the counsellors, against the power and force of all nobility, and the faithful subjects and people of the whole realm. As for envy, wrath, murder, and desire of blood, and covetousness of other men's goods, lands, and livings, they are the inseparable accidents of all rebels, and peculiar properties that do usually stir up wicked men unto rebellion.

Now such as by riotousness, gluttony, drunkenness, excess of apparel, and unthrifty games, have wasted their own goods unthriftily, the same are most apt unto, and most desirous of rebellion, whereby they trust to come by other men's goods unlawfully and violently. And where other gluttons and drunkards take too much of such meats and drinks as are served to tables, rebels waste and consume in short space all corn in barns, fields, or elsewhere, whole garners, whole storehouses, whole cellars, devour whole flocks of sheep, whole droves of oxen and kine. And as rebels that are married, leaving their own wives at home, do most ungraciously; so much more do unmarried men, worse than any stalands* or horses (being now by rebellion set at liberty from correction of laws, which bridled them before), which abuse by force other men's wives and daughters, and ravish virgins and maidens most shamefully, abominably, and damnably.

Thus all sins, by all names that sins may be named, and by all means that all sins may be committed and wrought, do all wholly upon heaps follow rebellion, and are to be found altogether amongst rebels. Now whereas pestilence, famine, and war, are by the holy Scriptures declared to be the greatest worldly plagues and miseries that likely can be, it is evident that all the miseries which all

* 'stallions'

55

these plagues have in them do wholly all together follow rebellion; wherein, as all their miseries be, so is there much more mischief than in them all.

For it is known that in the resorting of great companies of men together, which in rebellion happeneth both upon the part of true subjects, and of the rebels, by their close lying together, and corruption of the air and place where they do lie, with ordure and much filth in the hot weather, and by unwholesome lodging, and lying often upon the ground, specially in cold and wet weathers in winter, by their unwholesome diet, and feeding at all times, and often by famine and lack of meat and drink in due time, and again by taking too much at other times: it is well known, I say, that as well plagues and pestilences, as all other kinds of sickness and maladies, by these means grow upon and amongst men, whereby more men are consumed at the length, than are by dint of sword suddenly slain in the field. So that not only pestilences, but also all other sickness, diseases, and maladies do follow rebellion, which are much more horrible than plagues, pestilences, and diseases, sent directly from God, as hereafter shall appear more plainly.

And as for hunger and famine, they are the peculiar companions of rebellion; for whiles rebels do in short time spoil and consume all corn and necessary provision, which men with their labours had gotten and appointed upon, for their finding the whole year after; and also do let all other men, husbandmen, and others, from their husbandry, and other necessary works, whereby provision should be made for times to come, who seeth not that extreme famine and hunger must needs shortly ensue and follow rebellion? Now whereas the wise King and godly prophet, David, judged war to be worse than either famine or pestilence, for that these two are often suffered by God, for man's amendment, and be not sins of themselves: but wars have always the sins and mischiefs of men upon the one side or other joined with them, and therefore is war the greatest of these worldly mischiefs: but of all wars, civil war is the worst, and far more abominable yet is rebellion than any civil war, being unworthy the name of any war, so far it exceedeth all wars in all naughtiness, in all mischief, and in all abomination. And therefore our Saviour Christ denounceth desolation and destruction to that realm, that by sedition and rebellion is divided in itself.

Now as I have shown before that pestilence and famine, so is it yet more evident that all the calamities, miseries, and mischiefs of war be more grievous, and do more follow rebellion, than any other war, as being far worse than all other wars. For not only those ordinary and usual mischiefs and miseries of other wars do follow rebellion, as corn, and other things necessary to man's use, to be spoiled, houses, villages, towns, cities, to be taken, sacked, burned, and destroyed, not only many wealthy men, but whole countries to be impoverished and utterly beggared, many thousands of men to be slain and murdered, women and maids to be violated and deflowered; which things when they are done by foreign enemies, we do much mourn, as we have great causes; yet are all these miseries without any wickedness wrought by any our countrymen. But when these mischiefs are wrought in rebellion by them that should be friends, by countrymen, by kinsmen, by those that should defend their country and countrymen from such miseries, the misery is nothing so great as is the mischief and wickedness, when the subjects unnaturally do rebel against their prince, whose honour and life they should defend, though it were with the loss of their own lives; countrymen to disturb the public peace and quietness of their country, for defence of whose quietness they should spend their lives; the brother to seek, and often to work, the death of his brother; the son of the father; the father to seek or procure the death of his sons, being at man's age, and by their faults to disherit their innocent children and kinsmen their heirs for ever, for whom they might purchase livings and lands, as natural parents do take care and pains, and be at great costs and charges; and universally, instead of all quietness, joy, and felicity, which do follow blessed peace and due obedience, to bring in all trouble, sorrow, disquietness of minds and bodies, and all mischief and calamities, to turn all good order upside down, to bring all good laws in contempt, and to tread them under feet; to oppress all virtue and honesty, and all virtuous and honest persons; and to set all vice and wickedness, and all vicious and wicked men at liberty; to work their wicked wills, which were before bridled by wholesome laws; to weaken, to overthrow, and to consume the strength of the realm, their natural country, as well by the spending and wasting of the money and treasure of the prince and realm, as by the murdering of the people of the same, their own countrymen, who should defend the honour of their prince, and liberty of their country, against the invasion of foreign enemies: and so, finally, to make their country, thus by their mischief weakened, ready to be a prey and spoil to all outward enemies that will invade it, to the utter and perpetual captivity, slavery, and destruction of all their countrymen, their children, their friends, their kinsfolk left alive, whom by their wicked rebellion they procure to be delivered into the hands of foreign enemies, as much as in them doth lie.

In foreign wars our countrymen in obtaining the victory win the praise of valiantness; yea, and though they were overcome and slain, yet win they an honest commendation in this world, and die in a good conscience for serving God, their prince, and their country, and be children of eternal salvation; but in rebellion, how desperate and strong soever they be, yet win they shame here in fighting against God, their prince, and country, and therefore justly do fall headlong into Hell, if they die, and live in shame and fearful conscience, though they escape.

But commonly they be rewarded with shameful deaths, their heads and carcases set upon poles, or hanged in chains, eaten with kites and crows, judged unworthy the honour of burial; and so their souls, if they repent not, as commonly they do not, the devil harrieth them into Hell in the midst of their mischief. For which dreadful execution St Paul showeth the cause of obedience, not only for fear of death, but also in conscience to Godward, for fear of eternal damnation in the world to come.

Wherefore, good people, let us, as the children of obedience, fear the dreadful execution of God, and live in quiet obedience, to be the children of everlasting salvation. For as Heaven is the place of good obedient subjects, and Hell the prison and dungeon of rebels against God and their prince; so is that realm happy where most obedience of subjects doth appear, being the very figure of Heaven: and contrariwise, where most rebellions and rebels be, there is the express similitude of Hell, and the rebels themselves are the very figures of fiends and devils, and their captain the ungracious pattern of Lucifer and Satan, the prince of darkness; of whose rebellion, as they be followers, so, shall they of his damnation in Hell undoubtedly be partakers; and as undoubtedly children of peace, the inheritors of Heaven with God the Father, God the Son, and God the Holy Ghost, to whom be all honour and glory for ever and ever. Amen.

VIII

The following extract from 'The Sermon against Excess of Apparel' presents a picture of Tudor fashions in dress and the preachers' attitude towards it.

All may not look to wear like apparel, but everyone according to his degree, as God hath placed him. Which, if it were observed, many one doubtless should be compelled to wear a russet-coat, which now ruffleth in silks and velvets, spending more by the year in sumptuous apparel, than their fathers received for the whole revenue of their lands. But, alas! nowadays, how many may we behold occupied wholly in pampering the flesh, taking no care at all, but only how to deck themselves, setting their affection altogether on worldly bravery, abusing God's goodness when he sendeth plenty, to satisfy their wanton lusts, having no regard to the degree wherein God hath placed them. The Israelites were contented with such apparel as God gave them, although it were base and simple. And God so blessed them, that their shoes and clothes lasted them forty years; yea, and those clothes which their fathers had worn, their children were contented to use afterward. But we are never contented, and therefore we prosper not; so that most commonly he that ruffleth in his sables, in his fine furred gown, corked slippers, trim buskins, and warm mittens, is more ready to chill for cold, than the poor labouring man, which can abide in the field all the day long, when the north wind blows, with a few beggarly clouts about him. We are loth to wear such as our fathers have left us; we think not that sufficient or good enough for us. We must have one gown for the day, another for the night; one long, another short; one for winter, another for summer; one through-furred, another but-faced; one for the working day, another for the holy day; one of this colour, another of that colour; one of cloth, another of silk or damask. We must have change of apparel, one afore dinner, and another after; one of the Spanish fashion, another Turkey; and, to be brief, never content with sufficient. Our Saviour Christ bade his disciples they should not have two coats; but the most men, far unlike to his scholars, have their presses so full of apparel, that many know not how many sorts they have. . . . The proud and haughty stomachs of the daughters of England are so maintained with divers disguised sorts of costly apparel, that, as Tertullian, an ancient father, saith, there is left no difference in apparel between an honest matron and a common strumpet. Yea, many men are become so effeminate, that they care not what they spend in disguising themselves, ever desiring new toys, and inventing new fashions. Therefore, a certain man, that would picture every countryman in his accustomed apparel, when he had painted other nations, he pictured the Englishman all naked, and gave him cloth under his arm and bade him make it himself as he thought best, for he changed his fashion so often that he knew not how to make it. Thus, with our fantastical devices we make ourselves laughing-stocks to other nations; while one spendeth his patrimony upon pounces* and cuts,† another bestoweth more on a dancing-shirt than might suffice to buy him honest and comely apparel for his whole body. Some hang their revenues about their necks, ruffling in their ruffs, and many a one jeopardeth his best joint to maintain himself in sumptuous raiment. And every man, nothing considering his estate and condition, seeketh to excel others in costly attire. Whereby it cometh to pass, that, in abundance and plenty of all things, we yet complain of want and penury, while one man spendeth that which might serve a multitude, and no man distributeth of the abundance which he hath received, and all men excessively waste that which should serve to supply the necessities of others. There hath been very good provision made against such abuses, by divers good and wholesome laws; which, if they were practised as they ought to be of all true subjects, they might in some part serve to diminish this raging and riotous excess in apparel: but, alas! there

* Holes pinked or cut out for ornamenting a garment.
† The edges of a garment slashed for decoration.

appeareth amongst us little fear and obedience, either of God or man. Therefore must we needs look for God's fearful vengeance from Heaven, to overthrow our presumption and pride ...

But it will be here objected, and said of some nice and vain women, that all which we do in painting our faces, in dyeing our hair, in embalming our bodies, in decking us with gay apparel, is to please our husbands, to delight his eyes, and to retain his love towards us. Oh vain excuse, and most shameful answer, to the reproach of thy husband! What couldst thou more say to set out his foolishness, than to charge him to be pleased and delighted with the devil's tire? Who can paint her face, and curl her hair, and change it into an unnatural colour, but therein doth work reproof to her Maker who made her? As though she could make herself more comely than God hath appointed the measure of her beauty. What do these women, but go about to reform that which God hath made? not knowing that all things natural are the work of God, and things disguised and unnatural be the works of the devil: and as though a wise and Christian husband should delight to see his wife in such painted and flourished visages, which common harlots most do use, to train therewith their lovers to naughtiness; or, as though an honest woman could delight to be like an harlot for pleasing of her husband. Nay, nay, these be but vain excuses of such as go about to please rather others than their husbands. And such attires be but to provoke her to show herself abroad, to entice others: a worthy matter. She must keep debate with her husband to maintain such apparel, whereby she is the worse housewife, the seldomer at home to see her charge, and so neglect his thrift, by giving great provocation to her household to waste and wantonness, while she must wander abroad to show her own vanity, and her husband's foolishness. By which her pride, she stirreth up much envy of others, which be as vainly delighted as she is. She doth but deserve mocks and scorns, to set out all her commendation in Jewish and ethnic apparel, and yet brag of her Christianity. She doth but waste superfluously her husband's stock by such sumptuousness, and sometimes she is the cause of much bribery, extortion, and deceit in her husband's dealings, that she may be the more gorgeously set out to the sight of the vain world, to please the devil's eyes, and not God's, who giveth to every creature sufficient and moderate comeliness, wherewith we should be contented, if we were of God. What other thing dost thou by those means, but provokest others to tempt thee, to deceive thy soul, by the bait of thy pomp and pride ? What else dost thou, but settest out thy pride, and makest of the undecent apparel of thy body, the devil's net, to catch the souls of them which behold thee ? O thou woman, not a Christian, but worse than a paynim, thou minister of the devil! why pamperest thou that carrion flesh so high, which sometime doth stink and rot on the earth as thou goest ? Howsoever thou perfumest thyself, yet cannot thy beastliness be hidden, or overcome with thy smells and savours, which do rather deform and misshape thee, than beautify thee. What meant Solomon to say of such trimming of vain women, when he said, *A fair woman, without good manners and conditions, is like a sow which hath a ring of gold upon her snout*; but that the more thou garnish thyself with these outward blazings, the less thou carest for the inward garnishing of thy mind, and so dost but deform thyself by such array, and not beautify thyself ?

IX

From 'The Sermon against Idleness'. It contrasts the idleness which causes beggary and poverty with the hard work which results in thrift and contentment – the familiar argument that social evils are the result of personal moral weakness.

But what shall we need to stand much about the proving of this, that poverty followeth idleness ? We have too much experience thereof (the thing is the more to be lamented) in this realm. For a great part of the beggary that is among the poor can be imputed to nothing so much as to idleness, and to the negligence of parents, which do not bring up their children either in good learning, honest labour, or some commendable occupation or trade, whereby, when they come to age, they might get their living. Daily experience, also, teacheth that nothing is more enemy or pernicious to the health of man's body than is idleness : too much ease and sleep, and want of exercise. But these and such like incommodities, albeit they be great and noisome, yet because they concern chiefly the body and external goods, they are not to be compared with the mischiefs and inconveniences, which through idleness happen to the soul, whereof we will recite some. Idleness is never alone, but hath always a long tail of other vices hanging on, which corrupt and infect the whole man after such sort, that he is made at length nothing else but a lump of sin. *Idleness*, saith Jesus Sirach, *bringeth much evil and mischief*. St Bernard calleth it the mother of all evils, and step-dame of all virtues; adding, moreover, that it doth prepare, and, as it were, tread the way to Hell-fire. Where idleness is once received, there the devil is ready to set in his foot, and to plant all kind of wickedness and sin, to the everlasting destruction of man's soul. Which thing to be most true, we are plainly taught in the thirteenth of Matthew, where it is said, that *the enemy came while men were asleep, and sowed naughty tares among the good wheat* . . .

When man through idleness, or for default of some honest occupation or trade to live upon, is brought to poverty and want of things necessary, we see how easily such a man is induced for his gain to lie, to practise how he may deceive his neighbour, to forswear himself, to bear false witness, and oftentimes to steal and murder, or to use some other ungodly mean to live withal; whereby not only his good name, honest reputation, and a good conscience, yea, his life is utterly lost, but also the great displeasure and wrath of God, with divers and sundry grievous plagues, are procured. Lo here the end of the idle and sluggish bodies, whose hands cannot away with honest labour: loss of name, fame, reputation, and life, here in this world; and without the great mercy of God, the purchasing of everlasting destruction in the world to come. Have not all men then good cause to beware and take heed of idleness, seeing they that embrace and follow it have commonly of their pleasant idleness, sharp and sour displeasures? Doubtless, good and godly men, weighing the great and manifold harms that come by idleness to a commonwealth, have from time to time provided with all diligence, that sharp and severe laws might be made for the correction and amendment of this evil. . . . In this realm of England, good and godly laws have been divers times made, that no idle vagabonds and loitering runagates should be suffered to go from town to town, from place to place, without punishment, which neither serve God nor their prince, but devour the sweet fruits of other men's labour, being common liars, drunkards, swearers, thieves, whoremasters, and murderers, refusing all honest labour, and give themselves to nothing else but to invent and do mischief, whereof they are more desirous and greedy than is any lion of his prey. To remedy this inconvenience, let all parents and others, which have the care and governance of youth, so bring them up either in good learning, labour, or some honest occupation or trade, whereby they may be able in time to come not only to sustain themselves competently, but also to relieve and supply the necessity and want of others. . . . *It is the gift of God*, as Solomon saith, *when one eateth and drinketh, and receiveth good of his labour*. Secondly, when one liveth of his own labour, so it be honest and good, he liveth of it with a good conscience; and an upright conscience is a treasure inestimable. Thirdly, he eateth his bread not with brawling and chiding, but with peace and quietness, when he quietly laboureth for the same, according to St Paul's admonition. Fourthly, he is no man's bondman for his meat's sake, nor needeth not for that to hang upon the good-will of other men; but so liveth of his own, that he is able to give part to others. And to conclude, the labouring man and his family, whiles they are busily occupied in their labour, be free from many temptations and occasions of sin, which they that live in idleness are subject unto. And here ought artificers and labouring men, who be at wages for their work and labour, to consider their conscience to God, and their duty to their neighbour, lest they abuse their time in idleness, so defrauding them which be at charge both with great wages, and dear commons. They be worse than idle men indeed, for that they seek to have wages for their loitering. It is less danger to God to be idle for no gain, than by idleness to win out of their neighbours' purses wages for that which is not deserved. It is true, that Almighty God is angry with such as do defraud the hired man of his wages; the cry of that injury ascendeth up to God's ear for vengeance. And as true it is that the hired man, who useth deceit in his labour, is a thief before God. *Let no man*, saith St Paul to the Thessalonians, *subtilly beguile his brother, let him not defraud him in his business; for the Lord is a revenger of such deceits*. Whereupon he that will have a

good conscience to God; that labouring man, I say, which depend-
eth wholly upon God's benediction, ministering all things sufficient for his living, let him use his time in a faithful labour, and
when his labour by sickness or other misfortune doth cease, yet
let him think, for that in his health he served God and his neighbour truly, he shall not want in time of necessity. . . . Let all
masters of households reform this abuse in their families; let
them use the authority that God hath given them; let them not
maintain vagabonds and idle persons, but deliver the realm and
their households from such noisome loiterers, that idleness, the
mother of all mischief, being clean taken away, almighty God
may turn his dreadful anger away from us, and confirm the covenant of peace upon us for ever, through the merits of Jesus Christ,
our only Lord and Saviour: to whom with the Father and the
Holy Ghost be all honour and glory, world without end. Amen.

4

THOMAS LEVER (1521–77)

THOMAS LEVER, who was born at Little Lever in Lancaster in 1521, became a leader of the extreme Puritan party of reform in Cambridge University. He made a reputation by his sharp rebukes of the courtiers when preaching before Edward VI and in 1551 he became Master of St John's College, Cambridge. Because of his Puritan convictions and his support for the cause of Lady Jane Grey, he fled to Zurich after Queen Mary's accession. On the continent he imbibed fresh draughts of Puritan doctrine and on his return to England in 1559 he became Rector and Archdeacon of Coventry. In 1564 he was appointed to a Canonry in Durham but his persistence in nonconformity, especially over the wearing of the surplice, led to the deprivation of his Canonry in 1567, although he retained his other preferments.

X

From a sermon preached at Paul's Cross, 13 December 1550, denouncing the corruptions of contemporary society, such as the neglect of education and profiteering in town and country.

If you had any eyes you should see and be ashamed that in the great abundance of lands and goods taken from the abbeys, colleges and chantries for to serve the King in all necessaries, and charges, especially in provision of relief for the poor and for maintainance of learning, the King is so disappointed that both the poor be spoiled, all maintenance of learning decayed, and you only enriched. But for because you have no eyes to see with, I will declare that you may hear with your ears and so perceive and know, that whereas God and the King hath been most liberal to give and bestow, there you have been most ungrateful to dispose and deliver. For according unto God's word and the King's pleasure, the universities which be the schools of all godliness and virtue, should have been nothing decayed, but much increased and amended by the reformation of religion.

As concerning God's word for the upholding and increasing of the universities, I am sure that no man knowing learning and virtue doth doubt. And as for the King's pleasure, it did well appear in that he established unto the universities all privileges granted before his time, and also in all manner of payments required of the clergy, as tithes and first fruits, the universities be exempted. Yes and the King's Majesty that dead is, did give unto the University of Cambridge at one time two hundred pounds yearly to the exhibition and finding of five learned men to read and teach divinity, law, physic, Greek and Hebrew.*

At another time thirty pounds yearly *in liberam et puram eliemosinam*. In free and pure alms. And finally for the first foundation of a new college so much as should serve to build it and replenish it with more scholars and better livings than any other college in the University before that time had.

By the which every man may perceive that the King's giving many things and taking nothing from the University was very desirous to have them increased and amended. Howbeit all they that have known the University of Cambridge since that time that it did first begin to receive these great and manifold benefits from the King's Majesty, at your hands, have just occasion to suspect that you have deceived both the King and the University, to enrich yourselves. For that before you did begin to be the disposers of the King's liberality towards learning and poverty, there were in houses belonging to the University of Cambridge two hundred students of divinity, many very well learned: which now be clean gone, house and man, young towards scholars and old fatherly Doctors, not one of them left: one hundred also of other sort, that having rich friends or being beneficed men did live of themselves in hostelries or inns, be either gone away or else fain to creep into colleges, and put poor men from bare livings. Those both be all gone, and a small number of poor, godly, diligent students

* At Cambridge in 1540, and at Oxford in 1546, Henry VIII had established the Regius professorships in theology, medicine, civil law, Hebrew and Greek, each endowed with an annual salary of £40.

now remaining only in colleges be not able to tarry to continue their study in the University for lack of exhibition and help. There be divers there which rise daily between four and five of the clock in the morning, and from five until six of the clock, use common prayer with an exhortation of God's word in a commune chapel, and from six unto ten of the clock use ever either private study or commune lectures. At ten of the clock they go to dinner, whereas they be content with a penny piece of beef among four having a little porridge made of the broth of the same beef, with salt and oatmeal, and nothing else.

After this slender dinner they be either teaching or learning until five of the clock in the evening, when they have a supper not much better than their dinner. Immediately afterwards, they go either to reasoning in problems or unto some other study, until it be nine or ten of the clock, and being without fire are fain to walk or run up and down half an hour to get a heat on their feet when they go to bed.

These be men not weary of their pains, but very sorry to leave their study: and sure they be not able some of them to continue for lack of necessary exhibition and relief. These be the loving saints which fear God, taking great pains in abstinence, study, labour and diligence, with watching and prayer. Wherefore, as Paul for the Saints and brethren at Jerusalem, so I for your brethren and Saints at Cambridge, most humbly beseech you make your collections amongst you rich merchants of this city, and send them your oblations unto the University, so shall you be sure to please God, to comfort them, and provide learned men to do much good throughout all this realm . . .

Look whether that there was not a great number of both learned and poor that might have been kept, maintained, and relieved in the universities: which lacking all help or comfort, were compelled to foresake the university, leave their books, and seek their living abroad in the country? Yea, and in the country many grammar schools founded of a godly intent to bring up poor men's sons in learning and virtue, now be taken away by reason of the greedy covetousness of you that were put in trust by God and the King to erect and make grammar schools in many places: and had neither commandment nor permission to take away the schoolmasters living in any place. Moreover much charitable alms was there in many places yearly to be bestowed in poor towns and parishes upon God's people, the King's subjects: which alms to the great displeasure of God and dishonour of the King, yea and contrary to God's word and the King's laws, you have taken away. I know what you do say and brag in some places: that you have done as you were commanded with as much charity and liberality towards both poverty and learning, as your commission would bear and suffer . . .

Take heed unto the King's statutes, the Acts of Parliament: there you shall find that the nobles and commons do give and the King doth take into his hands abbeys, colleges and chantries for erecting of grammar schools, the godly bringing-up of youth, the further augmenting of the universities, and better provision for the poor.* This shall you find in the Acts of Parliament, in the King's statutes: but what shall be found in your practice and in your deeds ? Surely the pulling-down of grammar schools, the devilish drowning of youth in ignorance, the utter decay of the universities, and most uncharitable spoil of provision that was made for the poor . . .†

When did ever any officers in authority show such rebellious and proud minds, as was of late plainly perceived in very many of the communality ? I put the case that they be so covetous, that one of their greedy guts had swallowed up a whole abbey, house, lands and goods. And if you had had powers unto your wills, you had devoured whole countries, houses and goods, men and beasts, corn and cattle, as you did begin.

Some of them keep their farms in their own hands, and many of you keep your own corn in your own barns. Yea, marry, why

* Refers to the Acts of 1536 and 1539 for the Dissolution of the Monasteries, and the Chantries Acts of 1545 and 1547. In the case of the latter it was provided that the money should be applied to public and charitable purposes, and indeed a small part of the proceeds were used for this. The vast majority of the money, however, went into the pockets of Edward VI's advisors.

† 'Lever's indictment of the failure to refound the schools disendowed under the Chantries Act was followed by the re-establishment, in 1551-2, of a dozen or more schools with endowments . . .' S. T. Bindoff, *Tudor England*, 1950, p. 140.

should we not keep our corn in our own barns? Foresooth, you may not now keep it for dread of God, obedience to the King's Majesty, and pity of your poor neighbours . . .

He that has no corn thinks he has no part, nor is not guilty, in this matter: but I can tell that there are many of them that neither have, nor will have, corn, which make corn most dear. I have heard now that even this last year there were certain acres of corn growing on the ground bought for eight pounds: he that bought it for eight sold it for ten. He that gave ten pounds sold it to another above twelve pounds: and at last, he that carried it out of the ground paid thirteen pounds. Likewise I heard that certain quarters of malt were bought after the price of three shillings and fourpence a quarter to be delivered in a certain market town upon a certain day. This bargain was so often bought and sold before the day of delivery came that the same malt was sold to him that should receive it there and carry it away after six shillings a quarter. Look and see how much a craftsman or any other honest man that must spend corn in his house, by this manner of bargaining payeth, and how little the husbandman that tilleth the ground and payeth the rent receiveth: then you may see and perceive it must needs be hard for either of them to keep a house, the craftsman paying so much and the husbandman taking so little.

There is a like manner of bargaining of them that be leasemongers,* for leasemongers make the tenants to pay so much and the landlord to take so little that neither of them is well able to keep house. I hear say that within a few miles of London an honest gentleman did let his ground by lease to poor honest men after two shillings and fourpence an acre: then cometh a leasemonger, a thief, and extortioner, deceiving the tenants, buyeth their leases, puts them from the grounds, and causeth those that have it from him now to pay after nine shillings, or as I heard say, nineteen shillings, but I am ashamed to name so much. How be it that covetous extortioners are ashamed of no deed, be it never so evil. And as I hear say, there be many leasemongers in London that heighten the rent of bare houses: and as corn, lands, tenements and houses, so in all manner of wares, there be such buyers and sellers as cause the providers and makers of the wares to take

* Those who bought and sold leases for profit.

so little and the occupiers of the wares to pay so much that neither of them both is able to live. All the merchants of mischief that go betwixt the bark and the tree. Betwixt the husbandman that getteth the corn and the householder that occupieth corn, betwixt the landlord that letteth farms and the tenants that dwell in the farms. And betwixt the craftsman that maketh or the merchant that provideth wares and other men that occupieth wares. I say these merchants of mischief coming betwixt the bark and the tree do make all things dear to the buyers: yet wonderful vile and of small price to many that must needs set or sell that which is their own honestly come by ...

Take away all merchantmen from any town or city and you shall leave almost no provision of things that be necessary. Take away leasemongers, regrators* and all such as by buying and selling make things more dear, and when they be gone all things will be more plenty and better cheap. Now may you see who they be that make a great dearth in a great plenty. For who is it that heighteneth the price of corn? The husbandman that getteth plenty of corn by tilling of the ground? No: the regrator that buyeth corn to make it dear, growing upon the ground. Who raiseth the rents, joineth house to house, and heapeth farms together? The gentleman, that by gaining of leases, letteth forth his own lands into other men's hands? No, the leasemongers, that by selling leases, buyeth and bringeth other men's lands into their own hands. Who maketh all manner of wares and merchandise to be very dear? The merchant venturer, which, with faithful diligence to provide for the commonwealth, carrieth forth such things as may well be spared, and bringeth home such wares as must needs be occupied in this realm? No, the merchant of mischief that by crafty conveyance for his own gain carrieth away such things as may not be spared and bringeth again such wares as are not needful. Take heed you merchants of London that you be not merchants of mischief, conveying away so much old lead, wool, leather and such substantial wares as would set many Englishmen to work and do every man good service, and bringing home silks and sables, fur and foolish feathers to fill the realm full of such baggage as will never do rich or poor good and necessary

* 'profiteers'

service. Be ye sure, if this realm be rich, you shall not need to be poor; if this realm be poor, you shall not be able to keep and enjoy your riches. Take heed then that your merchandise be not a serving of foolish men's fancies, which will destroy the realm: but let it be a providing for honest discreet men's commodities, which will be the upholding and enriching of you and of the whole realm. Take heed unto your vocations prelates and preachers, magistrates and officers, landlords and tenants, craftsmen and merchants – all manner of men take heed unto yourselves and to your conversation and living . . .

Show the nobility that they have oppressed the commonalty, keeping them under in fear and ignorance, by power and authority, which might and should have been lovingly learned by their obedience and duty to both God and the King by preaching of the Gospel. Show the nobility that they have extorted and famished the commonalty by the heightening of fines and rents of farms and decaying of hospitality and good housekeeping. Show the commonalty that they be both traitors and rebels, murmuring and grudging against mine ordinances: tell the commonalty that the ox draweth, the horse beareth, the tree bringeth forth fruits and the earth corn and grass to the profit and comfort of man, as I have ordained them: but they of the commonalty of England buy and sell, make bargains and do all things to the grief and hindrance of man, contrary to my commandment. Tell the commonalty that they take one another's farm over their heads, they thrust one another out of their houses, they take leases unto themselves and let them dearer unto others: they buy corn and wares to make others pay more dear for it: they hurt and trouble, eat up and devour one another. Tell all England, high and low, rich and poor, that they everyone prowling for themselves be servants unto Mammon, enemies unto God, disturbers of the commonwealth and destroyers of themselves. And for all this let them know that I have no pleasure in the death of a sinner. *Sed magis ut convertatur et vivat*, but rather I give him respite and send him warning that he may turn and live comfortably here on earth and joyfully in Heaven for ever. Therefore if any in England do turn and amend he shall save himself.

5

EDWYN SANDYS (*c.* 1516–88)

EDWYN SANDYS was born probably in 1516 and rose to become
Archbishop of York in 1575. He was Master of St Catherine's
Hall, Cambridge, in 1547. An anti-Romanist and a leader of the
Protestant Reformation, he supported Lady Jane Grey on the
death of Edward VI. For this action he was imprisoned in the
Tower and deprived of his Mastership. When released he fled to
the continent. He returned to England at the accession of Eliza-
beth, and at once received preferment. He refused the See of
Carlisle but accepted Worcester in 1559, where he zealously pro-
moted the Puritan cause. He became Bishop of London in 1570
and five years later he was translated to the Archbishopric of York.
He was learned, disputatious and obstinate.

XI

From 'A Sermon preached before Parliament' (no date) on the text:

Moreover as for me, God forbid that I should sin against the Lord
in ceasing to pray for you: but I will teach you the good and the right
way.

Only fear the Lord, and serve him in truth with all your heart: for
consider how great things he has done for you. (*1 Sam. xii, 23–4*).

It stresses the importance of upright magistrates and the proper en-
forcement of law; it condemns some of the commercial practices of the
day and the sins and indulgences of private men.

The prince is set as the head over the body, as the chief shepherd
over the flock. These titles are given to princes and governors, to
put them in mind, not only of their honour, and pre-eminence,
but of their charge and office also. But the prince cannot do this
alone: it is a burden too heavy for one to wield. And therefore he

must, according to the counsel which Jethro gave unto Moses, 'choose out of all the people men wise and fearing God, lovers of the truth, such as hate covetousness, and out of them make rulers over thousands, hundreds, fifties, and tens, that they may sit and judge the people at all seasons.' Magistrates should be chosen out of all the people for their worthiness. It is unmeet that such things as should follow deserts be procured by other sinister means. Magistrates should be wise men, furnished with learning, understanding, good skill, and long experience; men that fear God, religious lovers of his truth, favourers of the Gospel, and of all such as live in the fear of God; true and upright dealers, such as will steadfastly fasten their eyes upon the causes brought before them, and not regard the face of any man; lastly, haters of covetousness, bribes, and rewards. Good officers should thus be qualified. And, to the end that magistrates may be such, it must be provided that there may be choice of officers without sale of offices. It is not probable that he, which obtaineth such a room for a price, will leave it freely, or deal justly in it. A greater corruption than this cannot enter into a commonwealth. For by this mean both the prince and people are deceived. To punish the evil, to maintain the good, to overlook the whole, and to choose and appoint forth worthy officers for the government of the commonwealth, this is the duty of a prince that feareth God. That prince which doth this serveth God in truth. . . . Kings and princes in their several dominions have such power through the providence of Almighty God, by whose appointment they wear their crowns, that their ordinances be not lightly broken, unless themselves be careless to have them kept. For, by reason of the majesty that God hath given them, they are feared of all estates and conditions of men. They can throw down whom they will; and whom they will they can advance. They have the chain and the rein in their hands: they can draw others whither they will, but others are not able to draw them unless they list. This power, and strength, and glory, which God hath given unto kings, and whereby they are able to lead the world as it were in a string, leaveth them utterly without excuse, if they use it not to the benefit of the commonwealth. They cannot serve God in truth, and give the bridle to their subjects to sin without restraint. These times of greatest and gravest consultation are fit occasions, wherein princes may most effectually show how heartily and truly they fear the Lord. These are the times to provide chains, that is to say, good statutes and laws to hold all men within compass, and to bind together the scattered parts of the commonwealth. When the great council of Rome entered into the senate, to consult for the good government and defence of the empire; first they went and sacrificed to Jupiter, and there every man offered up and left behind him his private affections, promising that their consultation should only tend to the common benefit. Leave you all private affections likewise: cast them behind you: seek not your own commodity. Let it appear that you love your country. God, the prince, and the common-wealth, require a faithful performance of this service at your hands. Seek by law the sincere setting forth, the maintenance and continuance, of God's true religion. Let this be your first and principal care; and so shall ye serve the Lord in truth.

Seek by law to repress the gainsayers, and the enemies of this truth. This liberty, that men may openly profess diversity of religion, must needs be dangerous to the commonwealth. . . . Let conformity and unity in religion be provided for; and it shall be as a wall of defence unto this realm.

And as these things are especially to be regarded; as our prin-cipal care must be for the highest matters, sincerity and unity in religion; so we may not neglect or pass over smaller things, which need redress. For, as diseases and sores in the basest and vilest parts of the body do grieve and may endanger the chiefest, unless they be cured betimes; so the least abuses, by sufferance, may work the greatest harm. Gorgeous apparel and sumptuous diet, with such like matters, may seem small things; but they are the causes of no small evils. They eat up England; and are therefore to be repressed by strait laws. It is a part of true service done unto God to see even unto these things.

We may seem to cast our eyes very low, when we look into the dealings of every officer under the prince. Yet every one must be seen unto. They wax suddenly rich by the spoil of the prince. Reform it by law, that all may walk in truth. If merchants, with other artificers, and meaner trades, do enrich themselves by im-poverishing others through deceitful shifts; the commonwealth

suffereth damage by their uneven dealings. If we will have God
served in truth, we must by law reform them.

That biting worm of usury, that devouring wolf, hath consumed many: many it hath pulled upon their knees, and brought
to beggary; many such as might have lived in great wealth, and in
honour not a few. This canker hath corrupted all England. It is
become the chief chaffer* and merchandise of England. We shall
do God and our country true service by taking away this evil.
Repress it by law; else the heavy hand of God hangeth over us
and will strike us.

That vile sin of adultery, in God's commonwealth punished
with death, so overfloweth the banks of all chastity, that, if by
sharp laws it be not speedily cut off, God from heaven with fire
will consume it. Prevent God's wrath: bridle this outrage: so shall
you serve the Lord in truth.

There is nothing more hurtful to the commonwealth than these
corner† contracts, without consent of parents; contrary to the
word of God, the law of nature, the law civil, and all right and
reason. The inconveniences that follow are not sufferable.
Euaristus, a bishop of Rome, saith, 'It is not wedlock, but whoredom, when the consent of parents is wanting.' God cannot be
better served, than if by law ye restrain this unlawful contracting.
The children of this inconvenient marriage may scarcely be
termed lawful. The devil, that hath ever hated wedlock, and loveth
whoredom, was the first author of this great disorder. God grant
you understanding hearts and willing minds, faithfully and in
truth to travail to repress and take away these evils.

And, as evil is to be controlled by law, so that which is good is
also by law to be procured. God hath made us many ways rich.
For what we have, freely at his hands we have it. But he himself is
become very poor; insomuch that, for want of relief, he is forced
to beg; and, for want of lodging and meat, he lieth and dieth in our
streets. This great ingratitude God cannot but revenge. O, what
shame is this to a Christian commonwealth, in a reformed
country! Obstinate Jews would never show themselves so unthankful. Their ancient law, forbidding beggars, is even to this
day most straitly kept amongst them. Laws in this behalf have

* 'trade'   † i.e. 'done in a corner'

been provided; but as they wanted perfection, so have they in manner in no point or anywhere had execution. Serve God in truth: provide that Christ crave not. Such as will not feed him here he will never feed in his kingdom. Thus have I, point by point, let you see disorders and wants in the commonwealth. Ye have authority by law to reform them. Consider dutifully of it, and serve God truly as ye ought, always remembering the saying of the prophet Isaiah, 'Woe be to them that make wicked laws'.

XII

From 'A Sermon preached at St Paul's Cross' (no date) on the text: 'But the end of all things is at hand: be ye therefore sober, and watch unto prayer' (*1 Peter iv, 7*). *It refers to extravagances in eating, drinking and dress.*

As this inward sobriety of mind and judgement is required, so are we exhorted likewise to an outward sobriety, which consisteth in diet, in apparel, in gesture, and in speech. Be sober in diet. Nature is contented with a little: but, where sobriety wanteth, nothing is enough. The body must have sufficient, lest it faint in the midst of necessary duties: but beware of gluttony and drunkenness. And Christ saith, 'Take ye heed, overload not your hearts with these burdens of excess.' Be not drunken with wine. These lessons are fit for England, where ancient sobriety hath given place to superfluity; where many such rich men are, as fare daintily day by day. God grant their end be not like his, who, riotously wasting here the creatures of God, wanted afterwards a drop of water when he would gladly have had it! John Baptist was content with a simple diet, Christ with very slender fare; but there are of us, I fear me, whose god is their belly, and whose felicity is meat and drink. Our excess this way is intolerable and abominable: we strive to equal almost Vitellius, who had served unto him at one feast 2,000 fishes, and 7,000 birds; and Heliogabalus, that monster of the world, who at one supper was served with 600 ostriches. There is no bird that flieth, no fish that swimmeth, no beast that moveth, which is not buried in our bellies. This excess is an enemy both to wealth and health: it hath cut off much housekeeping, and brought many men to extreme beggary; and as many great diseases are cured by abstinence, so fullness hath been the cause of sundry strange and unwonted sicknesses. Aurelian, the Emperor, did never send for physician in time of his sickness, but cured himself only by thin diet. And as immoderate feeding doth much hurt to the body, so it is more noisome to the mind. For as the ground, if it receive too much rain, is not watered, but drowned, and turneth into mire, which is neither fit for tillage nor for yielding of fruit; so our flesh, over-watered with wine, is not fit to admit the spiritual plough, or to bring forth the celestial fruits of righteousness. The herbs that grow about it will be loathsome and stinking weeds; as brawling, chiding, blasphemy, slander, perjury, hatred, manslaughter, and suchlike bad works of drunkenness and darkness. Are not these unsavoury fruits enough to make us abhor the tree ? A drunken body is not a man, but a swine, fit for devils to enter into. For these sins are against nature, which, being moderately refreshed, is satisfied; being stuffed, is hurt, violated, and deformed. God hath given us his creatures soberly to use, and not so shamefully to abuse: we should, if we did well, feed the body to serve and not to rule, to obey, and not to lead, the spirit. 'I chastise my body,' saith St Paul, 'and bring it into servitude.' Is it not perilous, trow you, to pamper and make strong our adversary ? or have we a greater or stronger enemy than our rebellious flesh! Full-bellied drunkards are no better than traitors in this spiritual war. . . . We have the blessed apostle of Christ, the servant of God, to put us in mind of sobriety in diet. Nor in diet only, but also in attire. 'A man's apparel, laughter, and gait, doth show his nature.' In apparel this is to be observed, that, avoiding vanity and pride therein, every man wear according to his calling. John Baptist wore a rough coat of camel's hair; but Solomon used rich and glorious apparel; and yet both used that which did become them. There is no more holiness in a friar's cowl, than in a shepherd's cloak: yet that is comely in one, which is not seemly in another. St Paul is very earnest with women, and requireth them to go in sober apparel, decking themselves 'with shame-facedness and modesty, not with broidered hair, or with gold, or pearls, or sumptuous attire, but as becometh women that profess the fear of God'. And St Peter telleth them, that their godly mother Sarah went soberly apparelled. Sarah was a good woman, a rich woman, and a noble woman: such as follow her footsteps need not be ashamed. Yet do I not condemn all other apparel: yea, even such apparel as is costly and gorgeous may be fit for some states and personages. I do not doubt but that Hester and Judith did wear gold, and were gorgeously decked. But if Paul and Peter did live in our days, they would not spare the vanity of our women, much less of our men. The vain and monstrous apparel of all other countries and nations England hath scraped together, and in a bravery put it on; the estimation whereof is this: a light wavering mind, matched with a vain proud heart, desireth a light, vain, strange, proud, and monstrous apparel, to cover and clad it withal. But sobriety is content with that which is seemly. Be sober in your apparel. . . . There be two grand enemies of hospitality. The one is covetousness, the other profuseness. Nigardliness would not suffer Nabal, that rich carl, to bestow a piece of bread to relieve the necessity of David, a king. 'Shall I take my bread and my water and the flesh of my beasts that I have killed for my shearers, and give it to men whom I know not either who or whence they are?' Others, with the prodigal son, waste that unthriftily, wherewith they should relieve the poor and comfort strangers: some of them being eaten up, as they say, with three H. H. H.: horses, hawks, and harlots; some with vain apparel, casting away as much upon a garment, as would almost ransom a king; some with building, some with banqueting; some by one mean, and some by another: whereby it is come to pass that hospitality itself is waxen a stranger, and needeth harbour: we have shut it quite and clean out of doors.

6

HENRY SMITH (*c.* 1550–91)

Born in Leicestershire in about 1550, Henry Smith was ordained to the ministry but, because of scruples with regard to subscription to the Articles, he determined not to undertake a pastoral charge. In 1587 he was elected Lecturer of St Clement Danes, London, but in the following year he was suspended from preaching by the bishop because he had not subscribed to the Articles of Religion and had spoken against the Prayer Book. Thomas Fuller, the seventeenth-century Church historian, said that he was commonly called 'the silver-tongued Smith'* and à Wood said that he was 'esteemed the miracle and wonder of his age, for his prodigious memory, and for his fluent, eloquent and practical way of preaching'.†

XIII

The following extracts are from 'The first Sermon on Usury' (no date or place), preached on the text: 'A soft answer turneth away wrath; but grevious words stir up anger. . . . A fool despiseth his father's instruction: but he that regardeth reproof is prudent' (Prov. xv, 1 and 5). An illustration of the contemporary attitude of churchmen to usury.

Usury is the sin which God will try now whether you love better than his Word; that is, whether you will leave it if he forbid it. For if he flatly forbid it and yet you will fully retain it, then you love usury better than God's Word. Therefore one saith well that our usurers are heretics, because after many admonitions, yet they maintain their error and persist in it obstinately, as Papists do in Popery. For this cause I am glad that I have an occasion to grapple

---

* Thomas Fuller, *Church History*, Bk. ix, 16, p. 142.
† Anthony á Wood, *Athenae Oxoniensis*, i, p. 603.

with this sin, where it has made so many spoils; and where it has so many patrons: for it is said that there be more of this profession in this city than there be in all the land beside . . .

First, I will define what usury is. Secondly, I will show you what usury doth signify. Thirdly, I will show the unlawfulness of it. Fourthly, I will show the kinds of it. Fifthly, I will show the arguments which are alleged for it. Sixthly, I will show the punishment of it. Seventhly, I will show you what opinion we should hold of them which do not lend upon usury, but borrow upon usury. Lastly, I will show you what they should do which have got their riches by usury.

Touching the first, usury is that gain which is gotten by lending, for the use of the thing which a man lendeth, covenanting before with the borrower to receive more than was borrowed; and therefore one calls the usurer a legal thief, because before he steals, he tells the party how much he will steal, as though he stole by the law . . .

Now all the Commandments of God are fulfilled by love, which Christ noteth, when he draweth all the Commandments to one Commandment, which is, *Love God above all things, and thy neighbour as thyself:* as if he should say, he which loveth God, will keep all the Commandments which respect God: and he which loveth his neighbour will respect all the Commandments which respect his neighbour: therefore to maintain love, God forbiddeth all things which hinder this love; and amongst the rest he forbiddeth usury as one of her deadliest enemies. For man cannot love and be a usurer, because usury is a kind of cruelty, and a kind of extortion, and a kind of persecution; and therefore the want of love doth make usurers: for if there were love, there would be no usury, no deceit, no extortion, no slandering, no revenging, no oppression: but we should live in peace and joy and contentment, like the angels: whereby you see, that all our sins are against ourselves: for if there were no deceit, we should not be deceived; if there were no slander, we should not be slandered; if there were no envy, then we should not be envied; if there were no extortion, then we should not be injured; if there were no usury, then we should not be oppressed. Therefore God's law had been better for us than our own law: for if his law did stand, then we should not be deceived, nor slandered, nor envied, nor injured, nor oppressed. God hath commanded every man to lend freely; and who would not borrow freely? Therefore they which brought in usury, brought in a law against themselves ...

As the name of the Devil doth declare what an enemy he is: so the name of usury doth declare what an enemy she is. That you may know usury for a biter, her name doth signify biting. . . . . All usury signifieth biting, to show that all usury is unlawful.

Now you have heard what usury is and of what it is derived; you shall hear the unlawfulness of it.

First, it is against the law of charity, because charity biddeth us to give every man his own and to require no more than our own: but usury requireth more than our own and gives not to other their own. Charity rejoiceth to communicate her goods to others and usury rejoiceth to gather other men's goods to herself.

Secondly, it is against the law of nations; for every nation hath some law against usury and some restraint against usurers, as you shall hear when we speak of the punishment.

Thirdly, as it is against the law of nations, so it is against the law of nature; that is, the natural compassion which should be amongst men. You see a river when it goeth by an empty place, it will not pass until it hath filled that empty place, and then it goeth forward to another empty place and filleth it; and so to another empty place and filleth it; always filling the places that are empty. So should we; the rich should fill the poor, the full should fill the hungry, they which abound should fill them which want; for the rich are but God's almoners, and their riches are committed to them of God, to distribute and do good, as God doth himself ...

Fourthly, it is against the law of God. First, it is forbidden in *Exodus xxii* where it is said, *If thou lend money unto my people*, that is, *to the poor with thee, thou shalt not oppress them with usury*. Here is usury called oppression; therefore if oppression is a sin, usury is a sin too. Secondly, it is forbidden *Leviticus xxv, 26*, where it is said, *Thou shalt not give thy money to usury, nor lend thy victuals for increase*. Here you may see that men may be usurers of victuals and other things, as well as of money. Thirdly, it is forbidden in *Deuteronomy xxiii*, where it is said, *Thou shalt not lend unto thy brother upon usury*. And lest you should say that he meaneth but one kind of usury, he showeth that he means all kinds of usury; for after in the nineteenth verse he says, *As usury of money, usury of victuals, usury of corn, or usury of anything that is given to usury:* because some are no usurers of money, but some are usurers of victuals, some are usurers of cloth, some are usurers of corn, some are usurers of wine, some are usurers of oil, and some of one thing and some of another; and none would be accounted usurers but they which lend money unto usury: therefore God forbiddeth so precisely usury of anything, showing that all usury is unlawful . . .

Christ expounding the Commandment which forbiddeth to steal, saith, *Lend freely*, showing that usury, because she lendeth not freely, is a kind of theft, and the usurers a kind of thieves, or else this exposition were not right. Therefore *Zaccheus*, as though he had stolen other men's goods, when he began to repent, he restored them again four-fold; even as thieves are enjoined to restore four-fold for that which they have stolen, so *Zaccheus* restored four-fold, as though he had stolen. It seemeth that *Zaccheus* was no great thief, because he restored four-fold for all that he had gotten wrongfully: for he got but the fourth part of his goods wrongfully at the most, or else he could not have restored four-fold again. But now, if some should restore four-fold for all that they have gotten wrongfully, they should restore more than they have, because all which usurers get, they get wrongfully; for their occupation is a sin: and therefore one saith, Because they cannot restore four-fold here, they shall suffer a hundred-fold hereafter . . .

Now you have heard the unlawfulness of usury, you shall hear how many kinds there be of it. As other crafts are called mysteries, so I may fitly call it the Mystery of Usury; for they have devised more sorts of usury than there be tricks at cards. I cannot reckon half and I am afraid to show you all, lest I should teach you to be usurers while I dissuade you from usury. Yet I will bring forth some, and the same reasons which are alleged against these shall condemn all the rest.

Some will not take usury, but they will have the use of your pasture, or your land, or your orchard, or your team, or your kine, until you pay the money again, which in that time will grow to a greater gain to the usurer and a greater loss to the borrower than if he had paid more money than other usurers are wont to take.

Some will not take usury, but they will take plate and vessels, and tapestry and bedding, and other household stuff, to use and wear until the money come home, which will lose more in wearing than the interest of the money would come to. This usury is forbidden in the second of *Amos*, where God complaineth, saying, *They lie down upon the clothes which are laid to pledge*: showing that we should not lie down upon such clothes; that is, we should not use or wear the thing which is laid to pledge.

Some will take no usury, but they will take a pawn, which is better than the money which they lend; and then they will covenant that if he bring not the money again by such a day he forfeiteth his pawn; which day the usurer knoweth that the poor man is not able to keep, and so he keepeth the pawn for his money, which is worth twice his money. This usury is forbidden in *Leviticus xxv*, where it is said, *Thou shalt not take usury or vantage*. As if he should say, Thou shalt not take the forfeiture; for then thou takest vantage, when thou takest more than thou lendeth.

Some will not take usury, but they will buy something at a small price and then covenant with the borrower that he buy the same again of the same price at such a day, which day the usurer knoweth that the borrower is not able to keep and so he getteth for a little that which the other might have sold for much more. This usury is condemned in the first chapter to the *Thessalonians*, the fourth verse, where it is said, *Let no man defraud or circumvent his brethren in any thing*.

Some will not take usury, but they will lend their money to occupiers upon condition to be partakers in their gains but not in their losses. So one takes all the pains and abideth all the venture, and the other that takes no pains reapeth half the profit. This usury is forbidden in *2 Thessalonians ii, 10*, where it is said, *He which will not work, let him not eat*.

Some will not take usury; but if he be a labourer or mason, or a carpenter, which borroweth of him, he will covenant with him for so many day's work, he shall labour with him so many days or so many weeks for no money, but the loan of money. This usury is condemned in *Luke x, 7*, where it is said, *The labourer is worthy of his hire.*

Some will not take usury; but if you have not present money to pay for their wares they will set a high price on them for the forebearing of the time, and so they do not only sell their wares, but they sell time too; that is, they do not only sell their own, but they sell God's own ...

XIV

From a sermon entitled 'The Poor Man's Tears' (no date or place) on the text: 'Whosoever shall give to drink unto one of these little ones a cup of cold water only in the name of a disciple, verily I say unto you, he shall in no wise lose his reward' (*Matt. x, 42*). *It stresses the duty of the rich to give charity to the poor.*

Alms is a charitable relief given by the godly to the sick, to the lame, the blind, the impotent, the needy, the hungry and poorest persons, even such as are daily vexed with continual want, to whom even of duty, and not of compassion, we ought to impart some part of that which God hath mercifully bestowed upon us. For as we daily seek for benefits at God's hand, which he doth continually give us, so ought we therewith to relieve the poor, since God hath so commanded us. The performance whereof we ought not to drive off from time to time, but to do it when they desire to have it done. For the true obedience of God doth forbid us to prolong or drive off the doing of good things. ... O let us take heed that our hearts be not hardened against the poor nor that we give our alms to get glory of the world, but so let us give our alms that the one hand may not know what the other doeth. Yea, we ought to give with such equality that our poor neighbours may be relieved, to whom indeed we ought to become contributors, as *Job* was. All people have not one belly: for as one chimney may be hot, so another may be cold; one pot moist with liquor, when another may be dry; one's purse empty, when another's is full; so one poor man's belly full, and another's empty. That is a good commonwealth that looketh to every member in the commonwealth; and those men are worthy of riches that look daily to the feeding of their poor neighbours. Let therefore the tears of the poor admonish you to charity, that when *Dives* hath dined *Lazarus* may have the crumbs.

Now let us proceed and consider what we must give and to whom we must give. In the text we are willed to give, though it be but a cup of cold water or a piece of bread. This containeth matter both for the taker and the giver. Bread will serve beggars and they must be no choosers, yet bread will not serve some beggars, that boldly upon upon Gads-Hill, Shooters-Hill, and such like places, take men's horses by the heads and bid them deliver their purses. For these fellows are of the opinion of the *Anabaptists* that every man's goods must be common to beggars, which ought to be suppressed by godly policy. As for the other sort of beggars and other poor persons, they must be content to take up their cross and endeavour themselves patiently to suffer their ordinary grievances and remember that man's nature may be satisfied with a little.

As touching how much we should give, we are taught that if we have much we should give accordingly; if we have but little, give what we can spare. Saint *Luke* counselleth us, if we *have two coats* we must *give one to him that hath none; and of meat likewise*. But as touching this question little need to be spoken when our own covetous hearts are ready enough to frame excuses.

Some will make a question of their alms and say they know not what the party is that demandeth relief or beggeth alms of them. Oh! say some, I suspect he is an idle person, dishonest, or perhaps an unthrift, and therefore refuse to give any relief at all. To this I answer, they are needless doubts, for we ought to relieve them, if we know them not for such persons; and let their bad deeds fall on their own necks, for if they perish for want we are in danger of God's wrath for them, but to give unto such as we know of lewd behaviour, thereby to continue them in their wickedness, were very offensive. We are not still tied to one place for giving our charity, but it stretcheth far; for we are commanded not only to relieve our own countrymen, but also strangers and such as dwell in foreign nations . . .

The tears of men, women and children are grievous and pitiful, and tears give cause of great compassion, especially the tears of such as therewith are constrained to beg for their relief. But if the tears of the rich for the loss of their goods, or the tears of parents for the death of their children, or the tears of kind-natured persons for the loss of friends, or other wrongs sustained ought generally to be regarded and pitied, then much more should the tears of those breed great compassion in the hearts of Christians whom beggary and extremity of miserable hunger constraineth to shed tears in most grievous and lamentable sort. Oh! what shall a man say unto those pitiful faces which are made moist through the extremity of hunger, wherein are most bitter and sharp effects, a thing above all extremes ? . . .

Tears are the last thing that man, woman, or child can move by, and where tears move not nothing will move. I therefore exhort you, by the lamentable tears which the poor do daily shed through hunger and extreme misery, to be good to them, to be charitable and merciful to them and to relieve those whom you see with misery distressed.

The Scripture saith, *Give to every one that asketh.* God gave herbs and other food unto every living thing. Every commonwealth that letteth any member of it perish for hunger is an unnatural and uncharitable commonwealth. But men are nowadays so full of doubts, through a covetous desire for themselves, that they cannot abide to part with anything for the poor, notwithstanding that God hath promised that he will not forget the work and love which you have showed in his name to the poor and distressed.

Some will say for their excuse that they are overcharged by giving to a number of persons and therefore they cannot give to so many beggars, for by so doing they might soon become beggars themselves. *David* answered this objection very well and saith thus, *I never saw the just man forsaken, nor his seed beg their bread;* whereby he meant that in all the time he had lived . . . he scarcely ever saw that, upon an upright heart in giving, a man was brought to beggary.

There are a number that will deny a poor body a penny and plead poverty to them, though they seem to stand in never so great extremes, when in a far worser sort they will not stick immediately to spend ten or twenty shillings. The rich worldling makes no conscience to have ten or twenty dishes of meat at his table, when in truth the one half might sufficiently satisfy nature and the rest run to the relief of the poor, and yet in the end he might depart better refreshed with one dish than commonly he is with twenty. Some will not stick to have twenty coats, twenty houses, twenty farms, yea twenty lordships, and yet go by a poor person whom they see in great distress and never relieve him with one penny, but say, God help you, I have not for you. There are lawyers that will not stick to undo twenty poor men, and merchants that make no conscience to eat out twenty others, that have their hundreds out at usury, their chests crammed full with crowns and their coffers full of golden gods and glittering angels, that will go by twenty poor, miserable, hungry, impotent and distressed persons, and yet not bestow one penny on them; and though they do most shamefully ask it, yet can they most shamefully deny it and refuse to perform it . . .

If the proud would leave their superfluity in apparel, their excess in embroidery, their vanity in cuts, guards and pounces,* their excess in spangling, their fantastical feather and needless bravery, the greater part would suffice towards the relief of the poor, and yet they have insufficient to suffice nature.

Let the glutton seek only to suffice nature and leave his daily surfeiting in belly-cheer, then might the poor be fed with that which he oftentimes either loathsomely vomits forth or which worketh as an instrument to shorten his own life.

Let the whoremonger leave off his dalliance and his inordinate expenses for maintaining his wickedness and it shall be good for his body and better for his soul; yea, his purse shall be heavier and he thereby better able to relieve the poor.

Let every artificer and tradesman live orderly, avoiding superfluous expenses, not spending his money vainly at dice, tables, cards, bowling, betting and such like, but live as becometh civil Christians in the fear of God; they may have sufficient for the maintenance of themselves and their family, and yet the poor may be by them sufficiently relieved.

Let us consider that we who have our beginning from God ought generally to bend our actions towards the pleasing of God;

* i.e. garments slashed, trimmed and cut for ornamentation.

and doing as he commandeth us we please him; for if we help the poor we help him; and doing all charitable actions to the poor he accounteth it as done to himself.

Let us generally learn not to condemn or despise the poor, but according to our abilities help them and consider their extremes, and at any hand not disdain and upbraid them with the titles of base rogues or such like, but in all godly Christian means cherish and comfort them with such charitable relief as we may in reason afford unto them, yea, and consider of their care as if it were our own.

7

JOHN STOCKWOOD (d. 1618)

JOHN STOCKWOOD was a schoolmaster and a divine. He was
Minister of Battle, Sussex, in 1571, became headmaster of the
free grammar school at Tonbridge, Kent, in or before 1578, and
Vicar of Tonbridge some seven years later. He was a celebrated
and powerful preacher.

XV

*The sermon from which the following extract is taken was preached
at St Paul's Cross, 24 August 1578, on the text:*

There was a certain man in Caesarea called Cornelius, a centurion
of the band called the Italian band,

A devout man, and one that feared God with all his house, which
gave much alms to the people, and prayed to God alway.

He saw in a vision evidently about the ninth hour of the day an
angel of God coming in to him, and saying unto him, Cornelius.

And when he looked on him, he was afraid, and said, What is it,
Lord? And he said unto him, Thy prayers and thy alms are come up
for a memorial before God.

And now send men to Joppa, and call for one Simon, whose sur-
name is Peter: He lodgeth with one Simon, a tanner, whose house is by
the sea side: he shall tell thee what thou oughtest to do.

And when the angel which spake unto Cornelius was departed, he
called two of his household servants, and a devout soldier of them that
waited on him continually;

And when he had declared all these things unto them, he sent them
to Joppa. (*Acts x, 1–8*).

*It comments on theatres and other amusements, exhorts schoolmasters
in their duties, and calls upon the Lord Mayor of London to 'clean
up' the city.*

You here in London have good experience of that which a little before I spake, namely, that as God commonly more plentifully blesseth the greater cities, so, for their contempt, they have more plentiful taste of his plagues before other places. For tell me, I pray you, what contagious sickness or dangerous disease is there but for the most part you have the first and the greatest visitation with it? And do you think that we of the country escape scotfree? Yet for all this, what is our behaviour toward the Word of eternal life? Will not a filthy play, with the blast of a trumpet, sooner call thither a thousand than an hour's tolling of a bell bring to the sermon a hundred? Nay, even here in the city, without it be at this place and some other certain ordinary audience, where shall you find a reasonable company? Whereas, if you resort to the theatre, the Curtain* and other places of plays in the city, you shall on the Lord's day have these places, with many others that I cannot reckon, so full as possible they can throng, besides a great number of other lets to pull from the hearing of the Word, of which I will speak hereafter. And do you think that so long as these enormities are suffered the plague and such other like infectious sicknesses, which in the xxviii of Deuteronomy the Lord threateneth to send as scourges for the contempt of his Word, shall cease and diminish among you? Nay, they be means for them to rage more fiercely and to cause God to send new plagues among them, for as we are witty to commit new sins so the Lord daily prepareth new punishments to correct us withal, insomuch that he visiteth our new sins with such new and strange diseases as the names are unknown to us and never heard of by our forefathers.... I cannot but commend the laudable policy and diligent endeavour of the Right Honourable my Lord Mayor and the worshipful Aldermen his brethren for the preventing of infection, by commanding men's houses to be kept sweet and the theatres clean, with other suchlike ways. But believe me, dear brethren, the plague cannot be carried away in a dung cart. What availeth it to have sweet houses and stinking souls? pleasant smelling chambers and grievous savoring minds? clean and fair theatres and foul and filthy hearts and consciences? As I do not dislike these outward cleansings, so I beseech you, let everyone of us labour for the inward purging and scouring of our souls . . .

* The Curtain was a theatre built in 1577.

We . . . on the Lord's day must have fairs kept, must have bear-baiting, bull-baiting, . . . must have bawdy interludes, dicing, carding, tabling, dancing, drinking. . . . I dare boldly stand to avouch it, that there is no day in the week wherein God is so much dishonoured as on that day on which he should be best served. And must we for these abuses think at the Lord's hands to escape unscathed ? . . .

Most humbly and reverently, in the fear of God [I] request you, Right Honourable my Lord Mayor of this worthy City of London, with the worshipful Master Sheriffs and Aldermen, as the Lord hath laid upon you and the persons of public magistrates, that you will keep in your several wards a careful and diligent watch to meet with all such abuses as highly offend God and are directly against her Majesty's laws; amongst the rest, these filthy whore-dom and beastly drunkenness, outrageous and unreasonable dicing and carding, and horrible profanation of the Lord's day, in flocking and thronging to bawdy plays by thousands, whereas they ought to be occupied in hearing the Word of the Lord. As for whoredom, it is common; drunkenness is in every tavern; dicing and carding in most of your ordinary tabling places; re-sorting to plays in the time of sermons a thing too manifest. For the other, as I have them by report, so I wish them false. If they be true, I desire to have them punished with severity. Then shall you show yourselves religious and zealous Cornelians*, in living not only godly yourselves, but also bringing others belonging to your charge to be honest, virtuous and godly likewise. Thus doing, the Lord will bless with many blessings both you and your poor city, which for Christ's sake I beseech him to do . . .

Give me leave, I beseech you, a little to direct my speech unto those whom in respect of their office it chiefly concerneth to bring up youth. I mean schoolmasters, for among all the diseases that these our days and times are grievously sick withal there is none wherewith they are either more generally or more dangerously infect than with this – that the most part of schoolmasters, like as fathers and householders, think it no part of their duty to meddle with instructing their scholars and pupils in the Word of the Lord and the principles of Christian religion. . . . Some of you think

* A reference to the text of the sermon.

overmuch gentleness to be the way and others continual and tyrannical scourging and whipping to be the way, whereas indeed you are both sorts far and wide out of the way. For the one with too much leniency encourageth them to a lewd licentiousness and looseness of manners; the others, thinking by cruel and butcherly beating to win reformation, engender in them such a mislike and loathing of learning that they abhor with as deadly hatred the school-house as we do those things which are most loathsome and noisome to us. I like well of gentleness, if it be such as by it manners be not corrupted and spilled, and, on the other side, I allow of reasonable correction, so as it be used as the last remedy – that is, when no other will serve. But the first, the best and the chiefest way is to begin with teaching your youth the fear of the Lord . . .

When as the Lord in his mercy hath sent us the Gospel with peace and quiet, [the devil] useth pleasure and prosperity to draw men unto vanity. How this way he prevaileth both in country and city our present times afford too plentiful examples, and the time to come in another world will yield unto the frequenters of such lewdness plentiful punishment. There be not many places where the Word is preached besides the Lord's day (I would to God there were), yet even that day the better part of it is horribly profaned by devilish inventions, as with Lords of Misrule, Morris dancers, May-games, insomuch that in some places they shame not in the time of divine service to come and dance about the church; and without, to have men naked dancing in nets, which is most filthy, for the heathen that never had further knowledge than the light of nature have counted it shameful for a player to come on the stage without a slop*; and therefore, amongst Christians, I hope such beastly business shall not be let escape unpunished, for which end I recite it, and can tell, if I be called, where it was committed within these few weeks. What should I speak of beastly plays, against which out of this place every man crieth out? Have we not houses of purpose built with great charges for the maintenance of them, and that without the liberties, as who would say, There, let them say what they will say, we will play. I know not how I might with the godly learned especially

* 'breeches'

more discommend the gorgeous playing place erected in the fields* than to term it, as they please to have it called, a Theatre, that is even after the manner of the old heathenish Theatre at Rome, a show place of all beastly and filthy matters, to the which it cannot be chosen that men should resort without learning thence much corruption. For if he that beheld but the filthy picture of *Jupiter* in a shower of golden rain descending unto *Dianae* could thereby encourage himself unto filthiness, shall we think that flocks of as wild youths of both sexes, resorting to interludes, where both by lively gesture and voices there are allurements unto whoredom, they can come away pure and not inflamed with concupiscence? I will not here enter this disputation, whether it be utterly unlawful to have any plays, but will only join in this issue, whether in a Christian commonwealth they be tolerable on the Lord's day . . .

 * On the Southwark banks of the Thames; probably refers to the erection of the Curtain in 1577.

8

THOMAS WHITE (*c.* 1550–1624)

THOMAS WHITE was born about 1550 in Bristol and became Vicar of St Dunstan-in-the-West in 1575. Ten years later preferment came rapidly and in the four years, 1590–93, he secured stalls in Salisbury Cathedral, in Christ Church, Oxford, and in St George's Chapel, Windsor. He erected the hospital in Bristol for the poor and under his will he founded Sion College, London, as a corporation of all the clergy within the City of London and its suburbs. He was 'a noted and frequent preacher of God's word'.

XVI

From 'A Sermon preached at Paules Cross', 3 November 1577, on the text:

Woe to her that is filthy and polluted, to the oppressing city:
She obeyed not the voice; she received not correction; she trusted not in the Lord; she drew not near to her God.
Her princes within her are roaring lions; her judges are evening wolves; they gnaw not the bones till the morrow. (*Zeph. iii, 1–3*).

An attack on the vices of the city, with special reference to theatres and play-going, to usury and creditors, and to the eating and sleeping habits of 'the great'.

Because I spake of Sabbaths, know you every day is a Christian Sabbath, yet one among the rest was especially commanded to the Jews, and commended unto us both to rest our bodies and our beasts; but the chief end was for Israel to go to the Sanctuary and for us to come to the house of prayer. ... Assuredly we come nothing near the Jews in this point, for on our Sabbaths all manner of games and plays, banquetings and surfeitings are very rife. If any man have any business in the world, Sunday is counted an idle day. If he have none, then it is bestowed in other pleasures. *Trahit sua quenque luptas,* Every man followeth his own fancy. And the wealthiest citizens have houses for the nonce: they that have none make shift with alehouses, taverns and inns, some rowing on the water, some roving in the field, some idle at home, some worse occupied; that what you get evilly all the week is worst spent on the Sabbath day, according to the proverb, Ill gotten, all spent. Blame not your servants if they follow your example, for your prodigality makes them unthrifty. But what account, how answer you? Is this the Lord's day or no? If it be, how intolerable, nay how accursed and most condemnable, are these outrageous *Bachanalia, Lupanaria* – I cannot tell what to call them – such as heathen men were ever ashamed of (I am sure), and therefore practised better matters, although profane exercises. But ours favours so of *Venus* court and *Bacchus* kitchen that it may rightly be entitled an abominable and filthy city, and without doubt London shall justify her elder sister Jerusalem if in time she turn not to the Lord. I say nothing of divers other abuses, which so carry away thousands and drown them in the pernicious vanities of the world. Look but upon the common plays in London and see the multitude that flocketh to them and followeth them. Behold the sumptuous theatre houses, a continual monument of London's prodigality and folly. But I understand they are now forbidden because of the plague. I like the policy well if it hold still, for a disease is but bodged or patched up that is not cured in the cause, and the cause of plague is sin, if you look to it well, and the cause of sin are plays; therefore the cause of plagues are plays *Quicquid est causa causa est causa causati.* Shall I reckon up all the monstrous birds that breed in this nest? Without doubt I am ashamed, I should surely offend your chaste ears, but the old world is matched and Sodom overcome, for more horrible enormities and swelling sins are set out by those stages than every man thinks for, so some would believe, if I should paint them out in their colours. Without doubt you can scarcely name me a sin that by that sink is not set agog – theft and whoredom, pride and prodigality, villainy and blasphemy. These three couples of hellhounds never cease barking there, and bite many, so as they are incurable ever after, so that many a man hath the lewder wife, and many a wife the lewder husband by it; and it cannot otherwise be but that which robbeth flatly the Lord of all his honour, and is directly against the whole first table of his laws, should make no bones of breach of the second also, which is towards our neighbour only. Wherefore, if thou be a father thou lovest thy child; if thou be a master thou lovest thy servant; and thou be what thou canst be, thou lovest thyself that hauntest those schools of vice... theatres of all lewdness. If it be not suppressed in time, it will make such a tragedy that all London may well mourn while it is London, for it is no playing time (and every man bethink him well) but time to pray rather. But faith is fainted, and when the Son of Man comes, shall he find faith upon the earth ? Blessed is the servant who when his master cometh shall find doing, not playing but working, and doing not evil but good, for that is our duty that are God's servants, but Satan's slaves do run another race . . .

Of the several sorts of wicked branches all sprouting out of this poisoned body [i.e. usury], covetousness being the root of all, I leave to speak at large: as of masters detaining servants' wages, it is a cruelty and comes of covetousness, a roaring sin which shall make the sinners howl for it if they repent not in time. Remember you have a master in heaven, and let not the hireling's wages tarry with thee all night, as many make them reap their labour for their pains. Such grubbers these be, which grind the faces of the poor, and lurch them as they list, using them worse than many a man would a beast. They cost more and are as dear in Christian eyes as thou, and more precious too, and thou keep that way, for the end thereof is destruction. This is a great fault of gentlemen in the country, and some in the city too, as hardhearted and merciless as the beast. Take heed, lest in the bitterness of their grief they curse thee and their cry come up unto the Lord.

I say nothing of creditors, which may well be called executors, for spoiling of orphans, infants and widows, which are their own carvers, and beggar and beguile them to whom the right belongs. And here methinks I see the secret judgement of God on goods ill-gotten. As David saith, thou scrapest and canst not tell for whom thou rakest into thy clutches and knoweth not who shall possess them, perhaps thy executor, perhaps a stranger, sometimes thy enemy and sometimes thine own son, that consume and scatter abroad what thou with toil and turmoil . . . hast miserably scratched together in all the days of thy life. It is flown in a year, yea sometimes in an hour, if they fall kindly to it, as many masters do . . .

The prophet Amos saith of them of his time that they lie in beds of ivory, not so costly as wood at that time, as is to be found in the beds of our age, comparing time with time and place with place, as howsoever they bettered us in the wood, we pass them all for curious work. The prophet names no down beds neither – perhaps feathers was the only use. But now niceness is more dainty than so, covetousness more cunning for the turn. They drinking of wine in bowels doth show that curious-wrought goblets and counterfeit hypocrisy was not then known of old. They anointed themselves with sweet odours, but we perfume ourselves with the dearest musk. They did eat fat calves out of their stalls and the younglings out of their flock, but we are fond beyond them, for veal and mutton is too gross for our diet; nay, the sea with all his fish, the air with all his birds, and the earth with all her beasts cannot satisfy our beastly appetites. A cook among profane men was a strange art and banished out of some commonweals as a superfluous science to make men eat more than needs, but in England it is a great occupation and in London a very rich company. I speak it not against the necessary use of them, but against the needless abuse of such as are cunning and curious and very costly to no purpose. He is counted the finest cook nowadays that can invent new fashions and new disguises. None of all this could Amos charge Israel withal, and with all this is England too truly to be charged . . .

9

JOHN HOSKINS (1579–1631)

JOHN HOSKINS became a Fellow of New College, Oxford, in 1600 and in 1612 he was appointed a Prebendary of Hereford and Rector of Ledbury. At about the same time he became Chaplain to King James I.

XVII

From a 'Sermon preached at Paul's Cross', probably in 1615, on the text: 'Woe to the crown of pride, to the drunkards of Ephraim, whose glorious beauty is a fading flower, which are on the head of the fat valleys of them that are overcome with wine' (*Isa. xxviii, 1*). *The preacher's view of fashions in dress and cosmetics.*

Daughters of England (for so must I speak), build not turrets or castles on your heads, with *braided hair and gold put about*. There can be no fences or fortresses of your chastity, rather they are allurements of your enemy, if not tokens and trophies of his victory. The Persian king, having many wives, appointed this or that city to find this or that wife a tire* or a bonnet and others to supply her with another ornament. The Prince of the world, I fear, having set up his proud banners amongst us and conquered us, hath imposed a heavier tribute upon us, one of our cities must maintain most of his concubines. For could I conceive it or you hear it without grief of heart, our ancient, substantial, fundamental trades belonging unto clothing go down, and they that fill our cities are *Nuguiendi*, triflers, or as the civil law names some, *Gyneciarii*, such as provide for that woman's wardrobe in the third of *Esay*. The men that are busied and the charge that is employed about these painful and difficult toys would serve for many new Plantations, but for the waste of precious hours, *dum*

* 'head-dress'

99

moliuntur, dum comuntur, while they are tiring and trimming themselves, tis more lamentable than credible, I dare be bold to say, kingdoms might be conquered whilst ruffs are a-pinning. Proud imaginations may pervert my meaning, yet though my speeches were racked they would not confess one syllable against civil decency, *mundus erit qui non offendet sorbidus*, that is, comeliness which doth not offend by sluttish negligence. The garnishments of pride have no communion or agreement with the garments of comeliness. Comeliness would never bid a woman go beyond her condition; only pride, being no lawful queen, usurpeth here a crown, as some that are scarce ladies wear coronets. Comeliness would never bid a woman pass the bounds of her ability; only pride sets us walking in the middle of our wealth. . . . Comeliness would never make more of jewels than of children; but, alas, nowadays the pride of matrons stalks along the streets, clothed with the spoils of children and posterity. Besides all this, honest comeliness will not offer occasion of suspicion; but the garish ceremonies of pride cannot but carry bad signification, so covering the body that they discover the mind. . . . Neither may you daughters of England (so must I still speak) abuse God's creation, attempt to control or correct his workmanship, adding to that face, which Saint *James* termeth natural, the borrowed features of a face artificial, for *Esay* crieth here, *Woe to the crown*, and we must cry, Woe to the face of pride. Was it not enough that unnatural niceness hath hid their breasts and refused to give their own bowels suck? Must pride hide their face too? No wonder then if husbands grow jealous of their wives and know not their children, whilst wives so disfigure themselves like courtesans that children hardly know their mothers. And can they then say that this is to please their husbands? No sooner are they varnished, but they foresake their home. . . . Among the wise, their pleasing humour takes none effect or success at all, for when their time, their colours, their pains and their inventions are wasted, *facies dicetur an ulcus*, shall we call it a face or shall we call it an impostume? *Jezebel* (I am sure) proves *Jezebel*, when all is done, fit for nothing but to look out at a window towards the place and instruments of her destruction, unfit to stir or travel in her vocation. Drops of rain or the sweat of her own brows will soil her countenance. Unfit to blush and be ashamed of her wantonness, the rising of the blood will fret her countenance. Unfit to mourn or repent for her wickedness, the tears of her eyes will wrinkle her countenance. Unfit to lift up her face towards heaven for pardon and forgiveness, God may justly say he knows not that countenance, he knoweth it not with approbation. *Jezebel, Jezebel*, thou shalt know what he will know by just visitation. . . . God shall uncase thee, *God shall smite thee, thou whited wall*. Walls and not women have need of such plastering . . .

I do the less marvel that women should deny their age to please men when men have almost denied their sex to please women. Some spend whole mornings in purging, powdering and perfuming themselves, as though there were good reason so to do; others in anointing their head or plaiting their locks, as if they had rather the commonwealth than their hair should be disordered; others in frizzling their tuffs and curling their foretops, as though one hair scorned to dwell by another. Most men so form and fashion themselves to the variable excess of outlandish attire that women shall have much ado to be more vain or fantastical, as if few believed the Lord in *Zephaniah. I will visit all such as are clothed in strange apparel.* . . . Amongst us the compendious course is taken of gathering our credit near unto us into clothes, which lay scattered in hospitality before, and in attendants. The city wonders at the country that the poor sheep should eat up men; the country wonders again at the city that suits of apparel should devour serving-men. Nor hath this pride turned away men's followers only; it hath likewise banished all affection of charity. A poor man were as good go beg of an image or a monument as of these gorgeous idols which represent nothing but apparel. *They have not for him*, they say, *They have not for him*, when the jewels in their ears, the rings on their fingers and roses on their shoes give their mouths the lie. Their superfluities might supply his necessities. But what speak I of the poor? Give my plainness leave to press the comparison. Our Liege Lord and gracious Sovereign (whom God preserve for ever) requires a support at our hands. We are not for him but for ourselves. The crown of the King must want; the crown of pride must not want. Let her assure herself, as long as there is a prophet in Israel, and a Providence in Heaven, she shall both hear and feel a *woe*; *Woe to the crown of pride, etc.*

10

JOHN DONNE (1573–1631)

JOHN DONNE, who is best known as one of the greatest of English poets, was the son of a prosperous ironmonger and was not ordained until 1615, when he was forty-three. Before then he was known in London as 'a great visitor of ladies, a great frequenter of plays, a great writer of conceited verses'. He took part in the Earl of Essex's expeditions to Cadiz in 1596 and to the Azores in 1597. He was brought up a Roman Catholic and became an Anglican in about 1598. After his ordination he became Chaplain to James 1 and in 1621 he was appointed Dean of St Paul's, London. His sermons, which attracted vast congregations, represent some of the best prose of the period.

XVIII

From a sermon preached on 2 February 1623 (no place) on the text: 'Render therefore to all their dues: tribute to whom tribute is due; custom to whom custom; fear to whom fear; honour to whom honour' (*Rom. xiii, 7*). *Topics referred to include the payment of dues to the Crown, forgery, honour to superiors and charity to inferiors.*

To [the Sovereign] we consider first a real, and substantial, and then a circumstantial and ceremonial debt. The substantial debt is paid in a faithful, in a ready and cheerful paying of those debts, those tributes, and customs (as the Apostle calls them here) which belong to the King, and he that makes no conscience in defrauding the public, he that withholds part of this debt, whensoever he can, he would pay that which he pays in counterfeit money, if he durst: he that deceives, because he sees he can scape with that deceit, he would coin too, if he saw too, that he could scape for that coining. A principal reason that makes coining and adulterat-

ing of money capital in all states, is not so much because he that
coins usurps the Prince's authority (for every coiner is not a
pretender to the Crown), nor because he diminishes the Prince's
majesty (for what is the Prince the worse in that his face is stamped
by another in base metal, than when that is done by himself, or
when his face is graved in any stone that is not precious ?), as
because he that coins injures the public: and no man injures the
public more than he who defrauds him, who is God's steward for
the public, the King. In matter of clothes and apparel, God wrought
a miracle in private men's cases, in continuing and enlarging the
children of Israel's clothes in the wilderness: in matter of meat he
wrought a miracle in private men's behalf too, in feeding so
many, with so few loaves, and fishes; and so he did for drink too,
in a miraculous providing of wine at the Marriage; for meat, and
drink, and clothes are things necessary for every man: but because
money is not so, if these other things may otherwise be had (as some
nations have lived, by permutation of commodities, without
money), therefore God never wrought a miracle in matter of
money, in any private man's case; but because money is the
most necessary of all, to the public, to the Prince, therefore he
wrought a miracle for that; and for that, only then, when that
money was to be employed upon tribute to Caesar; no miracle in
matter of money but for tribute. As it is a sign of subjection to see a
man stand bareheaded, so it may be a declination towards a worse
condition, to see a state bare-headed, to see the Prince, the head,
kept bare, by being either defrauded of that which is ordinarily
due to him, or denied that which becomes also due in the payment,
though it were extraordinarily given in the grant . . .

Due respect be given to every man, in his place; for when
young men think it the only argument of a good spirit, to behave
themselves fellowly, and frowardly to great persons, those greater
persons, in time, take away their respect from princes, and at
last (for in the chain of order, every link depends upon one another) God loses the respect and honour due to him; private men
lessen their respect of magistrates, and magistrates of princes, and
princes and all, of God. And therefore, that which St *Chrysostom*
says of the highest rank, *Non putes Christianae philosophiae digni-
tatem laedi*, reaches to all sorts, Let no man think that he departs

from the dignity of a Christian, in attibuting to every man that which appertains to the dignity of his place ...

Every wife hath a superior at home, so hath every child, and every servant, and every man a superior somewhere, in some respect, that is, in a spiritual respect: for so, not only the King, but the highest spiritual person hath a superior for absolution. And to this superior respectively, every man owes a ceremonial respect, as a debt, though this debt be not so far, as to accompany him, or to encourage him in his ill purposes, for that is too high a ceremony, and too transcendent a complement, to be damned for his sake, by concurring with my superior in his sins. And then, they, whose office is it to direct even their superiors by their counsel, (as that office may in cases belong to a wife, to a child, to a servant, as *Job* professes it was in his family), have also a ceremonial duty in that duty, which is to do even that with sweetness, with respect, with reverence. It was a better rule in so high a business, then a man would look for at a Friar's hands, which St *Bernard* hath, *Abseque prudentia & benevolentia, non sunt perfecta consilia*: no man is a good counsellor, for all his wisdom, and for all his liberty of speech, except he love the person whom he counsels: If he do not wish him well, as well as tell him his faults, he is rather a satirist, and a calumniator, and seeks to vent his own wisdom, and to exercise his authority, than a good counsellor ...

Now this hath led us to our other list of human creditors, that is, our inferiors, and to render to them also their dues; for, to them we said at beginning, there was due counsel, if they were weak in understanding; and there was due relief if they were weak in their fortunes. For the first, there are some persons in so high place in this world, as that they can owe nothing to any temporal superior, for they have none: but there is none so low in this world, but he hath some lower than he is, to pay this debt of counsel and advise to: at least the debt of prayer, for him, if he will not receive the debt of counsel to him. But in this place (for haste) we contract ourselves to the debt of relief to the poor: amongst whom, we may consider one sort of poor whom we ourselves have made poor, and damnified, and then our debt is restitution; and another sort, whom God, for reasons unknown to us hath made poor, and there our debt is alms. For the first of these (those whom thou hast damnified and made poor) thou needst not come to the Apostle's question of the blind man, *Did this man sin or his parents, that he is born blind?* Did this man waste himself in housekeeping, or in play, or in wantonness, that he is become poor? *Neither he sinned, nor his parents,* says Christ; neither excess, nor play, nor wantonness hath undone this man, but thy prevarication in his cause, thy extortion, thy oppression: and now he starves, and thou huntest after a popular reputation of a good housekeeper with his meat; now he freezes in nakedness, and thy train shines in liveries out of his wardrobe; every constable is ready to lay hold upon him for a rogue, and thy son is knighted with his money. *Sileat licèt fama, non silet fames,* says good and holy *Bernard,* fame may be silent, but famine will not: perchance the world knows not this, or is weary of speaking of it, but those poor wretches that starve by thy oppression know it, and cry out in his hearing, where thine own conscience accompanies them, and cries out with them against thee. Pay this debt, this debt of restitution, and pay it quickly; for nothing perishes, nothing decays an estate more, nothing consumes, nothing enfeebles a soul more, than to let a great debt run on long.

But if they be poor of God's making, and not of thine (as they are to thee, if thou know not why, or how they are become poor) (for though God have inflicted poverty upon them for their sins, that is a secret between God and them, that which God hath revealed to thee, is their poverty, and not their sins) then thou owest them a debt of alms, though not restitution: though thou have nothing in thy hands which was theirs, yet thou hast something which should be theirs; nothing perchance which thou hast taken from them, but something certainly which thou hast received from God for them; . . . So that whether they be poor of God's making, or poor of your making, *Reddite debitum,* pay the debt you owe, to the one by alms, to the other by restitution.

II

THOMAS ADAMS (d. 1653)

WHAT little is known of Thomas Adams comes from the title pages and epistles dedicatory to his works. From these we know that in 1612 he was 'a preacher of the Gospel at Willington', Bedfordshire. In 1614 he became Vicar of Wingrove, Bucks. He was a great preacher and was described by Robert Southey as 'the prose Shakespeare of puritan theologians'.

XIX

From a sermon entitled 'The Gallant's Burden' (no date or place) on the text:

The burden of Dumah. He calleth to me out of Seir, Watchman, what of the night? Watchman, what of the night?

The watchman said, The morning cometh, and also the night: if ye will enquire, enquire ye: return, come (*Isa. xxi, 11–12*).

It contains references to usury, drunkenness, and the impotence of the law.

Be there not usurers that say to the gold in secret, Thou art my confidence? *Populus me sibilat, at mihi plaudo ipse domi*, – The world hisseth at me, but I hug and applaud my own soul, and fat my spirits in the sight of my bags. Is there never a broker to comfort himself, in the distress of his conscience, with 'Usury is no sin, many learned men are of this opinion.' But I ask him if his conscience can be so satisfied; would he not willingly give one hundred-pound bag to be secured in this point? ... These two are not unfitly compared to two millstones: the usurer is the nether stone, that lies still; he sits at home in his warm furs, and spends his time in a devilish arithmetic, in numeration of hours, days, and moneys, in subtraction from others' estates, and multiplication of his own, till they have divided the earth to themselves, and themselves to hell; the broker runs round like the upper millstone, and betwixt both these the poor is grinded to powder . . .

Is this all? No; *Vidi ebriosorum sitim, et vomentium famem*, – I have seen drunkenness reeling from tavern to tavern, and, not seldom, from thence to his stews. It was the sin, nay, the shame of beggars; it is now the glory, the pride of gallants. They should daily be transformed to the image of God; they come nearer to beasts, let me say, to devils; for St Bernard saith, *Ebrietas est manifestissimus daemon*, – Drunkenness is a most manifest devil. They that are possessed with Satan, or with drunkenness, fall alike into the fire, into the water; they gnash alike, alike they foam; and as all the disciples could not cast out that one sort of devils, so nor all the preachers this, Matthew xvii, 16, 21.

Gluttony is not much less general, no less evil. Drunkenness makes a man so giddy he cannot stand, and gluttony so pursy that he cannot go. That old verse and rule is forgotten in our feasts –

> Too soon, too fine, too daintily,
> Too fast, too much, is gluttony.

There is an appetite natural; when the stomach can extract no more juice from meats received, it covets more. There is an appetite sensual; when the rich says, 'My soul, eat,' not my body. Nay, are not some in this city like those Horace speaks of? When their estate can reach but to herrings, they long for fresh salmon. We desire the strength of bodies and the length of days; our full dishes forbid it. If ever that verse was true, now is the time –

> Non plures gladio, quam cecidere gula; –
> The enemy's sword kills not more than their own throat.

Swearing and whoredom I will join together, as most sins go by couples: so the prophet, 'The land is full of adulterers, and for oaths the land mourneth.' Add unto swearing the twin-born brother of it, cursing; a sin that makes God (the *summum bonum*) the base executioner of our revenge. How strange, when men grieve us, to turn our teen* upon God, and rend him to pieces! Blasphemers against mortal princes are killed with the sword, and

* 'grief'

all their estates confiscate; against the Prince of Heaven it is not regarded . . .

Were these the sins of Edom, and are they not the sins of England? The sins, said I? Nay, the gods of England! For the usurer adores his metals, the epicure his junkets*, the drunkard his gallons, the voluptuous his lusts, the adulterer his harlots, the proud and gallant Edomite his gay clothes and studied carriage: and as the Israelites cried to their calf made of golden ear-rings, 'These are thy gods, O Israel!', Exodus xxxii, 4; so we may speak it with horror and amazement of these foolish, bestial, devilish sins, 'These are thy gods, O England!' Weak, wretched, unhelpful gods! For shame! What, where are we? Could Edom ever be worse? Have we devoured so many years of peace, ease, plenty, and saturity (if I may so call it) of God's word, and are we still so lame, lean, and ill-favoured in our lives? What shall I say? Hath the sweet Gospel, and the sober preaching of it, made us sensual, senseless, impudent, frantic, as the nature of that country is wonderful, if true, that rain causeth dust, and drought dirt? Have the sweet dews of Hermon made the hill of Zion more barren? Hath the sun of plenty, from the filth of security, bred monsters of sins? Have God's mercies made us worse? What shall I say?

Good laws are made; the life-blood of them is the execution. The law is else a wooden dagger in a fair sheath, when those that have the charge imposed, and the sword in their hands, stand like the picture of St George, with his hand up, but never striking. We complain not of the higher magistrates, from the benches of whose judgement impiety departs not without disgrace, without strokes. The blame lies on inferior officers, who think their office well discharged if they threaten offenders: these see, and will not see. Hence beggars laze themselves in the fields of idleness; hence taverns and tap houses swarm with unthrifts, of whom, whether they put more sin into their bellies, or vomit more forth, is a hard question; I mean, whether their oaths or ebrieties exceed. Hence we look to have vagrants suppressed, idleness whipped, drunkenness spoke withal; but the execution proves too often like the judges' feast – the guests set, the tables furnished, meat in the

* 'feasts'

dishes, wine in flagons; but putting forth their hands to take them, they apprehend nothing but air . . .

XX

From a sermon entitled 'The White Devil or the Hypocrite Uncovered', preached at St Paul's Cross, 7 March 1612, on the text: 'This he said, not that he cared for the poor; but because he was a thief, and had the bag, and bare what was put therein' (*John xii, 6*). *Eating, drinking, fine buildings, dishonesty in trade, profiteering, enclosures, and usury are among the subjects which received the preacher's condemnation.*

But let me tell you what indeed is waste:

1. Our immoderate diet – indeed not diet, for that contents nature – this is waste. . . . There are many shrewd contentions between the appetite and the purse: the wise man is either a neutral or takes part with his purse. To consume that at one banquet which would keep a poor man with convenient sustenance all his life, this is waste . . .

2. Our unreasonable ebrieties:

> Tenentque
> Pecula saepe homines, et inumbrant ora coronis.

They take their fill of wine here, as if they were resolved, with Dives they should not get a drop of water in hell. Eat, drink, play; *quid aliud sepulchro bovis inscribi poterat ?* – what other epitaph could be written on the sepulchre of an ox ? *Epulonum crateres, sunt epulonum carceres* – their bowls are their bolts; there is no bondage like to that of the vintage. The furnace beguiles the oven, the cellar deceives the buttery; we drink away our bread, as if we would put a new petition into the Lord's prayer, and abrogate the old: saying no more, with Christ, 'Give us this day our daily bread,' but, 'Give us this day our daily drink'; *quod non in diem, sed in mensem sufficiti* – which is more than enough for a day, nay, would serve a month. Temperance, the just steward, is put out of office: what place is free from these alehouse recusants, that think better of their drinkingroom than Peter thought of Mount Tabor ?

Bonum est esse hic – 'It is good being here', Matthew xvii, 4, *ubi nec Deus, nec doemon* – where both God and the devil are fast asleep. It is a question whether it be worse to turn the image of a beast to a god, or the image of God to a beast; if the first be idolatry, the last is impiety. A voluptuous man is a murderer to himself, a covetous man a thief, a malicious a witch, a drunkard a devil; thus to drink away the poor's relief, our own estate: *Ad quid perditio haec ?* – 'Why is this waste ?'

3. Our monstrous pride, that turns hospitality into a dumb show: that which fed the belly of hunger now feeds the eye of lust; acres of land are metamorphosed into trunks of apparel; and the soul of charity is transmigrated into the body of bravery: this is waste. We make ourselves the compounds of all nations: we borrow of Spain, Italy, Germany, France, Turkey and all; that death, when he robs an Englishman, robs all countries. Where lies the wealth of England ? In three places: on citizens' tables, in usurers' coffers, and upon courtiers' backs. God made all simple, therefore woe to these compounded fashions! God will one day say, *Hoc non opus meum, nec imago mea est* – This is none of my workmanship, none of my image. One man wears enough on his back at once to clothe two naked wretches all their lives: *Ad quid*, etc. – 'Why is this waste ?'

4. Our vainglorious buildings, to emulate the skies, which the wise man calls 'the lifting up of our gates too high', Proverbs xvii, 19. Houses built like palaces; tabernacles that, in the master's thought, equal the mansion of Heaven; structures to whom is promised eternity, as if the ground they stood on should not be shaken, Hebrews xii, 16. Whole towns depopulate to rear up one man's walls; chimneys built in proportion, not one of them so happy as to smoke; brave gates, but never open; sumptuous parlours, for owls and bats to fly in: pride began them, riches finished them, beggary keeps them; for most of them moulder away, as if they were in the dead builder's case, a consumption. Would not a less house, Jeconiah, have served thee for better hospitality ? Jeremiah xxii. Our fathers lived well under lower roofs; this is waste, and waste indeed, and these worse than the devil. The devil had once some charity in him, to turn stones into bread, Matthew iv, 3; but these men turn bread into stones, a trick beyond the

devil: *Ad quid perditio hoec ?* – 'Why is this waste ?'. . . But some of you rob Peter to pay Paul: take tenths from the church, and give not the poor the twentieths of them. It is not seasonable, nor reasonable charity, to undo whole towns by your usuries, enclosings, oppressions, impropriations; and for a kind of expiation, to give three or four the yearly pension of twenty marks: an almshouse is not so big as a village, nor thy superfluity whereout thou givest, like their necessity whereout thou extortest; he is but poorly charitable that, having made a hundred beggars, relieves two . . .

5. There is thievery . . . among tradesmen: and who would think it ? Many, they say, rob us, but we rob none; yes, but they think that *verba lactis* will countenance *fraudem in factis* – smooth words will smother rough deeds. This web of theft is many ways woven in a shop or warehouse, but three especially:

First, By a false weight, and no true measure, whose content or extent is not justifiable by law, Deuteronomy, xxv, 13; or the cunning conveyances in weighing or meting, such as cheat the buyer. Are not these pretty tricks to pick men's purses ? The French word hath well expressed them; they are legerdemains. Now had I not as good lose my purse on Salisbury plain as in London Exchange ? Is my loss the less, because violence forbears, and craft picks my purse ? The highway thief is not greater abomination to God than the shop-thief, Proverbs xi, 1; and for man, the last is more dangerous: the other we knowingly fly, but this laughs us in the face whiles he robs us.

Secondly, By insufficient wares, which yet, with a dark window and an impudent tongue, will appear good to the buyer's eye and ear too. Sophistry is now fled from the schools into shops; from disputation to merchandising. He is a silly tradesman that cannot sophisticate his wares, as well as he hath done his conscience; and wear his tongue with protestations barer than trees in autumn, the head of old age, or the livings of churchmen. Oaths indeed smell too rank of infidelity; marry, we are Protestants, and protest away our souls: there is no other way to put off bad wares, and put up good moneys. Are not these thieves ?

Thirdly, By playing, or rather preying, upon men's necessities: they must have the commodity, therefore set the dice on them; *vox latronis*, the advantage taken of a man's necessity is a trick beyond Judas. Thou shouldest rather be like Job, 'a foot to lame necessity', Chapter xxix, 15, and not take away his crutch. Or perhaps God hath put more wit into thy brains than his, thou seest further into the bargain, and therefore takest opportunity to abuse his plainness: thou servest thyself in gain, not him in love; thou mayest, and laugh at the law, but there is a law thou hast transgressed, that, without Jesus Christ, shall condemn thee to hell . . .

6. There is more store of thieves yet: covetous landlords, that stretch their rents on the tenter-hooks of an evil conscience, and swell their coffers by undoing their poor tenants. These sit close, and stare the law in the face, yet, by their leave, they are thieves. I do not deny the improvement of old rents, so it be done with old minds, – I mean, our forefathers' charity, – but with the devil, to set right upon the pinnacles, and pitch so high a price of our lands that it strains the tenants' heartblood to reach it, is theft, and killing theft. What all their immoderate toil, broken sleep, sore labours can get, with a miserable diet to themselves, not being able to spare a morsel of bread to others, is a prey to the landlords' rapine: this is to rob their estates, grind their faces, suck their blood. These are thieves.

7. Engrossers,* that hoard up commodities, and by stopping their community raise the price: these are thieves. Many block-houses in the city, monopolies in the court, garners in the country, can testify there are now such thieves abroad. We complain of a dearth; sure the heavens are too merciful to us that are so unmerciful one towards another. Scarcity comes without God's sending: who brings it then? Even the devil and his brokers, engrossing misers. The commonwealth may often blow her nails, unless she sit by an engrosser's fire: her limbs may be faint with hunger, unless she buy grain at an engrosser's price. I confess this is a sin which the law takes notice of, but not in the full nature, as theft. The pick-purse, in my opinion, doth not so much hurt as this general robber; for they rob millions. These do not, with Joseph, buy up the superfluity of plenty to prevent a dearth, but hoard up the store of plenty to procure a dearth: rebels to God, trespassers to nature, thieves to the commonwealth. If these were

* Those who buy in large quantities, with a view to securing a monopoly.

apprehended and punished, neither city nor country should complain as they do. Meantime the people's curse is upon them, and I doubt not but God's plague will follow it, if repentance turn it not away: till when, they are private thieves.

8. Enclosers; that pretend a distinction of possessions, a preservation of woods, indeed to make better and broader their own territories, and to steal from the poor commons: these are horrible thieves. The poor man's beast is his maintenance, his substance, his life; to take food from his beast, is to take the beast's food from his belly: so he that encloseth commons is a monstrous thief, for he steals away the poor man's living and life; hence many a cottager, nay, perhaps farmer, is fain (as the Indians do to devils) to sacrifice to the lord of the soil a yearly bribe for a *ne noceat*. For though the law forbids such enclosures, yet *quod fieri non debet, factum valet* – when they are once ditched in, say the law what it will, I see no throwing out. Force bears out what fraud hath borne in. Let them never open their mouths to plead the commonwealth's benefit; they intend it as much as Judas did when he spake for the poor. No, they are thieves, the bane of the common good, the surfeit of the land, the scourge of the poor; good only to themselves, and that in opinion only, for they do it ' to dwell alone', Isaiah v, 8: and they dwell alone indeed, for neither God nor good angel keeps them company; and for a good conscience, it cannot get through their quicksets. These are thieves, though they have enclosed their theft, to keep the law out and their wickedness in: yet the day shall come their lands shall be thrown out, their lives thrown out, and their souls thrown out; their lands out of their possessions, their lives out of their bodies, their souls out of heaven, except repentance and restitution prevail with the great Judge for their pardon. Meantime they are thieves.

9. Many taphouse-keepers, taverners, victuallers, which the provident care of our worthy magistrates hath now done well to restrain; if at least this Hydra's heads do not multiply. I do not speak to annihilate the profession: they may be honest men, and doubtless some are, which live in this rank; but if many of them should not chop away a good conscience for money, drunkenness should never be so welcome to their doors. The dissolute wretch sits there securely, and buys his own sickness with a great expense,

which would preserve the health of his poor wife and children at home, that lamentably moan for bread whiles he lavisheth all in drink. Thus the pot robs him of his wits, he robs himself of grace, and the victualler robs him of his money. This theft might yet be borne, but the commonwealth is here robbed too. Drunkenness makes so quick riddance of the ale that this raiseth the price of malt, and the good sale of malt raiseth the price of barley: thus is the land distressed, the poor's bread is dissolved into the drunkard's cup, the markets are hoised up.* If the poor cannot reach the price, the maltmaster will; he can utter it to the taphouse, and the taphouse is sure of her old friend, drunkenness. Thus theft sits close in a drinking-room, and robs all that sail into that coast. I confess they are (most of them) bound to suffer no drunkenness in their houses, yet they secretly acknowledge that if it were not for drunkenness, they might shut up their doors, as utterly unable to pay their rents. These are thieves . . .

12. The twelfth and last sort of thieves (to make up the just dozen) are the usurers. This is a private thief like Judas, and for the bag like Judas, which he steals from Christ like Judas, or rather from Christians, that have more need, and therefore worse than Judas. This is a man made out of wax: his *Paternoster* is a pawn; his creed is the condition of this obligation; his religion is all religation, a binding of others to himself, of himself to the devil: for look how far any of the former thieves have ventured to hell, the usurer goes a foot further by the standard. The poet exclaims against this sin –

Hinc usura vorax, avidumque, in tempore foenus, etc.

describing in that one line the names and nature of usury. *Foenus, quasi foetus.* It is a teeming thing, ever with child, pregnant, and multiplying. Money is an unfruitful thing by nature, made only for commutation; it is a preternatural thing it should engender money; this is *monstrosus partus*, a prodigious birth. *Usura, quasi propter usum rei.* The nature of it is wholly devouring: their money to necessity is like cold water to a hot ague, that for a time refresheth, but prolongs the disease. The usurer is like the worm we call the timber-worm (*Teredo*) which is wonderful soft to touch, but hath

* 'raised' (i.e. prices are raised).

teeth so hard that it eats timber; but the usurer eats timber and stones too. The prophet hedgeth it in between bribery and extortion: 'In thee have they taken gifts to shed blood: thou hast taken usury and increase, and thou hast greedily gained of thy neighbours by extortion, and hast forgotten me, saith the Lord. Therefore I have smitten my hands at thy dishonest gain,' &c., Ezekiel xxii, 12, 13. You hear God's opinion of it. Beware this dishonest gain; take heed lest this casting your money into a bank cast not up a bank against you; when you have found out the fairest pretexts for it, God's justice shall strike off all: 'Let no man deceive you with vain words: for such things God's wrath will fall on the children of disobedience,' Ephesians v, 6. Infinite colours, mitigations, evasions, distinctions are invented, to countenance on earth heaven-exploded usury: God shall then frustrate all, when he pours his wrath on the naked conscience. God saith, 'Thou shalt not take usury': go now study paintings, excuses, apologies, dispute the matter with God; hell-fire shall decide the question. 'I have no other trade to live on but usury.' Only the devil first made usury a trade. But can this plea in a thief, 'I have no other trade to live on but stealing,' protect and secure him from the gallows?

The usurer then is a thief; nay, a double thief, as the old Roman law censured them, that charged the thief with restitution double, the usurer with fourfold; concluding him a double thief. Thieves steal sometimes, usurers always. Thieves steal for necessity, usurers without need. The usurer wounds deeper with a piece of paper than the robber with a sword. Many a young gentleman, newly broke out of the cage of wardship, or blessed with the first sunshine of his one-and-twenty, goes from the vigilance of a restraining governor into the tempting hand of a merciless usurer, as if he came out of God's blessing into the warm sun. Many a man, that comes to his lands ere he comes to his wits, or experience of their villainy, is so let blood in his estate by usury, that he never proves his own man again . . .

12

ROBERT SANDERSON (1587–1663)

ROBERT SANDERSON was born in Yorkshire and was ordained in
1611. He held several benefices, became Chaplain to Charles I,
and in 1642 was appointed Regius Professor of Divinity at Oxford.
He refused to accept the Solemn League and Covenant, with the
result that he was deprived of his professorship in 1648 and for a
time was imprisoned. After the Restoration he became Bishop of
Lincoln, but he died three years after his appointment.

XXI

*From 'Ad Populum', a sermon preached at St Paul's Cathedral, 4
November 1621, on the text: 'Brethren, let every man, wherein he
is called, therein abide with God' (1 Cor. vii, 24). It deals with the
evils of idleness and vagrancy, and insists that charity should not be
indiscriminate.*

It is the sin of many of the gentry, whom God hath furnished with
means and abilities to do much good, to spend their whole days
and lives in an unprofitable course of doing either nothing, or as
good as nothing, or worse than nothing. I cannot be so either stupid,
as not to apprehend, or rigorous, as not to allow, a difference in
the manner of employment, and in other circumstances thereto
belonging, between those that are nobly or generously born and
bred, and those of the meaner and ordinary rank. Manual and
servile and mechanic trades and arts are for men of a lower condition. But yet no man is born, no man should be bred, unto idleness. There are generous and ingenuous and liberal employments,
sortable to the greatest births and educations. For some man whom
God hath blessed with power and authority in his country, with
fair livings and large revenues, with a numerous family of servants, retainers, and tenants, and the like, it may be a sufficient

calling, and enough to take up his whole time, even to keep hospitality, and to order and overlook his family, and to dispose of his lands and rents, and to make peace, and preserve love and neighbourhood among them that live near or under him. He that doth but this as he ought to do, or is otherwise industrious for the common good, must be acknowledged a worthy member of the commonwealth; and his course of life, a calling, although perhaps not so toilsome, yet *in suo genere* as necessary and profitable, as that of the husbandman, merchant, lawyer, minister, or any other.

But for our mere or parcel* gallants, who live in no settled course of life, but spend half the day in sleeping, half the night in gaming, and the rest of their time in other pleasures and vanities, to as little purpose as they can devise, as if they were born for nothing else but to eat and drink, and snort and sport, who are spruce and trim as the lilies – Solomon in all his royalty was not clothed like one of these – yet they neither sow, nor reap, nor carry into the barn, they neither labour nor spin, nor do anything else for the good of human society: let them know, there is not the poorest contemptible creature, that crieth oysters and kitchen-stuff in the streets, but deserveth his bread better than they; and his course of life is of better esteem with God and every sober wise man, than their's . . .

Consider this, you that are of noble or generous birth. *Look unto the rock, whence you were hewn*; and to the pit, whence you were digged. Search your pedigrees, collect the scattered monuments and histories of your ancestors, and observe by what steps your worthy progenitors raised their houses to the height of gentry or nobility. Scarce shall you find a man of them that gave any accession, or brought any noted eminency, to his house, but either serving in the camp, or sweating at the bar, or waiting at the Court, or adventuring on the seas, or trucking in his shop, or some other way industriously bestirring himself in some settled calling and course of life. You usurp their arms if you inherit not their virtues; and those ensigns of honour and gentry, which they by industry achieved, sit no otherwise upon your shoulders than as rich trappings upon asses' backs, which serve but to render the

* 'partial'

poor beast more ridiculous. If you, by brutish sensuality, and spending your time in swinish luxury, stain the colours and embase the metals of those badges of your gentry and nobility which you claim by descent, think, when we worship or honour you, we do but flout you; and know, the titles we in courtesy give you, we bestow upon their memories whose degenerate offspring you are, and whose arms you unworthily bear; and they do no more belong to you than the reverence the good man did to Isis belonged to the ass that carried her image.

The third sort of those that live unprofitably and without a calling, are our idle sturdy rogues and vagrant town's-end beggars, the very scabs, and filth, and vermin of the commonwealth. I mean such as have health, and strength, and limbs, and are in some measure able to work and take pains for their living, yet rather choose to wander abroad the country, and to spend their days in a most base and ungodly course of life; and, which is yet more lamentable, by I know not what connivance, contrary to all conscience, equity, and law, are suffered. . . . I think never kingdom had more wholesome laws in both kinds, I mean both for the competent relief of the orderly poor, and for sharp restraint of disorderly vagabonds, than those provisions which in many of our own memories have been made in this land. But *Quid leges sine moribus* . . . ? Those laws are now no laws, for want of due execution; but beggars are beggars still, for want of due correction. *Et vetabitur semper, et retinebitur*: the saying is truer of rogues and gypsies in England, than ever it was of mathematicians in Rome. You, to whose care the preservation of the justice, and thereby also the peace of the land, is committed, as you tender the peace and justice of the land, as you tender your own quiet and the safety of your neighbours, as you tender the weal of your country and the honour of God, breathe fresh life into the languishing laws by severe execution; be rather cruel to these vipers than to the state. So shall you free us from the plague, and yourselves from the guilt, and them from the opportunities, of infinite sinful abominations.

But we are unreasonable to press you thus far, or to seek to you or any others for justice in this matter, having power enough in our own hands to do ourselves justice upon these men, if we would but use it. Even by making a strait covenant with our ears, not to heed them; and with our eyes, not to pity them; and with our hands, not to relieve them. Say I this altogether of myself? Or saith not the Apostle even the same? He that will not labour, let him not eat: relieve him not. But hath not Christ required us to feed the hungry, and to clothe the naked, and to be free and charitable to the poor? Nothing surer. God forbid any man should preach against charity and almsdeeds. But remember, that as God approveth not alms or any other work, if without charity, so nor charity itself, if without discretion. *Honour widows*, saith St Paul, but those *that are widows indeed*: so relieve the poor, but relieve those that are poor indeed. Not everyone that asketh, not everyone that wanteth, nay more, not everyone that is poor, is poor indeed; and he that in his indiscreet and misguided charity should give to everyone that asketh, or wanteth, or is poor, meat, or clothing, or alms, would soon make himself more hungry, and naked, and poor, than he that is most hungry, or naked, or poor. The poor, whom Christ commendeth to thee as a fit object for thy charity, the poor indeed, are those that want not only the things they ask, but want also means to get without asking. A man that is blind, or aged, and past his work; a man that is sick, or weak, or lame, and cannot work; a man that desireth it, and seeketh it, and cannot get work; a man that hath a greater charge upon him than his honest pains can maintain; such a man as one of these, he is poor indeed. Let thine ears be open, and thine eyes open, and thy bowels open, and thy hands open, to such a one: it is a charitable deed, and a *sacrifice of sweet smelling. With such sacrifices God is well pleased.* Forget not thou to offer such sacrifices upon every good opportunity; and be well assured God will not forget in due time to reward thee. But for a lusty, able, upright man, as they style him in their own dialect, that had rather beg, or steal, or both, than dig, he is no more to be relieved as a poor man than a woman that hath poisoned her husband is to be honoured as a widow. Such a woman is a widow, for she hath no more an husband than any other widow hath; but such a woman is not a widow indeed, as St Paul would be understood, not such a widow as he would have honoured: it is alms to hang up such a widow, rather than to honour her. And I dare say, he that helpeth one of these sturdy beggars to the stocks, and the whip, and the house of correction, not only deserveth better of the commonwealth, but doth a work of greater charity in the sight of God, than he that helpeth him with meat, and money, and lodging. For he that doth this, corrupteth his charity by a double error. First, he maintaineth, and so encourageth, the other in idleness, who, if none would relieve him, would be glad to do any work rather than starve. And secondly, he disableth his charity, by misplacing it, and unawares robbeth the poor, whilst he thinketh he relieveth them. As he that giveth any honour to an idol robbeth the true God, to whom alone all religious honour is due, so he that giveth any alms to an idle beggar robbeth the truly poor, to whom properly all the fruits of our alms are due. And so it cometh to pass often-times, as St Ambrose sometimes complained, that the mainten-ance of the poor is made the spoil of the loiterer . . .

XXII

From 'Ad Magistratum', a sermon preached at the Nottingham Assizes, 1634, on the text: 'Behold, here I am: witness against me before the Lord, and before his anointed: whose ox have I taken? or whom have I defrauded? whom have I oppressed? or of whose hand have I received any bribe to blind mine eyes therewith? and I will restore it you' (*1 Sam. xii, 3*). *It deals with the effect of bribery upon justice.*

Bribery is properly a branch of oppression. For if the bribe be exacted or but expected, yet so as that there can be little hope of a favourable or but so much as a fair hearing without it, then is it a manifest oppression in the receiver, because he maketh an ad-vantage of that power, wherewith he is intrusted for the adminis-tration of justice, to his own proper benefit; which ought not to be, and is clearly an oppression. But if it proceed rather from the voluntary offer of the giver, for the compassing of his own ends, then is it an oppression in him, because thereby he getteth an advantage in the favour of the Court against his adversary and to his prejudice. For observe it, the greatest oppressors are ever the greatest bribers, and freest of their gifts to those that may bestead them in their suits. Which is one manifest cause, besides the secret and just judgement of God upon them, why oppressors seldom thrive in their estates near the proportion of their gettings. Even because so much of what cometh in by their oppressions goeth out again for the upholding of their oppressions. It was not for nothing you may well think, that Solomon so yoked these two things together, oppressing the poor and giving to the rich, in Proverbs xxii. *He that oppresseth the poor to increase his riches, and he that giveth to the rich, shall surely come to want.* As he hath a spring one way, so he hath a drain another way, which keepeth him from rising to that excess of height he aimeth at . . .

Of the commonness of which sin, especially in inferior officers, who are ever and anon trucking for expedition, it would be impertinent to speak from this text, wherein Samuel speaketh of it only as it might concern himself who was a judge. Of the heinousness of it in the sight of God, and the mischief it doth to the commonwealth, when it is found in judges and magistrates, I shall forbear to speak, the time being withall now well nigh spent, because, out of the confidence I have of the sincerity of those that now hear me, I deem the labour needless. Only I cannot, the text offering it, but touch somewhat at that property which Samuel here ascribeth to a bribe, of blinding the eyes. Solomon speaketh much of the powerful operation of gifts and bribes, how they pacify anger, procure access into the presence of great persons, and favour from them, and sundry the like, which are all of easy understanding, and the truth of them, as well as the meaning, obvious . . .

But then what is it to blind the eyes ? or how can bribes do it ? Justice is not unfitly portrayed in the form of a man with his right eye open to look at the cause, and his left eye shut or muffled that he may not look at the person. Now a gift putteth all this out of order, and setteth it the quite contrary way. It giveth the left eye liberty, but too much, to look asquint upon the person, but putteth the right eye quite out, that it cannot discern the cause. . . . And the reason of all this is, because gifts, if they be handsomely conveyed, and not tendered in the name, nor appearing in the likeness of bribes, for then wise and righteous men will reject them with disdain, and shake their hands and laps from receiving them; but I say, if they come as presents only, and by way of kindness and respect, they are sometimes well accepted, and that deservedly, even of wise and righteous men, as testimonies of the love and observance of the givers. And then the nature of ingenuous persons is such, that they cannot but entertain a good opinion of those that show good respect unto them; and are glad when any opportunity is offered them whereby to manifest such their good opinion, and to requite one courtesy with another. Whereby it cometh to pass, that gifts, by little and little, and by insensible degrees, win upon the affections of such men as are yet just in their intentions and would not willingly be corrupted, and at the last over-master them. And the affections once thoroughly possessed, it is then no great mastery to do the rest, and to surprise the judgement. The good magistrate, therefore, that would save his eyes and preserve their sight, had need not only to hate bribes, but to be very jealous of presents, lest some of those things which he receiveth but as gifts be yet meant him for bribes. But especially to suspect those gifts as so meant, where the quantity and proportion of the gift, considered and compared with the quality and condition of the giver, may cast any just cause of suspicion upon them; but to conclude them absolutely so meant, if they be sent from persons that have business in the Courts.

13

JEREMY TAYLOR (1613–67)

JEREMY TAYLOR was born in Cambridge and after ordination his preaching attracted the notice of Archbishop Laud, who nominated him to a Fellowship at All Souls' College, Oxford. Shortly afterwards he became Chaplain to Charles I and in 1638 he was appointed Rector of Uppingham, Rutland. He left the benefice in 1642 to become a chaplain in the Royalist Army and was taken prisoner in 1645. After his release he retired to Wales, where he lived as Chaplain to Lord Carbery at Golden Grove. Here many of his best works were written, including the famous *Holy Living* (1650) and *Holy Dying* (1651). In 1660 he was appointed Bishop of Down and Connor (to which was added the Diocese of Dromore in 1661) and Vice-Chancellor of Dublin University. In his preaching and writing he displayed an aversion to both dissenters and Roman Catholics. Taylor's fame rests mainly on his devotional writings and on his work on moral theology, *Ductor Dubitantum* (1660). His sermons were lucid, cautious and devout, making use of a great deal of imagery and illustration.

XXIII

This extract is from a sermon entitled 'The House of Feasting, or the Epicure's Misery' (no date or place) on the text: 'If after the manner of men I fought with beasts at Ephesus, what advantageth me if the dead rise not? let us eat and drink; for tomorrow we die' (1 Cor. xv, 32). It stresses the evils of drink.

I pray consider what a strange madness and prodigious folly possesses many men, that they love to swallow death and diseases and dishonour, with an appetite which no reason can restrain. We expect our servants should not dare to touch what we have forbidden to them; we are watchful that our children should not swallow poisons, and filthiness, and unwholesome nourishment; we take care that they should be well-mannered and civil and of fair demeanour; and we ourselves desire to be, or at least to be accounted, wise, and would infinitely scorn to be called fools; and we are so great lovers of health that we will buy it at any rate of money or observance; and then for honour, it is that which the children of men pursue with passion, it is one of the noblest rewards of virtue, and the proper ornament of the wise and valiant; and yet all these things are not valued or considered, when a merry meeting, or a looser feast, calls upon the man to act a scene of folly and madness and healthlessness and dishonour. We do to God what we severely punish in our servants; we correct our children for their meddling with dangers, which themselves prefer before immortality; and though no man think himself fit to be despised, yet he is willing to make himself a beast, a sot, and a ridiculous monkey, with the follies and vapours of wine; and when he is high in drink or fancy, proud as a Grecian orator in the midst of his popular noises, at the same time he shall talk such dirty language, such mean low things, as may well become a changeling and a fool, for whom the stocks are prepared by the laws and the just scorn of men. Every drunkard clothes his head with a mighty scorn, and makes himself lower at that time than the meanest of his servants; the boys can laugh at him when he is led like a cripple, directed like a blind man, and speaks like an infant imperfect noises, lisping with a full and spongy tongue, and an empty head, and a vain and foolish heart: so cheaply does he part with his honour for drink or loads of meat; for which honour he is ready to die rather than hear it to be disparaged by another, when himself destroys it as bubbles perish with the breath of children. Do not the laws of all wise nations mark the drunkard for a fool, with the meanest and most scornful punishment? and is there anything in the world so foolish as a man that is drunk? But good God! what an intolerable sorrow hath seized upon great portions of mankind, that this folly and madness should possess the greatest spirits, and the wittiest men, the best company, the most sensible of the word 'honour', and the most jealous of losing the shadow, and the most careless of the thing? Is it not a horrid thing that a wise or a crafty, a learned or a noble person, should dishonour himself as a fool, destroy his body as a murderer, lessen his estate as a prodigal, disgrace every good cause that he can pretend to by his relation, and become an appellative of scorn, a scene of laughter or derision, and all for the reward of forgetfulness and madness? for there are in immoderate drinking no other pleasures.

Why do valiant men and brave personages fight and die rather than break the laws of men or start from their duty to their prince, and will suffer themselves to be cut in pieces rather than deserve the name of a traitor or perjured, and yet these very men, to avoid the hated name of glutton or drunkard and to preserve their temperance, shall not deny themselves one luscious morsel, or pour a cup of wine on the ground when they are invited to drink by the laws of the circle or wilder company?

Methinks it were but reason, that if to give life to uphold a cause be not too much, they should not think too much to be hungry and suffer thirst for the reputation of that cause; and therefore much rather that they would think it but duty to be temperate for its honour, and eat and drink in civil and fair measures, that themselves might not lose the reward of so much suffering, and of so good a relation, nor that which they value most be destroyed by drink.

There are in the world a generation of men that are engaged in a cause which they glory in, and pride themselves in its relation and appellative: but yet for that cause they will do nothing but talk and drink; they are valiant in wine, and witty in healths, and full of stratagem to promote debauchery; but such persons are not considerable in wise accounts. That which I deplore is, that some men prefer a cause before their life, and yet prefer wine before that cause, and by one drunken meeting set it more backward in its hopes and blessings than it can be set forward by the counsels and arms of a whole year. God hath ways enough to reward a truth without crowning it with success in the hands of such men. In the meantime they dishonour religion, and make truth be evil-spoken of, and innocent persons to suffer by their very relation, and the cause of God to be reproached in the sentences of erring and abusing people; and themselves lose their health and their reason, their honour and their peace, the rewards of sober counsels, and the wholesome effects of wisdom.

Árcanum neque tu scrutaberis illius unquam;
Commissumque teges, et vino tortus et ira.

Wine discovers more than the rack, and he that will be drunk is not a person fit to be trusted: and though it cannot be expected men should be kinder to their friend or their prince or their honour, than to God and to their own souls and to their own bodies; yet when men are not moved by what is sensible and material, by that which smarts and shames presently, they are beyond the cure of religion and the hopes of reason; and therefore they must 'lie in hell like sheep, death gnawing upon them, and the righteous shall have dominion over them in the morning' of the resurrection.

Seras tutior ibis ad lucernas:
Haec hora est tua, cum furit Lyaeus,
Cum regnat rosa, cum madent capilli.

Much safer it is to go to the severities of a watchful and a sober life; for all that time of life is lost, when wine, and rage, and pleasure, and folly, steal away the heart of a man, and make him go singing to his grave.

I end with the saying of a wise man, 'He is fit to sit at the table of the Lord, and to feast with saints, who moderately uses the creatures which God hath given him; but he that despises even lawful pleasures, οὐ μόνον συμπότης τῶν θεῶν ἀλλὰ καὶ συνάρχων shall not only sit and feast with God, but reign together with him, and partake of his glorious kingdom.'

14

ISAAC BARROW (1630–77)

ISAAC BARROW was born in London in 1630. Although he was a Royalist he became a Fellow of Trinity College, Cambridge, in 1649. He was a mathematician and classical scholar and at the Restoration, in 1660, he was appointed Professor of Greek at Cambridge and, in 1663, Lucasian Professor of Mathematics. He became Master of Trinity College, Cambridge in 1673. He was also Chaplain to Charles II. He was one of the most successful preachers of his day although his sermons were of quite inordinate length.

XXIV

From a sermon, 'Of Industry in our general Calling, as Christians' (no place or date) on the text: 'Not slothful in business; fervent in spirit; serving the Lord' (Rom, xii, 11). Each man has been placed in his state of life by God. He should therefore be industrious in his calling and not attempt to rise above his station.

So hath the great Author of order distributed the ranks and offices of men in order to mutual benefit and comfort, that one man should plough, another thrash, another grind, another labour at the forge, another knit or weave, another sail, another trade, another supervise all these, labouring to keep them all in order and peace; that one should work with his hands and feet, another with his head and tongue; all conspiring to one common end; the welfare of the whole, and the supply of what is useful to each particular member; every man so reciprocally obliging and being obliged; the prince being obliged to the husbandman for his bread, to the weaver for his clothes, to the mason for his palace, to the smith for his sword; those being all obliged to him for his vigilant care in protecting them, for their security in pursuing the work, and enjoying the fruit of their industry.

So every man hath a calling and proper business; whereto that industry is required, I need not much to prove, the thing itself in reason and experience being so clearly evident: for what business can be well dispatched, what success can be expected to any undertaking, in what calling can any man thrive, without industry? What business is there that will go on of itself, or proceed to any good issue, if we do not carefully look to it, steadily hold it in its course, constantly push and drive it forward? It is true, as in nature, so in all affairs, *Nihil movet non motum*, nothing moveth without being moved.

Our own interest should move us to be industrious in our calling, that we may obtain the good effects of being so in a comfortable and creditable subsistence; that we may not suffer the damages and wants, the disappointments and disgraces ensuing on sloth: but the chief motive should be from piety and conscience; for that it is a duty which we owe to God. For God having placed us in our station, he having apportioned to us our task, we being in transaction of our business his servants; we do owe to him that necessary property of good servants, without which fidelity cannot subsist; for how can he be looked on as a faithful servant, who doth not effectually perform the work charged on him, or diligently execute the orders of his master?

St Paul doth enjoin servants, that they should *in all things obey their masters*, with conscientious regard to God, as therein performing service to God, and expecting recompense from him: and of princes he saith, that they, in dispensation of justice, enacting laws, imposing taxes, and all political admininstrations, are *the ministers of God*, προσκαρτεροῦντες, *attending constantly upon this very thing*: and if these extremes, the highest and lowest of all vocations, are services of God; if the highest upon that score be tied to so much diligence, then surely all middle places, upon the same account of conscience towards God, do exact no less.

If he that hath one talent, and he that hath ten, must both improve them for God's interest; then he that hath two, or three, or more, is obliged to the same duty proportionably.

Everyone should consider the world as the family of that great Paterfamilias, *of whom the whole family in heaven and earth is named*, and himself as an officer or servant therein, by God's will and designation constituted in that employment, into which Providence hath cast him; to confer, in his order and way, somewhat towards a provision for the maintenance of himself, and of his fellow-servants. Of a superior officer our Lord saith, *Who is that faithful and wise servant, whom his Lord hath made ruler over his household, to give them their meat in due season?* So the greatest men are as stewards, treasurers, comptrollers, or purveyors; the rest are inferior servants, in their proper rank and capacity.

And he that with diligence performeth his respective duty (be it high and honourable, or mean and contemptible in outward appearance) will please God, as keeping good order, and as being useful to his service; so that, upon the reckoning, God will say to him, *Well done, good and faithful servant, thou hast been faithful over a few things; I will make thee ruler over many things: enter thou into the joy of the Lord.* But he that doeth otherwise (behaving himself carelessly or sluggishly in his business) will offend God, as committing disorder, and as being unprofitable.

He committeth disorder, according to that of St Paul; *We hear there are some, which walk among you disorderly, not working at all.* His sentence and doom will be, according to our Lord, *O thou wicked and slothful servant – Cast the unprofitable servant into utter darkness;* which words are spoken in relation to one, who being a flatterer, or sluggard in his calling, did not improve the special talent entrusted with him for God's service.

In fine, if we are conscientiously industrious in our vocation, we shall assuredly find the blessing of God thereon; and that he thereby will convey good success, comfort, competent wealth, a fair reputation, all desirable good unto us; for as all these things are promised to industry, so the promise especially doth belong to that industry, which a man doth exercise in an orderly course of action in his own way; or rather in God's way, wherein divine providence hath set him.

An irregular or impertinent laboriousness, out of a man's calling or sphere; a being diligent in other men's affairs, invading their office (as if I a priest will be trading, a layman preaching), may not claim the benefit of those promises, or the blessings of industry: but a husbandman, who, with conscientious regard to God, and confidence in him, is painful in tilling his ground, may expect a good crop; a merchant, who (upon the same principle, with the like disposition) earnestly followeth his trade, may hope for safe voyages and good markets; a prince carefully minding his affairs may look for peace and prosperity to his country; a scholar studying hard may be well assured of getting knowledge, and finding truth; all, who with honest diligence constantly do pursue their business, may confidently and cheerfully hope to reap the advantages suitable to it from the favourable blessing of God. So that we have all reason to observe the Apostle's precept, *Not to be slothful in business.*

XXV

From a sermon entitled 'Of Quietness, and doing our own business' (no date or place) on the text: 'That ye study to be quiet, and to do your own business, and to work with your own hands, as we commanded you' *(1 Thess. iv, 11). The actions of a man's superiors are not to be questioned by others, for they are answerable to God alone. The mysteries of state cannot be understood by vulgar people. Each person must attend to his own business and not to that of others.*

We should not, without call or allowance, meddle with our superiors, so as to advise them, to reprehend them, to blame or inveigh against their proceedings; for this is to confound the right order of things, to trespass beyond the bounds of our calling and station, to do wrong, not only to them, but to the public, which is concerned in the upholding their power and respect: it is indeed a worse fault than assuming the ensigns of their dignity, or counterfeiting their stamps; for that is but to borrow the semblance, this is to enjoy the substance of their authority.

Nothing in this busy and licentious age is more usual, than for private men to invade the office, to exercise the duties, to canvass and control the actions of their superiors; discussing what they ought to do, and prescribing laws to them; taxing what is done by them; murmuring at their decrees, and inveighing against their proceedings: everyone is finding holes in the state, and picking quarrels with the conduct of political affairs: everyone is reforming and settling the public according to models framed in his own conceit. Things, saith one, are out of order; the constitution is very defective, and ought to be corrected; such a law in all reason should be repealed, and such an one enacted; here our statesmen were out of their politics, and there our lawgivers failed in point of equity or prudence. No, clamours another no less eagerly, all things stand as well as can be; nothing can be amended, or ought to be altered; our establishment in all respects is more perfect than Plato's commonwealth, or the state of Utopia. Thus doth each man appoint himself counsellor of state, and turns legislator without any call from the King, or choice of the country: every one snatcheth at the sceptre, and invests himself with the senator's robe: every one acteth a prince and a bishop, or indeed is rather a censor and controller of both orders; not considering the wrong he committeth, nor the arrogance he practiseth, nor the mischiefs which naturally ensue upon such demeanour: for to direct or to check governors is in effect to exauctorate* or depose them, substituting ourselves in their room: and what greater injury can we do them or the public? To fix or reverse laws belongeth to the highest authority and deepest wisdom, which it is enormous presumption for us to arrogate to ourselves: by attempting such things we confound the ranks of men, and course of things; we ruffle the world, we supplant public tranquillity; and what greater mischief than this can we do among men?

It is the business and duty of those whom God hath constituted his representatives and ministers to deliberate and conclude what is to be done; and for the due performance of their charge they are accountable to their master, not to us; *Nobis obsequii gloria relicta est*; our duty and our privilege (for so it is, if we could understand it, it being far more easy and safe) it is to submit and obey with quiet and patience; if we do more, we are therein irregular, and no less undutiful to God than to our superiors; we forget those divine rules and precepts; *Where the word of a king is, there is power; and who may say to him, What doest thou? Submit yourselves to every ordinance of man for the Lord's sake. Do all things without murmurings and disputings.* We consider not what judgements are denounced upon those whose character it is *to despise government, to be presumptuous and self-willed, not to be afraid to speak evil of dignities.*

* To deprive of office, divest of authority.

We do not weigh the nature of the things we meddle with, nor the advantages of the persons whom we tax, nor our own incapacity to judge rightly about them. There is a kind of sacredness in the mysteries of state: as the mysteries of faith do surpass natural reason, so do those of state transcend vulgar capacity: as priests by special grace are qualified best to understand the one, so are princes by like peculiar assistance enabled to penetrate the former. He that employeth them in that great work of governing the world, and maketh them instruments of his providence, is not wanting in affording to them direction and aid needful for the discharge of their duty; whence their judgements of things are somewhat more than human, and their words may with us pass for oracular; *A divine sentence*, the wise King said, *is in the lips of the king; his mouth transgresseth not in judgement*. According to the ordinary reason of things, they are best able to judge of such things, being, by reason of their eminent station, able to discern more and farther than others; having by experience and constant practice acquired a truer insight into things, and a better skill to manage them: whereas we being placed beneath in a valley, can have no good prospect upon the grounds and causes of their resolutions and proceedings: we, for want of sufficient use and exercise, cannot skill to balance the contrary weights and reasons of things; to surmount the difficulties and rubs, to unfold the knots and intrigues, which occur in affairs of that kind; we cannot expect those special influences of light and strength from Heaven towards judging of affairs, which do not properly concern us: wherefore we are altogether incompetent judges, and impertinent dealers about those things; it is great odds, that in doing so we shall mistake and misbehave ourselves; we consequently do vainly and naughtily to meddle with them. If the love of public good doth transport us, let us restrain ourselves.

15

JOHN TILLOTSON (1630-94)

JOHN TILLOTSON was a Yorkshireman and in his earlier years was a nonconformist, being present at the Savoy Conference (1660) as an observer on the nonconformist side. He was appointed Preacher at Lincoln's Inn in 1663 where he soon secured attention by the quality of his preaching. After the Revolution of 1688 he was installed as Dean of St Paul's, and in 1691 he became Archbishop of Canterbury. He was anti-Romanist and was a supporter of the 'comprehension' of all Protestant dissenters, other than Unitarians, within the Church of England. 'He was not only the best preacher of the age,' wrote Gilbert Burnet, 'but seemed to have brought preaching to perfection. His sermons were so well heard and liked, and so much read, that all the nation proposed him as a pattern and studied to copy after him.' He reformed the style of preaching and transformed its content. In place of involved, elaborate discourses, teeming with metaphor and imagery, his sermons displayed ease of delivery, clarity and simplicity. In place of dispensing abstract theological discourse, Tillotson addressed men's reason, feelings and commonsense.

XXVI

From a sermon, 'On the Rule of Equity to be observed among men', preached at Cripplegate, September 1661, on the text: 'All things, whatsoever ye would that men should do to you, do ye even so to them; for this is the law and the prophets' (*Matt. vii, 12*). *An example of the typical seventeenth- and eighteenth-century 'commonsense' and prudential attitude towards trade and commerce, with as much stress on what is humanly possible in a free market in an imperfect world as upon absolute Christian ethical principles.*

Now if any shall desire to be more particularly satisfied, what that exact righteousness is, which in matter of contracts ought to be observed betwixt man and man? I must confess this is a difficult question, and to be handled very modestly by such as acknowledge themselves unacquainted with the affairs of the world, and the necessities of things, and the particular and hidden reasons of some kind of dealings; for he who is ignorant of these may easily give rules which will not comply with the affairs of the world. He may complain of that which cannot be otherwise, and blame some kind of dealings which are justifiable from particular reasons, not obvious to any man, who is unseen in the way of trade. Besides, there are many cases fall under this question, which are very nice, but of great consequence; and the greater caution and tenderness ought to be used in the resolution of them, because they are matters of constant practice, and the greatest part of mankind are concerned in them. Now it is a dangerous thing to mistake in those things, in which many persons are interested, especially if they be things of such a vast difference, as good and evil, right and wrong are: for if that be determined to be lawful, which is unlawful, men are led into sin; if that be determined to be unlawful, which is lawful, men are led into a snare: for if this determination be to the prejudice of men in their callings, it is a hundred to one but common example and private interest will make many continue in that practice; and then the mischief is this – though men do that which is lawful and right, yet they are staggered by the authority and confidence of him, who hath determined it unlawful; and so have some reluctance in their consciences in the doing of it; and this, by accident, becomes a great sin to them. And when upon a sick-bed, or any other occasion, they come to be touched with the sense of sin, this will be matter of greater horror and affrightment to them than a real sin, which they committed ignorantly, and were afterwards convinced of. Upon all these considerations, I ought to proceed with great wariness in the answering of this question. Therefore I shall content myself with speaking those things which are clear and evident, though they be but general, rather than venture out of my depth, by descending into particulars, and such things as are out of my notice.

I shall, therefore,

1. Lay down the general rule.

II. Some propositions, which may tend to the explication of it.

III. Some special rules for the directing of our commerce and intercourse.

I. The general rule is this: that which it is not unreasonable for me to desire to gain by another, when I am to sell, that I should allow another to gain by me, when I am to buy; and that which is not unreasonable another should gain by me, when I am to buy, that, and no more, I may gain by another, when I am to sell.

II. The propositions, which I shall lay down for the further explication of this rule, are these:

1. In buying and selling, such a proportion of gain may be taken, and ought to be allowed, as is mutually and universally best. And this every man is presumed to desire, because this will be certainly good for everyone; whereas, if it be not universally good, it may be bad for anyone; if it be not mutually so, it will be bad for me by turns.

2. That proportion of gain, which allows a reasonable compensation for our time, and pains, and hazard, is universally and mutually best. If the compensation be unreasonably great, it will be bad for the buyer; if unreasonably little, it will be bad for the seller; if equal and reasonable, it will be good for all.

3. That proportion of gain, which, in common intercourse and use of bargaining among those who understand what they buy and sell, is generally allowed, ought to be esteemed a reasonable compensation. This is evident, because the common reason of mankind doth best determine what is reasonable. Therefore, those who speak of commutative justice, and place it in the equality of things contracted for, need explaining; for value is not a thing absolute and certain, but relative and mutable. Now to fix the value of things, as much as may be, this rule is commonly given – *Tanti unumquodque valet, quanti vendi potest*; 'Everything is worth so much as it may be sold for': which must not be understood too particularly, as if the present and particular appetite of the contractor were to be the rule; for everything is not worth so much as any body will give for it; but so much as, in common intercourse among knowing persons, it will give. For this I take for a truth, that, in the ordinary plenty of commodities, there is an ordinary and usual price of them known to the understanding

persons of every profession. If I be out in this, the matter of gain will be more uncertain than I thought of.

4. A reasonable compensation doth not consist in an indivisible point, but hath a certain latitude, which likewise is to be determined by the common intercourse and practice of men. Suppose ten in the hundred be the usual gain made of such a commodity, eleven the highest, nine the lowest; the latitude is betwixt nine and eleven.

5. Every man engaged in a way of commerce is presumed to understand, unless the contrary be evident. So that, keeping within the latitude of a lawful gain, I may use my skill against another man in driving a bargain; but if his want of skill be evident, that is, sufficiently known to me, I must use him as I would do a child, or other unskilful person; that is, fairly.

6. Where the price of things alters (as it often doth almost in all things), no other rule can be given but the common and market-price. There are some things which are fixedly certain, as coin. There I have no latitude at all; I may not put off a piece of money for more than its value, though a person, out of ignorance, would take it for more. There are some commodities, which in ordinary plenty, being of ordinary goodness, have an unusual price. Here I have but little latitude, viz. that of the market. In the rising and falling of commodities, I have a greater latitude; but usually, in these cases, the market sets some kind of price, unless I be the sole master of a commodity; and here the latitude is the greatest, and my own reason and moderation must limit me. And if any ask, why I make the market the rule, seeing this seems to be as if I should say, Let every man get as much as he can, for so men in the market do; I answer, The market is usually more reasonable than the particular appetites of men; and though every man be apt to get as much as he can, yet men generally have an appetite to sell, as well as to sell dear, and that checks this; and men are brought to moderation, because they are unwilling to lose custom: so that he who governs himself by the market prices, not catching at particular advantages, seems to me to follow the safest rule.

7. There are some things allowed in common intercourse, which are so rigorous, that they are hardly just, which are rather tolerable than commendable. I will give one instance instead of many: a

man hath a small piece of ground lying within another man's estate: he is willing to sell, but requires, possibly, forty or sixty years' purchase, or more, according to the particular appetite of the purchaser. This seems not to be so agreeable to this great rule of equity. I doubt not but some advantage may be made in this case, and I will not set any peremptory limits: I shall only say this in general, we should set a moderate value upon another man's appetite and convenience.

8. It is to be feared, that something very like unrighteousness is woven into the mysteries of most trades; and, like Phidias's image in Minerva's shield, cannot be defaced without the ruin of it. I think this is not a groundless jealousy, but the confession and complaint of the most knowing and understanding persons in most human affairs. I shall instance only in the slightness of work, the imbasing of commodities, and setting them off by indirect advantages. I can only bewail this; for unless the world could generally be convinced of this, it is not like to be amended. Perfection is not to be looked for in this imperfect state; we must be content if things are passable.

9. Nevertheless, we ought to aspire after as great a degree of righteousness and equity, as the condition of human affairs will admit. We should bend all our endeavours to the bettering of the world, and not only avoid all unrighteousness, but draw back, as much as in us lies, from the indirect practices of the world, and from all appearance of unrighteousness.

III. The more particular rules are these:

1. Impose upon no man's ignorance or unskilfulness. Thou mayest set a just value upon thine own commodity, but not a price upon another man's head. I mean, thou mayest not rate a man's want of understanding, or set a tax upon his ignorance; therefore, take no advantage of children, or any other incompetent persons; and do not only use them with justice, but with ingenuity, as those that repose a trust in you, and cast themselves upon your equity. And here are some questions to be resolved.

Quest. 1. If a man be otherwise skilful in his calling, may not I take advantage of his ignorance of a particular circumstance, wherein the contract is concerned?

Ans. I will tell you how Tully resolves this in a particular case:

'A man (says he) brings a ship of corn from Alexandria to Rhodes, in a time of great famine; he may have what price he will; he knows of a great many more ships, that will be there next day: may he conceal this from the Rhodians?' He determines peremptorily he may not. If we will be worse than heathens – I say no more.

Quest. 2. But may we not take advantage of the ignorance of the seller, though not of the buyer? The difference is, he that offers to sell anything, at such a price, is willing so to part with it; now there is no wrong to him that is willing.

I answer, A man is so far willing, as he is knowing: Aristotle tells us, that ignorance is a sort of unwillingness. If a man, out of forgetfulness, or want of consideration, or sufficient understanding of his own calling, mistake himself, I may not make a prize of this man's weakness: for he is only willing to sell it so upon supposition he remembers right, and understands himself aright; but the thing being really worth more, he is absolutely unwilling, and I am injurious to him in taking advantage.

Quest. 3. May I not sell secret faults and vices in a commodity?

Ans. If the faults be such as men take for granted do often happen, and notwithstanding them they do not account any man to have deceived them, then they are faults pardoned by common consent; but if they be such, as I am grieved at, and think myself not fairly dealt withal, when they happen, then some think it is enough to allow for them in the price. But I think Tully hath determined it better: *Ne quid omnino quod venditor novit, emptor ignoret*, 'That the buyer should not be left ignorant of anything that the seller knows.' And this seems reasonable, for I know not but another man may value those faults higher than I do; however, it is not so fair for me to make another man's bargain.

2. Impose upon no man's necessity. If a man must needs buy now, or of thee, because none else is near, make no advantage of this.

3. When God's providence hath put into thy hands some great opportunity and advantage (as by the intervention of some unexpected law, by a sudden war or peace betwixt nations, or by some other casualty) do not stretch it to the utmost. *Fortunam reverenter habe*; 'Use this providential advantage modestly'; con-

sidering that He, whose blessing gave thee this opportunity, can blast thee a thousand ways.

4. Use plainness in all your dealings. This the Roman laws called, *bona fide agere*. Do not disparage another man's commodity, or raise your own besides truth; this is sinful. Do not insinuate a commendation or disparagement indirectly, thereby to lead a man into an error, that you may draw on a bargain the more easily. Do not (as your phrase is) ask or bid much out of the way; for if this be not simply unlawful, yet it doth not become an honest man. We commend the Quakers, because they are at a word in all their dealings: we would be loath not to be counted as good Christians as they are. Let us then do as good things as they do, especially when we account those things praiseworthy; and I am sure this is no ways contrary to justice, and honesty, and truth. I know nothing that gives so real a reputation to that sect as this practice: and would it not adorn those, who account themselves the more sober Christians ? If we praise this in others, let us practise it in ourselves. We are apt to value ourselves much by our orthodox judgements; but let us take heed that sectaries do not confute us by their orthodox lives. For the sake of religion, next to your consciences, in all your dealings tender your reputation: for *quod conscientia est apud Deum, id fama est apud homines*: 'that which conscience is in reference to God, that our reputation is in respect of men'.

5. In matters of vanity and fancy, and things which have no certain estimation, use moderation; and so much the rather, because in these thou art left to be thy own judge.

6. Do not go to the utmost of things lawful. He that will always walk upon the brink, is in great danger of falling down: he that will do the utmost of what he may, will sometime or other be tempted to what he should not; for it is a short and easy passage from the utmost limits of what is lawful, to what is evil and unlawful. Therefore, in that latitude, which you have of gain, use favour towards the poor and necessitous, ingenuity towards the ignorant and unskilful, and moderation towards all men.

7. Where you have any doubt about the equity of dealings, choose you the safest part, and that which will certainly bring you peace. For not only a good conscience, but a quiet conscience, is to

be valued above gain. Therefore in matters of duty do the most; in matters of privilege and divisions of right, and proportions of gain, where there is any doubt, choose the least, for this is always safe.

Thus I have laid down the rule and explained it, and have given as particular directions, as I could safely adventure to do. I must now leave it to every man to apply it more particularly to himself, and to deal faithfully with his own conscience in the use of it. Circumstances, which vary cases, are infinite; therefore, when all is done, much must be left to the equity and chancery of our own breasts. I have not told you how much in the pound you may gain, and no more; nor can I. A man may make a greater gain at one time than another of the same thing; he may take those advantages, which the change of things and the providence of God gives him, using them moderately. A man may take more of some persons than of others; provided a man use all men righteously, he may use some favourably. But I have on purpose forborne to descend to too many particularities; among other reasons, for the sake of Sir Thomas More's observation concerning the casuists of his time, who, he saith, by their too particular resolutions of cases, did not teach men *non peccare*, 'not to sin', but did show them, *quam prope ad peccatum liceat accedere sine peccato*; 'how near men might come to sin, and yet not sin'.

XXVII

From a sermon preached before the Queen at Whitehall, 6 September 1691, on the text: 'Speak unto all the people of the land, and to the priests, saying, When ye fasted and mourned in the fifth and seventh month, even those seventy years, did ye at all fast unto me, even unto me?' (*Zech. vii, 5*). *It deals with the slackness and maladministration of justice and the general lack of morals among ordinary people.*

Thus ought we, the people of this sinful land, upon this solemn day of fasting and humiliation, to set our sins in order before us with all their heinous aggravations; and in the bitterness of our souls to lament and bewail that general prevalence of impiety and vice, which hath overspread the nation, and diffused itself through all ranks and degrees of men, magistrates, ministers, and people. I shall speak something more particularly concerning each of these.

The sins of the magistrates, and those that are in authority. They that make laws for others, and are to see to the execution of them, ought to be strict observers of them themselves. For it must needs put a man not a little out of countenance, to be severe upon those faults in others, of which he knows himself to be notoriously guilty. And yet how many are there, whose place and duty it is to correct the vices and immoralities of others, who are far from being examples of virtue themselves ? and, therefore, it is no wonder that there is so lame and unequal a distribution of justice in the nation, and that magistrates are so cold and slack in the discountenancing of vice and impiety, and in putting the good and wholesome laws made against them in execution: as against the profanation of the Lord's day, by secular business, by vain sports and pastimes, which, by the very nature of them, are apt to dissolve the minds of men into mirth and pleasure, and to carry them off from all serious thoughts of God and religion, and from the meditations of another world; and to give the devil an advantage, and an opportunity, which he never fails to take, to steal the good seed, the word of God, which they have heard that day, out of their hearts, and to make it of none effect: and, which is yet worse, by lewd and sinful practices, which are unlawful at any time, but upon that day are a double breach and violation of God's law.

And, likewise, by neglecting to put in execution the laws against profane swearing and cursing, for which the land mourns, and against drunkenness, and adultery, and fornication, which are so common, and so impudently committed among us; whether they be civil or ecclesiastical laws: and it is hard to say which of them are most remissly executed.

And, to mention no more, by neglecting to prosecute that horrible sin of murder, so frequently now committed in our streets, beyond the example of former ages, with that severity and impartiality, which is necessary to free the nation from the guilt of that crying sin, which calls so loud to heaven for vengeance.

And all this, notwithstanding the magistrates are under the oath of God to put the laws in due execution against all these crimes, so far as they come to their knowledge, and fall under their cognizance.

The sins of the people: amongst whom there is almost an universal corruption and depravation of manners; insomuch, that impiety and vice seem to have overspread the face of the nation; so that we may take up that sad complaint of the prophet, concerning the people of Israel, and apply it to ourselves; that we 'are a sinful nation, a people laden with iniquity, a seed of evildoers; that the whole head is sick, and the whole heart faint; and that from the sole of the foot, even to the head, there is no soundness in us, but wounds, and bruises, and putrifying sores'.

We may justly stand amazed to consider, how the God of all patience is provoked by us every day; to think how long he hath borne with us, and suffered our manners; our open profaneness and infidelity; our great immoralities, and gross hypocrisy; our insolent contempt of religion, and our ill-favoured counterfeiting of it, for low and sordid ends; and, which is the most melancholy consideration of all the rest, we seem to be degenerated to that degree, that it is very much to be feared, there is hardly integrity enough left amongst us to save us.

And then if we consider further our most uncharitable and unChristian divisions, to the endangering both of our reformed religion, and of the civil rights and liberties of the nation: our incorrigibleness under the judgement of God which we have seen abroad in the earth, and which have in a very severe and terrible manner been inflicted upon these kingdoms, that the inhabitants thereof might learn righteousness: our insensibleness of the hand of God, so visible in his late providences towards us, and in the many merciful and wonderful deliverances which from time to time he hath wrought for us.

XXVIII

From a 'Sermon on the Education of Children' (no date or place) on the text: 'Train up a child in the way he should go: and when he is old, he will not depart from it' (*Prov. xxii, 6*). *An example of the typical attitude towards the education of children, with emphasis on obedience, modesty and diligence.*

The good education of children consists, not only in forming their minds in the knowledge of God and their duty, but more especially in endeavouring with the greatest care and prudence to form their lives and manners to religion and virtue. And this must be done by training them up to the exercise of the following graces and virtues:

First, to obedience and modesty; to diligence and sincerity; and to tenderness and pity, as the general dispositions to religion and virtue.

Secondly, to the good government of their passions, and of their tongue; and particularly to speak truth, and to hate lying as a base and vile quality; these being as it were the foundations of religion and virtue.

Thirdly, to piety and devotion towards God; to sobriety and chastity with regard to themselves; and to justice and charity towards all men; as the principal and essential parts of religion and virtue.

First, as the general dispositions to religion and virtue, we must train them up,

1st, to obedience. Parents must take great care to maintain their authority over their children; otherwise they will never regard their commands, nor hearken to and follow their instructions. If they once get head, and grow stubborn and disobedient, there is very little hope left of doing any great good upon them.

2dly, to modesty, which is a fear of shame and disgrace. This disposition, which is proper to children, is a marvellous advantage to all good purposes. 'They are modest,' says Aristotle, 'who are afraid to offend; and they are afraid to offend who are most apt to do it': as children are, because they are much under the power of their passions, without a proportionable strength of reason to govern them and keep them under.

Now modesty is not properly a virtue, but it is a very good sign of a tractable and towardly disposition, and a great preservative and security against sin and vice: and those children, who are much under the restraint of modesty, we look upon as most hopeful and likely to prove good: whereas immodesty is a vicious temper broke loose and got free from all restraint: so that there is nothing left to keep an impudent person from sin, when fear of shame is gone: for sin will soon take possession of that person whom shame hath left. He that is once become shameless hath prostituted himself. Therefore preserve this disposition in children, as much as is possible, as one of the best means to preserve their innocence, and to bring them to goodness.

3dly, to diligence; ... Train up children to diligence if ever you desire they should excel in any kind. 'The diligent hand (saith Solomon) maketh rich'; rich in estate, rich in knowledge. 'Seest thou a man diligent in his business,' as the same wise man observes, 'he shall stand before princes, he shall not stand before mean (or obscure) men.' And again, 'the hand of the diligent shall bear rule, but the slothful shall be under tribute.' Diligence puts almost everything into our power, and will in time make children capable of the best and greatest things.

Whereas idleness is the bane and ruin of children; it is the unbending of their spirits, the rust of their faculties, and as it were the laying of their minds fallow; not as husbandmen do their lands, that they may get new heart and strength, but to impair and lose that which they have. Children that are bred up in laziness are almost necessarily bad, because they cannot take the pains to be good; and they cannot take pains, because they have never been inured and accustomed to it; which makes their spirits restive, and when you have occasion to quicken them and spur them up to business, they will stand stock still.

Therefore never let your children be without a calling, or without some useful, or at least innocent employment, that will take them up; that they may not be put upon a kind of necessity of being vicious for want of something better to do. The devil tempts the active and vigorous into his service, knowing what fit and proper instruments they are to do his drudgery: but the slothful and idle, nobody having hired them and set them on work, lie in his way, and he stumbles upon them as he goes about; and they do as it were offer themselves to his service; and having nothing to do, they even tempt the devil himself to tempt them, and to take them in his way.

4thly, to sincerity; which is not so properly a single virtue, as the life and soul of all other graces and virtues: and without which, what show of goodness soever a man may make, he is unsound and rotten at the heart. Cherish therefore this disposition in children, as that which, when they come to be men, will be the great security and ornament of their lives, and will render them acceptable both to God and man.

5thly, to tenderness and pity: which when they come to engage in business and have dealings in the world, will be a good bar against injustice and oppression; and will be continually prompting us to charity, and will fetch powerful arguments for it from our own bowels.

To preserve this goodness and tenderness of nature, this so very human and useful affection, keep children, as much as is possible, out of the way of bloody sights and spectacles of cruelty; and discountenance in them all cruel and barbarous usage of creatures under their power; do not allow them to torture and to kill them for their sport and pleasure; because this will insensibly and by degrees harden their hearts, and make them less apt to compassionate the wants of the poor and the sufferings and afflictions of the miserable.

Secondly, as the main foundations of religion and virtue, children must be carefully trained up to the government of their passions, and of their tongues; and particularly to speak truth, and to hate lying as a base and vile quality.

1st, to the good government of their passions. It is the disorder of these, more especially of desire, and fear, and anger, which betrays us to many evils. Anger prompts men to contention and murder: inordinate desire, to covetousness and fraud and oppression: and fear many times awes men into sin, and deters them from their duty.

Now if these passions be cherished, or even but let alone in children, they will in a short time grow headstrong and unruly, and when they come to be men will corrupt the judgement, and turn good-nature into humour, and the understanding into prejudice, and wilfulness: but if they be carefully observed and prudently restrained, they may by degrees be managed and brought under government; and the inordinacy of them being pruned away, they may prove excellent instruments of virtue.

Therefore be careful to discountenance in children anything that looks like rage and furious anger, and to show them the unreasonableness and deformity of it. Check their longing desires after things pleasant, and use them to frequent disappointments in that kind; that when you think fit to gratify them they may take it for a favour, and not challenge everything they have a mind to as their due; and by degrees may learn to submit to the more prudent choice of their parents, as being much better able to judge what is good and fit for them.

And when you see them at any time apt out of fear to neglect duty, or to fall into any sin, or to be tempted by telling a lie to commit one fault to hide and excuse another, which children are very apt to do; the best remedy of this evil will be to plant a greater fear against a less, and to tell them what and whom they should chiefly fear – 'not him who can hurt and kill the body, but him who after he hath killed can destroy both body and soul in hell.'

The neglect of children in this matter, I mean in not teaching them to govern their passions, is the true cause why many that have proved sincere Christians when they came to be men, have yet been very imperfect in their conversation, and their lives have been full of inequalities and breaches, which have not only been matter of great trouble and disquiet to themselves, but of great scandal to religion; when their light, which should shine before men, is so often darkened and obscured by these frequent and visible infirmities.

2dly, to the government of their tongues. To this end teach children silence, especially in the presence of their betters. As soon as they are capable of such a lesson, let them be taught not to speak but upon consideration, both of what they say, and before whom. And above all, inculcate upon them that most necessary duty and virtue of speaking truth, as one of the best and strongest bands of human society and commerce: and possess them with the baseness and vileness of telling a lie: for if it be so great a provocation to give a man the lie, then surely to be guilty of that fault must be a mighty reproach ...

To the government of the tongue does likewise belong the restraining of children from lewd and obscene words, from vain

and profane talk, and especially from horrid oaths and impreca-
tions: from all which they are easily kept at first, but if they are
once accustomed to them, it will be found no such easy matter
for them to get quit of these vile habits. It will require great attention and watchfulness over themselves, to keep oaths out of their
common discourse: but if they be heated and in passion, they
throw out oaths and curses as naturally as men that are highly provoked fling stones, or any thing that comes next to hand, at one
another: so dangerous a thing is it to let anything that is bad in
children to grow up into a habit.

Thirdly, as the principal and essential parts of religion and
virtue, let children be carefully bred up.

1st, to sobriety and temperance in regard to themselves; under
which I comprehend likewise purity and chastity. The government of the sensual appetite, as to all kind of bodily pleasures, is
not only a great part of religion, but an excellent instrument of it,
and a necessary foundation of piety and justice. For he that cannot
govern himself is not like to discharge his duty either to God or
men. And therefore St Paul put sobriety first, as a primary and
principal virtue, in which men are instructed by the Christian
religion, and which must be laid as the foundation both of piety
towards God, and of righteousness to men. 'The grace of God,'
for so he calls the gospel, 'that brings salvation unto all men, hath
appeared; teaching us that denying ungodliness and worldly lusts,
we should live soberly, and righteously, and godly in this present
world.' It first teaches us to live soberly: and unless we train up
children to this virtue, we must never expect that they will live
righteously or godly in this present world.

Especially, children must be bred up to great sobriety and temperance in their diet, which will retrench the fuel of other inordinate appetites. It is a good saying I have met with somewhere,
Magna pars virtutis est bene moratus venter, 'a well-mannered and
well-governed appetite', in matters of meats and drinks, 'is a great
part of virtue'. I do not mean that children should be brought up
according to the rules of a Lessian diet*, which sets an equal stint
to all stomachs; and is as senseless a thing as a law would be which

* The Jesuit, Leonard Lessius (1554–1623), prescribed a diet of 14 oz. of
food a day.

should enjoin that shoes for all mankind should be made upon one and the same last.

2dly, to a serious and unaffected piety and devotion towards God, still and quiet, real and substantial, without much show and noise; and as free as may be from all tricks of superstition, or freaks of enthusiasm; which, if parents and teachers be not very prudent, will almost unavoidably insinuate themselves into the religion of children; and when they are grown up will make them appear, to wise and sober persons, fantastical and conceited; and render them very apt to impose their own foolish superstitions and wild conceits upon others, who understand religion much better than ourselves.

Let them be taught to honour and love God above all things, to serve him in private, and to attend constantly upon his public worship, and to keep their minds intent upon the several parts of it, without wandering and distraction; to pray to God as the fountain of all grace and the giver of every good and perfect gift; and to acknowledge him, and to render thanks to him, as our most gracious and constant benefactor, and the great patron and preserver of our lives; to be careful to do what he commands, and to avoid what he hath forbidden; to be always under a lively sense and apprehension of his pure and all-seeing eye, which beholds us in secret; and to do everything in obedience to the authority of that great lawgiver, who is able to save and to destroy, and with an awful regard to the strict and impartial judgement of the great day.

3dly, to justice and honesty: to defraud and oppress no man; to be as good as their word, and to perform all their promises and contracts; and endeavour to imprint upon their minds the equity of that great rule, which is so natural, and so easy, that even children are capable of it – I mean, that rule which our blessed Saviour tells us is the law and the prophets, namely, that we should do to others as we would have others do to us, if we were in their case and circumstances, and they in ours.

16

WILLIAM BEVERIDGE (1637–1708)

WILLIAM BEVERIDGE was born at Barrow in Leicestershire. At Cambridge University he specialized in oriental languages and in 1661 he was ordained. He was instituted as Vicar of Ealing and, in 1672, he became Vicar of St Peter's, Cornhill. He was appointed Archdeacon of Colchester in 1681. He declined the Bishopric of Bath and Wells when it was offered to him in 1691. This apparently gave offence at Court and it was not until 1704 that he was offered, and accepted, the See of St Asaph. He was not a great preacher.

XXIX

From a sermon on 'The Duty of Temperance and Sobriety' (no date or place) on the text: 'Take heed to yourselves, lest at any time your hearts be overcharged with surfeiting, and drunkenness, and cares of this life, and so that day come upon you unawares' (*Luke xxi,* 34). *It gives a vivid description of the evils of drunkenness and the terrible fate of drunkards.*

For every cup you take too much... in that it is too much, it is plainly more than will do you good; and what is not good, must needs be bad for you, both as to your souls and bodies. Your bodies suffer more than you are aware of by it; by it your strength is impaired, your natural heat abated, your stomachs overcharged, your brains disordered, your blood inflamed, and your whole bodies overspread with the seeds of all manner of distempers. 'Who hath woe?' saith the wise man, 'Who hath sorrow? Who hath contentions? Who hath babbling? Who hath wounds without cause? Who hath redness of eyes? They that tarry long at the wine; they that go to seek mixed wine.' And as we read in Ecclesiasticus, 'Drunkenness increaseth the rage of a fool till he offend; it diminisheth strength, and maketh wounds.' The same is found true by daily experience. Look upon a man in drink! what an hideous creature is he now become! More like a brute than man. His colour is changed, his eyes stare, his tongue falters, his head and his hand shake, his breath is short, his knees weak, so that he staggers to and fro, and at length perhaps falls down into a kennel, the fittest place for such brutes to lie in. Insomuch that the very sight of a drunken man is enough to make all men abhor and loathe the very thoughts of being drunken. And yet this is nothing in comparison of what they must needs feel inwardly. For if you look into their inward parts, you might there see their stomachs are sick, their lungs pant, their hearts beat, their heads ache, their blood ferments and boils, and at length breaks forth into a fever, or some other mortal distemper, which usually shortens their days, and puts an end to their miserable life by a more miserable death; which follows so naturally upon excessive drinking, that it is almost a miracle that any common drunkards live out half their days. And if any of them do happen to hold out to the usual age of men, it must be imputed unto God, either to his mercy waiting for their repentance, which is very rare: or else to his justice, continuing them longer in this world, to punish them the more severely in the next; which he hath given them sufficient warning of, by making this sin itself in some measure its own punishment; and so beginning to punish them for it, so soon as ever they have committed it; as they always experience, and sometimes have confessed, being forced to do so by the pains and diseases their bodies are afterwards tormented with. And it would be well for them if it went no farther: but drunkenness disorders the soul as much as it doth the body; or rather disordering the body, it disorders the soul too. For the soul, whilst it is united to the body, making use of the animal spirits that are in it, as its instruments whereby it performs its several operations; when they are out of tune, the soul can do nothing as it ought, no more than an artificer can work without tools, or such as are not fit for his purpose. But excessive drinking causeth such fumes and vapours in the stomach, which flying up into the brain, where the animal spirits chiefly reside, put them all out of order, either scattering them out of their places, or overpowering them so as to make them stupid and unactive, no way fit for the soul to make use of. Hence, some by drinking to excess, are deprived of all sense and reason, as if they had no souls at all, but were mere stocks, fit for nothing but to be cast into the fire and burnt, as they will be ere long. And though it doth not go so far, but they have still something like reason left them, yet it serves them to very little purpose. They cannot think a wise thought, understand nothing clearly, nor judge of anything aright. Their imaginations are disturbed, their consciences stupefied, and their passions all in a hurry, all irregular and extravagant; so that at present they are in a kind of delirium or frenzy, not knowing what they say, or what they do, or what is done to them; as the wise man excellently describes it, where forewarning men of drunkenness, he saith by that, 'Thou shalt be as he that lieth down in the midst of the sea, or as he that lieth upon the top of a mast. They have stricken me, shalt thou say, and I was not sick; they have beaten me, and I felt it not. When shall I awake ? I will seek it yet again.' And although this delirium continues in its height only while the liquor is working in their brains, yet their brains are thereby so clouded, their understanding so darkened, and all their faculties so discomposed, that they are never wise when sober, as the wise man observes, saying, 'Wine is a mocker, strong drink is raging; and whosoever is deceived thereby, is not wise'; or, as the word in the original signifies, 'shall not be wise'; so that as no wise man will be ever drunk, so no drunkard is ever a wise man.

By this, therefore, we may see into the reason which our Saviour here gives wherefore he would not have your hearts overcharged with drunkenness, even 'lest that day', the great Day of Judgement, 'come upon you unawares'. Your eternal state depending upon the issue of the proceedings upon that day, he often cautions you to prepare yourselves, and have your accounts ready against that time, whensoever it shall happen. And here in a more particular manner he adviseth you to have a care of drunkenness, as that which will make you put the evil day far from you, till at length it come unawares upon you, and surprise you when you do not so much as think of it, much less can be ready and prepared for it. For when your hearts are overcharged with drunkenness, it is impossible you should be fit to do that which is the greatest work you have to do; for indeed you can do nothing at all, not the least thing that is, as ye ought to do it. You cannot pray or meditate upon God; you cannot exercise any repentance or faith in Christ. But why do I speak of such things, which a drunkard is no more able to do than a brute beast is. He cannot so much as mind his particular calling, nor do any worldly business without spoiling it: all that he is fit for is to sin, and that, I confess, he is always fit for. Fit for it, did I say? Yea, he is desperately bent upon it, impetuously inclined to sin; to all sin, one as well as another: to lust, fury and revenge; to swearing, cursing, lying, brawling, fighting, murder, anything that comes in his way. There is no sin but some have committed it in their drink; and if there be any that a drunken man doth not commit, it is not because he would not, but because he could not. He had not an opportunity; otherwise he would have committed that as well as any other. For a man in such a condition hath no sense of the difference betwixt good and evil; for 'wine', as the prophet speaks, 'hath taken away his heart'. His reason, his understanding, his conscience is gone; and therefore all sins are alike to him. Hence it is that this sin never goes alone, but hath a great train of other sins always following it: insomuch that it cannot so properly be called one single sin, as all sins in one.

Wherefore, as ever ye desire to avoid any sin at all, ye must be sure to avoid drunkenness, which will so expose you to all manner of sin, that you can never be secure from falling into any whatsoever. And as you must avoid the sin itself, so likewise all that are addicted to it. It is not mine, but the wise man's counsel, 'Be not among wine-bibbers.' And St Paul commands, 'If anyone be a drunkard, with such an one not to eat.' It is not enough that you be not drunk with them, but you must not so much as drink with them, nor eat with them, nor keep them company any more than ye needs must; and that both for their sakes and your own: for their sakes, that so they may be ashamed of themselves and of their sin, when they see all sober men abhor and shun them like so many wild beasts: and for your own sake, lest you by degrees learn it of them, and become like to them, the worst sort of cattle upon the face of the earth, that only cumber the ground, doing good to none, and worst of all to themselves who live like brutes; and it would be well for them if they could die so too, so as never to live again. But that cannot be; live again they must, and that for ever; but where? In Heaven? No surely, they can never come thither. For God hath

expressly decreed, that 'no drunkard shall ever inherit the Kingdom of Heaven'. Indeed, what should they do there ? There is
neither wine nor strong drink to be had; and therefore Heaven
would seem a sad place to them. But they need not fear being sent
thither; they have God's word for it, that they shall not, and therefore they may believe it.

But where then must they live ? In a place more fit and proper
for them, even in hell; where they will meet with their old companions again, not to be merry, but to weep, and wail, and gnash
their teeth together; where they shall have drink enough, but it
shall be only fire and brimstone; where they shall be drunk continually, but it shall be with nothing else but the fury and vengeance of Almighty God: where, for the many hogsheads of good
liquor they consumed upon earth, they shall not have so much as
one drop of water to cool their inflamed tongues; where all their
drunken bouts will return upon them, and afflict and torment
them over again. In short, where 'the worm dieth not, and the fire
is not quenched'. This shall be the potion of their cup to drink in
the other world, who give themselves up to drunkenness in this.

Now put these things together; how that drunkenness consumes a great part of that little time that God hath allotted you
upon earth: it wastes your estates, and reduceth both yourselves
and families into extreme poverty, or at least into great danger of
it: it abuseth those good creatures to your own damage, which
God hath given for your benefit and advantage: it impairs the
health of your bodies, and breeds all manner of diseases in them:
it blots out the image of God that was enstamped upon you, and
makes you like to the beasts which perish: it deprives you of your
reason, or at least of the right use and exercise of it: it exposeth you
to all sorts of vice and wickedness that mankind is capable of committing: it maketh you unfit for all lawful and necessary employments, whether sacred or civil: and at last throws you down into
the bottomless pit, there to live with the devil and his fiends for
ever. Put, I say, these things together, and then judge ye whether
it be not the height of folly and madness for any man to allow himself in such a sin as this ? Whether they, who have been hitherto
addicted to it, had not best to leave it off, and all others to take heed
of ever falling into it, as they tender their own good and welfare.

17

FRANCIS ATTERBURY (1662–1732)

FRANCIS ATTERBURY was born in Buckinghamshire and became a Tory High Churchman. He was much involved in academic controversy at Oxford, but in 1691 he was appointed Lecturer of St Bride's, London, Chaplain to William and Mary and Preacher at Bridewell Hospital. He became the champion of Convocation against the Crown and of the rights of the Lower House against the Bishops. In 1701 he was appointed Archdeacon of Totnes, in 1704 Dean of Carlisle and, in 1711, Dean of Christ Church, Oxford. Finally, he was consecrated Bishop of Rochester in 1713, an office which he held with the Deanery of Westminster. In 1717, Atterbury, who always had Jacobite leanings, entered into direct communication with the Jacobites on the continent, and three years later was implicated in a Jacobite plot. He was arrested, imprisoned in the Tower and in 1723 he was deprived of all his offices and banished from the country. He never returned. Atterbury was regarded as one of the foremost preachers of the day, possessing a gift for oratory and a graceful manner.

XXX

From 'A Spittal Sermon', preached before the Lord Mayor at St Bride's Church, 26 April 1709, on the text: 'Likewise a Levite, when he was at the place, came and looked on him, and passed by on the other side' *(Luke x, 32). It lists the various groups of people who are in need of rich men's charity.*

There is a variety in the tempers even of good men, with relation to the different impressions they receive from different objects of charity. Some persons are more easily and sensibly touched by one sort of objects, and some by another: but there is no man, who, in the variety of charities now proposed, may not meet with that which is best suited to his inclination, and which of all others he would most desire to promote and cherish. For here are the wants of grown men and children; of the soldier, the seaman, and the artificer; of the diseased, the maimed, and the wounded; of distracted persons and condemned criminals; of sturdy wandering beggars and loose disorderly livers; nay, of those who counterfeit wants of all kinds, while they really want nothing but due correction and hard labour; at one view represented to you. And surely, scarce any man, who hath an heart capable of tenderness, can *come and look on* all these sad spectacles at once; and then *pass by on the other side*, without extending a merciful hand to relieve any of them.

Some may delight in building for the use of the poor; others in feeding and clothing them, and in taking care that manual arts be taught them: some, in providing physic, discipline, or exercise for the bodies; others in procuring the improvement of their minds by useful knowledge: some may please themselves in redressing the mischiefs occasioned by the wicked poor; others, in preventing those mischiefs, by securing the innocence of children, and by imparting to them the invaluable blessing of a virtuous and pious education: finally, some may place their chief satisfaction in giving secretly what is to be distributed: others, in being the open and avowed instruments of making and inspecting such distributions. And whoever is particularly disposed to any one or more of these methods of beneficence may, I say, within the compass of those different schemes of charity, which have been proposed, find room enough to exercise his Christian compassion. To go over them particularly –

Hast thou been educated in the fear of God, and a strict practice of virtue? was thy tender age fenced and guarded every way from infection by the care of wise parents and masters? and shall not a grateful relish of thy own great felicity in that respect, render thee ready and eager to procure the same happiness for others, who equally need it? shall it not make thee the common guardian, as it were, of poor orphans, whose minds are left as unclothed and naked altogether, as their bodies; and who are exposed to all the temptations of ignorance, want, and idleness?

Art thou a true lover of thy country? zealous for its religious and civil interests ? and a cheerful contributor to all those public expenses which have been thought necessary to secure them, against the attempts of the common enemy and oppressor ? is the near prospect of all the blessings of peace welcome and desirable to thee ? and wilt thou not bear a tender regard to all those, who have lost their health and their limbs in the rough service of war, to secure these blessings to thee ? Canst thou see any one of them lie by the way, as it were, *stripped, and wounded, and half-dead*; and yet *pass by on the other side*, without doing as much for thy friend, as that good *Samaritan* did for his enemy, when he had *compassion on him*, and *went to him, and bound up his wounds, pouring in oil and wine, and brought him to an inn* (or *house of common reception*, so the word, Πανδοχεῖον, signifies) and *took care of him*.

Have thy reasoning faculties been eclipsed at any time by some accidental stroke ? by the mad joys of wine, or the excess of religious melancholy ? by a fit of apoplexy, or the rage of a burning fever ? and hast thou, upon thy recovery, been made sensible, to what a wretched state that calamity reduced thee ? and what a sad spectacle, to all thy friends and acquaintance, it rendered thee ? And shall not this affliction, which thou hast felt thyself, or perhaps observed in others, who were near and dear to thee; shall it not lead thee to commiserate all those, who labour under a settled distraction ? who are shut out from all the pleasures and advantages of human commerce, and even degraded from the rank of reasonable creatures ? wilt thou not make their case thine ? and take pity upon them, who cannot take pity upon themselves ? wilt thou not contribute, to the best of thy power, either towards restoring the defaced image of God upon their souls; or (if that cannot be done) towards supporting them, for a while, under a charitable confinement, where human nature may be rescued from that contempt, to which such objects expose it ?

Once more; hast thou suffered at any time by vagabonds and pilferers ? hath the knowledge or opinion of thy wealth exposed thee to the attempts of more dangerous and bloody villains ? have thy unquiet slumbers been interrupted by the apprehension of nightly assaults, such as have terrified, and perhaps ruined some of thy unfortunate neighbours ? learn from hence duly to esteem and promote those useful charities, which remove such pests of human society into prisons and workhouses, and train up youth in the ways of diligence, who would otherwise take the same desperate courses: which reform the stubborn by correction, and the idle by hard labour; and would, if carried to that perfection of which they are capable, go a great way towards making life more comfortable than now it is, and property itself more valuable.

These are the several ways of beneficence, which you are now called upon to practise. Many arguments might be urged to induce you to it: but I am sensible I detain you too long; and therefore shall use but one; however, such a one as is equal to many, and cannot but have great weight with all that call themselves Christians. It is this – that our blessed Saviour went before us, in the practice of every one of these *four* instances of well-doing, which I have now recommended to you.

18

JONATHAN SWIFT (1667–1745)

JONATHAN SWIFT was born in Ireland, was ordained priest in 1695 and was appointed Dean of St Patrick's, Dublin, in 1713, where he remained until his death. He was a frequent visitor to this country, where he was much at home in literary and political circles. He was a brilliant pamphleteer and satirist and he is most popularly remembered as the author of *Gulliver's Travels* (1726) and *A Tale of a Tub* (1704). He was a Whig in politics although he found difficulty in supporting his party's attitude towards the non-conformists. He was a thorough-going pessimist, savage in his satire and worldly and ambitious in his outlook. For the last six years of his life he was sick, physically and mentally. As a preacher he eschewed emotion and 'refinements of style and flights of wit'. His sermons had vigour, economy and clarity and they emphasized conduct and the practical everyday duties of life.

XXXXI

From a sermon 'On the Poor Man's Contentment' (no place or date, but probably between 1717 and 1720) on the text: 'Not that I speak in respect of want: for I have learned, in whatsoever state I am, therewith to be content' (Phil. iv, 11). Although Swift's sphere of work was Ireland, the sentiments expressed in this sermon are typical of many English clergymen. In the face of the grave inequalities in wealth and station and the real suffering of the poor, Swift, who hated injustice, nevertheless still asserts that the poor are more blessed than the rich and have more cause for happiness.

The great question, long debated in the world is, whether the rich or the poor are the least miserable of the two? It is certain, that no rich man ever desired to be poor, and that most, if not all, poor men desire to be rich; from whence it may be argued, that, in all appearance, the advantage lieth on the side of wealth, because both parties agree in preferring it before poverty. But this reasoning will be found to be false: for, I lay it down as a certain truth, that God Almighty hath placed all men upon an equal foot, with respect to their happiness in this world, and the capacity of attaining their salvation in the next; or, at least, if there be any difference, it is not the advantage of the rich and the mighty. Now since a great part of those, who usually make up our congregations, are not of considerable station, and many among them of the lower sort, and since the meaner people are generally and justly charged with the sin of repining and murmuring at their own condition, to which, however, their betters are sufficiently subject (although, perhaps, for shame, not always so loud in their complaints), I thought it might be useful to reason upon this point in as plain a manner as I can. I shall therefore show, first, that the poor enjoy many temporal blessings, which are not common to the rich and the great, and, likewise, that the rich and the great are subject to many temporal evils, which are not common to the poor.

But, here I would not be misunderstood; perhaps, there is not a word more abused than that of the poor, or wherein the world is more generally mistaken. Among the number of those who beg in our streets, or are half starved at home, or languish in prison for debt, there is hardly one in a hundred who doth not owe his misfortunes to his own laziness or drunkenness, or worse vices.

To these he owes those very diseases which often disable him from getting his bread. Such wretches are deservedly unhappy; they can only blame themselves; and when we are commanded to have pity on the poor, these are not understood to be of the number.

It is true, indeed, that sometimes honest, endeavouring men are reduced to extreme want, even to the begging of alms, by losses, by accidents, diseases, and old age, without any fault of their own: but these are very few, in comparison of the other; nor would their support be any sensible burden to the public, if the charity of well-disposed persons were not intercepted by those common strollers, who are most importunate, and who least deserve it. These, indeed, are properly and justly called the poor, whom it should be our study to find out and distinguish, by making them partake of our superfluity and abundance.

But neither have these anything to do with my present subject: for by the poor I only intend the honest, industrious artificer, the meaner sort of tradesmen, and the labouring man, who getteth his bread by the sweat of his brow, in town or country, and who make the bulk of mankind among us.

First, I shall therefore show, first, that the poor (in the sense I understand the word) do enjoy many temporal blessings, which are not common to the rich and great; and likewise, that the rich and great are subject to many temporal evils, which are not common to the poor.

Secondly, from the arguments offered to prove the foregoing head, I shall draw some observations that may be useful for your practice.

1. As to the first: health, we know, is generally allowed to be the best of all earthly possessions, because it is that, without which we can have no satisfaction in any of the rest, for riches are of no use, if sickness taketh from us the ability of enjoying them, and power and greatness are then only a burden. Now, if we would look for health, it must be in the humble habitation of the labouring man, or industrious artificer, who earn their bread by the sweat of their brows, and usually live to a good old age with a great degree of strength and vigour.

The refreshment of the body by sleep is another great happiness of the meaner sort. Their rest is not disturbed by the fear of thieves and robbers, nor is it interrrupted by surfeits of intemperance. Labour and plain food supply the want of quieting draughts; and the wise man telleth us, that the sleep of the labouring man is sweet. As to children, which are certainly accounted of as a blessing, even to the poor, where industry is not wanting; they are an assistance to their honest parents, instead of being a burden; they are healthy and strong, and fit for labour; neither is the father in fear, lest his heir should be ruined by an unequal match; nor is he solicitous about his rising in the world, further than to be able to get his bread.

The poorer sort are not the objects of general hatred or envy; they have no twinges of ambition, nor trouble themselves with party quarrels, or state divisions. The idle rabble, who follow their ambitious leaders in such cases, do not fall within my description of the poorer sort; for, it is plain, I mean only the honest industrious poor in town or country, who are safest in times of public disturbance, in perilous seasons, and public revolutions, if they will be quiet, and do their own business; for artificers and husbandmen are necessary in all governments: but in such seasons, the rich are the public mark, because they are oftentimes of no use, but to be plundered; like some sort of birds, who are good for nothing but their feathers; and so fall a prey to the stronger side.

Let us proceed on the other side to examine the disadvantages that the rich and the great lie under, with respect to the happiness of the present life.

First then; while health, as we have said, is the general portion of the lower sort, the gout, the dropsy, the stone, the colic, and all other diseases are continually haunting the palaces of the rich and the great, as the natural attendants upon laziness and luxury. Neither does the rich man eat his sumptuous fare with half the appetite and relish, that even the beggars do the crumbs which fall from his table: but, on the contrary, he is full of loathing and disgust, or at the best of indifference in the midst of plenty. Thus their intemperance shortens their lives, without pleasing their appetites.

Business, fear, guilt, design, anguish, and vexation are continually buzzing about the curtains of the rich and the powerful and will hardly suffer them to close their eyes, unless when they are dozed with the fumes of strong liquors.

It is a great mistake to imagine that the rich want but a few things; their wants are more numerous, more craving, and urgent, than those of poorer men: for these endeavour only at the necessaries of life, which make them happy, and they think no farther: but the desire of power and wealth is endless, and therefore impossible to be satisfied with any acquisitions.

If riches were so great a blessing as they are commonly thought, they would at least have this advantage, to give their owners cheerful hearts and countenances; they would often stir them up to express their thankfulness to God, and discover their satisfaction to the world. But, in fact, the contrary to all this is true. For where are there more cloudy brows, more melancholy hearts, or more ingratitude to their great benefactor, than among those who abound in wealth? And indeed, it is natural that it should be so, because those men who covet things that are hard to be got, must be hard to please; whereas a small thing maketh a poor man happy; and great losses cannot befall him.

It is likewise worth considering, how few among the rich have procured their wealth by just measures; how many owe their fortunes to the sins of their parents, how many more to their own? If men's titles were to be tried before a true court of conscience, where false swearing, and a thousand vile artificers (that are well known, and can hardly be avoided in human courts of justice) would avail nothing; how many would be ejected with infamy and disgrace? how many grow considerable by breach of trust, by bribery and corruption? How many have sold their religion, with the rights and liberties of themselves and others, for power and employments?

And, it is a mistake to think, that the most hardened sinner, who oweth his possessions or titles to any such wicked arts of thieving, can have true peace of mind, under the reproaches of a guilty conscience, and amidst the cries of ruined widows and orphans.

I know not one real advantage that the rich have over the poor, except the power of doing good to others: but this is an advantage which God hath not given wicked men the grace to make use of. The wealth acquired by evil means was never employed to good ends; for that would be to divide the kingdom of Satan against itself. Whatever hath been gained by fraud, avarice, oppression, and the like, must be preserved and increased by the same methods. ... We must therefore conclude, that wealth and power are in their own nature, at best, but things indifferent, and that a good man may be equally happy without them, provided that he hath a sufficiency of the common blessings of human life to answer all the reasonable and virtuous demands of nature, which his industry will provide, and sobriety will prevent his wanting. *Agur*'s Prayer, with the reasons of his wish, are full to this purpose. 'Give me neither poverty nor riches; feed me with food convenient for me. Lest I be full and deny thee, and say, Who is the Lord? Or, lest I be poor, and steal, and take the name of my God in vain.'

From what hath been said, I shall, in the second place, offer some considerations, that may be useful for your practice.

And here I shall apply myself chiefly to those of the lower sort, for whose comfort and satisfaction this discourse is principally intended. For, having observed the great sin of those, who do not abound in wealth, to be that of murmuring and repining, that God hath dealt his Blessings unequally to the sons of men, I thought it would be of great use to remove out of your minds so false and wicked an opinion, by showing that your condition is really happier than most of you imagine.

First, therefore, it hath been always agreed in the world, that the present happiness of mankind consisted in the ease of our body and the quiet of our mind; but, from what hath been already said, it plainly appears, that neither wealth nor power do in any sort contribute to either of these two blessings. If on the contrary, by multiplying our desires, they increase our discontents, if they destroy our health, gall us with painful diseases, and shorten our life; if they expose us to hatred, to envy, to censure, to a thousand temptations, it is not easy to see why a wise man should make them his choice, for their own sake, although it were in his power. Would any of you, who are in health and strength of body, with moderate food and raiment earned by your own labour, rather choose to be in the rich man's bed, under the torture of the gout, unable to take your natural rest, or natural nourishment, with the additional load of a guilty conscience, reproaching you for injustice, oppressions, covetousness, and fraud? No; but you would take the riches and power, and leave behind the inconveniencies that attend them; and so would every man living. But that is more than our share, and God never intended this world for such a place of rest as we would make it; for the Scripture assureth us, that it was only designed as a place of trial. Nothing is more frequent, than a man to wish himself in another's condition; yet he seldom doth it without some reserve: he would not be so old; he would not be so sickly; he would not be so cruel; he would not be so insolent; he would not be so vicious; he would not be so oppressive; so griping; and so on. From whence it is plain, that, in their own judgement, men are not so unequally dealt with, as they would at first sight imagine: for, if I would not change my condition with another man, without any exception or reservation at all, I am in reality more happy than he.

Secondly, you of the meaner sort are subject to fewer temptations than the rich; and therefore your vices are more unpardonable. Labour subdueth your appetites to be satisfied with common things; the business of your several callings filleth up your whole time; so that idleness, which is the bane and destruction of virtue, doth not lead you into the neighbourhood of sin: your passions are cooler, by not being inflamed with excess, and therefore the gate and the way that lead to life are not so strait or so narrow to you, as to those who live among all the allurements to wickedness. To serve God with the best of your care and understanding, and to be just and true in your dealings, is the short sum of your duty and will be the more strictly required of you, because nothing lieth in the way to divert you from it.

Thirdly, it is plain, from what I have said, that you of the lower rank, have no just reason to complain of your condition; because, as you plainly see, it affordeth you so many advantages, and freeth you from so many vexations, so many distempers, both of body and mind, which pursue and torment the rich and powerful.

Fourthly, you are to remember and apply, that the poorest person is not excused from doing good to others, and even relieving the wants of his distressed neighbour, according to his abilities, and if you perform your duty in this point, you far outdo the greatest liberalities of the rich, and will accordingly be accepted of by God, and get your reward: for, it is our Saviour's own doctrine, when the widow gave her two mites, the rich give out of their abundance; that is to say, what they give; they do not feel it in their way of living: but the poor man, who giveth out of his little stock, must spare it from the necessary food and raiment of himself and his family. And therefore our Saviour adds, 'That the widow gave more than all who went before her; for she gave all she had, even all her living'; and so went home utterly unprovided to supply her necessities.

Lastly, as it appeareth from what hath been said, that you of the lower rank have, in reality, a greater share of happiness, your work of salvation is easier, by your being liable to fewer temptations; and as your reward in Heaven is much more certain, than it is to the rich, if you seriously perform your duty, for yours is the Kingdom of Heaven; so your neglect of it will be less excusable, will meet with fewer allowances from God, and will be punished with double stripes. For, the most unknowing among you cannot plead ignorance in what you have been so early taught, I hope, so often instructed in, and which is so easy to be understood. I mean the art of leading a life agreeable to the plain and positive laws of God. Perhaps you may think you lie under one disadvantage, which the great and rich have not; that idleness will certainly reduce you to beggary; whereas those who abound in wealth, lie under no necessity either of labour or temperance to keep enough to live on. But this is indeed one part of your happiness, that the lowness of your condition, in a manner, forceth you to what is pleasing to God, and necessary for your daily support. Thus your duty and interest are always the same.

To conclude; since our blessed Lord, who instead of a rich and honourable station in this world, was pleased to choose his lot among men of the lower condition; let not those on whom the bounty of providence hath bestowed wealth and honours, despise the men who are placed in an humble and inferior station; but rather, with their utmost power, by their countenance, by their protection, by just payment for their honest labour, encourage their daily endeavours for the virtuous support of themselves and their families. On the other hand, let the poor labour to provide things honest in the sight of all men; and so, with diligence in their several employments, live soberly, righteously and godly in this present world, that they may obtain that glorious reward promised in the Gospel to the poor, I mean, the Kingdom of Heaven.

19

JOSEPH BUTLER (1692–1752)

JOSEPH BUTLER was born at Wantage, the son of Presbyterian parents. When he went to Oxford in 1715 he became an Anglican and was ordained three years later. From 1718 to 1726, he was Preacher at the Rolls Chapel, where he delivered a series of sermons which won him his reputation as a preacher. In 1722 he was instituted as Rector of Houghton-le-Skerne, near Darlington, but three years later he was presented to the wealthy benefice of Stanhope, Durham. Here he led a secluded life while he wrote his famous *Analogy of Religion* (1736), the greatest theological work of the time. In 1738 he became Bishop of Bristol, the poorest See in England, but from 1740 he also held the Deanery of St Paul's, London, along with his Bishopric. While he was at Bristol he came into conflict with John Wesley and George Whitfield. In 1750 he was translated to the See of Durham. 'Butler,' it has been said, 'ranks among the greatest exponents of national theology and ethics in England since the Reformation.'

XXXII

From a sermon preached at St Bride's, London, before the Lord Mayor and the Governors of several hospitals in London, in Easter Week 1740, on the text: 'The rich and poor meet together; the Lord is the maker of them all' (*Prov. xxii, 2*). *The rich have a trust and a privilege to care for the poor. The various public charities in London.*

It is not only true, that the rich have the power of doing a great deal of good, and must be highly blameable for neglecting to do it: but it is moreover true, that this power is given them by way of trust, in order to their keeping down that vice and misery, with which the lower people would otherwise be quite overrun. For without instruction and good influence they, of course, grow rude and vicious, and reduce themselves to the utmost distresses; often to very terrible ones without deserving much blame. And to these must be added their unavoidable distresses, which yet admit of relief. This their case plainly requires, that some natural provision should be made for it: as the case of children does, who, if left to their own ways, would almost infallibly ruin themselves. Accordingly Providence has made provision for this case of the poor: not only by forming their minds peculiarly apt to be influenced by their superiors, and giving those superiors abilities to direct and relieve them; but also by putting the latter under the care and protection of the former: for this is plainly done, by means of that intercourse of various kinds between them, which, in the natural course of things, is unavoidably necessary. . . . He who has distributed men into these different ranks, and at the same time united them into one society, in such sort as men are united, has, by this constitution of things, formally put the poor under the superintendency and patronage of the rich. The rich then are charged, by natural providence, as much as by revealed appointment, with the care of the poor: not to maintain them idle; which, were it possible they could be so maintained, would produce greater mischiefs than those which charity is to prevent; but to take care, that they maintain themselves by their labour; or in case they cannot, then to relieve them; to restrain their vices, and form their minds to virtue and religion. This is a trust, yet it is not a burden, but a privilege, annexed to riches. And if everyone discharged his share of the trust faithfully, whatever be his share of it, the world would be quite another place from what it is. But that cannot be, till covetousness, debauchery, and every vice, be unknown among the rich. Then, and not before, will the manners of the poor be, in all respects, what they ought to be, and their distresses find the full relief, which they ought to find . . .

Amongst the peculiar advantages of public charities above private ones, is also to be mentioned, that they are examples of great influence. They serve for perpetual memorials of what I have been observing, of the relation which subsists between the rich and the poor, and the duties which arise out of it. They are standing admonitions to all within sight or hearing of them, to 'go and do likewise'. Educating poor children in virtue and religion, relieving the sick, and correcting offenders in order to their amendment, are, in themselves, some of the very best of good works. These charities would indeed be the glory of your city, though their influence were confined to it. But important as they are in themselves their importance still increases, by their being examples to the rest of the nation; which, in process of time, of course copies after the metropolis. It has indeed already imitated every one of these charities; for of late, the most difficult and expensive of them, hospitals for the sick and wounded, have been established; some within your sight, others in remote parts of the kingdom. You will give me leave to mention particularly that in its second trading city*; which is conducted with such disinterested fidelity and prudence, as I dare venture to compare with yours. Again, there are particular persons very blameably unactive and careless, yet not with good dispositions, who, by these charities, are reminded of their duty, and 'provoked to love and to good works'. And let me add, though one is sorry any should want so slight a reason for contributing to the most excellent designs, yet if any are supposed to do so merely of course, because they see others do it, still they help to support these monuments of charity, which are a continued admonition to the rich, and relief to the poor: and herein all good men rejoice, as St Paul speaks of himself in a like case, 'yea, and will rejoice'.

As all human schemes admit of improvement, all public charities, methinks, should be considered as standing open to proposals for it; that the whole plan of them, in all its parts, may be brought to as great perfection as is possible. Now it should seem that employing some share of the children's time in easy labour, suitable to their age, which is done in some of our charity schools, might be done in most others of them, with very good effect; as it is in all those of a neighbouring kingdom.† Then as the only purposes of punishments less than capital are to reform the offenders themselves, and warn the innocent by their example, everything which should contribute to make this kind of punishments answer these purposes better than it does, would be a great improvement.

* Bristol, where Butler was born.
† Ireland.

And whether it be not a thing practicable, and what would contribute somewhat towards it, to exclude utterly all sorts of revelmirth from places where offenders are confined, to separate the young from the old, and force them both, in solitude, with labour and low diet, to make the experiment, how far their natural strength of mind can support them under guilt and shame and poverty; this may deserve consideration. Then again, some religious instruction particularly adapted to their condition would as properly accompany those punishments which are intended to reform, as it does capital ones. God forbid that I should be understood to discourage the provision which is made for it in this latter case: I heartily wish it were better than it is; especially since it may well be supposed, as the state of religion is at present among us, that some condemned malefactors may have never had the doctrine of the Gospel enforced upon their consciences. But since it must be acknowledged of greater consequence, in a religious as well as civil respect, how persons live, than how they die; it cannot but be even more incumbent on us to endeavour, in all ways, to reclaim those offenders who are to return again into the world, than those who are to be removed out of it: and the only effectual means of reclaiming them, is to instil into them a principle of religion. If persons of authority and influence would take things of this and a like kind under their consideration, they might perhaps still improve these charities; which are already, I truly believe, under a better management than any other of so large a compass in the world.

XXXIII

From a sermon on the text: 'Above all things have fervent charity among yourselves: for charity shall cover the multitude of sins' (*1 Pet. iv, 8*). *It was preached on 31 March 1748, in St Lawrence Jewry, London, before the President and Governors of the 'London Infirmary, for the Relief of Sick and Diseased Persons, especially Manufacturers, and Seamen in Merchant Service, etc.'. The importance of providing for the sick who are poor. We should look with benevolence, not with severity, on the poor. Even those who by their own fault are poor and sick have a claim on men's charity. The limitations of the London Infirmary.*

Though nothing, to be called an objection in the way of argument, can be alleged against thus providing for poor sick people in the properest, indeed the only way in which they can be provided for; yet persons of too severe tempers can, even upon this occasion, talk in a manner, which, contrary surely to their intention, has a very malignant influence upon the spirit of charity – talk of the ill-deserts of the poor, the good uses they might make of being let to suffer more than they do, under distresses which they bring upon themselves, or however might, by diligence and frugality, provide against; and the idle uses they may make of knowing beforehand that they shall be relieved in case of those distresses. Indeed there is such a thing as a prejudice against them, arising from their very state of poverty, which ought greatly to be guarded against; a kind of prejudice, to which perhaps most of us, upon some occasions, and in some degree, may inattentively be liable, but which pride and interest may easily work up to a settled hatred of them; the utter reverse of that amiable part of the character of Job, that he was 'a father to the poor'. But it is undoubtedly fit, that such of them as are good and industrious should have the satisfaction of knowing beforehand, that they shall be relieved under diseases and casualties: and those, it is most obvious, ought to be relieved preferably to others. But these others, who are not of that good character, might possibly have the apprehension of those calamities in so great a degree, as would be very mischievous, and of no service, if they thought they must be left to perish under them. And though their idleness and extravagance are very inexcusable, and ought by all reasonable methods to be restrained; and they are highly to be blamed for not making some provision against age and supposable disasters, when it is in their power; yet it is not to be desired, that the anxieties of avarice should be added to the natural inconveniences of poverty.

It is said that our common fault towards the poor is not harshness, but too great lenity and indulgence. And if allowing them in debauchery, idleness, and open beggary; in drunkenness, profane cursing and swearing in our streets, nay in our houses of correction; if this be lenity, there is doubtless a great deal too much of it. And such lenity towards the poor is very consistent with the most cruel neglects of them, in the extreme misery to which those vices reduce them. Now though this last certainly is not our general fault; yet it cannot be said everyone is free from it. For this reason, and that nothing, which has so much as the shadow of an objection against our public charities, may be entirely passed over, you will give me leave to consider a little the supposed case above-mentioned, though possibly some may think it unnecessary, that of persons reduced to poverty and distress by their own faults.

Instances of this there certainly are. But it ought to be very distinctly observed, that in judging which are such, we are liable to be mistaken: and more liable to it, in judging to what degree those are faulty, who really are so in some degree. However, we should always look with mildness upon the behaviour of the poor: and be sure not to expect more from them than can be expected, in a moderate way of considering things. We should be forward not only to admit and encourage the good deserts of such as do well, but likewise as to those of them who do not, be ever ready to make due allowances for their bad education, or, which is the same, their having had none; for what may be owing to the ill example of their superiors, as well as companions, and for temptations of all kinds. And remember always, that be men's vices what they will, they have not forfeited their claim to relief under necessities, till they have forfeited their lives to justice.

Our 'heavenly Father is kind to the unthankful and to the evil; and sendeth His rain on the just and on the unjust'. And, in imitation of him, our Saviour expressly requires, that our beneficence be promiscuous. But we have moreover the Divine example for relieving those distresses which are brought upon persons by their own faults; and this is exactly the case we are considering. Indeed the general dispensation of Christianity is an example of this; for its general design is to save us from our sins, and the punishments which would have been the just consequence of them. But the Divine example in the daily course of nature is a more obvious and sensible one. And though the natural miseries which are foreseen to be annexed to a vicious course of life are providentially intended to prevent it, in the same manner as civil penalties are intended to prevent civil crimes; yet those miseries, those natural penalties admit of and receive natural reliefs, no less than any other miseries, which could not have been foreseen or prevented. Charitable providence then, thus manifested in the course of nature, which is the example of our heavenly Father, most evidently leads us to relieve not only such distresses as were unavoidable, but also such as people by their own faults have brought upon themselves. The case is, that we cannot judge in what degree it was intended they should suffer, by considering what, in the natural course of things. would be the whole bad consequences of their faults, if those consequences were not prevented, when nature has provided means to prevent great part of them. We cannot, for instance, estimate what degree of present sufferings God has annexed to drunkenness, by considering the diseases which follow from this vice, as they would be if they admitted of no reliefs or remedies; but by considering the remaining misery of those diseases, after the application of such remedies as nature has provided. For as it is certain, on the one side, that those diseases are providential corrections of intemperance, it is as certain, on the other, that the remedies are providential mitigations of those corrections; and altogether as much providential, when administered by the good hand of charity in the case of our neighbour, as when administered by self-love in our own. Thus the pain, the danger, and other distresses of sickness and poverty remaining, after all the charitable relief which can be procured; and the many uneasy circumstances which cannot but accompany that relief, though distributed with all supposable humanity; these are the natural corrections of idleness and debauchery, supposing these vices brought on those miseries. And very severe corrections they are; and they ought not to be increased by withholding that relief, or by harshness in the distribution of it. Corrections of all kinds, even the most necessary ones, may easily exceed their proper bound: and when they do so, they become mischievous; and mischievous in the measure they exceed it. And the natural corrections which we have been speaking of would be excessive, if the natural mitigations provided for them were not administered. . . .

I must congratulate you upon the great success the good spirit of beneficence has given to the particular good work before us; great, I think, beyond all example for the time it has subsisted. Nor would it be unsuitable to the present occasions to recount the particular of this success. For the necessary accommodations which have been provided, and the numbers who have been relieved, in so short a time, cannot but give high reputation to the London Infirmary. And the reputation of any particular charity, like credit in trade, is so much real advantage, without the inconveniences to which that is sometimes liable. It will bring in contributions for its support; and men of character, as they shall be wanted, to assist in the management of it; men of skill in the professions, men of conduct in business, to perpetuate, improve, and bring it to perfection. So that you, the contributors to this charity, and more especially those of you by whose immediate care and economy it is in so high repute, are encouraged to go on with 'your labour of love', not only by the present good, which you see is here done, but likewise by the prospect of what will probably be done, by your means, in future times, when this infirmary shall become, as I hope it will, no less renowned than the city in which it is established.

But to see how far it is from being yet complete, for want of contributions, one need only look upon the settled rules of the house for *admission of patients*. See there the limitations which necessity prescribes, as to the persons to be admitted. Read but that one order, though others might be mentioned, that *none who are judged to be in an asthmatic, consumptive, or dying condition be admitted on any account whatsoever*. Harsh as these words sound, they proceed out of the mouth of Charity itself. Charity pronounces it to be better that poor creatures, who might receive much ease and relief, should be denied it, if their case does not admit of recovery rather than that others, whose case does admit of it, be left to perish. But it shocks humanity to hear such an alternative mentioned; and to think, that there should be a necessity, as there is at present, for such restrictions, in one of the most beneficent and best managed schemes in the world. May more numerous or larger contributions, at length, open a door to such as these; that what renders their case in the highest degree compassionable, their languishing under incurable diseases, may no longer exclude them from the house of mercy!

20

THOMAS WILSON (1663–1755)

THOMAS WILSON was born at Burton, Cheshire, and was educated at Trinity College, Dublin, for the medical profession. In 1684, however, he was ordained and, after holding several parochial appointments, he was appointed Bishop of Sodor and Man in 1698, where he remained for fifty-seven years. He not only discharged his episcopal duties with ability, but was also a church builder, farmer and the founder of public libraries. In 1722 he suspended his Archdeacon for heresy, and after the Archdeacon's appeal to the governor, Wilson was imprisoned. In 1725, however, the case was decided in his favour. His devotional writings were much read and he was an acceptable preacher.

XXXIV

From a Charity Sermon entitled 'Continuance in Well-doing Remembered and Enforced', given at St Dunstan's, 16 February 1723, on the text: 'Let us not be weary in well-doing; for in due season we shall reap, if we faint not' (Gal. vi, 9). The advantages and dangers in educating the poor.

Because the corruption of human nature is such, that children are very hardly persuaded to see their interest, or to be at the pains to learn the way that leadeth unto life, there have therefore been proper encouragements thought of, and provided, out of the charitable contributions which from time to time have been collected. Some are *clothed*; some are *clothed and fed*; all are provided with books, and all are instructed in the principles of the Christian religion; and such as are towardly, and answer the end of their education, have a certain prospect of being further taken care of.

Now, if this is not a work of *well-doing*, we must despair of ever proving any thing to be so. And therefore good men ought not to be discouraged by the objections of wicked men and unbelievers. They will rather take their objections into consideration; and where any corruption or evil consequence has crept into this good design, they will take care to amend and prevent it for the future. For instance: such as have the immediate care of instructing them will make it their great business to be always instilling into them the great duties of *humility* and *gratitude*, that they may not forget the condition from whence they were taken, nor the Providence that has raised up means of procuring for them a Christian education.

It is but too natural, *it must be confessed*, for children that have been thus educated, *and very often for their parents too*, because they *have had* an orderly education, to think them *too good for servile employments*; never considering, that they must, *very probably*, have continued in the very *lowest rank and condition* without any distinct knowledge of God, and without any qualifications for a laudable employment, all the days of their life, had not God and good Christians provided better for them.

Now, to make this a pretence for their not being useful in their generation, *in any honest employment whatever*, which the providence of God, or the wisdom of the trustees for these charities shall assign them, is such *an ingratitude*, such a *forgetfulness*, as should by all means be guarded against; otherwise the consequence *most certainly* will be, that the children of many of those charitable persons who have contributed to *their* better education, must be obliged to accept of those meaner services and offices of life, which they think themselves too good for. And this at last will be a discouragement to this pious work.

And *this*, as was before said, should be the great concern of those to whom their education is entrusted to prevent, as much as may be, *that their hearts may not be lifted up above their condition*; but that they be often put in mind of the condition they would have been in, of *poverty*, *ignorance*, and *infidelity*, *it may be*, had not they been delivered by this happy providence; that pride will very ill become those who have been raised by charity; that *He* who had all things in his power, made choice of the cross; and though all nature was at his command, yet he was content with a very little, to teach us to be resigned in every condition of life; and lastly, that he who has more than he deserves (*and who can say he has not ?*) has no reason to complain, or think himself overlooked, if he has not the place he aims at.

Let us but guard against *this objection*, and it will not be in the power of *evil men*, or of *evil spirits*, to bring an accusation against you, as if you were not engaged in *well-doing*. And you have no reason to fear their malicious calumnies, nor be concerned, at the reproach which bad men would fling upon you, or upon the work you are engaged in.

They that speak against this work do, in effect, say, that to teach children the fear of God, and the knowledge of their duty, is to make them useless in their generation; that to teach them to be dutiful to their parents, will make them worse children; to be true and just in their dealings, will make them worse servants; to do their duty in that state of life which the providence of God shall assign them, will make them less useful to the world. In short; that religion is not consistent with the duties of a civil life; and that, provided the rich can but have the labour and bodies of the poor at their service, it is no matter what becomes of their souls. These are some of the wild reasonings, and consequences of the arguments, of *those* that are enemies to the charity schools. They are too absurd to be confuted seriously.

21

THOMAS SHERLOCK (1678–1761)

THOMAS SHERLOCK was ordained in 1701 and was appointed Master of the Temple three years later. His reputation as a preacher dated from this appointment. After being made Chaplain to Queen Anne in 1711, he was elected Master of St Catherine's Hall, Cambridge, in 1714. He then became Dean of Chichester (1715) and was heavily involved in the controversy, known as the 'Bangorian Controversy', aroused by the views of Benjamin Hoadly, Bishop of Bangor, on the nature of the visible Church. Sherlock himself became Bishop of Bangor in 1728 and was translated to Salisbury in 1734. Finally, he was appointed Bishop of London in 1748. Sherlock was ambitious and popular, industrious and efficient. Of his preaching it was said that he spoke 'with such strength and vehemence that he never failed to take possession of his whole audience and secure their attention'.

XXV

From a sermon entitled 'The Case of the Insolvent Debtors and the Charity due to them, considered', preached before the Lord Mayor at St Bride's London, 22 April 1728, on the text:

And his fellowservant fell down at his feet, and besought him, saying, Have patience with me, and I will pay thee all.
And he would not: but went and cast him into prison, till he should pay the debt. (*Matt. xviii, 29–30*).

A condemnation of the attitude of society towards the insolvent debtor.

There are many ways which men practise in oppressing the poor, which might properly fall under this consideration; but I shall confine myself to that single instance, to which the text relates, the hardheartedness and cruelty, which men use towards their poor insolvent debtors. And I the rather choose to speak to this case, because men are apt to imagine that conscience has nothing to do in it, and that they are secure from any guilt, so long as they follow in a legal manner the method prescribed by the law. Perhaps too, for a like reason, this iniquity has been less reproved, than it deserves, by the preacher; for fear he should be thought to condemn the law of his country.

I have no such fear; nor do I mean to condemn the law of my country, or to charge it with the cruelty of those who abuse it. If the law itself is severe, the more reason there is to be cautious in the use of it; but if men will turn the law, which was given them for the security of their property, into an instrument of oppression and revenge, the law is free, but they are guilty. And, without doubt, there have been many legal proceedings in courts of justice, which, when they come to be re-examined in a higher court, the judge and the jury shall be praised for executing the law faithfully, and yet the prosecutor condemned for violence and oppression . . .

When the debtor is chargeable with no fault, or fraud, but is disabled by mere poverty to satisfy his debts; to use the extremity of the law against such a man, is not only cruel and inhuman, but, as far as I can judge, contrary to the true meaning and design of the law itself. For the law which gives power over the body of the debtor, is not a criminal law, ordained for the punishment of offenders; but is a law made to secure men in their properties, and to guard them against the arts and contrivances of such as would injure them in their just demands. To use the law, therefore, where it cannot possibly have any effect towards securing your property, but can serve only to harass and torment a poor unfortunate man, is perverting the law, and making it subservient to purposes very different from those, for the sake of which it was ordained. The law does not entrust private men with the execution, or relaxation of its penalties for crimes and offences; but in the present case, every man may imprison, or release from prison his debtor as he pleases; a plain evidence that this law was meant as a defence of private rights, and not as a punishment for criminals.

Is it then a general rule, that the law can never with good conscience be executed against insolvent debtors; there may possibly, be exceptions, and more than I can foresee; but I think they must all be attended with this circumstance, that there be a prospect of recovering the debt, though the debtor himself be insolvent. It may so happen, that he who has nothing of his own, may have wealthy friends and relations; and though friends are not often willing, for the sake of justice, to pay the debts of a relation, yet, for the honour of the family, or out of personal regard to the relation, they will pay the money as the price of his redemption from a gaol. Many cases may be imagined where a rich relation ought in reason to pay the debt, rather than the poor creditor to lose it. In such cases, there may be a reason to justify or excuse the proceeding.

Some think that no severity is too great to be used towards such as have spent their estates riotously to the injury of their creditors. And indeed little is to be said in behalf of such persons. Yet still it is worth considering, whether you would choose to be judge and executioner in your own cause. And if the case be really so desperate, that you can aim at nothing by the execution of the law, but the punishment of the man who has wronged you; I am sure it is the safer way to leave the punishment to him, who has said, *Vengeance is mine, and I will repay.*

But the case which I have principally in view stands clear of these exceptions. The unfortunate persons, with whom the gaols are crowded, are, for the most part, such as have neither money nor friends to assist them; such as have fallen into poverty by misfortunes, by a decay in their business, or perhaps by the largeness of a family, which their utmost diligence could not support. Were they at liberty, they might probably be of use to themselves, and their poor families, and also to their creditors, by following their honest callings and employments. But now their strength consumes in vain, they starve in prison, and their children out of it, or are thrown upon the parish for a miserable maintenance; and no benefit or advantage accrues, or can prossibly accrue to the person who confines them.

Men are often urged to deal thus severely with others, by the grief and anguish which attend the disappointment they meet with in their just expectation; and being themselves sufferers, they think no treatment too bad for those to whom they impute their own distress. But could men consider calmly how much misery they bring into the world, and how many must partake in the sad effects of their resentment, I am persuaded that humanity and compassion, virtues to which this country never was a stranger, would in great measure prevent this evil.

When the father of a poor family, who have nothing to depend on for their subsistence but his labour and industry, is torn from them, what can the poor widow and orphans do? For a widow *she is*, and orphans *they are*, to all the intents and purposes of sorrow and affliction. It is well if they take no worse employment than begging; oftentimes they are tempted to pilfer or steal, or to prostrate themselves for bread; and happy is it for them, if they meet with no worse fortune, than to fall into your hands to be corrected and reformed.

In the meantime the wretched father sees himself undone, and his family dispersed and ruined. His spirits sink under sorrow, and despair eats out his strength and life; that should you in time relent and release him, it is ten to one but the relief comes too late. He is no longer the same man; before his imprisonment he was active and strong, and had spirit to go through his labour; he is broken in mind and body, and not able to improve to any advantage that liberty, which at last you are willing to allow him.

22

JOHN WESLEY (1703–91)

JOHN WESLEY was born at Epworth Rectory, Lincolnshire, and was founder of what came to be called the Methodist Movement. Wesley himself, who was ordained in 1725, remained a priest of the Church of England until his death. He was elected Fellow of Lincoln College, Oxford, in 1726, and gathered round him a group of earnest, devout and scholarly men who became known as 'Methodists'. In 1735 he and his brother, Charles, visited Georgia under the auspices of the Society for the Propagation of the Gospel. After his return in 1737 he had a vivid experience of conversion and the rest of his life was spent in evangelistic work. As most of the churches were closed to him, Wesley preached in the open air, travelling the whole of the country for this purpose, averaging 8,000 miles a year. He had a great capacity for leadership and organization and was recognized as an outstanding preacher. In politics he was a Tory and his concern for religious enthusiasm outweighed any concern over social inequality.

XXXVI

From a sermon preached before the Society for the Reformation of Manners on 30 January 1763 at the Chapel in West Street, Seven Dials, London, on the text: 'Who will stand up for me against the evildoers? or who will stand up for me against the workers of iniquity?' *(Ps. xciv, 16). A description of the establishment, aims and achievements of a Society founded to prevent the profanation of the Lord's day.*

A few persons in London, towards the close of the last century, united together, and, after a while were termed, *The Society for Reformation of Manners;* and incredible good was done by them for near forty years. But then, most of the original members being gone to their reward, those who succeeded them grew faint in their mind, and departed from the work: so that a few years ago the Society ceased; nor did any of the kind remain in the kingdom.

It is a Society of the same nature which has been lately formed. I purpose to show, first, the nature of their design, and the steps they have hitherto taken: secondly, the excellency of it; with the various objections which have been raised against it: thirdly, what manner of men they ought to be who engage in such a design: and, fourthly, with what spirit, and in what manner, they should proceed in the prosecution of it. I shall conclude with an application both to them, and to all that fear God.

I am, first, to show the nature of their design, and the steps they have hitherto taken.

It was on a Lord's day, in August 1757, that, in a small company who were met for prayer and religious conversation, mention was made of the gross and open profanation of that sacred day, by persons buying and selling, keeping open shop, tippling in ale-houses, and standing or sitting in the streets, roads, or fields, vending their wares as on common days; especially in Moorfields, which was then full of them every Sunday, from one end to the other. It was considered, what method could be taken to redress these grievances; and it was agreed, that six of them should, in the morning, wait upon Sir John Fielding* for instruction. They did so: he approved of the design, and directed them how to carry it into execution.

They first delivered petitions to the Right Honourable the Lord Mayor, and the Court of Aldermen; to the Justices sitting at Hick's Hall, and those in Westminster; and they received from all these honourable benches much encouragement to proceed.

It was next judged proper to signify their design to many persons of eminent rank, and to the body of the clergy, as well as the ministers of other denominations, belonging to the several churches and meetings in and about the cities of London and Westminster; and they had the satisfaction to meet with a hearty consent and universal approbation from them.

They then printed and dispersed, at their own expense, several thousand books of instruction to constables and other parish

---

* Sir John Fielding was a magistrate, blind from birth, who was much concerned to reduce the amount of vice and lawlessness in the country.

officers, explaining and enforcing their several duties: and to prevent, as far as possible, the necessity of proceeding to an actual
execution of the laws, they likewise printed and dispersed, in all
parts of the town, dissuasives from Sabbath-breaking, extracts
from Acts of Parliament against it, and notices to the offenders.

The way being paved by these precautions, it was in the beginning of the year 1758, that, after notices delivered again and again,
which were as often set at nought, actual informations were made
to the magistrates against persons profaning the Lord's day. By
this means they first cleared the streets and fields of those notorious offenders who, without any regard either to God or the King,
were selling their wares from morning to night. They proceeded
to a more difficult attempt, the preventing tippling on the Lord's
day, spending the time in alehouses, which ought to be spent in
the more immediate worship of God. Herein they were exposed to
abundance of reproach, to insult and abuse of every kind; having
not only the tipplers, and those who entertained them, the alehouse keepers, to contend with, but rich and honourable men,
partly the landlords of those alehouse keepers, partly those who
furnished them with drink, and, in general, all who gained by their
sins. Some of these were not only men of substance, but men of
authority; nay, in more instances than one, they were the very
persons before whom the delinquents were brought. And the
treatment they gave those who laid the informations naturally
encouraged 'the beasts of the people' to follow their example,
and to use them as fellows not fit to live upon the earth. Hence they
made no scruple, not only to treat them with the basest language,
not only to throw at them mud or stones, or whatever came to
hand, but many times to beat them without mercy, and to drag
them over the stones or through the kennels. And that they did not
murder them, was not for want of will; but the bridle was in their
teeth.

Having, therefore, received help from God, they went on to
restrain bakers likewise, from spending so great a part of the Lord's
day in exercising the works of their calling. But many of these were
more noble than the victuallers. They were so far from resenting
this, or looking upon it as an affront, that several, who had been
hurried down the stream of custom to act contrary to their own

conscience, sincerely thanked them for their labour, and acknowledged it as a real kindness.

In clearing the streets, fields, and alehouses of Sabbath-breakers, they fell upon another sort of offenders, as mischievous to society as any; namely, gamesters of various kinds. Some of these were of the lowest and vilest class, commonly called 'gamblers'; who make a trade of seizing on young and inexperienced men, and tricking them out of all their money; and after they have beggared them, they frequently teach them the same mystery of iniquity. Several nests of these they have rooted out, and constrained not a few of them honestly to earn their bread by the sweat of their brow, and the labour of their hands . . .

Increasing in number and strength, they extended their views, and began, not only to repress profane swearing, but to remove out of our streets another public nuisance, and scandal of the Christian name – common prostitutes. Many of these were stopped in their mid career of audacious wickedness. And, in order to go to the root of the disease, many of the houses that entertained them have been detected, prosecuted according to law, and totally suppressed. And some of the poor desolate women themselves, though fallen to

> The lowest line of human infamy,

have acknowledged the gracious providence of God, and broke off their sins by lasting repentance. Several of these have been placed out, and several received into the Magdalen Hospital.

If a little digression may be allowed, who can sufficiently admire the wisdom of Divine Providence, in the disposal of the times and seasons so as to suit one occurrence to another? For instance: just at a time when many of these poor creatures, being stopped in the course of sin, found a desire of leading a better life, as it were in answer to that sad question, 'But if I quit the way I now am in, what can I do to live? For I am not mistress of any trade; and I have no friends that will receive me': – I say, just at this time, God has prepared the Magdalen Hospital.* Here those who have no trade, nor any friends to receive them, are received with all tenderness; yea, they may live, and that with comfort, being provided with all things that are needful 'for life and godliness'.

* Founded 1758.

But to return. The number of persons brought to justice, from August 1757, to August 1762, is . . .   9,596

From thence to the present time:

For unlawful gaming, and profane swearing	40
For Sabbath-breaking	400
Lewd women, and keepers of ill houses	550
For offering to sale obscene prints	2

In all 10,588

In the admission of members into the Society, no regard is had to any particular sect or party. Whoever is found, upon inquiry, to be a good man, is readily admitted. And none who has selfish or pecuniary views will long continue therein; not only because he can gain nothing thereby, but because he would quickly be a loser, inasmuch as he must commence subscriber as soon as he is a member. Indeed, the vulgar cry is, 'These are all Whitefieldites.'* But it is a great mistake. About twenty of the constantly subscribing members are all that are in connexion with Mr Whitefield; about fifty are in connexion with Mr Wesley; about twenty, who are of the established Church, have no connexion with either; and about seventy are Dissenters; who make, in all, an hundred and sixty. There are, indeed, many more who assist in the work by occasional subscriptions.

These are the steps which have been hitherto taken in prosecution of this design. I am, in the second place, to show the excellence thereof, notwithstanding the objections which have been raised against it. Now, this may appear from several considerations. And, first, from hence – that the making an open stand against all the ungodliness and unrighteousness which overspread our land as a flood, is one of the noblest ways of confessing Christ in the face of his enemies. It is giving glory to God, and showing mankind that, even in these dregs of time,

> There are who faith prefer,
> Though few, and piety to God.

And what more excellent than to render to God the honour due unto his name ? to declare, by a stronger proof than words, even

* The followers of George Whitefield, Methodist evangelist, with whom at one time Wesley worked.

by suffering, and running all hazards, 'Verily there is a reward for the righteous; doubtless there is a God that judgeth the earth?'

How excellent is the design to prevent, in any degree, the dishonour done to his glorious name, the contempt which is poured on his authority, and the scandal brought upon our holy religion by the gross, flagrant wickedness of those who are still called by the name of Christ! to stem, in any degree, the torrent of vice, to repress the floods of ungodliness, to remove, in any measure, those occasions of blaspheming the worthy name whereby we are called, is one of the noblest designs that can possibly enter into the heart of man to conceive.

And as this design thus evidently tends to bring 'glory to God in the highest', so it no less manifestly conduces to the establishing 'peace upon earth'. For as all sin directly tends both to destroy our peace with God, by setting him at open defiance, to banish peace from our own breasts, and to set every man's sword against his neighbour; so whatever prevents or removes sin does, in the same degree, promote peace, – both peace in our own soul, peace with God, and peace with one another. Such are the genuine fruits of this design, even in the present world. But why should we confine our views to the narrow bounds of time and space? Rather pass over these into eternity. And what fruit of it shall we find here? Let the Apostle speak: 'Brethren, if one of you do err from the truth, and one convert him,' not to this or that opinion, but to God; 'let him know that he which converteth the sinner from the error of his way, shall save a soul from death, and hide a multitude of sins.' (James v. 19, 20) ...

But it is objected, 'However excellent a design this is, it does not concern *you*. For are there not persons to whom the repressing these offences, and punishing the offenders, properly belong? Are there not constables, and other parish officers, who are bound by oath to this very thing?' There are. Constables and church-wardens, in particular, are engaged by solemn oaths to give due information against profaners of the Lord's day and all other scandalous sinners. But if they leave it undone – if, notwithstanding their oaths, they trouble not themselves about the matter, it concerns all that fear God, that love mankind, and that wish well to their King and country, to pursue this design with the very same vigour as if there were no officers existing; it being just the same thing, if they are of no use, as if they had no being.

'But this is only a pretence: their real design is to get money by giving informations.' So it has frequently and roundly been affirmed; but without the least shadow of truth. The contrary may be proved by a thousand instances: no member of the Society takes any part of the money which is by the law allotted to the informer. They never did from the beginning; nor does any of them ever receive anything to suppress or withdraw their information. This is another mistake, if not wilful slander, for which there is not the least foundation.

'But the design is impracticable. Vice is risen to such a head, that it is impossible to suppress it; especially by such means. For what can a handful of poor people do, in opposition to all the world?' 'With men this is impossible, but not with God.' And they trust not in themselves, but him. Be then the patrons of vice ever so strong, to him they are no more than grasshoppers. And all means are alike to him: it is the same thing with God 'to deliver by many or by few'. The small number, therefore, of those who are on the Lord's side, is nothing; neither the great number of those that are against him. Still he doeth whatever pleaseth him; and 'there is no counsel nor strength against the Lord'.

XXXVII

From a sermon entitled 'The Use of Money' (no place or date) on the text: 'And I say unto you, make to yourselves friends of the mammon of unrighteousness; that, when ye fail, they may receive you into everlasting habitations' (*Luke xvi, 9*). *Provided he does not sin himself or cause hurt to his neighbour, it is right for a man to gain all he can. There are references to commercial practices, to drunkenness and luxury, and to the medical profession.*

It is of the highest concern, that all who fear God know how to employ this valuable talent;* that they be instructed how it may answer these glorious ends, and in the highest degree. And, perhaps, all the instructions which are necessary for this may be reduced to three plain rules, by the exact observance whereof

* i.e. money.

we may approve ourselves faithful stewards of 'the mammon of unrighteousness'.

The first of these is, (he that heareth, let him understand!) 'Gain all you can.' Here we may speak like the children of the world: we meet them on their own ground. And it is our bounden duty to do this: we ought to gain all we can can, without buying gold too dear, without paying more for it than it is worth. But this it is certain we ought not to do; we ought not to gain money at the expense of life, nor (which is in effect the same thing) at the expense of our health. Therefore, no gain whatsoever should induce us to enter into, or to continue in, any employ, which is of such a kind, or is attended with so hard or so long labour, as to impair our constitution. Neither should we begin or continue in any business which necessarily deprives us of proper seasons for food and sleep, in such a proportion as our nature requires. Indeed, there is a great difference here. Some employments are absolutely and totally unhealthy; as those which imply the dealing much with arsenic, or other equally hurtful minerals, or the breathing an air tainted with streams of melting lead, which must at length destroy the firmest constitution. Others may not be absolutely unhealthy, but only to persons of a weak constitution. Such are those which require many hours to be spent in writing; especially if a person write sitting, and lean upon his stomach, or remain long in an uneasy posture. But whatever it is which reason or experience shows to be destructive of health or strength, that we may not submit to; seeing 'the life is more' valuable 'than meat, and the body than raiment': and, if we are already engaged in such an employ, we should exchange it, as soon as possible, for some which, if it lessen our gain, will, however, not lessen our health.

We are, secondly, to gain all we can without hurting our mind, any more than our body. For neither may we hurt this: we must preserve, at all events, the spirit of an healthful mind. Therefore, we may not engage or continue in any sinful trade; any that is contrary to the law of God, or of our country. Such are all that necessarily imply our robbing or defrauding the King of his lawful customs. For it is, at least, as sinful to defraud the King of his right, as to rob our fellow-subjects: and the King has full as much right to his customs as we have to our houses and apparel. Other businesses there are which, however innocent in themselves, cannot be followed with innocence now; at least not in England; such, for instance as will not afford a competent maintenance without cheating or lying, or conformity to some custom which is not consistent with a good conscience: these, likewise, are sacredly to be avoided, whatever gain they may be attended with provided we follow the custom of the trade; for, to gain money, we must not lose our souls. There are yet others which many pursue with perfect innocence, without hurting either their body or mind; and yet, perhaps, you cannot: either they may entangle you in that company which would destroy your soul; and by repeated experiment it may appear that you cannot separate the one from the other; or there may be an idiosyncrasy – a peculiarity in your constitution of soul (as there is in the bodily constitution of many), by reason whereof that employment is deadly to you, which another may safely follow. So I am convinced, from many experiments, I could not study, to any degree of perfection, either mathematics, arithmetic, or algebra, without being a Deist, if not an Atheist: and yet others may study them all their lives without sustaining any inconvenience. None, therefore, can here determine for another; but every man must judge for himself, and abstain from whatever he in particular finds to be hurtful to his soul.

We are, thirdly, to gain all we can, without hurting our neighbour. But this we may not, cannot do, if we love our neighbour as ourselves. We cannot, if we love everyone as ourselves, hurt anyone *in his substance*. We cannot devour the increase of his lands, and perhaps the lands and houses themselves, by gaming, by overgrown bills (whether on account of physic, or law, or anything else) or by requiring or taking such interest as even the laws of our country forbid. Hereby all pawnbroking is excluded: seeing, whatever good we might do thereby, all unprejudiced men see with grief to be abundantly over-balanced by the evil. And if it were otherwise, yet we are not allowed to 'do evil that good may come'. We cannot, consistent with brotherly love, sell our goods below the market-price; we cannot study to ruin our neighbour's trade, in order to advance our own; much less can we entice away, or receive, any of his servants or workmen whom he has need of. None can gain by swallowing up his neighbour's substance, without gaining the damnation of hell!

Neither may we gain by hurting our neighbour *in his body*. Therefore we may not sell anything which tends to impair health. Such is, eminently, all that liquid fire, commonly called drams, or spirituous liquors. It is true, these may have a place in medicine; they may be of use in some bodily disorders; although there would rarely be occasion for them, were it not for the unskilfulness of the practitioner. Therefore, such as prepare and sell them only for this end may keep their conscience clear. But who are they? Who prepare them only for this end? Do you know ten such distillers in England? Then excuse these. But all who sell them in the common way, to any that will buy, are poisoners general. They murder His Majesty's subjects by wholesale, neither does their eye pity or spare. They drive them to hell, like sheep. And what is their gain? Is it not the blood of these men? Who then would envy their large estates and sumptuous palaces? A curse is in the midst of them: the curse of God cleaves to the stones, the timber, the furniture of them! The curse of God is in their gardens, their walks, their groves; a fire that burns to the nethermost hell! Blood, blood is there: the foundation, the floor, the walls, the roof, are stained with blood! And canst thou hope, O thou man of blood, though thou art 'clothed in scarlet and fine linen, and farest sumptuously every day'; canst thou hope to deliver down thy *fields of blood* to the third generation? Not so; for there is a God in heaven: therefore, thy name shall soon be rooted out. Like as those whom thou hast destroyed, body and soul, 'thy memorial shall perish with thee!'

And are not they partakers of the same guilt, though in a lower degree, whether surgeons, apothecaries, or physicians, who play with the lives or health of men, to enlarge their own gain? who purposely lengthen the pain or disease, which they are able to remove speedily? who protract the cure of their patient's body, in order to plunder his substance? Can any man be clear before God who does not shorten every disorder 'as much as he can', and remove all sickness and pain 'as soon as he can'? He cannot: for nothing can be more clear, than that he doest not 'love his neighbour as himself'; than that he does not 'do unto others, as he would they should do unto himself'.

This is dear-bought pain. And so is whatever is procured by hurting our neighbour *in his soul*; by ministering, suppose, either directly or indirectly, to his unchastity or intemperance; which certainly none can do, who has any fear of God, or any real desire of pleasing him. It nearly concerns all those to consider this, who have anything to do with taverns, victualling-houses, opera-houses, play-houses, or any other places of public, fashionable diversion. If these profit the souls of men, you are clear; your employment is good, and your gain innocent; but if they are either sinful in themselves, or natural inlets to sin of various kinds, then, it is to be feared, you have a sad account to make. O beware, lest God say in that day, 'These have perished in their iniquity, but their blood do I require at thy hands!'

These cautions and restrictions being observed, it is the bounden duty of all who are engaged in worldly business to observe that first and great rule of Christian wisdom, with respect to money. 'Gain all you can.' Gain all you can by honest industry. Use all possible diligence in your calling. Lose no time. If you understand yourself, and your relation to God and man, you know you have none to spare. If you understand your particular calling, as you ought, you will have no time that hangs upon your hands. Every business will afford some employment sufficient for every day and every hour. That wherein you are placed, if you follow it in earnest, will leave you no leisure for silly, unprofitable diversions. You have always something better to do, something that will profit you, more or less. And 'whatsoever thy hand findeth to do, do it with thy might.' Do it as soon as possible: no delay! No putting off from day to day, or from hour to hour! Never leave anything till tomorrow, which you can do today. And do it as well as possible. Do not sleep or yawn over it: put your whole strength to the work. Spare no pains. Let nothing be done by halves, or in a slight and careless manner. Let nothing in your business be left undone, if it can be done by labour or patience.

Gain all you can, by commonsense, by using in your business all the understanding which God has given you. It is amazing to observe how few do this; how men run on in the same dull track with their forefathers. But whatever they do who know not God, this is no rule for you. It is a shame for a Christian not to improve upon *them* in whatever he takes in hand. You should be continually learning, from the experience of others, or from your own experience, reading, and reflection, to do everything you have to do better today than you did yesterday. And see that you practise whatever you learn, that you may make the best of all that is in your hands.

Having gained all you can, by honest wisdom, and unwearied diligence, the second rule of Christian prudence is, 'Save all you can'. Do not throw the precious talent into the sea: leave that folly to heathen philosophers. Do not throw it away in idle expenses, which is just the same as throwing it into the sea. Expend no part of it merely to gratify the desire of the flesh, the desire of the eye, or the pride of life.

Do not waste any part of so precious a talent, merely in gratifying the desires of the flesh; in procuring the pleasures of sense, of whatever kind; particularly, in enlarging the pleasure of tasting. I do not mean, avoid gluttony and drunkenness only: an honest heathen would condemn these. But there is a regular, reputable kind of sensuality, an elegant epicurism, which does not immediately disorder the stomach, nor (sensibly at least) impair the understanding; and yet (to mention no other effects of it now) it cannot be maintained without considerable expense. Cut off all this expense! Despise delicacy and variety, and be content with what plain nature requires.

Do not waste any part of so precious a talent, merely in gratifying the desire of the eye, by superfluous or expensive apparel, or by needless ornaments. Waste no part of it in curiously adorning your houses; in superfluous or expensive furniture; in costly pictures, painting, gilding, books; in elegant rather than useful gardens. Let your neighbours, who know nothing better, do this: 'let the dead bury their dead'. But 'what is that to thee?' says our Lord: 'follow thou me'. Are you willing? Then you are able so to do!

Lay out nothing to gratify the pride of life, to gain the admiration or praise of men. This motive of expense is frequently interwoven with one or both of the former. Men are expensive on diet, or apparel, or furniture, not barely to please their appetite, or to gratify their eye, or their imagination, but their vanity too. 'So long as thou doest well unto thyself, men will speak good of thee.' So long as thou art 'clothed in purple and fine linen, and farest sumptuously every day', no doubt many will applaud thy elegance of taste, thy generosity, and hospitality. But do not buy their applause so dear. Rather be content with the honour that cometh from God.

Who would expend anything in gratifying these desires, if he considered, that to gratify them is to increase them? Nothing can be more certain than this: daily experience shows, the more they are indulged, they increase the more. Whenever, therefore, you expend anything to please your taste or other senses, you pay so much for sensuality. When you lay out money to please your eye, you give so much for an increase of curiosity – for a stronger attachment to these pleasures which perish in the using. While you are purchasing anything which men use to applaud, you are purchasing more vanity. Had you not then enough of vanity, sensuality, curiosity, before? Was there need of any addition? And would you pay for it too? What manner of wisdom is this? Would not the literally throwing your money into the sea be a less mischievous folly?

And why should you throw away money upon your children, any more than upon yourself, in delicate food, in gay or costly apparel, in superfluities of any kind? Why should you purchase for them more pride or lust, more vanity, or foolish and hurtful desires? They do not want any more; they have enough already; nature has made ample provision for them: why should you be at farther expense to increase their temptations and snares, and to pierce them through with more sorrows?

Do not leave it to them to throw away. If you have good reason to believe they would waste what is now in your possession, in gratifying, and thereby increasing, the desire of the flesh, the desire of the eye, or the pride of life; at the peril of theirs and your own soul, do not set these traps in their way. Do not offer your sons or your daughters unto Belial, any more than unto Moloch. Have pity upon them, and remove out of their way what you may easily foresee would increase their sins, and consequently plunge them deeper into everlasting perdition! How amazing then is the infatuation of those parents who think they can never leave their children enough! What! cannot you leave them enough of arrows, firebrands, and death? not enough of foolish and hurtful desires? not enough of pride, lust, ambition, vanity? not enough of everlasting burnings? Poor wretch! thou fearest where no fear is.

23

SAMUEL HORSLEY (1733–1806)

SAMUEL HORSLEY was born in London and, after his ordination, he became Rector of Newington Butts in Surrey in 1759. His interest in astronomy and geometry led him to be elected a Fellow to the Royal Society and its Secretary from 1773 to 1784. After being Archdeacon of St Albans for seven years, he was consecrated Bishop of St David's in 1778. In 1793 he was translated to the See of Rochester, which he held with the Deanery of Westminster, and from there he went to the Bishopric of St Asaph. He was an energetic bishop, somewhat dictatorial in his manner, generous and of considerable academic ability.

XXXVIII

From a sermon preached on the Anniversary of the Institution of the Magdalen Hospital* on 22 April 1795, on the text: 'Every man that hath this hope in him purifieth himself, even as he is pure' (*1 John iii, 3*). *A condemnation of the usual attitude of society towards 'the fallen woman'.*

This principle appears indeed to have been well understood and very generally adopted in the policy of all civilized nations; in which the preservation of female chastity, in all ages and in all parts of the world, hath been an object of prime concern. Of various means that have been used for its security, none seem so well calculated to attain the end, nor have any other proved so generally successful, as the practice which hath long prevailed in this and other European countries, of releasing our women from the restraints imposed upon them by the jealousy of Eastern manners; but under this indispensable condition, that the female,

* 'The Magdalen Hospital for the Reception of Penitent Prostitutes', founded 1758.

in whatever rank, who once abuses her liberty to bring a stain upon her character, shall from that moment be consigned to indelible disgrace, and expelled for the whole remainder of her life from the society of the virtuous of her own sex. But yet, as imperfection attends on all things human, this practice, however generally conducive to its end, hath its inconveniences, I might say its mischiefs.

It is one great defect, that by the consent of the world (for the thing stands upon no other ground), the whole infamy is made to light upon one party only in the crime of two; and the man, who for the most part is the author, not the mere accomplice of the woman's guilt, and for that reason is the greater delinquent, is left unpunished and uncensured. This mode of partial punishment affords not to the weaker sex the protection which in justice and sound policy is their due against the arts of the seducer. The Jewish law set an example of a better policy and more equal justice, when, in the case of adultery, it condemned both parties to an equal punishment; which indeed was nothing less than death.

A worse evil, a mischief, attending the severity, the salutary severity upon the whole, of our dealing with the lapsed female, is this – that it proves an obstacle almost insurmountable to her return into the paths of virtue and sobriety, from which she hath once deviated. The first thing that happens, upon the detection of her shame, is that she is abandoned by her friends, in resentment of the disgrace she hath brought upon her family; she is driven from the shelter of her father's house; she finds no refuge in the arms of her seducer – his sated passion loathes the charms he hath enjoyed; she gains admittance at no hospitable door; she is cast a wanderer upon the streets, without money, without a lodging, without food. In this forlorn and hopeless situation, suicide or prostitution is the alternative to which she is reduced. Thus, the very possibility of repentance is almost cut off; unless it be such repentance as may be exercised by the terrified sinner in her last agonies, perishing in the open streets, under the merciless pelting of the elements, of cold and hunger, and a broken heart. And yet the youth, the inexperience, the gentle manners, once, of many of these miserable victims of man's seduction, plead hard for mercy, if mercy might be consistent with the safety of the treasure we so sternly guard. We have high authority to say, that these fallen women are not, of all sinners, the most incapable of penitence – not the most unlikely to be touched with a sense of their guilt – not the most insusceptible of religious improvement; they are not of all sinners, the most without hope, if timely opportunity of repentance were afforded them: sinners such as these, upon John the Baptist's first preaching, found their way into the Kingdom of Heaven before the Pharisees, with all their outward show of sanctity and self-denial.

This declaration of our Lord justifies the views of this charitable institution, which provides a retreat for these wretched outcasts of society – not for those only who by a single fault, seldom without its extenuations, have forfeited the protection of their nearest friends; but even for those, generally the most unpitied, but not always the most undeserving of pity among the daughters of Eve, whom desperation, the effect of their first false step, hath driven to the lowest walks of vulgar prostitution. In the retirement of this peaceful mansion – withdrawn from the temptations of the world – concealed from the eye of public scorn – protected from the insulting tongue of obloquy – provided with the necessaries of life, though denied its luxuries – furnished with religious instruction, and with employment suited to their several abilities – they have leisure to reflect on their past follies; they are rescued from despair, that worst enemy of the sinner's soul; they are placed in a situation to recover their lost habits of virtuous industry – the softness of their native manners, and to make their peace with their offended God.

The best commendation of this charity is the success with which its endeavours, by God's blessing, have been crowned. Of three thousand women admitted since the first institution, two thirds, upon a probable computation formed upon the average of four years, have been saved from the gulf in which they had well nigh sunk, restored to the esteem of their friends, to the respect of the world, to the comforts of the present life, and raised from the death of sin unto the life of righteousness and the hope of a glorious immortality.

Happier far their lot than that of their base seducers! who, not checked, like these, in their career of guilty pleasure by any frowns or censures of the world, 'have rejoiced themselves in their youth' without restraint – 'have walked', without fear and without thought, 'in the ways of their heart, and in the sight of their eyes' – and at last perhaps solace the wretched decrepitude of a vicious old age with a proud recollection of the triumphs of their early manhood over unsuspecting woman's frailty; nor have once paused to recollect, that 'God for these things will bring them into judgement'. But with him is laid up the cause of ruined innocence: he hath said, and he will make it good, 'Vengeance is mine, and I will repay.'

XXXIX

From a sermon preached 'for the Deaf and Dumb Asylum'*, 1796, on the text: 'And they were beyond measure astonished, saying, He hath done all things well; he maketh both the deaf to hear, and the dumb to speak' *(Mark vii, 37). It commends the work of the Asylum in teaching the deaf and dumb to speak.*

It is now some years since a method has been found out, and practised with considerable success, of teaching persons deaf and dumb from the birth to speak: But it was not till the institution of this Asylum, in the year 1792, that the benefit of this discovery was extended in any degree to the poor; the great attention, skill, and trouble, requisite in the practice, putting the expense of cure far beyond the reach of the indigent, and even of persons of a middling condition. The Directors of this charity, who are likely, from their opportunities, to have accurate information upon the subject, apprehend that the number of persons in this lamentable state is much greater than might be imagined.

In this Asylum, as many as the funds of the charity can support, are taught, with the assistance of the two senses of the sight and the touch, to speak, read, write, and cast accounts. The deafness seems the unconquerable part of the malady; for none deaf and dumb from the birth have ever been brought to hear. But the calamity of the want of the sense of hearing is much alleviated –

---

* 'The Asylum for the Support and Encouragement of the Deaf and Dumb Children of the Poor', founded 1792.

comparatively speaking, it is removed, by giving the use of letters and of speech; by which they are admitted to the pleasure of social conversation, are made capable of receiving both amusement and instruction from books, are qualified to be useful both to themselves and the community, and, what is most of all, the treasures of that knowledge which maketh wise unto salvation are brought within their reach. The children admitted are kept under the tuition of the house five years, which is found to be the time requisite for their education. They are provided with lodging, board, and washing; and the only expense that falls upon the parent or the parish is in the article of clothing. The proficiency of those admitted at the first institution, in November 1792, exceeds the most sanguine expectations of their benefactors; and the progress of those who have been admitted at subsequent periods is in full proportion to the time. The number at present exceeds not twenty. There are at this time at least fifty candidates for admission; the far greater part of whom the slender finances of the society will not permit to be received.

I am persuaded that this simple statement of the object of the charity, the success with which the good providence of God has blessed its endeavours, within the narrow sphere of its abilities, and the deficient state of its funds, is all that is necessary or even proper for me to say to excite you to a liberal contribution for the support of this excellent institution, and the furtherance and extension of its views. You profess yourselves the disciples of that Master who during his abode on earth in the form of a servant went about doing good – who did good in that particular species of distress in which this charity attempts to do it, – and who, seated now at the right hand of God, sends down his blessing upon those who follow his steps, and accepts the good that is done to the least of those whom he calls his brethren as done unto himself.

24

THOMAS WHITAKER (1759–1821)

THOMAS WHITAKER was ordained in 1785, but remained without pastoral charge until 1797, when he was licensed to the Perpetual Curacy of Holme, Lancashire. He became Vicar of Whalley, Lancs., in 1809 and Vicar of Blackburn in 1818.

XL

From a 'Sermon Preached at the Consecration of the Chapel of Salesbury, in Lancs.', 8 September 1807, on the text: 'For he loveth our nation and hath built us a synagogue' (Luke vii, 5). One of the first clerical criticisms of the evil effects of the industrial revolution on the vast populations in the manufacturing towns.

In our situation, care and foresight, and an intimate acquaintance on the part of Government with local circumstances, are to supply the absence of that singular distribution which the Almighty measured out with his own immediate hand to the chosen people.

Among these local circumstances, one of the most important, and surely no little solecism in political economy, is a well-known fact, that one of the most populous districts in the kingdom is surrounded by the most extensive deserts.

The difficulty of providing for a population so disproportionate, not only to the produce of the neighbourhood in which it is collected, but even of the kingdom at large, under any sudden cessation of employment, or any extraordinary failure in the annual produce of the earth, cannot but fill every reflecting mind with the most serious apprehensions. Shut out as we are from the granaries of Europe, and debarred as the rest of Europe is likely to be from our manufactures, an island never free from the risk of famine with half the number of its present inhabitants, may, before the close of one unproductive year, present its governors with the alternative of working a miracle to provide bread, or of encountering the despair of a famished people.

This, however, is but a partial view of the subject: the following considerations are intended to show more generally, that in the manufacturing districts we have already overstepped the point within which population contributes to happiness; and that the primaeval blessing, 'be fruitful, and multiply, and replenish the earth', has its limits far within the physical possibilities of habitation and subsistence.

We have lived to prove that mankind may know too much for their own good. In the ruder ages of society men suffer from the want of arts and of the instruments of life: in times of vicious refinement, like the present, they are undone by the multiplication and abuse of them. The most improved state of the arts has a direct tendency to the increase of moral depravity. On the other hand, the happiest era of commerce in this country was an era of very inferior attainments in knowledge; for mediocrity in skill begat mediocrity in risks, in losses, in expectations, and, what is no trivial advantage to society, in gains themselves. All these circumstances were favourable to the spirit of that religion, which forbids ambition, anxiety, and excessive exertion for the attainment of any earthly object, warning us 'to let our moderation be known unto all men, for the Lord is at hand'.

Such was the calm unenterprising state of commerce, when a single discovery in mechanics, seized and applied with all the eagerness of discerning avarice, produced an immediate revolution in manners, the effects of which, though very conspicuous in every rank within their circuit, I shall principally consider as they affect the poor . . .

I contend . . . that under the mask of blessings, commercial habits have brought along with them a train of curses, the most hideous that ever visited mankind.

Of these the first in order, and perhaps in magnitude, is, that beside an abundant provision for the necessaries of life, every man, and almost every child, has a weekly superfluity of time and money at his own disposal.

The old state of things, which maintained as nearly as possible a weekly balance between the wants and earnings of a family, was entirely on the side of morals and religion. A situation in which a man must labour every day in the week excepting one for his daily bread, is one in which he will probably neither be too proud nor too careless to pray for it – sensible of his dependence, he will wait upon Providence by faith, and eat his meat with thankfulness.

But with superfluities, men in this condition are never to be trusted: they will not accumulate; and as their amusements either are sensual, or worse, the application of their superfluities must be pernicious.

The next effect produced by the new order of things has been to 'undomesticate' the people.

Until of late, children worked under the roof and eye of their parents: their application to the arts of trade was never exclusive; the daughters were frequently called off to little domestic offices, and the sons to the periodical operations of husbandry. Thus both sexes were prepared for the situations which in more advanced life they were destined to fill, as fathers, mothers, or household servants. But the inordinate requirements of modern commerce absorb every hour, and every faculty of its votaries; precluding the acquirement of domestic knowledge, and that practical readiness in the application of it which never can be learned but in childhood; they superadd helplessness to extravagance, and take away the best preventative of profligacy abroad which is comfort at home. Add to all this that habits of cleanliness, a quality nearly allied both to health and virtue, are unlearned and lost for life in places where, by the sordid avarice of parents, children are made to pass, not through fire to Moloch, but through filth to Mammon. These observations apply with peculiar weight to the untaught and unhappy female:

> – Empty of all good wherein consists
> Women's domestic honour, and chief praise,

she enters upon the important duties of a wife, a mother, and the mistress of an household, without neatness, without economy, without principles, without ideas.

An inconvenience akin to the last is severely felt by persons of an higher rank. The time has been, when it was deemed a privilege for the children of the poor to be received into superior families, many of which were schools of order and decorum; but the obligation is now inverted; domestics, instead of being governed, are to be cajoled into obedience; the right of a master to control their morals is sometimes expressly disclaimed; they know without the information of a great moralist, 'not that he keeps them, but that they keep him'; and thus a species of slavery is created unknown to every writer on natural or civil law, – the slavery of masters to their servants.

But to return – among the poor, parental discipline was always lax – it is now reduced almost to nothing. The misfortune of having no hope or object suspended till the death of the father always produced, at the approach of manhood in that class of society, an estrangement between parents and children resembling the dissolution of the $\Sigma \tau o \rho \gamma \eta$* which takes place at the same period in brutes. But now the certainty of employment, together with the little skill or strength required to direct movements which are everything but spontaneous, has begotten a prodigy indeed in the history of our species, a race of independent infants. Nay, even before the period of emancipation from the little which remains of parental authority, the ties of domestic attachment are broken; home is no more regarded with the tender fondness of childhood; the father is no longer looked up to as the protector from every injury, and the friend of every hour; the native bashfulness of that charming age is lost; intrepidity of front, and hardness of temper, are early acquired by children from living in a perpetual crowd; a growing opinion of self-importance is fostered by the habit of acquiring for themselves; and all these seeds, sown in the rank soil of the human heart, mature by just degrees, from a wayward childhood and a licentious youth, to a manhood headstrong and ungovernable, disobedient to man, and rebellious to God.

There is a kind of degree of profligacy which tends to depopulate; bad as they are, this is not true of the manners which I have been describing; for, though the constant intermixture of the two sexes in manufactories has a very injurious effect upon the chastity of both, the certainty of a provision in that rank will always lead to early marriage; and as the habits of manufacturers, though they tend to debilitate the constitution, are not found on the whole to

* 'love', 'affection'

abridge the term of human life, in such circumstances, from three to four contemporary generations will generally be found in the same line, where of old there were commonly no more than two.

Another inconvenience arising from the present state of society amongst us, is, the mode in which this increasing population is collected or distributed.

In choosing the sites of ancient towns and villages our fore-fathers courted the natural advantage of earth and air, or in other words fertility and shelter; under the new system, the two more active elements of fire and water are the attractive objects. Now, as the latter are usually found in greatest abundance where the former are most ungenial, groups of population have started up as by magic in situations neither very easy of access, nor open to observation. A great capital is indeed the scene of great atrocities, but it is always accessible to a prompt and vigorous police; on the contrary, the wide-spread population of farming districts cannot be placed under the same quick and jealous superintendence; but neither does the simplicity of their manners require it – this distribution of the people unhappily unites the inconveniences of both; sufficiently collected to foster and to encourage offences, and at the same time too remote from the administration of justice for prevention or for quick detection.

These remarks have not been made from an idle expectation, that establishments so deep-rooted, so entwined with the very foundations of society, will by any exertion of authority be extirpated – they are now perhaps, like some other evils, become necessary to our existence as a nation. Neither am I so sanguine as to entertain an hope, that in the present temper of mankind any vigorous or decisive effort of legislation will be made to reform or control them: but what laws cannot effect, religion can; at all events it is the last resource, and the multiplying of Churches is the only legitimate method of propagating religion – 'He loveth our nation and hath built us a synagogue.'

The necessity of some great and general effort for that purpose, will be proved by the following statement:

The population of this hundred at the era of the Reformation did not exceed 10,000 souls; seven years ago it was returned at 82,000, beside some considerable omissions; and such has been the increase during the last short interval, that it may now fairly be computed at 100,000. At the first of these periods there were in the same district at least twenty-four places of Religious Worship: there are now no more than thirty; and, what renders the disproportion in some chapelries still more enormous, ten at least of these are adequate to the accommodation of the inhabitants at present. But, to keep pace with such an increase of numbers, to check the progress of separation, or to counteract the increase of immorality, what provision has been made by the foundation of chapels on the establishment ? *The Building in which we are now assembled.* Yet these are no trifling objects; for in the same period, and within the same limits, ten conventicles have been licensed; nor can it be denied that sufficient attention has been paid to appetites more importunate than *Hunger and Thirst after Righteousness*, by multiplying *Synagogues* of another species, which they who *build*, and they who consecrate, can scarcely be said to *love our nation*.

Now were all the places of established worship conveniently situated, as they once were, or their congregations equally distributed, it is obvious to everyone who knows anything of their structures that they are collectively incapable of containing one fourth part of their congregations. In some it would be impossible, by any power of compression, to enclose a tenth part of the inhabitants.

These facts are so unlike anything which is elsewhere taking place, excepting perhaps in a few great commercial towns, that it cannot but be of importance to hold up a distinct and vivid representation of them. And when we take into the account that the same general principles may be applied to a population of at least half a million in this county alone, and little less in one immediately adjoining, the subject cannot but arrest the attention of every political reasoner, and of every lover of his country.

The manners of a people occupied in husbandry and pasturage are naturally favourable to established Government; they never speculate, they never act in great masses, their bodies are robust, their minds inactive. These qualities ensure obedience in civil life. An armed peasantry will also transfer, without effort and without a murmur, the uninquisitive obedience which they have learned in the farm, to the discipline of the camp. On the contrary; sedentary mechanics, though singly feeble, are collectively bold and unmanageable; their nerves are weak, their apprehensions lively, much of their time is spent in disquisitions above their capacities, the crude and mischievous publications of the day are swallowed by them in a mass; and while the poison of politics heats the mind, the poison of distilleries inflames the blood. Communicated to great manufactories, political disgusts vibrate through the whole body like an electric shock, and every talking demagogue has a willing and attentive audience already assembled at his hand.

In that great ferment of fanaticism which overturned both the throne and the altar in the seventeenth century, where was the frenzy highest, and where were the successive armies of rebellion raised and recruited? In the *Manufacturing Districts*. And in a late dreadful ebullition of political madness*, where were the emissaries of sedition most successful, and where the tesserae† of insurrection received with greatest avidity? In the *Manufacturing Districts*. I do not mean to accuse the body of the people of any strong or general tendency of the same kind at present; but it is sufficient for my purpose to prove, that, in the situations which I have been describing, they are so combined, and composed of such materials, as to be ready to explode whenever a single spark shall happen to fall upon them.

The views of political reasoners are for the most part limited by the present life: the deficiency of their system is indeed to be deplored; but even on their own grounds, attention to the religious principles of a people so numerous and collected becomes a point of prudence and of duty. Religion is the most powerful instrument which the politician has to work with. The enemies of Government have always understood the importance even of the shadow; how melancholy to see its friends overlook the substance! For active and systematic efforts to propagate the Gospel *at home*, would do more towards securing a peaceable and obedient commonalty, than hosts of armed men, of volumes of penal statutes. Secure the conscience, and you secure the man; make the people good Christians, and you make them faithful and dutiful subjects of course.

* i.e. the French Revolution.   † 'watchword'

25

THOMAS ARNOLD (1795–1842)

THOMAS ARNOLD was born in the Isle of Wight and became a fine classical scholar and Fellow of Oriel College, Oxford. He was ordained in 1818 and ten years later was appointed Headmaster of Rugby, where he initiated reforms which were copied by many other public schools. His system placed great emphasis on a high sense of duty, public service and the importance of personal character, based on the foundation of sound religious training. In 1841 he became Regius Professor of Modern History of Oxford. Thomas Arnold believed in the essential unity of Church and State and considered that the National Church should embrace all the various dissenting groups, should be more democratic and should give the laity a greater part in its affairs. It existed 'for the putting down of moral evils', and 'for the moral improvement of mankind'. Arnold had a passionate concern to relieve the conditions of the poor and to rectify injustices, yet he saw the ordering of society as it was in his day as the only just and practical one. It was not that he wished to preserve the *status quo*, but that the only instrument of change could be 'the aristocracy'. He was a powerful preacher, impressing his hearers by his force of character.

XLI

From a sermon preached in January 1831 on the text: 'And God saw everything that he had made, and, behold, it was very good' *(Gen. i, 31). The effect of the increasing population should be to encourage emigration. Labour will always be man's lot; it is indeed his greatest good. Rich and poor must live in harmony.*

When men do labour upon the ground, and thus make the earth yield her increase; when riches are thus acquired, useful arts discovered, knowledge abundantly obtained; when the condition of mankind, speaking now of their wordly welfare, is greatly improved, and each generation, availing itself of the experience and discoveries of its fathers, continues to advance beyond those which went before it; when all this happens, still God has provided that men shall not be able to free themselves from the necessity of labour. He has so ordered the course of the world, that the numbers of mankind increase faster than the food which their labour, aided by their improving knowledge, can provide for them. And the very improvements of their knowledge help on this increase. Greater cleanliness and comfort, greater care, and greater skill in medicine, are the means of saving a vast number of lives, and of prolonging them to old age, which amongst savages are cut off by sickness, neglect, and misery. And, again, as laws and manners become better and milder, acts of violence are less common, and even wars are rendered far less bloody; insomuch that, whereas, in the old times, whole nations were sometimes cut off by the sword; it is remarkable that in our days, war has added to the numbers of a people in some cases, much more than it has taken away: and in no instance has it had any effect worth noticing, in hindering the natural growth of population.

Thus the sentence of God still finds a way to fulfil itself, out of the very midst of our prosperity. The numbers of a people continually multiplying call continually for fresh exertions of labour and knowledge to provide for them; and thus all the sources of wealth which a country possesses are, one after another, found out and called into action. But when this has been done, and the numbers still go on increasing – and especially when any particular causes have made them increase even faster than is natural – then the land is not able to bear them, and God calls upon them by the voice of his providence, to go and bestow their labour upon other lands, that so the whole earth may be, in process of time, replenished and subdued. And because this labour is generally more unwelcome than any other – for men naturally love the land in which they were born and bred, and would not willingly go and live far away from it – therefore God calls us to it by the sharpest spur of necessity; men's condition in their own country being rendered so miserable by their increasing numbers, in spite of all their labour, that they have no choice left them, and are thus forced in a manner to execute God's purposes – which are, that man shall earn his bread by labour, and that not one part of the world only, but the whole face of the earth, shall be by this labour replenished and subdued.

I am sure that these are points most fit and most useful to be, at this moment, explained to the people of this country. Undoubtedly the present distress has been partly occasioned by other causes, which cannot with propriety be touched upon here. As it ill becomes this sacred place to deny or to disguise those political evils which have been brought on by the fault of man, so neither does it become it to dwell upon them: because our business here is not to think of men's dealings with us, but rather to consider our duties to them and to God – and God's dealings also with us. But, in the present case, we need not go to other causes. If one single word could remove all the political grievances that exist, the distress would, in a great measure, still remain the same, because it arises from the very order of God's providence, which has made the natural increase of a people's numbers become, after a certain time, a sure cause of suffering – that so men might be driven to foreign lands, and the whole earth might in time be inhabited and cultivated. Had it not been for this, the very land in which we now live might have been at this day a wilderness, and the human race might never have stirred beyond those countries in which the first patriarchs fixed their abode. But God wills that man's labour should never cease till the whole earth be filled; yet, while enforcing this by distress and suffering, he at the same time gives a blessing to it: for though distress may force a man to go to a distant country, yet he may go out in hope – his labour, when bestowed in God's appointed manner, will be sure of meeting with its return – and suffering is, in fact, only the needful spur to make an effort, unwelcome in itself, but which will surely lead to an improvement in his condition who makes it.

So, then, labour, which was one part of God's first sentence upon sin, will always be man's necessary portion; yet out of it, when rightly employed, he gains his greatest worldly good. And so death, which was the other part of the sentence, will always be our portion also; yet out of it, when rightly taken, we gain our greatest good of all: for, unless we put off this mortal frame, we cannot be clothed with immortality. Out of the earthly punishment comes our earthly good; out of the punishment which went beyond this earth comes our heavenly and everlasting good. But then the punishment must be rightly taken; that is, it is only a Christian death which has in it the seed of life eternal: otherwise, it is death, and death for ever. And now that evil in the world, and in ourselves, of which I spoke in the beginning of my sermon – that evil which makes God's works in their present state so unworthy of their original blessing – is an evil of two kinds, a natural evil, and a moral evil; or, in plainer words, distress and suffering in our outward condition, and the evil of wickedness and sin. I have said what I most fully believe – I will almost say what I know – to be the chief cause of the outward suffering: namely, that our numbers are so many, that, like the herdsmen of Abraham and Lot before they parted from one another, the land is not able to bear us, so that we cannot dwell together. And the remedy – I do not say the only one, but the chief one, and without which no other will be of any use – is even the same which has been practised from the earliest times for the furtherance of God's purposes; that they who are in distress in their own country should remove to plenty and to comfort in a new country. But for the other evil, that of sin and wickedness, which adds so greatly to our outward distress, neither may this be cured by any political improvements alone – and, unless it be cured, political improvements are, after all, of little value. If we had not a single grievance to complain of, do we think that all our temptations would be gone also; or, that if some were made less, others again would not rather become greater ? He must know very little of himself who does not know that his own heart, after all, is his worst enemy; that if all were peace and comfort without, he has still in his own evil nature, until it is changed by the Spirit of God, a worse root of bitterness within. But what says the last of God's prophets, when proclaiming the preparation for Christ's coming ? 'Remember ye the law of Moses my servant, with the statutes and judgements. Behold, I will send you Elijah the prophet, before the coming of the great and dreadful day of the Lord. And he shall turn the heart of the fathers to the children, and the heart of the children to their fathers; lest I come and smite the earth with a curse.' How every word of this is, indeed, a lesson to us now! To remember the eternal law – not that of forms and ceremonies, but that of the Spirit of holiness; the love of God, and of our neighbour, that he who, like Elijah, would do the work of a true reformer, should labour to turn the heart of the fathers to the children, and the heart of the children to the fathers – that is, should labour not only to keep alive the affections of domestic life, for that is not all that is intended, but to turn to one another the hearts of those who are as fathers and children in the state – of those who are in authority, and those subject to authority – of those who, from wealth, rank, knowledge, or character, are fitted to instruct, relieve, and improve, and those who, from poverty and ignorance, have great need that relief and instruction should be given them. Are the hearts of these two classes turned to one another at present? and if they are not ere long, is it not sure, to the extreme of certainty, that God will soon come and smite the earth with a curse – with that bitter curse which unkindly feelings, in their last excess, involve both in private life and in public? What is it, when they who should be fathers, show nothing of a father's care; when they who should be children, show nothing of childlike duty? God knows, and God be thanked for it, that there are many blessed exceptions – that in many cases the hearts of the rich and poor are knit to one another in Christian brotherhood. But I know, and you know also, that in too many cases it is far otherwise; that neglect and selfish carelessness on the one side, have led to suspicion and bitter hatred on the other; so that I have heard it said, that the rich and the poor are each other's natural enemies: and thus the poor look with suspicion even upon those who, in all sincerity, are trying to do them kindness, because they look upon them as belonging to the party of their enemies. This suspicion is shocking indeed, and most unjust; but it is not by showing disgust or anger that we can remove it.

Brethren, the truth ought to be spoken at this crisis without any scruple or reserve; only, let it not be thought that while speaking, in this matter especially, of the faults of others, the Christian minister does not feel how much he himself is included in the same reproach. We have been, and are now, far too neglectful of the poor and ignorant; we measure their wants by far too low a standard; we are content with doing far too little for them: the vile person is sometimes called liberal, and the churl said to be bountiful, because we take to ourselves too much credit for trifling services, which cost us little or nothing of self-denial. In one word, we do not enough study to catch the full spirit of His example, who, though he was their Lord and Master, yet washed his own disciples' feet, that we also might learn to wash one another's feet. These are our faults – neglect and selfish carelessness: for of hard-heartedness, or wilful oppression, I verily believe that the instances are most rare. These are our faults: and would that every one of us, by private and public prayer, and with all watchfulness, would strive to gain the full spirit of charity, to do away with them. But the poor have their faults too; and, although *we* may not well reprove them, while we labour under our own, yet, in the sight of God, who will judge us all without respect of persons, they are faults to be repented of and amended. They have not the charity which thinketh no evil, for they suspect evil, sometimes, where nothing but kindness is intended; they encourage others to think meanly of them, when they are so careless of truth, so long as anything is to be gained by a lie; they are great respecters of persons, and show a very low sense of justice and goodness, when they excuse acts of dishonesty, or even of violence, so long as they are committed by the poor against the rich. If the poor wish to be respected, let them hate falsehood and dishonesty, by whomsoever committed, and for whatever object. But these things are not subjects on which we may reproach one another: rather, let us bear our own burdens, without looking to those of our neighbours, and each ask forgiveness of God for our sins, and grace heartily to repent of them. Doubtless the times are awful; and evil of every sort, outward and moral – distress of nations, tumults, war, and, in our own bosoms, unbelief and uncharitableness – are threatening our happiness, here and hereafter. What the result may be, as far as regards the nation, or this world's prosperity, is kept among the hidden things of God. But it is among the things revealed for our comfort, that no labour of faith and love is ever lost for him who works it; that he in whom the Christian trusts is able to save to the uttermost those who come to him; and that, amidst all tribulations, he who shall endure to the end, the same shall be saved.

XLII

From a Charity Sermon preached for the benefit of an unnamed school (no date or place) on the text: 'Woe unto you, lawyers! For ye have taken away the key of knowledge: ye entered not in yourselves, and them that were entering in ye hindered' *(Luke xi, 52). The importance of educating the poor.*

He must indeed be blind, who does not see that society is endangered actually by the ignorance of the poor, and by their feeling of the suffering and degradation of their present condition. And what is far more to the purpose is, that this danger is now, in a considerable degree, our own fault; and a fault which will become daily more and more blamable, in proportion as we persist in it in spite of warning. No doubt, the increased knowledge and comforts of slaves will put an end to slavery; because slavery is an abuse and an injustice, which exists only through the weakness and degradation of those who suffer from it. And if the increased knowledge and improved feelings of the poor could put an end to poverty, as indeed they would greatly lessen it, and still more would temper its worst bitterness, who would not bless God, if he might be even one of the humblest instruments of so great a good! But to fear that the poor would destroy all distinctions of property, in the same manner as slaves would free themselves from slavery, is to put property and slavery on the same footing; to confound a good with an evil; a right with a wrong; a system, whose destruction would of necessity make the well-being of mankind impossible, with one whose destruction would highly promote it; it is, in short, to confound a thing which no good man will attack, with one which no good man will defend. And experience abundantly shows that property and slavery do rest upon a wholly different foundation; for history furnishes no instance, even amidst the wildest revolutions, of an attack on property, as such. I mean, that no scheme has ever been attempted for taking away the property of the rich, merely because they had too much, and giving it to the poor, merely because they had too little. There have not been wanting, indeed, at different times, a few individuals, half-desperate in wickedness, and half-crazed in folly, who have tried to propose such a thing; but the common sense of mankind, poor as well as rich, has instantly put down the notion, with mingled disgust at its injustice, and ridicule of its childish folly. Nor is it possible that it should ever find favour, unless through what might fitly be called the continued crime of society; I mean, from our allowing the poor to go on in such a state of ignorance and misery, that the folly of the plan would not be seen by them: and the inevitable wretchedness that it would occasion, as well as its extreme wickedness, would be a matter of indifference to men who had ceased to regard either God or man, from a conviction that their actual misery could not possibly be changed for the worse.

And now, to bring all this into a form more directly practical – if I am asked, what should any individual do upon this view of our social condition, or what good can he derive from considering it; it is not difficult, I think, to find an answer. First of all, with regard to the institution with which we are now more immediately concerned, and others of a similar kind; he who is deeply convinced that what is most wanted in our relations with the poor is not charity, in our common sense of the word, but charity in St Paul's sense of it – not beneficence and almsgiving, but brotherly kindness and sympathy – he will not only be more anxious to support them to the utmost by his subscriptions, and by his personal attention, but he will do this in a humbler and simpler spirit; that is, he will think that he is doing no great thing after all, but a very common and obvious duty, which he dares not to leave undone. Further, he will be relieved from a feeling which, I believe, has chilled the zeal of many in supporting schools for the poor, and has perplexed and pained the minds of more. The feeling which I speak of, is this: misled by the common language and accustomed to form a very low estimate of the intellectual wants of the poor, many persons confound reading and writing with education: they consider themselves as having been engaged in educating the poor; and then, when they see that their labours have produced little fruit, they are half bewildered when they hear it said that this is a plain proof that to educate the poor can do no good. Alas! in that sense of the word which could alone justify our expecting so much from it, I know of no provision hitherto made in England for the education of the poor, nor, perhaps, is it possible that any can be made. I never knew any poor man who could properly be said to be educated; except, in some rare instances, where men, breaking through all difficulties, have, by their own power of mind and indefatigable industry, succeeded in educating themselves. If we call our own children educated at the age when we commonly send them to school for the first time – if their education is completed at eight or nine years old – then may we call those educated who have been taught to read and write at our parish schools. But if reading and writing are not education, but the mere preparatory steps to it, then to talk of the education of the poor, is to talk of a thing which does not exist; and to expect an important moral and religious improvement from the machinery now in operation, is to look for a full crop of corn after sowing a single handful of seed. Even that handful may produce something; and they who have compared the results of our present schools with the means employed in them, and with the unfavourable circumstances of other kinds which counteract their influence, will be gratified much rather than disappointed – will rather thank God that the good effected has been so much, than wonder that, with such inadequate means, it is not more. All that has been done hitherto, then, should encourage, much more than discourage us; but he who has a high sense of what education really is, and how grievously the poor stand in need of it, will feel, that if the mere first steps to it have been found useful, the reality itself, which it is his bounden duty to try to introduce – the further it is carried, which to the utmost practicable extent it should be – may well be looked to as a source of still greater blessings.

26

SYDNEY SMITH (1771–1845)

SYDNEY SMITH was born in Essex and was ordained in 1794. He was one of the founders of the highly successful *Edinburgh Review* in 1802. He later settled in London where he was Preacher at the Foundling Hospital. Smith was a staunch Whig and was admitted to Holland House, the social centre of the Whig Party. He was renowned for his wit and for his social accomplishments. In 1813 he was forced to reside in his country parish at Foston, Yorkshire, where he cheerfully settled down to country life. In 1828 he was given a Prebend in Bristol Cathedral; in 1829 he was appointed to the benefice of Combe-Florey in Somerset, and finally, in 1831, he became a Canon of St Paul's Cathedral. Smith was a moral reformer with a deep aversion to radicals. In parochial life he was a philanthropist, was understanding in his judgement of immorality and lawlessness, and was concerned to improve the conditions of the poor. Although he had strong religious convictions, his outlook was secular and he had a distaste for 'enthusiasm' and clericalism. His sermons were popular, fresh and sometimes racy.

XLIII

From a sermon 'On the Sin of Adultery', preached at Berkeley Chapel, 1809, on the text: 'Thou shalt not commit adultery' (*Exod. xx, 14*). *It condemns the 'double standard' adopted by society towards this sin – condemnation of the woman and condonation of the man.*

Who is there who has not beheld with the purest pleasure the spectacle of a well-ordered family, than which life has none more comely, more cheerful, more serene ? the provident activity of a father; a mother breathing peace, and gentleness, and goodness, over all; the youthful ardour of children, their pleasant ways, their graceful shame, and their fondness, the recompense of amiable patience; then, that wise regularity which a family exhibits, that conspiracy of views and interests, and the strength of that affection, which nature teaches, and man allows and applauds. When human beings are thus gathered together, every good man wishes to them happiness and peace: they affect our feelings, they satisfy our reason, they call down our blessings and our prayers! This, then, is the pure and the holy scene upon which the adulterer breathes his polluted breath! – this is the freshness which he withers; this the fragrance which he taints: these are the children of Christ, among whom he carries anguish, and remorse, and everlasting shame! He enters into this house, as the serpent entered into God's garden, to tempt and to destroy, to banish the man and the woman from the Eden in which they dwell, and to fix a mark upon their race! The time also shall come, when God shall say to him, as he said to the serpent, 'Because thou hast done this, cursed art thou above all creatures, and beyond every beast of the field.' Look truly and plainly to what this crime is. A fellow-creature rendered unhappy for the rest of his existence, children banished from their home, a wretched woman consigned to perpetual degradation and shame. No year passes away that is not marked with some such ravages on human happiness; there is no cruelty and no crime which appeals so strongly to the heart, I will not say of every religious man only, but of every plain honest man, who conducts himself respectably in life, and draws the circle of justice round all he says, and all he does. It is monstrous that society, rigidly just to female vice, should have no indignation left for such deliberate villainy in men! that we should yield up our sense of right and wrong to the imposing plea of high birth and finished manners, and forgive a man for transgressing the plainest laws of God, because he falls in gracefully with all the rules and courtesies of social life. We may talk of recompense afforded by human laws, but what recompense can reach wounded affections? how can you break a man's heart, and repay him? or, count out in gold and silver the price of comfort and of peace? Give back that affection which these people swore to one another, before the altar of God; cause the man to look upon his betrothed wife as the comforter of his days; make him forget that he has been injured and disgraced; unload his heart, and light up in it, its ancient fondness:

then, when you have done this, go to the victim of your passion –
she will ask of you her feelings of innocence and security; she will
require at your hands her days of virtuous tranquillity, when she
knew no guilt; all the joys that she felt in the bosom of her family,
and the circle of her children; she will ask of you the love of her
husband, the support of her friends, and the respect of the world:
all these things this poor woman will require at your hands; and if
there be any good left in your heart, the generous and the noble
feelings of a man will rise up to judge you, and you will burn in the
hell of conscience. You forget that while this crime in you is called
bravery and spirit, while you are still suffered, by the laxity of
the world, to rear your head among honest men, that the partner of
your crime is for ever abandoned, for ever infamous, a penitent,
an outcast, and a wanderer; that no future regularity can restore
her to the world, or replace her in the rank of virtuous women. If
yours was the peril and yours the infamy, your vices would at least
be generous, though they could not be just; but no plea of honour,
of pity, or of religion, has power over the man whose heart is
hardened by constant pleasure; before which all sense of shame
and of restraint crumble into the dust. There are men mingling in
all large societies, who have, I believe, no other occupation on
earth but the gratification of their vices; who finding by plausible
manners an easy access to your family, will fill it with vice and
shame; will repay your unsuspecting benevolence, by ruining
your domestic happiness, and, in an instant, pull down that
temple of innocence and purity, which it has cost so many years to
build up.

To a tender-hearted man and a good Christian it is an ex-
quisitely painful sight to witness the wretched resources of a
woman, who pretends she can despise the world, and bear up
against the weight of public condemnation: she thinks she can
despise the world; alas! she knows not the strength of that world
she despises, nor the power of a whole community when they sit
in solemn judgement on the great duties of life. It is not by the
admiration of dissolute men that she can soothe her wounded feelings, and become respectable to herself: amid all her melancholy
affectation of gaiety there is a misgiving of heart, there is
something which whispers to this unhappy woman that she is

mistaken; that the world are right; that crime is not to be hid by levity, and by assurance; that the pride of her days and the peace of her soul are gone for ever and ever.

I have lived to see many things, which at the outset of life I could scarcely have believed to be possible, but I never yet saw a woman who could bear up under infamy and disgrace: they can suffer grief, and never utter a complaint; they can descend from wealth to poverty, and smile at the change; they can meet death on great occasions, as death ought to be met – but they cannot bear shame, and they cannot bear the consciousness of guilt: they are not fitted for it, they were never intended to endure it – we all see that the canker is there – the freshness and the fragrance are gone for ever, and the rest of life is passed in the silent agony of a broken heart, or in a precipitate career of vice and passion.

The business of the world devolves upon men: they are compelled to act, and they may forget the judgements of the world upon particular parts of their conduct; but women have no great and absorbing occupations to turn their minds from the contemplation of their own unhappiness. A guilty woman, secluded from the ordinary circle of frivolous amusement, has one picture constantly before her eyes – the picture of her own folly, her own ruin, and her own guilt: in the front of the picture solitude and contempt, in the distant scene God and eternity. Ambition does not take her away from herself; she cannot engage in the pursuit of wealth; day and night the same spectre rises up to say, 'Folly – ruin – wretchedness! It is all gone; all happiness is gone out of life; for you, there is no peace but in the silence of the grave.'

Another difference between the two sexes in the power of supporting disgrace is this: a man who does wrong may still (however unjustly) uphold himself by the splendour and importance of his talents and attainments; he may be necessary to mankind as a leader in peace or war; he may be a great discoverer; he may be endowed with the most beautiful powers of invention and composition; but women, restrained to the narrow circle of domestic life, must be innocent, or they will be nothing. If they cannot offer to mankind the spectacle of purity and righteousness, they have nothing else to offer which is great and estimable. We expect to find all things according to the genius and purpose of their nature.

If a flower be not fragrant, we cast it away; there must be a playful light in the diamond, and there must be concord in musical sounds. So, in a woman must there ever dwell the dignity and elevation of virtue. We expect to find her in the path of God, we turn with disgust from the foul passions which are engendered in the strife of the world; and we turn to women for the best spectacle this world can afford of purity, innocence, and peace. The only way to be happy is to follow common rules, and to do our duty to God and man: the wages of sin are always inadequate, but still it enhances wretchedness to be wretched for nothing; to see that we have lost the feelings of virtue, without reaping the rewards of wickedness. Look at the life of an adulteress. Is she commonly repaid by the gratitude of that person for whom she has sacrificed everything in this world and in the world to come ? It is from her very betrayer that she is, generally speaking, the most sure of meeting with contempt and disdain: he looked for a transient regard, and he has met with a permanent burden: the object of his crime is the sign of his disgrace and his misfortune: mutual reproach and aversion commonly terminate the wretched history of adulterous intercourse. When God is given up, all is given up; when the plain way is once deserted, life is sickly delusion and heart-rending grief.

Then let such a woman bring before her eyes the contempt and disdain which she meets with from her very children: for her crimes, they feel themselves covered with unjust and unmerited shame. Their first sensation, as they begin to mingle in the world, is a sensation of shame and anguish that they should owe their existence to such a mother: they enter into life marked, shamed, and degraded. The adulteress will find no shelter among her children, though she slept not that they might sleep; though their infant hands and eyes were never lifted up to her in vain; though she loved them with all her heart, and all her strength, and all her soul. A woman may perhaps bear the scorn of those who are her aliens in blood, but when our sons and our daughters – our strength, our comfort, and our hopes – when those whom we have watched and nourished rise up in judgement against us, life must become intolerable; and dreadful as is the thought of eternity, we shall pray to the God of mercy that we may go down quickly to the grave. 'Such lot,' says Solomon, 'shall the woman have who forsakes the guide of her youth, and forgets the covenant of her God; for her house inclines to death, and her paths to the grave. But a virtuous woman is far above rubies; strength and honour are her clothing, and she shall rejoice in the time to come. She openeth her mouth with wisdom, and in her tongue is the law of kindness. Her children rise up and call her blessed; her husband also he praiseth her. Favour is deceitful, and comeliness is vain, but a woman that feareth the Lord, she shall be praised.'

There is something extremely revolting in the meanness of this sin; in the duplicity, fraud, and evasion with which it is almost always accompanied. The adulterer sits at your table, and shares your feast, and calls himself your friend. He accepts your confidence, smiles on your children, and is alive to your interests. He is safe, because his ingratitude is too great for suspicion. The heart of man is naturally slow to believe in such complicated guilt; and this very confidence, which ought to preserve him from guilt, only screens him from detection. The life of an adulterer is falsehood after falsehood; a long system of hypocrisy; a calm tenour of ingratitude; a settled alienation from Christ; a deliberate sacrifice of good feelings, manly virtues, and religious duties. It is a life as pitiful as it is wicked; as unworthy of an elevated gentleman as it is of a good Christian; because, while it destroys great interests, and mars great affections, it is full of despicable fraud and intolerable meanness.

I have not long to express my sentiments in this place; it will be a satisfaction to me hereafter to remember that I have borne my share of testimony against that, which exposes the lives of women to indescribable wretchedness; which disturbs the order of life, and violates the clearest precepts of the Gospel.

XLIV

From a sermon on behalf of the Society for the Promotion of Prison Discipline* (no place or date, but probably about 1850) on the text:

For he hath looked down from the height of his sanctuary; from heaven did the Lord behold the earth;

* 'The Society for the Diffusion of Knowledge upon the Punishment of Death, and the Improvement of Prison Discipline', founded 1808.

To hear the groaning of the prisoners; to loose those that are appointed to death (*Ps. cii, 19–20*).

A description and criticism of prison conditions and proposals to alleviate them.

A question has been raised by some humane men, whether or not it is lawful to take away life as a punishment for crime. The argument has been carried on with great force and great ingenuity: the humane reasoner almost wishes that the objection to capital punishments could be made good, and that reason and reflection could be led to disapprove a practice at which every feeling of humanity trembles; but whatever be the difference of opinion among thoughtful men upon this important topic, there is one observation in which all men have agreed and *must* agree, and that is, that you yourself must not have taught the man you put to death the very crime for which he dies; that the executioner ought not to be the master; that the pupil ought not to be the victim; that the corruption worthy of death should not have been instilled by him in whose hands the instrument of death is placed. If there be cruelty upon earth – this it is! If there is a mockery of justice – that is it! What has been the state of our prisons before the late exertions of this valuable society, and what blood-guiltiness laid upon us? A young man led out to execution in the flower of his youth, and sent before his God and his Redeemer, with all the solemn and appalling forms of justice! – But what cruelty, you will ask, is there in all this? Was he not fairly tried? Yes. Was he not fairly heard? Certainly he was. Is there any doubt of his having committed the offence? None! But where did he learn to commit the offence? what blackened his soul? where did he acquire that portion of hell which drove him to murder and to rob? You found him when a boy in the commission of some trifling offence, and you placed him in prison, among grown-up thieves and murderers; and no one came to see the poor wretch; and no one warned him. Howard* was gone – and that blessed woman† who visits dungeons had not begun her labours of the Gospel; and day after day the poor youth was encouraged to

* John Howard (*c.* 1724–90), prison reformer.
† Elizabeth Fry (1780–1845), Quaker prison reformer.

murder and to steal – and the law smote him – and his soul is in the
torments of hell! This is the foundation of our Society! upon this
plea we ask for your association and your assistance, that we may
prevent crime, may prevent prisons from becoming the school of
crime; that we may classify, assort, and separate in prisons; that
we may avoid that awful responsibility and un-Christian feeling,
that the victim of the law has become a victim of the law through
our negligence, callousness, and coldness of heart; that we have
grudged the expense of preparing proper receptacles; that we have
grudged the time for inspection, and parental care; that the only
activity and alacrity we have shown is in the infliction of those
condign punishments which are never just but when everything
has been done to render them infrequent and improbable.

The next great object we have had in view, after classification, is
employment of convicted prisoners; employment so managed and
arranged, that without cruelty or oppression it may make a prison
a place of punishment, and a terror to the evil doer. Nor is
education of the young overlooked, so far as is compatible with the
wholesome severity of regular labour. Our object is not to turn
prisons into workshops where the ingenuity of the mechanic may
be promoted and rewarded; nor to let the idea go abroad among
the poor, that our prisons are schools, where their children may
obtain a better education from their crimes than they can do beyond the walls of prisons by their virtue. We wish so to manage
occupation, that it shall convey in some degree the feeling of
punishment; that it may be remembered with aversion, and
avoided with care. We wish so to manage the education of prisons,
that every interval of discipline should be used in giving life to the
dead hearts of criminals; in teaching cruel men not to destroy
human life; in unfolding to the ignorant, who never heard instruction, all that our blessed Saviour had unfolded to us, in the
good and holy work of redeeming. It is an awful and beautiful
sight to see instruction going on in gaols. Some hear it with sullen
indifference; but the thought of God sometimes strikes into the
heart of a poor wretch, like a vein of silver in a rock: hope animates
him; for a moment he is the sinner that repenteth! and if that
moment could be fixed, he might be led on to eternal life.

When the Society for Prison Discipline are anxious for education in gaols, remember of what ingredients gaols, and, above all, gaols in this metropolis, are composed; not of persons habituated to instruction; not of those who have been taught by their clergy, or learnt in established schools a lesson they have forgotten and neglected, but of persons turned out by their own parents from their earliest childhood into the streets to steal! who have never entered a church, who have never heard a pastor, who have never heard God's law mentioned but when it was broken, nor God's name invoked but when it was blasphemed. May not a man say when he is hurried on to execution, 'If I had ever heard this when I was young, if I had been only even tried with instruction, if any human being had noticed me, if a prayer book had been put into my hand, if any human being better, happier, and wiser than me, had cast upon me a look of compassion, or a word of counsel, I might have lived on the common life of man, and died the death of the just!'

I cannot take upon myself to say that all these improvements in prisons are wholly owing to this Society, but I am sure they are improvements for which this Society has always contended very zealously, and very ably; I am sure many of them have taken place partially since the institution of this Society, that the attention of Englishmen is now very strongly turned to these objects, and turned to them, I very firmly believe, in a great measure, from what the members of this Society have written and done.

The quantity of abuse which creeps into every human institution is quite incredible; but to those whose attention happens to be forcibly called to those particular points, the future historian will paint the reign that is past* (and deservedly paint it) as an age of civilization and refinement; and yet nearly eighteen years of that reign had elapsed when Howard gave the following account of English prisons, as he found them in the year 1777, in the general circuit which he made:

Many [he says] who go in in health, are in a few months changed to emaciated dejected objects; some are seen pining under diseases, expiring on the floors in loathsome cells of pestilential fevers. The prisoners have neither tools nor materials of any kind, but spend their

* The reign of George III.

time in sloth and profaneness. I have often weighed the daily prison allowance of food, and found it to be only from seven to eight ounces. Many prisoners are half starved: such of them as at their commitment were in health come out almost famished, and for weeks incapable of labour. In many gaols there is no allowance of straw: some lie upon rags, others upon the bare floor – debtors and felons, men and women, young and old – the felon and the misdemeanant – are all confined together. From my own observations [he says] made in 1773, 74, 75, I am fully convinced that many more prisoners were destroyed by the gaol fever than were put to death by all the public executions in the kingdom.'*

How many rich and how many good men were there at that period who sat down utterly ignorant of these matters, and said that all was well, and who would have dismissed as troublesome and exaggerated such an account as I have given you, and which we now *know* to have been an accurate statement of the truth. We must not flatter ourselves that everything in gaols is even now arranged as it ought to be; that there are not many things to amend and improve; that we are not called upon, as good men and Christians, to follow the great man who has preceded us, and by calm reflection and careful observation, and gentle degrees, to perfect this great engine of civil polity. Take, for instance, one great feature of Christian charity, and Samaritan compassion, produced in the last year by the recommendation and eloquent appeals of this Society. A human being whose term of imprisonment had expired, or who perhaps after long imprisonment had been acquitted, was discharged from prison, many days' journey from his home, without a morsel of bread, or any lawful means of acquiring any; so that the poor wretch, with all his new repentance and his weak faith, and rising hope in Christ, has been driven to some fresh act of villainy for his support; and after one taste of the fresh air, and one look at the sun, and one happy gaze at the cheerful bustle of life, has come back to his sadness and chains, and sees another year of life given up to the long sorrows of the prison. In the meantime his family and children, who have numbered the days, are waiting for him, and are beat down once more to the earth by the rude storms of life! There are many here present who

* *State of the Prisons in England and Wales, with Preliminary Observations and an Account of some Foreign Prisons*, 1777.

will say, they did not know these things, and that they never heard of them! But how are they to be heard of and known, if you will not do as we do, and descend to scenes of misery like this, and make yourselves familiar with them? I ask your contributions this day for the relief of ten thousand miseries which live and grow in prisons as their native soil; but I ask more! I ask you to join us – to be a member of the Society for the Promotion of Prison Discipline – to lend us your name, your authority, your time, your understanding, in a cause which wants and deserves them all! And I say to all my brethren, if you are wise, go into prisons sometimes, visit dungeons, come near to the captive! Do it for your soul's sake: it will put you in mind of the sin and wretchedness of life! It will teach you why the ministers of the Gospel so often call upon your charity! You will see then that the lower order of human beings want all the care, all the precepts, and all the inspection you can bestow upon them! I strongly counsel every pious Christian, every good man who wishes to perfect his soul, to seek diligently for the occasional sight of wretchedness in hospitals and prisons, and places of sorrow! It teaches you more than the writer, and more than the preacher, can teach you! It carries you forward to think of death, and of the grave; it makes you ask yourself why you were born, and for what purposes you live: it shames you out of a frivolous life of pleasure; it opens the new pleasure of compassion, and makes you resolve to live for the salvation of the wicked, and the comfort of the unhappy! You mistake if you suppose all these occupations are mere trouble and vexation. Is it nothing to establish order where everything was confusion? Is it no pleasure to see occupation substituted for idleness, reasonable piety instead of shocking profanation? health instead of disease, justice in lieu of cruelty and oppression? If there is a person upon earth whose feelings are to be envied, it is he who has found a prison a den of thieves; and turned it into a house of prayer.

27

FREDERICK ROBERTSON (1816–53)

FREDERICK ROBERTSON was born in London and hoped to
enter the army. Under pressure, however, he abandoned this
intention and was ordained in 1840. In 1847 he was appointed
Minister of Trinity Chapel, Brighton, where his influence as a
preacher extended far and wide. He preached extemporaneously
from notes, his sermons being intensely scriptural and displaying
his great gift of analysing motive and character. He had a powerful
influence with the working classes and gained their full confidence. In his sermons he had much to say about the social duties
of the rich and strongly condemned the social injustices of his
day. He died at the early age of thirty-seven.

XLV

*From a sermon entitled 'Judgement respecting Inheritance', preached
22 June 1851, on the text:*

And one of the company said unto him, Master, speak to my
brother, that he divide the inheritance with me.

And he said unto him, Man, who made me a judge or a divider over
you?

And he said unto them, Take heed, and beware of covetousness: for
a man's life consisteth not in the abundance of the things which he
possesseth (*Luke xii, 13–15*).

It deals with the relationship between the social classes.

The great problem which lies before Europe for solution is, or will
be this: whether the present possessors of the soil have an exclusive right to do what they will with their own, or whether a
larger claim may be put in by the workman for a share in the
profits? Whether Capital has hitherto given to Labour its just
part, or not? Labour is at present making an appeal, like that of

this petitioner, to the Church, to the Bible, to God. 'Master, speak unto my brother, that he divide the inheritance with me.'

Now in the *mere* setting of that question to rest, Christianity is not interested. That landlords should become more liberal, and employers more merciful: that tenants should be more honourable, and workmen more unselfish; that would be indeed a glorious thing – a triumph of Christ's cause; and any arrangement of the inheritance *thence* resulting would be a real coming of the Kingdom of God. But whether the soil of the country and its capital shall remain the property of the rich, or become more available for the poor – the rich and the poor remaining as selfish as before – whether the selfish rich shall be able to keep, or the selfish poor to take, is a matter, religiously speaking, of profound indifference. Which of the brothers shall have the inheritance, the monopolist or the covetous ? Either – neither – who cares ? Fifty years hence what will it matter ? But a hundred thousand years hence it *will* matter whether they settled the question by mutual generosity and forbearance.

I remark a third thing. Jesus refused to be the friend of one, because he was the friend of both. He never was the champion of a class, because he was the champion of humanity.

We may take for granted that the petitioner was an injured man – one at all events who thought himself injured: and Christ had often taught the spirit which would have made his brother right him: but he refused to take his part against his brother, just because he *was* his brother, Christ's servant, and one of God's family, as well as he.

And this was his spirit always. The Pharisees thought to commit him to a side when they asked whether it was lawful to give tribute to Caesar or not. But he would take no side as the Christ: neither the part of the government against the tax-payers; nor the part of the tax-payers against the government.

Now it is a common thing to hear of the rights of man; a glorious and a true saying: but, as commonly used, the expression only means the rights of a section or class of men. And it is very worthy of remark, that in these social quarrels both sides appeal to Christ and to the Bible as the champions of their rights, precisely in the same way in which this man appealed to him. One class appeal to the Bible, as if it were the great arbiter which decrees that the poor shall be humble and the subject submissive: and the other class appeal to the same Book triumphantly, as if it were exclusively on their side, its peculiar blessedness consisting in this, that it commands the rich to divide the inheritance, and the ruler to impose nothing that is unjust.

In either of these cases Christianity is degraded, and the Bible misused. They are not, as they have been made, O shame! for centuries, the servile defenders of rank and wealth, nor are they the pliant advocates of discontent and rebellion.

The Bible takes neither the part of the poor against the rich exclusively, nor that of the rich against the poor: and this because it proclaims a real, deep, true, and not a revolutionary brotherhood.

The brotherhood of which we hear so much is often only a one-sided brotherhood. It demands that the rich shall treat the poor as brothers. It has a right to do so. It is a brave and a just demand: but it forgets that the obligation is mutual; that in spite of his many faults, the rich man is the poor man's brother, and that the poor man is bound to recognize him and feel for him as a brother.

It requires that every candid allowance shall be made for the vices of the poorer classes, in virtue of the circumstances which, so to speak, seem to make such vices inevitable: for their harlotry, their drunkenness, their uncleanness, their insubordination. Let it enforce that demand: it may and must do it in the name of Christ. He was mercifully and mournfully gentle to those who through terrible temptation and social injustice had sunk; and sunk into misery at least as much as into sin. But, then, let it not be forgotten that some sympathy must be also due on the same score of circumstances to the rich man. Wealth has its temptations: so has power. The vices of the rich are his forgetfulness of responsibility, his indolence, his extravagance, his ignorance of wretchedness. These must be looked upon, not certainly with weak excuses, but with a brother's eye by the poor man, if he will assert a brotherhood. It is not just to attribute all to circumstances in the one case, and nothing in the other. It is not brotherhood to say that the labourer does wrong because he is tempted; and the man of wealth because he is intrinsically bad ...

Covetousness: the covetousness of all. Of the oppressed as well as of the oppressor; for the cry 'Divide' has its root in covetousness just as truly as 'I will not'. There are no innocent classes: no devils who oppress, and angels who are oppressed. The guilt of a false social state must be equally divided.

We will consider somewhat more deeply this covetousness. In the original the word is a very expressive one. It means the desire of having more – not of having more because there is not enough; but simply a craving after more. More when a man has not enough. More when he has. More, more, ever more. Give. Give. Divide. Divide.

This craving is not universal. Individuals and whole nations are without it. There are some nations, the condition of whose further civilization is, that the desire of accumulation be increased. They are too indolent or too unambitious to be covetous. Energy is awakened when wants are immediate, pressing, present; but ceases with the gratification.

There are other nations in which the craving is excessive, even to disease. Pre-eminent among these is England. This desire of accumulation is the source of all our greatness and all our baseness. It is at once our glory and our shame. It is the cause of our commerce, of our navy, of our military triumphs, of our enormous wealth, and our marvellous inventions. And it is the cause of our factions and animosities, of our squalid pauperism, and the worse than heathen degradation of the masses of our population.

That which makes this the more marvellous is, that of all the nations on the earth, none are so incapable of enjoyment as we. God has not given to us that delicate development which he has given to other races. Our sense of harmony is dull and rare, our perception of beauty is not keen. An English holiday is rude and boisterous: if protracted, it ends in ennui and self-dissatisfaction. We cannot enjoy. Work, the law of human nature, is the very need of an English nature. That cold shade of Puritanism which passed over us, sullenly eclipsing all grace and enjoyment, was but the shadow of our own melancholy, unenjoying, national character.

And yet, we go on accumulating as if we could enjoy more by having more. To quit the class in which they are and rise into that above, is the yearly, daily, hourly effort of millions in this land. And this were well if this word 'above' implied a reality: if it meant higher intellectually, morally, or even physically. But the truth is, it is only higher fictitiously. The middle classes already have every real enjoyment which the wealthiest can have. The only thing they have not is the ostentation of the means of enjoyment. More would enable them to multiply equipages, houses, books. It could not enable them to enjoy them more.

Thus, then, we have reached the root of the matter. Our national craving is, in the proper meaning of the term, covetousness. Not the desire of enjoying more, but the desire of having more.

And if there be a country, a society, a people, to whom this warning is specially applicable, that country is England, that society our own, that people are we. 'Take heed and beware of covetousness.' . . .

God is on the side of the poor, and the persecuted, and the mourners – a light in darkness, and a life in death. But the poverty, and the persecution, and the darkness are the condition on which they feel God's presence. They must not expect to have the enjoyment of wealth and the spiritual blessings annexed to poverty at the same time. If you will be rich, you must be content to pay the price of falling into temptation, and a snare, and many foolish and hurtful lusts, which drown men in perdition; and if that price be too high to pay, then you must be content with the quiet valleys of existence, where alone it is well with us: kept out of the inheritance, but having instead God for your portion, your all-sufficient and everlasting portion. Peace, and quietness, and rest with Christ.

28

JOHN WHITTAKER (c. 1790–1854)

JOHN WHITTAKER was born in Manchester and in 1822 was appointed Vicar of Blackburn. During his incumbency the parish church of Blackburn was rebuilt and twelve new churches were erected. He was a man of considerable learning and was particularly interested in astronomy.

XLVI

In 1839 the Chartists displayed their strength by appearing in certain churches, having beforehand sent the incumbent a request that he should preach on a certain text. On 4 August John Whittaker was invited by the Chartists to preach on the following text:

Go to now, ye rich men, weep and howl for your miseries that shall come upon you.

Your riches are corrupted, and your garments are moth-eaten.

Your gold and silver is cankered; and the rust of them shall be a witness against you, and shall eat your flesh as it were fire. Ye have heaped treasure together for the last days.

Behold, the hire of the labourers who have reaped down your fields, which is of you kept back by fraud, crieth: and the cries of them which have reaped are entered into the ears of the Lord of sabaoth.

Ye have lived in pleasure on the earth, and been wanton; ye have nourished your hearts, as in a day of slaughter.

Ye have condemned and killed the just; and he doth not resist you.

Be patient therefore, brethren, unto the coming of the Lord. Behold, the husbandman waiteth for the precious fruit of the earth, and hath long patience for it, until he receive the early and latter rain.

Be ye also patient; stablish your hearts: for the coming of the Lord draweth nigh. Grudge not one against another, brethren, lest ye be condemned: behold, the judge standeth before the door.

Take, my brethren, the prophets, who have spoken in the name of the Lord, for an example of suffering affliction, and of patience.

Behold, we count them happy which endure. Ye have heard of the patience of Job, and have seen the end of the Lord; that the Lord is very pitiful, and of tender mercy.

But above all things, my brethren, swear not, neither by heaven, neither by the earth, neither by any other oath: but let your yea be yea; and your nay, nay; lest ye fall into condemnation.

Is any among you afflicted ? let him pray. Is any merry ? let him sing psalms.

Is any sick among you ? let him call for the elders of the church; and let them pray over him, anointing him with oil in the name of the Lord:

And the prayer of faith shall save the sick, and the Lord shall raise him up; and if he have committed sins, they shall be forgiven him.

Confess your faults one to another, and pray one for another, that ye may be healed. The effectual fervent prayer of a righteous man availeth much (*Jas. v, 1–16*).

The Chartists turned up in force to hear him, but he left them in no doubt that he believed their cause to be wrong and that to apply this text to the rich in England was the height of injustice.

In all forms of human society, in all ages of national progression, or retrogression, there will be *particular* cases of wickedness – of rich men who have acquired wealth by dishonest means, who have wantonly oppressed the poor, who have, when they could do it safely, murdered the innocent. But the Apostle has put it *generally*, not alluded to *one*, to *some*, or even to *numerous* cases. He was contemplating *general* national depravity of this description.

And looking upon his meaning in this light – I must say, and I do so with an honest conscience and upon full conviction, that it would be the height of injustice and the grossest falsehood, it would be an act of flagrant false witness against our brethren, to apply any such description, with the most distant pretence of generality, to any body of men, rich or high in station, in a really Christian country. Still more extravagantly false and unfounded would it be in our own land, which is governed by equal laws, where civil rights and public guarantees of liberty are secured too firmly to be shaken, except by those who enjoy their benefit. I will fearlessly ask anyone, whether a person could possibly obtain credence from even the most credulous person in the country, if he were to accuse an English judge of having perverted justice or given an unfair sentence from the tribunal in consequence of a bribe. It would be scouted as a monstrous lie from one end of England to the other. Again, find me a country in the whole habitable globe, where as in England, to say nothing of the legal and compulsory provision made for the poor, there are such numbers of public institutions and organized charities instituted in the true spirit of genuine Christian charity, for the relief of the distressed, the necessitous, the aged, the helpless. Look at the infirmaries, the alms-houses, the hospitals, the colleges, the schools, the innumerable communities and societies formed for such purposes of charity, and the incalculable wealth poured forth abundantly for their support. These – these, come from *our* rich men – men whom God has blessed with plenty, and who, from love to God, who has delivered them from sin and death by the blood of his dear Son, are prompt and ready to impart freely of that plenty to aid and succour their distressed brethren in the Lord . . .

In applying our subject to some practical benefit, I shall now address myself to those who have of their own accord invited me to preach from this portion of Holy Scripture. I see an unusually large congregation before me, and I rejoice at the sight. But I have more than once spoken to larger and more formidable bodies in this place, though never to a more motley one. And on the present occasion I feel it absolutely necessary to direct to you some words of distinct explanation before I commence this address. The body to whom I allude, and from whom this invitation came, is, I well know, a very small one – so small, that it cannot, either by its numbers, influence or respectability, account for the present concourse. I believe, and I have good reason for the opinion, that if all their comrades were assembled, they could not muster in this populous parish much more than one hundred persons. They have given publicity and notoriety to their purpose of occupying the parish church this morning, in expectation, and indeed certainty, that they would be accompanied by a mixed multitude of persons, who, without any affinity or connexion with themselves, would seem to swell their numbers. I see before me, further, a very *mixed* congregation. Many of you, my brethren, belong to other congregations, and have been led hither by curiosity; not a few with the obvious intention of setting an example of devout and decorous behaviour, and thus affording a moral protection to the church and her minister. I see many youths, some of whom I can recognize, and could not fail to know by their prayer books, who ought, with the Sunday schools to which they belong, to have been this morning at another of our churches. But, I repeat it, the party which has caused this un-usual assemblage is contemptibly small, and their leaders and instigators are no more than two or three dissolute persons, whose characters, I am informed, (for they are unknown to me) are pretty generally known and appreciated. I wish it therefore to be most distinctly understood that, whatever may drop from my lips apparently harsh or severe in the way of reprimand, is addressed by no means to the whole of the present auditory, but to that small body which I have thus summarily described. They have thought fit, contrary to their ordinary usage, to pay a visit to their parish church. I am heartily glad to see them there. They have invited me to preach to them. I am delighted to have such an opportunity; and if anything could add to the satisfaction, it is their request to that effect. And although the manner and guise in which they have thought fit to present themselves, is certainly unusual and not quite seemly, I will not complain on that score, nor is it my in-tention to address one word of unkindness to them. I rejoice too much to behold them in the house of God, where I believe most of them are perfect strangers, to do anything of this nature.

Believe me, my dear friends – for dear you are, and dear are your immortal souls to me, (would they were more dear to your-selves!) – believe me, that I speak not to you in anger, though in much sorrow. What may have been your motive for this irruption into the house of prayer, singular and unusual as it has been, I pretend not to know. Your object has probably been vague enough and perfectly undefined. Some have come from curiosity, some in caprice and mere freak, some to annoy and distress the ordinary congregation, and a few perhaps to display an open disrespect of religion without an intention of listening to what may be said. But, though I know not, and perhaps the majority of you are equally ignorant of any reason for this extraordinary exhibition, I feel confident that, with respect to some of you, God had his own especial end to answer in bringing you here. The preacher of the Gospel, its authorized minister, is but his instrument: and his voice, his teaching, his testimony, his arguments and reproofs must all be perfectly unavailing, unless the Holy Spirit come down and give his effectual energy and divine grace to work out the conversion of the sinner's heart.

Such being my sincere feelings towards you, and such my sanguine hopes respecting you, I shall use great boldness of speech. Bear with me, then, for a few minutes, while I give you, in words of sure wisdom and true friendship, some salutary counsel, which you will find profitable both for the present world and that which is to come. My words are those of affection: pardon me, if they are strong. I speak the accents of truth: let that truth-fulness command your attention. I will not, and I cannot, com-promise God's truth in deference to, still less in fear of, man or any number of men. In short, I trust I fear God too much to fear you. I mean well towards you. I am not to be intimidated; and I *will* be heard.

I have to tell you then, first, that you are grossly deceived, most infamously and impudently deluded and practised upon by persons who have their own wicked and selfish ends to answer by your destruction. How far they may as yet have succeeded in your perversion, your own consciences will best determine. But a very few reflexions, if you will permit yourselves to entertain them, will and must suffice to convince you that this general statement is correct. If the case were otherwise, if it were any lawful, good, or godly cause, in which they wished to engage you, would it be the first requisite, their primary object, as it is, to eradicate all religious principle and belief from your minds? Would they in that case so labour, as they do, to persuade you, and make you fancy you believe, that revelation is a falsehood? Would they endeavour so zealously to untie all social obligations, to obliterate all traces of Christian charity and kindly feeling? Would they, if they had any good object in view, or any kind intention towards yourselves, argue that as, according to their teaching, you must die like the beasts that perish, therefore the most appropriate thing you can do is to live like beasts? Such doctrines as these, horrible and repugnant as they are to that remnant of divinity which is still allowed to cleave to fallen man and which still points to immortality, can be a fitting preparation for nothing but the most nefarious schemes and the most diabolical issue. And along with such spiritual instruction, allow me to inquire what is the conduct recommended to you by these your teachers for your moral guidance in this life. They tell you that all have equal rights to property as to its distribution, that is to say, all property in this world is at the disposal of those who can seize occupation of it by the strong hand. For the doctrine of equal rights to property, you perceive, necessarily amounts to nothing less than this. You are first to covet, next to demand, and then, if your demand be not conceded, you are directed to take by violence your neighbour's goods. Next, they would have you believe, though it is truly wonderful that they should imagine such extreme credulity of human folly to be possible, that ignorance and numbers are the fittest qualifications for the high, difficult, delicate and intricate duties of legislation – and that no genuine liberty can exist without this extremely philosophical arrangement. And they have also, by precept and example, encouraged you to threaten and menace the lives of your peaceful brethren, who do not assent to the unjust requisitions which they direct you to make on them.

You have many excuses, my friends. I do not, and I cannot believe that doctrines, so frantic and outrageously preposterous as these, to say nothing of their portentous wickedness, can have imposed on many of you. Beware in time. Mark your path, and watch well your footsteps; for evil is before you. I trust, and I hope, that I warn you in time. You have, as I observed, many excuses. One of these is ignorance – of which I have a sure proof. It is, after all, but an imperfect plea of excuse. But your deceivers can advance no such plea. If *you* see not their drift, you may depend upon it *they* see and contemplate afar off, with malicious glee and total want of sympathy, the far-spread ruin which they meditate, and of which you would be the first victims. This is not precisely the fittest place for axioms on politics or political economy. But some principles are so plain and simple, and their truth when stated so obvious, that they cannot be deemed irrelevant here. Attend to me.

Is it not manifest, that real liberty consists, not in the absence of all restraint, but in being bound by no more legal restrictions than are absolutely necessary for the general welfare of the entire community ?

And does it not thence necessarily follow, that freedom is a comparative term, and that no country can enjoy it save in proportion to the virtue of its people generally, and the moral restraints, thence ensuing, which render legal restrictions less requisite or obsolete ? No nation ever attained civil liberty by mere charters and acts of legislation. They were the effects and not the cause of national virtue. The inverse process has often been tried and has always failed.

Is it not plain also, that no equality of property *can* exist, so long as God endows man unequally with gifts mental and personal ? And is it not clear, that, if all were made equal in respect of property at some imaginary point of time, they could not, for the above reason, remain equal for a single week ? In very small communities, where such an agreement by mutual compact is made, it may be practicable. But it never was extensively attempted save once, and that was in the early Christian Church – not by the direct injunction, so far as we can ascertain, though with the implied assent of Christ's Apostles. And we have proof that this arrangement was abandoned and put an end to by the Apostles themselves, as the Church multiplied, because it was then found impracticable: it was proved by experience to be, on a large scale, an impossibility.

So much, in very brief terms, for the utter futility of the representations of those who deceive you. They would bring upon you the same anathemas which the Apostle denounced against the 'rich men' in our text, whom he called to 'howl' and 'weep' for the miseries that should come upon them. For the forcible seizure of your neighbour's property would seem as flagrant an offence as that of one who 'kept back by fraud' the 'hire of the labourers who had reaped down his fields'. And he who threatens the life of his unoffending and peaceable neighbour is somewhat nearly akin in spirit to one who 'condemns and kills the just, who does not resist him'.

So much, I say, for the machinations of your enemies and seducers. Depend upon it, that in every popular convulsion, such as that into which these designing men would seduce you, the poorer and labouring classes, having put themselves out of the reach of ordinary legal protection, are the first to suffer from its effects, and they suffer more severely than any other. From the earliest memorials of the human race it never was otherwise.

Again: the wealth of a nation, however strange some of you may think the assertion, does not consist of gold and silver, or any such perishing things. The precious metals are merely its conventional representatives in detailed transferences. But the wealth of a nation consists in the industry, mental or corporeal, of its people, and the security afforded by legal provision for the produce of that industry. Pearls and diamonds are less precious jewels than honest labour, content of mind, patience of heart, and a good conscience towards God and man. The happiness of a nation depends upon these several requisites, and, generally speaking, upon the virtuous, religious and moral character of its people. A nation that does not fear God and keep his commandments, never was, never will be, and never can be, happy.

Take these things to heart, my brethren. Be patient, and trust in the Lord. Be industrious, and he will reward you. Be pious, and he will be with you. Call upon him; and he will hear you. Be mindful of his covenant, and he will not forget you, but embrace you in the arms of his eternal mercies. 'Be patient, therefore, brethren, to the coming of the Lord. Stablish your hearts; for the coming of the Lord draweth nigh. Grudge not one against another, lest ye be condemned: behold the Judge standeth before the door.'

29

FREDERICK DENISON MAURICE (1805–72)

FREDERICK DENISON MAURICE was born in Norfolk, the son of a Unitarian minister. By 1836 he had accepted the Anglican faith and in 1834 was ordained. He was appointed Chaplain of Guy's Hospital in 1836 and six years later he became Professor of English Literature and History at King's College, London. In 1846 he was appointed Chaplain of Lincoln's Inn and Professor of Theology at King's College. He was dismissed from the latter post in 1853 because of his liberal views on the nature of eternal punishment. In 1864 he was appointed Professor of Moral Theology in the University of Cambridge and, in 1870, Vicar of St Edward's, Cambridge. He was a great theologian, seeing every question in the light of theology. His theology was practical, as is shown by his life-long concern for education and by the fact that he was one of the founders of the Christian Socialist Movement and of the Working Men's College in London (1854). Maurice was the theologian of the Christian Socialist Movement, witnessing to the social implications of the Incarnation. His sermons are highly theological and are somewhat involved in style.

XLVII

From a sermon entitled 'The Law of Christ the Law of Humanity', *preached at Lincoln's Inn, 14 March 1858, on the text: 'Bear ye one* *another's burdens, and so fulfil the law of Christ' (Gal. vi, 2).* *Economic and social competition is not 'a necessary and eternal law'.* *What ought to be supreme, for society as much as for individuals, is* *the law of Christ, which has been revealed in the Incarnation.*

Thus, for instance, a great many people seem to have convinced themselves, that when they strive one against another, which shall possess the greatest amount of money, or of the good things which money procures, they are obeying a necessary and eternal law, one which they cannot resist or transgress without ceasing to be men. You will hear it continually assumed that this strife and contention is just as much the principle which determines the movements of human society as gravitation is the principle which determines the movements of natural bodies; that it is just as ridiculous to complain of the perpetual jostling of men against each other, with all the sorrow and misery which it causes to thousands and tens of thousands, as to be angry that water does not flow up instead of down a hill. By violent efforts, it is said, under some strange, irregular influence, the ordinary course of men's feelings may for a time be changed – even reversed. But only a fanatic would think of making these irregular influences normal; only a madman would reconstitute the universe upon a dream. In some other planet, it is added, where the inhabitants are not men, but beings of quite a different race and propensities, a better principle than this of universal rivalry may exist. But all the energy and purpose of *our* life would be lost if this mighty stimulus were withdrawn. If the Mammon we worship demands a costly amount of human sacrifices, there is a compensation in the benefits he bestows upon us.

Now, that the tendency which these reasoners speak of exists in the nature of every man whatsoever, that it works most strongly in the man who has most activity, most of all the qualities which society requires in its members – that no circumstances which we can create or conceive of will extinguish it – I believe is undoubtedly true. And I believe a man owes much to those who keep him in mind of this fact, who say to him, 'Be assured this desire of being first yourself, this inclination to trip up your neighbour, is in you now, will be in you always. Change your place, your mode of life, every influence which seems to you to have begotten or nourished it, and you will have it still. When you fancy it is dead, and are acting upon that supposition, you shall see it starting up with greater freshness than ever. Social arrangements will not put an end to it: if they aim at such a result, there is great fear that they will weaken the individual energies of those for whom they are formed, and will be, after all, what the most ingenious social arrangements were said to be by the old sage, mere spider-webs, which entangle the weaker insects, and which the stronger break through. Education will not put an end to it; so far as it awakens the faculties, and gives them greater elasticity and freedom, this disposition to outrun others, to grasp what they have, to assert mastery over them, will be also awakened.' These observations, however we may shrink from them as disagreeable, are, it seems to me, true, and therefore should not be concealed from ourselves or from others.

But to boast, when we have made them, that we have proclaimed the *law* by which men are bound together as members of a commonwealth, is surely of all extravagant pretensions the most monstrous. We have been fortunate enough to perceive something which *hinders* them from living and working together – something which induces each man to interfere with the actions and purposes of his fellow-man – something that has been the secret of hostility in past time, and threatens to make that hostility perpetual. But who does not see that if you have lighted upon so strange and perplexing a fact in the order of the world, you are bound to show how society has gone on in spite of it ? The more vigour you attribute to this selfish rivalry – the more manifold you find its workings to be – the more you are bound to explain to yourself how it has been possible for human beings to exist together under such a condition. You must seek for some principle of cohesion which has been able to withstand this tremendous principle of repulsion; and you must confess, if you are a reasonable man, that that principle, however it may have been transgressed, however imperfectly it may have been acknowledged, is in truth the law of the universe, the law which all human laws and schemes of government implicately confess, when they appear most to set it at naught.

You may fancy that when I speak thus I am trying to convince you that religion, or, as it is sometimes called still more vaguely, *the religious principle*, has been necessary for the conservation of society, and is necessary for it still. But there is much confusion and mischief, I fear, lurking in the use of such language. It may mean that religion prevents a society from perishing, which has selfishness for its root, and which would naturally fall to pieces if it had not some supernatural power, or the dream of some supernatural power, to keep it together. Such a religion statesmen have unquestionably been desirous of, and priests have been found ready to supply them with it. But if by religion be meant the Gospel of Christ in a living, practical sense, it declines such an honour altogether. It does not exist to keep men comfortable in their contradictions, or to avert the consequences of them. It exists as a perpetual witness against those contradictions, and a perpetual prophecy of the result which must come from them. A society which has reached the point of confessing no principle but that of rivalry, no maxim but that of 'Every man for himself', may in its dying agonies ask help of the Gospel – but assuredly too late. What can it do to save a community which has been deliberately, systematically, setting aside its first and most notorious precepts – which has pronounced the principle, my text announces, to be no foundation of human life at all, but only an excuse for pretty sentences in commendation of charity and gentleness such as preachers deliver, and which it is respectable to listen to for a few minutes on a Sunday ? No! religion, or the religious principle, if it is worth anything – if it is not another name for the worship of the God of this world, of the Evil Spirit – cannot be the instrument of preventing or even delaying that destruction which the Righteous and True God has pronounced against all unrighteousness and untruth.

Either the Gospel declares what society is, and what it is not; what binds men together, what separates them, or it has no significance at all. Either it shows how a uniting principle may be an effectual, living principle – how those tendencies which lead to separation may be overcome – or it fails to do what it professes . . .

There is indeed a general notion that benevolence is a good and desirable quality; that it is a graceful thing, and even in some cases a needful thing to care for others as well as ourselves. But this benevolence is represented as the beautiful capital of a pillar, which rests upon the most earthly base. It is a habit which may improve and mitigate the evils of the world, but affirms them to be radical. Or else religious people say, that to bear one another's burdens is the law of the regenerate man, but that the world generally can only follow a selfish rule. Governments must try to make that rule as efficient for keeping up good order as they can.

A more hateful and accursed inference from a great truth was never suggested by the Spirit of Lies for the purpose of undermining and making ineffectual a maxim which he dares not openly contradict. Assuredly there is this great and eternal distinction between the new and old man, the regenerate and the unregenerate. But the new man is he who consents to follow the true law of humanity which is in Christ Jesus, and so to be at one with his fellow-men; the old man is he who obeys the inclinations of his nature, and so is at war with his fellows. The law of Christ is *not* the law of a select few, but the law for man. It would be so, though all men disobeyed it; it continues so, though those who ought to proclaim the good news to their fellow-creatures, that Christ has taken the nature of men, and died for men, prefer to wrap themselves up in a conceit of their own privileges, and to boast that they have been put into an extra-human, or inhuman, position. Whoever comes to think habitually that there is a different law for different classes of human creatures, will infallibly obey the lower and least troublesome law in his own ordinary practice. For his distinction is grounded on this knowledge, that two principles are contending in himself, and if he once believes that the good principle is his own, for which he can, under any pretext, take credit to himself, he will fall under the dominion of the evil. He will, in all his dealings with other men, act upon the low notions which he supposes are the only notions they can understand or recognize; he will not make good his claim to be regenerate and different from these men by bearing their burdens, and so fulfilling the law of Christ, but by the most arrogant contempt and bitter judgement of them. A Christian man must believe that the law of Christ is applicable to all persons and all cases, or he will very soon apply it really and practically to no persons and in no cases. He must acknowledge it as the human law, or it certainly will not be the law of his church, or circle, or caste; he must believe that it lies at the root of all politics and of all daily business, or he will not make it the guide of his individual conduct, not even of his most sacred and solemn transactions.

There is another way in which this general application of the principle is often evaded by good men: they think that Christ is to come some day to restore the world and set all right, but that in the meantime society is to be left to take its course, and to follow what evil maxims it chooses for itself. That Christ will one day be the acknowledged Ruler of this earth, and of all that dwell on it, no one who calls him Lord and Master can bear to doubt. 'I should utterly have fainted,' says the Psalmist, 'if I had not verily believed to see the goodness of God in the land of the living.' No man who feels the oppressions of the world, and tries to bear up against them, can help utterly fainting, if he does not verily believe that this earth shall not always be a den of robbers, but that its true Saviour and Helper shall himself purge it and restore it. But the men of old were able verily to believe this truth; because they verily believed, in their own day, that the universe was not the devil's but God's, and because they set themselves manfully to fight in that conviction against those who said it was the devil's, and tried to make it so, we must do the same. If this law of bearing one another's burdens is not the law by which all things and all men are governed now, it never will be. Our faith in its future establishment rests wholly on our belief in its present truth. And if it is true, then must we desire Him who has fulfilled it in his own life to fulfil it in all the members of his body.

This then is our position, brethren. We see society dragged along by that mighty power of competition which wise men commend, and declare to be the sovereign principle in the universe. We see some of the men who obey this impulse, exhibiting admirable zeal and energy, a zeal and energy in vanquishing circumstances which we hold to be worthy of all imitation and all cultivation. But we see that they do not after all wholly obey this impulse; that they are not merely selfish, that they are members of families, of social circles, in which, to a certain extent, yes, to a very considerable extent, they act upon the rule, 'Bear ye one another's burdens'.

And we see another sight which is more appalling. We see oftentimes their sons exhibiting very little of their strength, hardly any of their domestic feelings, yet thoroughly possessed by their doctrine. They desire to be before others, but the desire is not making them painstaking, thrifty pursuers of fortune. They covet to be rich, and they become gamblers. They will take what seems to them the shortest road to riches, heedless, of course, of all warnings, that it is a road full of pits, in which thousands are lost, while one gets his reward and finds it to be a wretched reward. You are not then really stirring up that enterprise, that hope, which you say, and say rightly, is so essential to a nation's strength and well-being. You are producing men who are restless today, will be listless tomorrow; pursuers of phantoms, often ugly phantoms, for awhile; indifferent, disappointed, heartless loungers, when they have missed the prize. Must you not make an effort to recover that which competition cannot give, if you will obtain any one of its advantages? Must you not try to strengthen the bonds of sympathy which it is threatening? Must not the thought of providing for others besides ourselves, for those who shall live when we are in our graves, be in some way awakened? But that thought has its ground in the law which binds men together, not in the law which sets them one against another. That is a lower exhibition of the law which is expounded in the text, the law which was fulfilled by Jesus Christ.

I have owned, brethren, that we have no right to reproach any other men – merchants, shopkeepers, lawyers – for thinking the world's law mightier and more generally applicable than the Divine law. We, the ministers of the Gospel, have most to answer for. We have sanctioned this unbelief. We have acted upon it. The Church ought to uphold the national life, the family of England, by its prayers, its confessions, its sacraments. We have spoken of these prayers, confessions, sacraments, as if they were themselves instruments and abettors of the selfish law, as if there was no force in them which could enable us to obey the other law. Oh! that this Lent we might repent altogether, you and we, of the sin of such unfaithfulness! Oh that we might, each for himself, knowing the plague of his own heart, and also with one heart and voice, own that we have not borne each other's burdens, and so fulfilled the law of Christ! Oh that we may indeed feel that his yoke is the easy yoke, and that we have put on ourselves the heavy one! Oh that we may come to Christ's Holy Sacrament, believing that he can feed us with the flesh and make us drink of the blood which he gave for the world, when he bore all our burdens; that he can quicken us with his Spirit, to bear each other's burdens!

30

SAMUEL WILBERFORCE (1805–73)

SAMUEL WILBERFORCE, a son of William Wilberforce, leader
of the movement for the abolition of the slave trade, was born at
Clapham. He was ordained in 1828 and was appointed Rector of
Brightstone in 1830. After holding the benefice of Alvestoke from
1840 he became Dean of Westminster in 1845. Later the same
year he was consecrated Bishop of Oxford and was translated to
the See of Winchester in 1869. He transformed, by his example,
the popular idea of a bishop from that of a leisured aristocrat to
that of an active and hard-working pastor and administrator. He
was a moderate High Churchman and as a bishop he had to cope
with the controversy around the Oxford Movement. He was a
man of great eloquence and social charm. His weakness lay in his
ambition and his desire to please everybody. Hence his nick-name,
'Soapy Sam'.

XLVIII

*From a sermon entitled 'I Have much People in this City', preached
at the Consecration of Christ Church, Denton, Manchester, 13
October 1853, on the text: 'I have much people in this city'
(Acts viii, 10). A vivid illustration, taken from Manchester, of the
Church's neglect of people in the industrial cities.*

To inquire for a few moments into the causes of our present state,
suffer me, at the outset, brethren, to ask you to consider whether
one chief cause of this want of Christian life in our great centres of
population has not been this, that we have never duly felt that
they were the places in which the moral and religious life ought
to be the most vigorous. Would this vast city be what it is, as to its
provision for the worship of God, if the vision voice which spake
to St Paul concerning Corinth, had indeed reached, with all its

clearness, to the heart of the great mass of the true servants of God who dwell within it? Have not too many of us rather acquiesced in the deep practical infidelity of supposing that great cities must, to a certain extent, be given up to wickedness; that we may hope to do some good in our rural and more scattered districts, but that in these vast hives of life, and industry, and production, and intellectual activity, it is almost useless to endeavour to make Christ's Church strong, and Christ's truth dominant. I, for one, do firmly believe, brethren, that there is in this city, for instance, an amount of true piety which, but for the palsying effect of some such secret admission that evil must be the master, would have led to nobler exertions for God and for man, which would have made this city, not only as it is, the metropolis of the world's industry, and the marvellous stronghold of an intellectual activity, at once various, robust, accurate, and subtle, but would also have made it a centre of all Christian influences, for this land first, and then, through it, for the whole earth. Oh, my brethren, that so it may be yet! And if it is to be so, here must be the beginning, we must feel the application to ourselves of the declaration, 'I have much people in this city', and then we shall give ourselves, according to our power, to work out its fulfilment. Now it is this example which, I think, is set before you here today. This church and these intended schools, what are they but a declaration that this world-mart is meant by God to be a Christian citadel? This is why this church is built with becoming grandeur, and finished with a beauty of its own; why it is not a mere building in which men can be collected, but one suited, in its proportions and solid stateliness, and in its costly materials, for the worship of the high God, who hath given us all things. For here is a declaration that God's house should be built, and God's work should be done, as it becomes the great wealth of this city to build and to do it; that there should be an example set of offering, not of the lame and the maimed to him, who has so mightily enriched us with silver and gold, and costly merchandise, and skilful hands, and able heads, and daring hearts, and above all, with the souls of men; but that there should be given to him as he has given to us.

And here, you may observe, we come directly to a second great cause of the languid state of the Church in these great cities, which springs by direct necessity from the former. For not perceiving that they ought to be the centres of the Church's life, we have acquiesced in their remaining unfurnished with those outward means of fabrics, schools, and endowments, which would enable her to reach their teeming multitudes. Only let me, in the briefest possible statement, lodge in your minds, one single set of figures as to this great city, and this point will be incontrovertibly established. Manchester contained in 1851, 452,158 souls. There was in the same year room in all its churches for 58,000 worshippers; there was none for that fearful residue of well nigh 400,000 neglected souls! Nor let us flatter ourselves that this is the neglect of past times altogether, and that our present efforts are greatly redressing the evil. So far from this being true, the evil gains upon us. In 1801, 16 per cent of the then population of Manchester could be received into its churches; but in 1851, after all which has been done, that fearfully low average has sunk to only 13 per cent, who can now be received into its churches. Now I need not weary you, my brethren, by dwelling upon the inevitable consequences of such a state of things. Men must, by the deepest laws of our nature, become careless, dissolute, and godless, who, with everything to excite their passions, and much to stimulate their intellect, are thus thrust out of the Church's keeping. In such men, even religion itself, when, through God's mercy, it does spring up in one heart or another, is too often a divided, darkened, spasmodic, unruly acting of the spiritual life, which is almost as threatening to the purity of the faith within the Church, as was the forerunning irreligion to her existence and security. But all this is surely self-evident. There is, however, another acting of this inefficient provision of the Church's machinery which I would just wish to suggest to you, because it does not so readily occur to every mind. When the Church is conquering a pagan city for Christ, her zeal is inflamed, and not deadened, by the sight which meets her everywhere, of the multitude of unbelievers. Their masses and their misery stir up her prayers, and arm her hands with the sharpest weapons for her merciful conflict. They are the guerdon God will give her, and to win them for her Lord her Apostles labour without fainting, and her martyrs bleed even with joy. But the effect upon the Church of an admitted heathendom within her borders, is the exact opposite of this. It benumbs, at every turn, her own life. Her sons grow to acquiesce in fierce divisions, in wide-spread carelessness, in utter ignorance of God, as conditions which are to be looked for within her pale. And this tells, at every turn, upon her own moral energies. She no longer regards the whole population as her proper charge; some are supposed to belong to separatists; some to no religion at all: she is supposed to be charged by God only with the gathered congregations who voluntarily attend in her courts – until at length some, at least, of her clergy grow to acquiesce in the common estimate; they measure their congregations, but they forget the multitude without. They receive parishes of 30,000 souls as their charge, and never faint under the burden. What must follow from such a state of things? Alas! that soon all is palsied and almost dead. The ever-present hum of the world's busy voice grows louder and louder around and within her courts; whilst alas! prayers wax feeble, sacraments become obscured, the religious life a taste, the purity of doctrine wanes, the winning example of a life of loving self-sacrifice is rare; and to eyes which can read the signs of coming judgement, the shaking of the candlestick foreshows its removal. Who amongst us is bold-hearted enough to deny that too many of such signs of evil may already be discerned amongst us?

Here, then, again, our duty is plain; today's work is one fulfilling of it which should be multiplied on every side. And suffer me, my brethren, as a comparative stranger amongst you, to say that everything seems to call on YOU for new and unparalleled exertions. Your great spiritual necessities – your unequalled vigour in all matters of intellectual life and practical efficiency; your new constitution as a separate diocese,* which gives you the opportunity of more centralized action, all are loud calls to you to pour in to the supply of the Church's necessity the wealth which God has allowed you, in this very place, so largely to collect. May he make this our assembling here, and the consideration of this great subject, however imperfectly it has been brought before you, an occasion of a new awakening.

But, my brethren, I should not be true to my deepest con-

* The See of Manchester was founded in 1846.

victions, if, after undertaking to touch, however lightly, upon the causes of this great evil of our religious state, I left you with the belief that I conceive all would be done by a mere increase, however vast, of our endowments, our schools and churches. No, my brethren, blessed as the work of this day surely is, yet it must, I think, make us feel, when we compare its utmost possible results with the wants of the population round us, that our Church does need, even beyond all such efforts, some new development of her internal spiritual powers, if she is, indeed, to grapple boldly with the greatest needs of this people ...

It is not merely that our great cities collect within their borders our greatest sins: this must be so; their multitudes must offer the same shelter for evil, which was formerly found in wastes and deserts; neither is it merely that these sins exhibit, from time to time, a peculiar intensity of wickedness; for it is of the very nature of a lapsed Christianity to assume this peculiarly malignant type of evil. But it is that the Church, in her own work, is comparatively powerless in these centres of life. It is, that she does not duly develop her own appropriate resistance to these evils; that she does not lift up visibly beside them a proportionate intensity of devotion, completeness of self-sacrifice, and manifested reality of spiritual life. Now, to supply all this, we want something more than a mere increase of churches and endowments. We want a quickening of the Church's internal spiritual vigour, we want greater gifts of grace, we want a deeper love for the purity of doctrine, we want a higher value for souls, a simpler faith in the cross, a life more pervaded with the presence of our Lord. This, of course, must be the gift of God; but then we must seek and we must prepare to receive his gifts: and what I ask you to weigh well and thoughtfully is this; is there not in our religious system great room for improvements, which, under the blessing of God, would tend to arouse the lethargic currents of our own life, and enable us to labour far more successfully for others? Of course, I can but touch upon this now and here; but let me ask you, can the Church now, as she ought to do, deliberate, resolve, and act on the particulars of her own special work? Are we not often hampered by a certain unbending rigidity of external form, marring the free action of the spirit? If this be not so, why else, I would ask you, for example, when pestilence threatens any district of our land, cannot our people be gathered, as others are, for special litanies and intercessions ? for short earnest services where men cannot attend long ones ? Why should these be withheld from us ? Why should not, again, the needs of our scattered multitudes at such times be met by short, moving services, through which, by God's grace, true devotion might be roused in many a slumbering soul ? Why are we to be so tied down that we cannot preach to our dying multitudes without having first read to them a service which, as yet, they cannot appreciate ? Is not all this so, because at the time when our present system was formed, this abridgement of liberty was necessary to keep down a dominant superstition, and, when it was last revised, to keep out a puritanical licence, and that now, amidst most pressing spiritual wants, we have no power, when the danger is different, of adapting that system to our wants ? Was it not, if the truth be spoken, from this cramping pressure of our system, that our Wesleyan brethren were almost forced to separate themselves from us, and so introduce the widening and all but infinite evils of division, if they would enjoy the spiritual assistances which they desired, and which we ought to have been able to afford them within our own communion. Will any reasonable man say that we can ever hope to regain our lost multitudes, without arousing, in our body, these slumbering powers of spiritual exertion ?

31

CHARLES KINGSLEY (1819–75)

CHARLES KINGSLEY was born in Devon and after his ordination in 1842 he became Curate of Eversley, Hants., and Vicar of the same parish in 1844. He was Professor of Modern History at Cambridge from 1860–69, when he was appointed Canon of Chester. He became Canon of Westminster in 1873. Kingsley was, for a time, a leading spirit in the Christian Socialist Movement and sympathized with the cause of the Chartists. In politics, however, he was far more of a Tory than a radical and was later accused of deserting the Socialist Movement. He became disillusioned with the working classes for not living up to his ideal for them. Impetuous and excitable, Kingsley was regarded as a leading exponent of 'muscular Christianity', strongly averse to all forms of asceticism and a critic of the principles of the Oxford Movement. He became a well-known novelist, his most popular works being *Westward Ho!* (1855), and *The Water Babies* (1863). In his preaching, Kingsley was fearlessly outspoken, indicting the social evils of his day and those he considered responsible for them. His style was direct, simple and vigorous. 'Kingsley delivered sermons like a man wrestling with demons' (Owen Chadwick).

XLIX

From a sermon entitled 'The Message of the Church to Labouring Men', preached in St John's Church, Charlotte Street, Fitzroy Square, London, 22 June 1851, on the text:

And he came to Nazareth, where he had been brought up: and, as his custom was, he went into the synagogue on the sabbath day, and stood up for to read.

And there was delivered unto him the book of the prophet Esaias. And when he had opened the book, he found the place where it was written,

The Spirit of the Lord is upon me, because he hath anointed me to preach the gospel to the poor; he hath sent me to heal the broken-hearted, to preach deliverance to the captives, and recovering of sight to the blind, to set at liberty them that are bruised,

To preach the acceptable year of the Lord.

And he closed the book, and he gave it again to the minister, and sat down. And the eyes of all them that were in the synagogue were fastened on him.

And he began to say unto them, This day is this scripture fulfilled in your ears (*Luke iv, 16–21*).

The message of Christ is freedom; forms of society which favour accumulation of capital in the hands of a few are contrary to the kingdom of God. Christianity proclaims freedom to the poor, the equality of all men and the eternal right of brotherhood. This was a sermon in a series arranged by the Rev. G. S. Drew during the Great Exhibition in Hyde Park. A crowd of working men came to hear Kingsley, and the Rev. G. S. Drew so strongly disagreed with the preacher's views that there occurred the incident referred to on page 27 supra.

Though man may forget the meaning of the very signs which God has preserved to him, yet to the poor there will be always in the Church a message from their Heavenly Father, in the Bible, which proclaims man's freedom – in baptism, which proclaims his equality – in the supper of the Lord which proclaims his brotherhood, and those, not as dim and distant possibilities, for which he is to crave and struggle of his own self-will, but as his absolute and eternal right, which God the father has given him – which God the Son has bought for him with his blood – and which God the Holy Spirit will give him strength and wisdom to take possession of and realize whensoever he casts himself humbly and loyally under the guidance of the God who made him.

I say that these three things, which exist, and always have existed, in the Christian Church, have borne witness, and do bear witness, for the many against the few, in a way in which nothing of man's invention could bear witness. I say that they declare that men are free, equal, brothers. I say that they taught *me* so. I say that they proclaim that every man or king who tries to enslave men, to be partial and unjust to one class or person, to cause division among the human brotherhood, contrary to the will and law of God, is accursed. These bear witness against all false priests, false teachers, false rulers. These have recalled in every age, and will recall in this age, as I trust in God, both laity and clergy to the example of him who died on the cross, who came to give healing to the broken-hearted, to preach deliverance to the captives, and recovering of sight to the blind; to set at liberty them that are bruised, to preach the acceptable year of the Lord, who counted not his own life dear to him, but gave it freely for those who hated him; who spent his life in healing sickness, in enlightening the blinded mind as well as the blinded body; who told men, for the first time those words had ever been heard on earth, that they should call no man master on earth, for one was their master, even God; one was their father, even God; and they were all brothers; whose prayer for them, the night before his crucifixion, was, that mankind might be all one – one in him, even as he was one with God the Father. Consider those three things, my friends – consider them as they stand now in England here, and see whether any witness for freedom, equality, and brotherhood which man can invent, bears the deep witness for them which they bear. The Bible is the right of the poorest man, as well as of the richest – of the simplest, as well as of the most educated – and of whom does the Bible tell him? Of a Divine Lord, in whose image man was created – a being all purity, all love, all patience, all wisdom, all power, from the earliest ages – the light who lightens every man who comes into the world, who emancipated and civilized into a great nation a horde of injured slaves, that they might bear witness through all time of his existence, of his love, and of his justice – who raised up from the lowest ranks of that nation prophets to rebuke the luxurious and the tyrannical, to proclaim his righteous wrath and fury against the devourers of the earth – who in his boundless love and mercy condescended to take upon himself human flesh, and be called the son of a carpenter, and toiled and suffered, houseless and despised, among the poor, the sick, the ignorant, the neglected – who gave himself up, for the sake of mankind, to utter shame and agony, and the death of the felon and the slave – who wrestled with death itself, the foe alike of rich and

poor, and tried its might, and conquered it, and rose again to proclaim that beyond the grave there was an eternity of endless justice,
love, and light, for those who had known in this world only darkness, neglect, and cruelty; and that he, the tender, the longsuffering, the foe of the scribe and the Pharisee, the friend of the
harlot and the sinner – that to him all power was given in heaven
and earth – that the human race was henceforth under his care –
that he was their guide, their teacher, their avenger – that the day
would come upon this earth when all the wildest dreams of poets
and of seers should be outrivalled by the blessed reality of the new
earth, wherein should dwell righteousness, of which the Lord
God, and he, the Lamb of God, should be the Light; when the
nations of the world should become the nations of God and of his
Christ, and there should be no more pain or death, no more
tyranny or misrule, no more lust or intemperance, no more
devouring struggle of man against man, or nation against nation –
no more weary widows or pining orphans – no more hard-handed
drudges, wearying themselves in the fire for very vanity – no more
idolatry or priestcraft to stand between the free soul of man and
the God who made him, but that mankind should see God face to
face, when he himself would wipe away tears from all eyes.

Is not that a gospel – a good news to the poor ? What cunning or
darkness of man's invention can darken the everlasting hope and
assurance of the suffering poor as long as the book which preaches
to them that good news is in their hands ?

Look again at baptism – a sacrament or sign – and *what* a sign!
Thoughtless men have sneered at it from its simplicity, and
laughed at the Church for attributing, as they say, miraculous
virtues to the sprinkling of a little water, as if the very simplicity
of the sign was not in itself a gospel, that is, good news to the poo r,
proclaiming that baptism is the witness of a blessing not meant
merely for the high-born, or the philosopher, or the genius, but,
like the rain of heaven and the running brook, free to all, even to
the poorest and to the most degraded: his right, as water is,
simply because he is a human being. Baptism works no miracle;
it proclaims a miracle which has been from all eternity. It proclaims that we are members of Christ, children of God, citizens of
a spiritual kingdom – that is, of a kingdom of love, justice, self-

sacrifice, freedom, equality. Those spiritual laws, says baptism, are the true ground and constitution of all human society, and not rank, force, wealth, expediency, or any outward material ground whatsoever; not they, but the Kingdom of God whose name is Love and Righteousness, which, if any nation or society of men seek first, all other outward and material blessings of health, wealth, and civilization, will be surely added to them, because they will be working in harmony with the laws of him who made the world of matter, as well as the laws of spirit. To take a single instance of what I mean – what is the plain and simple meaning of the baptismal sign, but washing – purification – and that alike of the child of the queen and the child of the beggar ? It testifies of the right of each, because the will of God for each is, that they should be pure. And what better witness do you want, my working friends, against that vile neglect which allows tens of thousands in our great cities to grow up hogs in body, soul, and spirit ? If we really believe the meaning of that baptismal sign, we should need few further arguments in favour of sanitary reform, for every savage in St Giles's would feel that he had a right to say, God's will is that my children should be pure washed without and within from everything that defiles and degrades man; my child is God's child – God's spirit is with it. It is the temple of the Living God, and whosoever defiles the temple of God, him will God destroy. God has promised to purify its spirit: how dare you interfere with God's work ? God's will is that its whole body, soul, and spirit, should be preserved blameless, and grow up to the full stature of a noble manhood. How dare you stand in the way of the will of God towards even óne of the meanest of his creatures ? How dare you, in your sectarian jealousy, your dread of that light which after all comes down from God, who is the Father of Light; how dare you, I say, refuse to allow his mind to be purified by education; how dare you, for the sake of your own private greed or party chicaneries, refuse to allow his body such purity as God has not denied even to the wild beast in his native forest ? How dare you, in the face of that baptismal sign of the sprinkled water, keep God's children exposed to filth, brutality, and temptation, which festers in your courts and alleys, making cleanliness impossible – drunkenness all but excusable – prostitution all but natural – self-respect and decency unknown? Again, my working friends, I speak the truth of God. In that font is a witness for education and for sanitary reform, which will conquer with the might of an archangel, when every other argument has failed to prove that the masses are after all not mere machines and hands to be used up in the production of a wealth of which they never taste, when their numbers are, as far as possible, kept down by economical and prudent rulers, to the market demand for – members of Christ, children of God, and inheritors of the Kingdom of Heaven.

And what, my friends, is the message of the Lord's supper? What more distinct sign and pledge that all men are equal? Wherever in the world there may be inequality, it ceases there. One table, one reverential posture, one bread, one wine, for high and low, for wise and foolish. That sacrament proclaims that all alike are brothers of each other, because they are all alike brothers of one – and he the son of a village maiden. That sacrament proclaims that all are equally his debtors – all equally in need of the pardon which he has bought for them – and that that pardon is equally ready and free to all of them. That sacrament proclaims that they all equally draw from him their life, their health, their every strength, and faculty of body, mind, and heart, all, therefore, equally bound to live for him, and therefore for those whom he loved, for whom he laboured, for whom he died – for whom he lives and reigns for ever – whose every suffering, and oppression, and neglect, he will avenge to the uttermost in the day of his wrath – in a word, for the people. That sacrament has told me – 'Men are thy brothers still. God has made them so; and thou canst not unmake it.' Oh, my dear friends, if the heartfelt experience of one man can bring home to your minds the power of that blessed sign, hear me, this night, and believe me, when I tell you, in the hearing of God the Father, and Jesus Christ, the poor man – that to that blessed sacrament and pledge of brotherhood, I at least owe all the little lukewarm love for the people, which I do trust and hope I feel. When I have been proud, it has humbled me, and said to me, 'These toilsome labourers, and stunted drudges, are as great in God's sight – greater, for aught thou knowest, than thou.' When I have been selfishly superstitious, it has said to me, 'Think thou not of thyself alone, in the presence of the Father of all, whose mercy is over all his works. Thou must worship with thy brothers; thou must claim teaching, light, life, only as a member of a body, or thou shalt have none of it.' When I have been inclined to enjoy myself at ease, and let the world run past me, heedless of its moans, Sunday after Sunday has that beloved sacrament rebuked me, and seemed to say to me with the voice of the Poor Man of Nazareth himself, 'Look what God would have these poor creatures be, and look what they are? Art thou not living in a lie, fighting against him whom thou professest to serve, if thou dost not devote thy every energy to give them those blessings of the Kingdom of God, of which they here have claimed their share, to educate, civilize, deliver them in body, mind, and heart?' When I have been inclined to take offence at people because they disagreed with me, because they seemed ungrateful or unjust to me – then, beyond all arguments, that blessed sign has recalled me to my senses, and said to me, 'See, these men with whom thou art angry *are* thy brothers after all. Their relation to thee is God-given and eternal. Thou didst not choose them – thou didst not join thyself to them. God chose them – God joined thee to them – and thou canst not alter his choice – thou canst not part thyself from them. Hate them, and turn from them if thou darest!'

Above all, when I have been inclined to give in to that subtlest of all temptations – the notion that one Gospel is required for the man of letters, and another for the labouring drudge – that he may pamper and glorify himself on art and science, and the higher and more delicate subjects of thought, while for the poor man a little reading and writing, and religion, is enough and to spare; then again, that sacrament has warned me 'Not so – one bread, one wine, for thee and them. One Lord, one pardon, one fountain of life, one guiding and inspiring spirit. They have not only the same rights, but the same spiritual wealth in them. If thou hast been put into circumstances, in which thou canst use thy gifts more freely than they can theirs, why is it but that thou mayest share thy superfluity with their need – that thou mayest teach them, guide them, nourish up into flower and greet the heaven-given seed of nobleness which lies in them as surely as in thee?

For after all, as that bread and that wine proclaim to thee – thou hast nothing of thine own – wit, scholarship, utterance – what hast thou which thou didst not receive ? Fool! instead of priding thyself on it as thine own property, confess it to be that which it is, the gift of God, who hath only bestowed it on thee as his steward – give it freely to all, as he hath given freely to thee.'

L

From a sermon 'On the Cholera', 1866 (no place), on the text: 'And there came a fear on all: and they glorified God, saying, That a great prophet is risen up among us; and, That God hath visited his people' (*Luke vii, 16*). *During the nineteenth century there were severe outbreaks of cholera in this country. Kingsley, like many other preachers, while acknowledging that cholera may be due to insanitary conditions, sees in it God's visitation upon man's lack of faith.*

God uses the powers of nature to do his work: of him it is written, 'He maketh the winds his angels, and flames of fire his ministers.' And so this minute and invisible cholera-seed is the minister of God, by which he is visiting from house to house, searching out and punishing certain persons who have been guilty, knowingly or not, of the offence of dirt; of filthy and careless habits of living; and especially, as has long been known by well-informed men, of drinking poisoned water. Their sickness, their deaths, are God's judgement on that act of theirs, whereby God says to men, You shall not drink water unfit for even dumb animals; and if you do, you shall die.

To this view there are two objections. First, the poor people themselves are not in fault, but those who supply poisoned water, and foul dwellings.

True; but only half true. If people demanded good water and good houses, there would soon be a supply of them. But there is not a sufficient supply; because too many of the labouring classes in towns, though they are earning very high wages, are contented to live in a condition unfit for civilized men; and of course, if they are contented so to do, there will be plenty of covetous or careless landlords who will supply the bad article with which they are satisfied; and they will be punished by disease for not having taken care of themselves.

But as for the owners of filthy houses, and the suppliers of poisoned water, be sure that, in his own way and his own time, God will visit them; that when he maketh inquisition for blood, he will assuredly requite upon the guilty persons, whoever they are, the blood of those five or six thousand of her Majesty's subjects who have been foully done to death by cholera in the last two months, as he requited the blood of Naboth, or of any other innocent victim of whom we read in Holy Writ. This outbreak of cholera in London, considering what we now know about it, and have known for twenty years past, is a national shame, scandal, and sin, which, if man cannot and will not punish, God can and will.

But there is another objection, which is far more important and difficult to answer. This cholera has not slain merely fathers and mothers of families, who were more or less responsible for the bad state of their dwellings; but little children, aged widows, and many other persons who cannot be blamed in the least.

True. And we must therefore believe that to them – indeed to all – this has been a visitation not of anger but of love. We must believe that they are taken away from some evil to come; that God permits the destruction of their bodies, to the saving of their souls. His laws are inexorable; and yet he hateth nothing that he hath made.

And we must believe that this cholera is an instance of the great law, which fulfils itself again and again, and will to the end of the world – 'It is expedient that one die for the people, and that the whole nation perish not.'

For the same dirt which produces cholera now and then, is producing always, and all day long, stunted and diseased bodies, drunkenness, recklessness, misery, and sin of all kinds; and the cholera will be a blessing, a cheap price to have paid, for the abolition of the evil spirit of dirt.

And thus much for this very painful subject – of which some of you may say – 'What is it to us? We cannot prevent cholera; and, blessed as we are with abundance of the purest water, there is little or no fear of cholera ever coming into our parish.'

That last is true, my friends, and you may thank God for it. Meanwhile, take this lesson at least home with you, and teach it your children day by day – that filthy, careless, and unwholesome habits of living are in the sight of Almighty God so terrible an offence, that he sometimes finds it necessary to visit them with a severity with which he visits hardly any sin; namely, by inflicting capital punishment on thousands of his beloved creatures . . .

For months past we have been praying that this cholera should not enter England, and our prayers have not been heard. In spite of them the cholera has come; and has slain thousands, and seems likely to slay thousands more. What plainer proof can there be to those who believe in the providence of God, and the rule of Jesus Christ our Lord, than that we are meant to learn some wholesome lesson from it, which we have not learnt yet? It cannot be that God means us to learn the physical cause of cholera, for that we have known these twenty years. Foul lodging, foul food, and, above all, natural and physical, foul water; there is no doubt of the cause. But why cannot we save English people from the curse and destruction which all this foulness brings? That is the question. That is our national scandal, shame, and sin at this moment. Perhaps the Lord wills that we should learn that; learn what is the moral and spiritual cause of our own miserable weakness, negligence, hardness of heart, which, sinning against light and knowledge, has caused the death of thousands of innocent souls. God grant that we may learn that lesson. God grant that he may put into the hearts and minds of some man or men, the wisdom and courage to deliver us from such scandals for the future.

But I have little hope that that will happen, till we get rid of our secret atheism; till we give up the notion that God only visits now and then, to disorder and destroy his own handiwork, and take back the old scriptural notion, that God is visiting all day long for ever, to give order and life to his own work, to set it right whenever it goes wrong, and re-create it whenever it decays. Till then we can expect only explanations of cholera and of God's other visitations of affliction, which are so superstitious, so irrational, so little connected with the matter in hand, that they would be ridiculous, were they not somewhat blasphemous. But when men arise in this land who believe truly in an ever-present God of order, revealed in his son, Jesus Christ; when men shall arise in this land, who will believe that faith with their whole hearts, and will live and die for it and by it; acting as if they really believed that in God we live, and move, and have our being; as if they really believed that they were in the kingdom and rule of Christ – a rule of awful severity, and yet of perfect love – a rule, meanwhile, which men can understand, and are meant to understand, that they may not only obey the laws of God, but know the mind of God, and copy the dealings of God, and do the will of God; and when men arise in this land, who have that holy faith in their hearts, and courage to act upon it, then cholera will vanish away, and the physical and moral causes of a hundred other evils which torment poor human beings through no anger of God, but simply through their own folly, and greediness, and ignorance.

LI

From a sermon entitled 'Human Soot', preached for the Kirkdale Ragged Schools, Liverpool, 1870, on the text: 'It is not the will of your Father which is in heaven, that one of these little ones should perish' (*Matt. xviii, 14*). *An indictment of the inhumanity of the commercial system as it was exemplified in a town like Liverpool.*

I am here to plead for the Kirkdale Industrial Ragged School, and Free School-room Church. The great majority of children who attend this school belong to the class of 'street arabs', as they are now called; and either already belong to, or are likely to sink into, the dangerous classes – professional law-breakers, profligates, and barbarians. How these children have been fed, civilized, christianized, taught trades and domestic employments, and saved from ruin of body and soul, I leave to you to read in the report. Let us take hold of these little ones at once. They are now soft, plastic, mouldable; a tone will stir young souls to the very depths, a look will affect them for ever. But a hardening process has commenced within them, and if they are not seized at once, they will become harder than adamant; and then scalding tears, and the most earnest trials, will be all but useless.

This report contains full and pleasant proof of the success of the schools; but it contains also full proof of a fact which is any-thing but pleasant – of the existence in Liverpool of a need for such an institution. How is is that when a ragged school like this is opened, it is filled at once: that it is enlarged year after year, and yet is filled and filled again? Whence comes this large population of children who are needy, if not destitute; and who are, or are in a fair way to become, dangerous? And whence comes the population of parents whom these children represent? How is it that in Liverpool, if I am rightly informed, more than four hundred and fifty children were committed by the magistrates last year for various offences; almost every one of whom, of course, represents several more, brothers, sisters, companions, corrupted by him, or corrupting him. You have your reformatories, your training ships, like your Akbar, which I visited with deep satisfaction yesterday – institutions which are an honour to the town of Liverpool, at least to many of its citizens. But how is it that they are ever needed? How is it – and this, if correct, or only half correct, is a fact altogether horrible – that there are now between ten and twelve thousand children in Liverpool who attend no school – twelve thousand children in ignorance of their duty to God and man, in training for that dangerous class, which you have, it seems, con-trived to create in this once small and quiet port during a century of wonderful prosperity . . .

I do not blame you, or the people of Liverpool, nor the people of any city on earth, in our present imperfect state of civilization, for the existence among them of brutal, ignorant, degraded, helpless people. It is no one's fault, just because it is everyone's fault – the fault of the system. But it is not the will of God; and therefore the existence of such an evil is proof patent and sufficient that we have not yet discovered the whole will of God about this matter; that we have not yet mastered the laws of true political economy, which (like all other natural laws) are that will of God revealed in facts. Our processes are hasty, imperfect, barbaric – and their result is vast and rapid production: but also waste, refuse, in the shape of a dangerous class. We know well how, in some manufactures, a certain amount of waste is profitable – that it pays better to let certain substances run to refuse, than to use every product of the manufacture; as in a steam mill, where it pays better not to consume the whole fuel, to let the soot escape, though every atom of soot is so much wasted fuel. So it is in our present social system. It pays better, capital is accumulated more rapidly, by wasting a certain amount of human life, human health, human intellect, human morals, by producing and throwing away a regular percentage of human soot – of that thinking, acting dirt, which lies about, and, alas! breeds and perpetuates itself in foul alleys and low public houses, and all dens and dark places of the earth.

But, as in the case of the manufactures, the Nemesis comes, swift and sure. As the foul vapours of the mine and the manufactory destroy vegetation and injure health, so does the Nemesis fall on the world of man; so does that human soot, these human poison gases, infect the whole society which has allowed them to fester under its feet.

Sad, but not hopeless! Dark, but not without a gleam of light on the horizon! For I can conceive a time when, by improved chemical science, every foul vapour which now escapes from the chimney of a manufactory, polluting the air, destroying the vegetation, shall be seized, utilized, converted into some profitable substance; till the black country shall be black no longer, the streams once more crystal clear, the trees once more luxuriant, and the desert which man has created in his haste and greed shall, in literal fact, once more blossom as the rose. And just so can I conceive a time when, by a higher civilization, formed on a political economy more truly scientific, because more truly according to the will of God, our human refuse shall be utilized, like our material refuse, when man, as man, even down to the weakest and most ignorant, shall be found to be (as he really is) so valuable, that it will be worth while to preserve his health, to develop his capabilities, to save him alive, body, intellect, and character, at any cost; because men will see that a man is, after all, the most precious and useful thing on the earth, and that no cost spent on the development of human beings can possibly be thrown away.

I appeal, then, to you, the commercial men of Liverpool, if there are any such in this congregation. If not, I appeal to their wives and daughters, who are kept in wealth, luxury, refinement, by the honourable labours of their husbands, fathers, brothers, on behalf of this human soot. Merchants are (and I believe that tney deserve to be) the leaders of the great caravan, which goes forth to replenish the earth and subdue it. They are among the generals of the great army which wages war against the brute powers of nature all over the world, to ward off poverty and starvation from the ever-teeming millions of mankind. Have they no time – I take for granted that they have the heart – to pick up the footsore and weary, who have fallen out of the march, that they may rejoin the caravan, and be of use once more ? Have they no time – I am sure they have the heart – to tend the wounded and the fever-stricken, that they may rise and fight once more ? If not, then must not the pace of their march be somewhat too rapid, the plan of their campaign somewhat precipitate and ill-directed, their ambulance train and their medical arrangements somewhat defective ? We are all ready enough to complain of waste of human bodies, brought about by such defects in the British army. Shall we pass over the waste, the hereditary waste of human souls, brought about by similar defects in every great city in the world ?

Waste of human souls, human intellects, human characters – waste, saddest of all, of the image of God in little children. That cannot be necessary. There must be a fault somewhere. It cannot be the will of God that one little one should perish by commerce, or by manufacture, any more than by slavery, or by war.

As surely as I believe that there is a God, so surely do I believe that commerce is the ordinance of God; that the great army of producers and distributors is God's army. But for that very reason I must believe that the production of human refuse, the waste of human character, is not part of God's plan; not according to his ideal of what our social state should be; and therefore what our social state can be. For God asks no impossibilities of any human being.

LII

From a sermon on 'Capital Punishment', Quinquagesima Sunday, 1872, on the text:

And God blessed Noah and his sons, and said unto them, Be fruitful, and multiply, and replenish the earth.

And the fear of you and the dread of you shall be upon every beast of the earth, and upon every fowl of the air, upon all that moveth upon the earth, and upon all the fishes of the sea; into your hand are they delivered.

Every moving thing that liveth shall be meat for you; even as the green herb have I given you all things.

But flesh with the life thereof, shall ye not eat.

And surely your blood of your lives will I require; at the hand of every beast will I require it, and at the hand of man; at the hand of every man's brother will I require the life of man.

Whoso sheddeth man's blood, by man shall his blood be shed: for in the image of God made he man (*Gen. ix, 1–6*).

It expresses approval of capital punishment; punishment has priority over amendment; the laws of a country are the copy of God's will.

You all know that there is nowadays a strong feeling among some persons about capital punishment; that there are those who will move heaven and earth to interfere with the course of justice, and beg off the worst of murderers, on any grounds, however unreasonable, fanciful, even unfair; simply because they have a dislike to human beings being hanged. I believe, from long consideration, that these persons' strange dislike proceeds from their not believing sufficiently that man is made in the image of God. And, alas! it proceeds, I fear, in some of them, from not believing in a God at all – believing, perhaps, in some mere maker of the world, but not in the living God which Scripture sets forth. For how else can they say, as I have known some say, that capital punishment is wrong, because 'we have no right to usher a man into the presence of his Maker'.

Into the presence of his Maker! Why, where else is every man, you and I, heathen and Christian, bad and good, save in the presence of his Maker already? Do we not live and move and have our being in God? Whither can we go from his spirit, or whither can we flee from his presence? If we ascend into Heaven, he is there. If we go down to Hell he is there also. And if the law puts a man to death, it does not usher him into the presence of his Maker, for he is there already. It simply says to him, 'God has judged you on earth, not we. God will judge you in the next world, not we. All we know is, that you are not fit to live in this world. All our duty is to send you out of it. Where you will go in the other world is God's matter, not ours, and the Lord have mercy on your soul.'

And this want of faith in a living God lies at the bottom of another objection. We are to keep murderers alive in order to convert and instruct and amend them. The answer is, We shall be most happy to amend anybody of any fault, however great: but the experience of ages is that murderers are past mending; that the fact of a man's murdering another is a plain proof that he has no moral sense, and has become simply a brute animal. Our duty is to punish not to amend, and to say to the murderer, 'If you can be amended, God will amend you, and so have mercy on your soul. God must amend you, if you are to be amended. If God cannot amend you, we cannot. If God will not amend you, certainly we cannot force him to do so, if we kept you alive for a thousand years.' That would seem reasonable, as well as reverent and faithful to God. But men nowadays fancy that they love their fellow creatures far better than God loves them, and can deal far more wisely and lovingly with them than God is willing to deal. Of these objections I take little heed. I look on them as merely loose cant, which does not quite understand the meaning of its own words, and I trust to sound, hard, English commonsense to put them aside.

But there is another objection to capital punishment, which we must deal with much more respectfully and tenderly; for it is made by certain good people, people whom we must honour, though we differ from them, for no set of people have done more (according to their numbers) for education, for active charity, and for benevolence, and for peace and good will among the nations of the earth. And they say, you must not take the life of a murderer, just because he is made in God's image. Well, I should have thought that God himself was the best judge of that. That, if God truly said that man was made in his image, and said, moreover, as it were at the same moment, that, therefore, whoso sheds man's blood, by man shall his blood be shed – our duty was to trust God, to obey God, and to do our duty against the murderer, however painful to our feelings it might be. But I believe these good people make their mistake from forgetting this; that if the murderer be made in God's image and likeness, so is the man whom he murders; and so also is the jury who convict him, the judge who condemns him, and the nation (the society of men) for whom they act.

And this, my dear friends, brings us to the very root of the meaning of law. Man has sense to make laws (which animals cannot do), just because he is made in the likeness of God, and has the sense of right and wrong. Man has the right to enforce laws, to see right done and wrong punished, just because he is made in the likeness of God. The laws of a country, as far as they are just and righteous, are the copy of what the men of that country have found out about right and wrong, and about how much right they can get done, and how much wrong punished. So, just as the men of a country are (in spite of all their sins) made in the likeness of God, so the laws of a country (in spite of all their defects) are a copy of God's will, as to what men should or should not do. And that, and no other, is the true reason why the judge or magistrate has authority over either property, liberty, or life. He is God's servant, the servant of Christ, who is King of this land and of all lands, and of all governments, and all kings and rulers of the earth. He sits there in God's name, to see God's will done, as far as poor fallible human beings can get it done. And, because he is, not merely as a man, but, by his special authority, in the likeness of God, who has power over life and death, therefore he also, as far as his authority goes, has power over life and death. That is my opinion, and that was the opinion of St Paul. For what does he say – and say not (remember always) of Christian magistrates in a Christian country, but actually of heathen Roman magistrates? 'Let every soul be subject unto the higher powers. For there is no power but of God: the powers that be are ordained of God. Whosoever therefore resisteth the power, resisteth the ordinance of God: and they that resist shall receive to themselves damnation.' Thus spoke out the tenderest-hearted, most Christ-like human being, perhaps, who ever trod this earth, who, in his intense longing to save sinners, endured a life of misery and danger, and finished it by martyrdom. But there was no sentimentality, no soft indulgence in him. He knew right from wrong; commonsense from cant; duty from public opinion; and divine charity from the mere cowardly dislike of witnessing pain, not so much because it pains the person punished, as because it pains the spectator. He knew that Christ was King of kings, and what Christ's kingdom was like. He had discovered the divine and wonderful order of men and angels. He saw that one part of that order was: 'the soul that sinneth, it shall die'.

But some say that capital punishment is inconsistent with the mild religion of Christ – the religion of mercy and love. 'The mild religion of Christ!' Do these men know of whom they talk? Do they know that, if the Bible be true, the God who said, 'Whoso sheddeth man's blood, by man shall his blood be shed', is the very same Being, the very same God, who was born of the Virgin Mary, crucified under Pontius Pilate – the very same Christ who took little children up in his arms and blessed them, the very same Word of God, too, of whom it is written, that out of his mouth goeth a two-edged sword, that he may smite the nations, and he shall rule them with a rod of iron, and he treadeth the wine press of the fierceness and wrath of Almighty God? These are awful words, but, my dear friends, I can only ask you if you think them too awful to be true?

32

EDWARD BOUVERIE PUSEY (1800–1882)

EDWARD PUSEY was born at the family seat of Pusey in Berkshire. After he had graduated at Oxford he spent two years at Göttingen studying the new developments in German Biblical Theology. In 1828 he was appointed Professor of Hebrew in the University of Oxford and Canon of Christ Church, and he held these offices to the end of his life. He became one of the foremost Tractarians and leader of the movement after J. H. Newman had joined the Church of Rome. He was a centre of theological controversy over such matters as the Real Presence of Christ in the Eucharist, auricular confession, and the use of the Athanasian Creed. In his early days Pusey was a liberal but later became resistant to movements of reform. He regarded poverty as a spiritual condition and, although he encouraged his followers to serve the Church in places where poverty was greatest, he gave them no insight into its causes and possible remedies. His preaching was very influential, although he possessed neither the voice nor the style of the orator, nor the brilliancy and lucidity of the popular preacher. The characteristics of his sermons were their earnestness, their spirituality and their practical nature.

LIII

From a sermon entitled 'The Value of Almsgiving in the Sight of God' preached between 1859 and 1872 on the text: ' The Lord hath made all things for himself: yea, even the wicked in the day of evil' *(Prov. xvi, 4). Ruthless economic competition exploits the poor; God did not create men for this, but made rich and poor for each other's benefit. The rich should offer the superfluity of their wealth to the poor. This sermon illustrates the Tractarians' lack of social concern.*

What is that almsgiving which has such omnipotence with God, which outweighs the justice of the All-Just, and changes the sentence of the Unchangeable? And (which is the aweful side of this) what is that mercy, which if we have not, we 'shall have judgement without mercy'? This question, whereon hangs our eternity, is of the more moment now, because, while in other days almsgiving has been neglected, to ours it has been reserved, in direct contradiction of God's word, to think that charity is needless, nay that it is pernicious. Selfishness is to be our charity. We are to expend on ourselves, forsooth, in order to find employment for the poor. Then, the model of Christian charity would be that rich man of the Gospel, whom our Lord selects for condemnation, he who was clothed in purple and fine linen, and fared sumptuously every day. Doubtless he encouraged the manufactures of Tyre and Sidon, and the weavers of Palestine, while he bound not up the sores of Lazarus; foreign commerce and domestic labour were promoted by the luxuries of his table and the rich ointment for his guests, while he fed not Lazarus with the crumbs which fell from it, nor poured oil into his wounds. Lazarus, according to this philosophy, might have laboured, or might have been supported by those who laboured for the rich man's luxuries. If he were uncared for, it was that there were not Dives enough to give employment to the poor. Miserable, flimsy, transparent hypocrisy! Were the employment of the poor our end, would they be less employed in manufacturing comforts for themselves, than in weaving luxuries for us? Are the poor less employed in building hospitals for their sick or convalescent, almshouses for their aged, homes for their orphans, schools for their children, churches, wherein they might worship God, than in labouring on what is to trick out the houses, or deck the tables or the persons of the rich? Heartless anti-Christian hypocrisy! A reckless, fraudful, competition, whose aim is to cheapen every luxury and vanity, in order that those at ease may spend on fresh accumulated luxuries and vanities what they withhold from the poor, lowers the price of the things which we crave for, by paring down the wages of the poor. The clothing of those at ease is often moistened by the tears of the poor, as they are worn down by the toil which supplies not bread for their children; it is dyed with the blood of that fearfully increasing class, redeemed together with us by the wasted blood of

Christ, who eke out by sin and self-profanation the scanty wages, which alone our love of luxuries and self-indulgence will spare to them; and then Christians are to hold themselves acquitted of their debt to their Redeemer in the persons of his poor; they are to be held to have given him meat and drink, to have clothed him, to have visited him, in these whom he has chosen as his representatives, of whom they never thought, except as provided for enough by their luxuries, into whose dwellings they sicken and loathe to enter!

They speak thus idly of misery who never saw it. Men, who had the hearts of men, could not penetrate into the courts and alleys of our large towns, or chambers poisoned by death or disease, where the voice of mercy was never heard, where, as in hell, no drop of mercy ever fell into their cup of wretchedness, and, in the face of that ghastly truth, dare to say that human misery is the fruit of human, nay rather, divine charity. We have had well-nigh no calamity, but an all-devouring luxury; the visitations of God have rather diminished distress. Whence then, on this theory, all this festering, thronged, accumulated misery?

No, unseared as you still are, you cannot think, my sons, that God, who, in his providence, constituted this variety of ranks and conditions, ordered all, by a narrow favouritism, for the self-pleasing of a few. You cannot think that he, who makes his unintelligent creation itself a picture of the mutual dependence and mutual supply of wants, uniting in one whole, by a wonderful harmony, things seemingly the most discordant and the most unconnected; knitting together in one the offices of all; maintaining in life everything which lives through the involuntary ministration of other created things, and, by its life or death, ministering to the life of others; you cannot think that he would have less of harmony in his intelligent creation, or has constituted you lords of all which, in his providence, he has allowed to pass into your hands, with no end save of self-enjoyment. He who made all things one over against another, made rich and poor for each others' benefit; nay, by how much more 'it is more blessed to give than to receive', the duty of almsgiving is more blessed to us than to them. All which we have is God's; he calls it ours, that we may have the dear happiness of giving it to him. The poor are more necessary to *us*, than we to them. We are necessary to them for their bodies; they are necessary to us for our souls. God has constituted the rich as the representatives, the substitutes, the cooperators with his providence, the agents and depositories and channels of his bounties to the poor; the witnesses to them of his unseen benevolence; the multipliers of their thanksgiving; their protectors against the worst temptations to crime for the relief of their indigence. The poor he has constituted the visible representatives to the rich of his Only Begotten Son, who, 'being rich', for us men and for our salvation, 'became poor'; who, in *their* earthly lot, exalted our human nature to the union with his divine, gave to it its true surpassing dignity, and now vouchsafes to unite to himself all human miseries, except sin, dignifying each by its relation to himself, and, in the poor, accepting as done to himself what is done to them. Their hands are to us the hands of Christ; the poor stretcheth out his hand; what we give, Christ receives; in giving to them, we give to ourselves; we give them temporal things, we receive, through them, eternal; we receive rather than give. For we give what we must soon part with; we receive, according to our condition in God's sight, his favour, in relation to our needs. If we are still out of God's grace and in danger of hell-fire, we receive grace to repent; if we be in God's grace, we receive 'grace upon grace', increased union with God here, increased light, deepened love, enlarged capacity of bliss, increased stores of everlasting glory. 'I remember not,' says St Jerome, 'that I ever read of one who died an evil death, who had willingly practised deeds of charity; for he hath many intercessors, and it is impossible that the prayers of many should not be heard.' Yea! He, our all-availing Intercessor himself receives our gifts, himself intercedes for us, himself prepares us for the everlasting habitations, in that unspeakable glory which, as now, he ascended to prepare for us with himself.

But then again (and the answer concerns our everlasting doom) where is the almsgiving which our God, our Redeemer, condescends to solicit of our hands, which he has so blended with his own redeeming love, to which he has promised an entrance into his own joy? Those who have distinguished most carefully, have laid down, that what, in a large construction, we *need*, is alone ours; 'our superfluities are the necessaries of the poor'. God, who knows the hearts of the rich, leaves us what we need for our health, our well-being, nay, our station in society and the good condition of those, his and our children, whom he has given us. He who has ordered this manifold variety of ranks to serve to his glory and to elicit a rich harmony of combined graces and thanksgiving to himself, the all-bounteous Giver of all, does not call on us to resign what he has lent us, if we wish to retain it. The substance he allows us to transmit, as we received it. But of that yearly increase, which his continual providence maintains to us, he always reserved a portion, whereby we should honour him as our Liege-Lord, and own ourselves but his tenants at his will. . .

I know not which gives the more terrifying view of the multiplicity of the luxuries of this day, the exceeding promises annexed by God's word and pronounced by our Judge on love for his poor, or the terrible woe pronounced by that same Judge on its neglect.

The punishment on its neglect witnesses how essential it is to our salvation; the largeness of God's promises on its fulfilment implies a largeness of bountifulness in those who are to win those promises and that love, beyond what we see anywhere, except perhaps among the poor themselves. Among the rich and those who dwell at ease, where is it ? The squalid misery of hundreds of thousands in our metropolis, the motherless children who take refuge from want in sin which is destructive of soul and body, the sick, unvisited and perishing slowly in their want, echo, through many a mile of forsaken human misery, 'where ?' Meanwhile, confessedly, whatever may, in this last half-century, have been amended, luxuries have, in every rank which can have them, largely increased, so that we seem to have two classes only, the children of luxury and the children of penury . . .

You do not see the suffering poor. Our modern refinement will not bear the sight of Lazarus, nor allow him to lie at the gate of the rich, to elicit the mercy of the merciful, or to receive the charity of our dogs. We remove out of sight the misery, which would be offensive to our delicacy, and which we will not make sacrifices to relieve. We proscribe mendicity: we cannot proscribe misery. The law can make it a crime to ask alms in the name of Jesus. It cannot do away with the presence of Jesus. Now too Jesus has to be sought, in order to be found. The deepest misery is the most retiring. To suffer, like our Lord, overlooked, despised, neglected of men, but precious in his sight, is most like to the earthly lot of the Redeemer of us all.

Whited sepulchres are the streets of our cities. They are beautiful outwardly, but within, but a few yards from all that pomp, luxury, and self-indulgence, which sweep unheeding by, Christ, as he himself says, lies, an hungered, athirst, naked, sick, unvisited: and in what unmitigated festering misery are the members of Christ! You would not knowingly deck your walls with pictures, while man, the image of God and the representative of Christ, you clothe not; you would not knowingly multiply delicacies upon yourselves, while men, like yourselves, members of Christ, and Christ in them, is an hungered. God looks graciously on each age; he allows you your enjoyments, and, in moderation, your amusements. He will account these things as the natural demands of your condition in life. But he does not allow you superfluities, to supply your passions, to enervate yourselves, to nourish the life of the senses, to dull the fineness of intellect, to strengthen self-indulgence, to weaken self-control, to injure your moral energy, to unfit you for every office of devoted self-denying duty, everything by which you can benefit humanity or serve your God. Not things lawful, but things unlawful, either in themselves or in their excess, dry up charity, because they dry up the heart. You cannot here know the poor, but you can know of those who know every poor man. The cry of the poor reacheth the ear of God. Let them not cry against you, 'Ours is it, which ye waste; what ye expend idly is mercilessly rent from us.' Woe to that man, whom the poor shall implead at the Judgement-seat of Christ. Woe to him, for whom they shall not plead. Mercy is the only companion of the departed. Blessed, eternally blessed we, if, when our souls were justly forfeited to the strict justice of God, Mercy accompany us to the eternal throne, Mercy plead our cause with the All-merciful, Mercy persuade our Judge to have mercy on us, and he, arrayed in the robe wherewith we have here clothed his poor, say to us those words of mercy, 'Inasmuch as ye have done it unto one of the least of these my brethren, ye have done it unto me.'

33

JOSEPH BARBER LIGHTFOOT (1828–89)

JOSEPH BARBER LIGHTFOOT was born in Liverpool and was ordained in 1854. He was a classical and Biblical scholar, and, after becoming Canon of St Paul's in 1871, was appointed Lady Margaret Professor of Divinity at Cambridge in 1875. He was one of the most outstanding Biblical scholars of his age and his work on the Bible and on the Early Fathers has stood the test of time. In 1879, after some reluctance, he accepted the See of Durham, where he proved to be an able pastor and a thorough administrator. He concerned himself with the social problems of his diocese and was popular with the workers.

LIV

From a sermon entitled 'The Hearing Ear and the Seeing Eye', preached at St James, Piccadilly, Second Sunday after Easter, 1873, on the text: 'The hearing ear, and the seeing eye, the Lord hath made even both of them' (*Prov. xx, 12*). *An interesting comment on the state of the nineteenth-century theatre as seen through the eyes of an Anglican clergyman.*

To purify, and not to stimulate at any cost – this, according to Aristotle, is the proper function of scenic representation. I desire no other definition. I make no larger demand. Let it be the aim of the tragic poet to purify one set of emotions, such as anger, fear, pity, by kindred representations of pathos and suffering; of the comic poet to purify another set – love, mirth, geniality and the like – by kindliness, by humour, if need be, by satire and by ridicule, but at all events to *purify*. This was the tendency of the English stage in the age of its greatest triumphs and in the person of its noblest dramatists, despite occasional coarsenesses of expression, the more to be deplored as blots on a fair picture. But can this definition be applied with any truth to the recent drama of this country? I am glad to think that there are some noble exceptions, of which this may indeed be said. All honour to those dramatic writers and those stage managers who have disdained to court popularity by flattering a vicious public taste. But as a rule, is purification either the aim or the tendency of the English stage at this moment? If so, how comes it that the clergyman is almost barred entrance into a theatre by general consent, and even worldly men would sneer if he should appear frequently within its walls? How comes it that the plots and the dialogue of pieces which are witnessed without a blush by thousands cannot be alluded to in the family circle, except under the disguise of some delicate euphemism or some carefully guarded periphrasis?

Test the present tendency of the theatre by this standard, and what results will the examination yield? Shall we say that it enlists all the activities of the mind and all the sympathies of the heart on the side of purity and honour and virtue? Shall we say that it shows a scrupulous respect for the chastity of growing youth and the fidelity of wedded life, holding up every violation of the one and every breach of the other to scorn, as mean and degrading; that it carefully abstains from inflaming any corrupt passion by a gesture or a look or a word suggestive of evil; that it is scrupulously modest in its appointments, its dresses, its movements; that its mirth and its repartee are not barbed with any taint of poison which will rankle and fester in the imagination; and that thus, while it attracts and amuses, it also chastens and elevates, doing its noble work all the more effectually because it teaches without seeming to teach, because it demands no effort, which is not also a delight, in the spectators?

Are these its moral effects? And do its intellectual influences correspond to these? Does it give a healthy tone to the mental faculties? Does it abhor all mean artifices, and aim at producing its effects by imagination, by humour, by careful construction of plots, by truthful delineation of character? Does it avoid mere sensationalism, striking right home to the mind, rather than dazzling the eye and fascinating the ear? Does it eschew mere burlesque, scorning to purchase an easy popularity by caricaturing any illustrious name or any important movement or any great work of genius, and thus by a false association of ideas debasing and vitiating the public taste? For what are sensationalism and burlesque but different kinds of mental intoxication, producing a delirious sense of excitement for the moment, but ending in the degradation and wreck of the faculties, where each fresh gratification begets a fresh craving, till the intellectual constitution is shattered by excessive indulgence in stimulants? . . .

There is perhaps little likelihood of a return to the coarseness of the past. But may not a still greater peril to the morals of England lurk under the insidious refinement which disguises its corrupt tendencies in graceful images, which trades on the fact that our noblest impulses lie very close to our basest passions, and thus leads astray by working on the amiable sensibilities of the heart? Mere coarseness carries with it its own antidote, for it repels all but vulgar and debased natures by its loathsomeness. It is the fatal association that blends the good with the evil, that makes vice palatable by culture and refinement, from which we have most to dread.

We have not fallen so low yet. Thank God, it is true. But in what direction are we moving? This is the really momentous question. Are we on an incline? For, if so, unless we arrest ourselves at once by a stern effort, then by an inevitable law of forces moral as well as physical, the descent will be accelerated, and the precipitation must come at last. I wish I could think it possible to answer this question in more than one way. But can any man who calmly reviews the last quarter of a century doubt that during this period a poisonous taint has been spreading through literature and society? The infection may have been communicated in the first instance from abroad; but it is naturalized, or almost naturalized, among us now. The degradation of the stage is only one token of a much more general corruption. The popular literature – the novels and poetry – the newspaper reports, even the shop-windows, tell the same tale. Subjects are discussed, and sights are exhibited, which would not have been tolerated a few years ago. And we, as patriots, look idly on, discussing the material defences of our country, as though no moral danger threatened her integrity; we, as Christians, fold our arms, as though we should never be called to account for any of these things, as though it were a light matter in ourselves or others to abuse the faculties and the senses which God has given us, forgetting the responsibility inculcated in the wise man's saying, 'The hearing ear, and the seeing eye, the Lord hath made even both of them.'

And yet what interests should appear more momentous either to the patriot or to the Christian than the purity of his country's literature? A bad law may be rescinded, a vicious institution may be abolished; but a corrupt work of genius is there, there for ever. Can there be any lesson more grave or more deeply pathetic than the confession of that epilogue in which the father of English poetry, at the close of his life, glancing back on the creations of his literary genius, retracts all that is tainted with grossness and levity, avowing his contrition and asking forgiveness through the mercy of Christ? And again; will not all right-minded men echo the tribute of respect which our great living poet has paid to his great predecessor, and thankfully acknowledge that the laureate wreath did indeed descend upon him greener from the brows of one who uttered nothing base? Who does not regret, even in Shakespeare, the occasional coarseness, possibly not his own, which blots the pages of dramas otherwise essentially pure and healthy and noble in their moral tone?

For indeed the responsibilities of literary genius are enormous, as the consequences are incalculable. Can any anguish be imagined more bitter to the awakened conscience of a penitent than the memory of some one human soul polluted, degraded, ruined by his means? To such a one any accumulation of suffering will seem a small price to pay for redeeming the past, if only he could bear all the burden himself, if only the past were not irredeemable. Such remorse might well drag down a spirit from on high. And yet what is one isolated case of degradation through personal companionship, compared with the noxious influence of a perverted literary genius, which pervades all classes and extends to all time? Who is so hardened that he would dare to face such a retrospect, if only for a moment he were gifted with a seraph's vision, and could see spread out before him the infinite, intricate consequences of his work in all their manifold and hideous forms? Who would not hold it better far to have lived obscure and died forgotten, than thus to have laid a whole world at his feet, dazzled with the brilliancy of his genius, and then, when the intoxication of popularity has passed away, then, when it is too late, to awaken to the awful reality ?

But, if the purity of our literature is threatened, the fault cannot be all on one side. There is a law of supply and demand in literature as well as in commerce. A corrupt drama is the reflection of a corrupt age. The author gives what the audience requires. Each acts and reacts upon the other, either debasing or elevating, as the tendency may be. The remedy therefore is in the hands of the people of England, more especially of the influential and cultivated classes of England.

34

HENRY PARRY LIDDON (1829–90)

HENRY PARRY LIDDON was born in Hampshire and after his ordination in 1852 he became curate of Wantage. He never lost the profound sympathy with the poor which his life as a curate aroused. He was a theologian and a Tractarian in his religious outlook, having been profoundly influenced by E. B. Pusey. He became the first Vice-Principal of Cuddesdon Theological College when it was founded in 1854. Five years later he was appointed Vice-Principal of St Edmund's Hall, Oxford. In 1864 he was given a Prebend at Salisbury. Finally, in 1870, he became Dean Ireland Professor of Exegesis at Oxford and Canon of St Paul's. His powerful preaching attracted large congregations of all ranks and conditions. His sermons, which were well constructed, full of intellectual depth and power, were characterized by passionate fervour and inordinate length, some taking no less than eighty minutes to preach.

LV

From a sermon entitled 'The Gospel and the Poor', preached on Whit Sunday 9 June 1876, on the text: 'The Spirit of the Lord is upon me, because he hath anointed me to preach the gospel to the poor; he hath sent me to heal the brokenhearted, to preach deliverance to the captives, the recovering of sight to the blind, to set at liberty them that are bruised' (*Luke iv, 18*). *The effect which poverty has on men and women.*

A first effect of poverty . . . is the confiscation of a poor man's best time and thought, from sheer necessity, to the task of providing food and clothing for himself and his family. Many men who are far from being poor have to work for a livelihood. But a man can work hard, if he can at will command a holiday. A man can work hard, if his work is also felt to be a source of refinement, of instruction, of discipline, of recreation; if it enlightens his mind, if it purifies his affections. As a rule, a poor man's work is not of this description: it is, from all points of view save that of the wages it yields, unremunerative, because it is more or less mechanical. It cannot be interrupted unless from sheer necessity; the poor man cannot afford to lose a day's wages, and therefore, though feeling depressed or ill, he cannot forego a day's work. As he works he is not thinking of his place in the moral universe, although he is at least capable of true nobility as is any other human being; he is thinking of the next meal, of the next pay-day, of the next rent-day. The next rent-day is probably his most distant horizon. Rarely can he aspire to win an independence, and so to purchase exemption from the necessity which is laid upon him of supporting existence by incessant toil. Who does not see how this liability must clog and depress the human spirit; how it chokes up the avenues through which even natural light and heat penetrate within the understanding and the heart? Some room must be made for religion amidst the thoughts and occupations of life before it can inspire or control them; and in the case of the poor man, who has to work hard for his daily bread, and to whom all mental effort is very serious, the difficulty of even getting a hearing for the good tidings which Christ our Lord has brought to earth from heaven is often great indeed.

Another effect of poverty is that it often blights those domestic scenes of happiness which prepare the way of religion in the soul. In the natural course of things, kindliness, courtesy, refinement, are the products of home life; the home is the centre and the manufactory of these natural graces. It is to his family that a man escapes when his day's toil is over. At home he forgets the passions and the rivalries, be they great or small, of his public life, whatever its sphere or scale of importance; at home the finer side of human nature has a chance of growing, as being sure of its nutriment and its welcome. At home a man knows, if nowhere else, what it is to be interpreted generously, to be trusted, to be loved; here he finds a field for the play of those affections in the exercise of which earthly happiness mainly consists. But for this two things are needed; competency and order. And how often are these wanting in the households of the poor! Many of us must have visited cabins in which a numerous family inhabits a single room; in which the young, the aged, the sick, the hale, the parents and children, herd together by day and by night; in which the mother, who should be a presiding genius of kindliness and of cleanliness, is the representative of ill-humour and of dirt; in which all that protects ordinary intercourse against coarseness, and ordinary tempers against irritation, and average health against disease, and modest efforts to improve against brutal interference, is too often absent; in which all is so crowded that there is no room for delicacy, for reserve, for the charities, for the properties of common life. Certainly –

> Haud facile emergunt, quorum virtutibus obstat
> Res angusta domi.

Worse off, it has been truly said, may be the poor man, whom civilization has made what he is, than was his savage ancestor; for worse his lot who lives in the back lane of a great city, where pure air, and light, and room, and cleanliness are denied him, than that of the man of another time, who roamed in the forest beneath the sky of heaven, and who could at least command, amid whatever disadvantages, the requisites for healthy animal existence, and for the unstinted play of pure affections. Yes! A comfortless home is often even more fatal to character than to health. It chills the affections; it sours the temper; it ends by doing more. Nothing is more common than to hear severe language applied to the poor man's habit of spending his evenings at the public house. But who of us, when by chance walking at night through the neglected quarters of a great town, has observed how, at more or less frequent intervals, the monotony of dreariness and squalor is broken by the brilliant lights and the ostentatious hospitalities of these establishments, can wonder that the poor man is attracted by the contrast which they present to all that characterizes his home, and that, yielding to their fatal welcome, he essays to drown in an hour of brute half-consciousness the memory of the griefs that too sorely embitter his domestic life? It is the road to ruin, without a doubt. But it is not for those of us who have never felt even the shadow of the troubles which are eating out his heart to cast a stone at him.

The worst result of poverty is that it often destroys self-respect. Self-respect is a different thing, as it is needless to add, from the most venial form of self-complacency. The forfeiture of self-respect does not necessarily take place when a poor man becomes a pensioner on the bounty of others. A man who receives from his fellow-man that assistance which, if their circumstances were reversed, he would gladly bestow, undergoes no moral damage in consequence; he is merely a party to a transaction which effects on a small scale an equitable redistribution of property. If, indeed, he prefers dependence to exertion: if, forgetful of the intrinsic nobleness of work, he attempts to purchase leisure by the servilities of beggary, then, beyond doubt, his manhood is impaired, and he is in a fair way to be and to do much that is fatal to the respect which a good man should entertain for the sanctities of his life. But of itself, dependence does not degrade. Children are not the worse for depending on their parents; servants are not injured by the kindness of their employers; tenants are not humiliated by the considerate liberality of the landlord; nor do we any of us suffer because we are all indebted for all that we are and have to the Eternal Bounty, and he knows us too well, and has too good a care of us, to have ordered anything really inconsistent with our true well-being. No, his dependence does not threaten the poor man's self-respect; but, especially in large centres of life, he is peculiarly exposed to the ravages of a passion which, if yielded to, degrades and brands the soul with a fatal certainty. Certainly, envy is no monopoly of the poor; it makes itself felt in all sections of society. . . . From their narrow and squalid homes they go abroad to gaze on the mansions of the great and wealthy; at their scanty meals they discuss the splendid banquets which can command every luxury but appetite; as they pursue their daily toil, they see around them men of their own race and age to whom life is made so easy as to become little less than a protracted weariness. Of those unchanging laws which will always create great inequalities in the circumstances of human lives they know little or nothing. Why should things be thus? Why should there be these immense contrasts, this unaccountable caprice – for such it must seem – in the distribution of life's prizes and blessings? These are questions which force themselves naturally enough into a poor man's mind; and the bitter thoughts which they breed lead him from time to time to take part in deeds of violence and blood. The outrage in a foreign capital last Sunday afternoon, which sent a thrill of pain and fear through the civilized world, was the product of social theories created by the passion that finds a ready stimulus in the circumstances of the poor.* A writer who has lately sketched with vivid power some of the approaches to the first French Revolution, has analysed generally with a master hand the explosive forces by which was shattered a social fabric that had lasted already for a thousand years. But he has apparently failed to point out how intimately the moral degradation of the men who trampled the old monarchy in the dust of Paris was due to the pent-up energy of a hidden passion, capable almost beyond any other of brutalizing the human soul.

Poverty of course is and means a great deal more than has thus been stated. But at least let us bear in mind that it involves, very commonly, the exhaustion of life by mechanical work, the degradation of character in the home and in the usual expedients to escape from it, and the loss of self-respect, and of all that that loss implies, through the continued, unappeased, ever-increasing envy of the lot of others. Not that poverty has not produced its heroes, who have vanquished its disadvantages with stern determination. We have here to consider, not the splendid exceptions, but the average result. And that result may, within limits, be counteracted by wise philanthropy and by wise laws. When a sufficient number of regular holidays are secured by law, as in bygone ages the Church did secure them by her festivals for the working poor; when the hours of daily labour are kept within reasonable limits; when homes have been provided for the people on any considerable scale in which the first conditions of healthy living shall be insisted on; when it shall have been made fairly possible for every poor man so to better his condition by work as to escape from poverty into comfort; and when education shall have done all that may be done towards furthering this result, legislation and philanthropy will have achieved what may be fairly required of

* Refers to the second attempt to assassinate the Emperor of Germany on Sunday, 2 June 1878.

them. Useful knowledge, practical kindness, and beneficent laws – these are not the Gospel; but, like philosophy, they are, or may be, its handmaids. They may make its task smooth and grateful; they may associate themselves with its victories, or they may prepare its way.

But for more important results a higher force is needed; nothing less than the Christian faith itself. The faith of Christ reverses the disadvantages of poverty with decisive force. It acts upon poverty not from without, but from within; it begins not with legislation, but with hearts and minds; not with circumstances, but with convictions. When this faith is received, it forthwith transfigures the idea of labour: labour is no longer deemed a curse, but a discipline; work of all kinds is sensibly ennobled by being done with and for Jesus Christ; and by this association it acquires the character of a kind of worship. When this faith is received, it sweetens, consecrates, elevates the affections of the husband, of the father, of the child; it sets the physical difficulties of a pauper household at defiance by referring them to the Holy Home of Nazareth; or it lifts the whole conception of human relationships into an atmosphere where the risks to which they are ordinarily exposed have ceased to exist. When this faith is embraced it changes the estimate of different conditions in life; the first become last, and the last first.

35

RICHARD CHURCH (1815–90)

RICHARD CHURCH was born in Lisbon and spent his earlier years in Florence. In 1838 he was elected Fellow of Oriel College, Oxford. He became Rector of Whatley, Somerset, in 1852, and twenty years later, in 1871, he was appointed to the Deanery of St Paul's. He was a Tractarian. His sermons were impressive and often dealt with moral and social questions.

LVI

From 'Pain and Remedy', a sermon preached on behalf of the London Dispensary*, at St Anne and St Agnes, with St John Zachary, Gresham Street, London, 1873, on the text: 'Jesus went about all Galilee, teaching in their synagogues, and preaching the gospel of the kingdom, and healing all manner of sickness and all manner of disease among the people' *(Matt. iv, 23). A description of the human suffering which exists beneath the surface of opulence and wealth; the duty of Christians to relieve it.*

Pain is for men to *bear*, in themselves; it is for them to *relieve*, in others. It is in this latter view that it appeals to us today. There stands before us this strange, appalling fact of our nature and condition – almost more appalling to men in health than to men themselves in suffering – that multitudes of our fellow-creatures round about us are, intermittently or continuously, languishing or agonizing in disease or pain. We see them not. We do not hear their groans and cries. Their pale faces, their hopeless eyes, their writhing forms, are hidden from us – hidden in dark alleys, and squalid courts, and mean and wretched lodgings. Yet there they are. Behind this screen of opulence and busy life, *there* they are. It does not require an effort of faith or imagination to realize all the

* Founded 1777.

misery which is going on not so far off while we are here: it only requires us to open our minds to what we know to be certain; it only needs to make leisure in our souls, to attend and to think of what there is no doubt about. This great mass of suffering and pain cries to us for help: all the more solemnly that the appeal is a silent one, and we are not allowed to see the suffering which yet we know exists. It makes its mute entreaty for relief. And it is not as if the entreaty were an idle one. It is as certain that there are remedies to be had, as it is certain that pain exists. And the power of opening these remedies to this suffering, God has placed, my brethren, *just* as we are willing to use it, in our hands.

I ask you, then, on behalf of all the pain and suffering which must be in a great city, to use this power. I ask you to do what you can to cooperate with an institution which exists to minister relief and healing to the numbers who could not otherwise obtain it. There is in this matter, between different classes of men, a tremendous equality and a tremendous inequality. The equality is that in the pangs and horrors of disease all of us are on a level. In the dreadful scale of human suffering – from its most homely to its severest forms, from a cold or a toothache or a headache to those extreme forms of torment which it makes us shudder even to think of; in those strange visitations of it which have a kind of tragic interest about them and are thought worthy of special record and special pity, and in its commonplace vulgar shapes, which, when we are not suffering ourselves, we are apt to smile at – in this liability to every kind of pain, in feeling its bitterness when it comes, all of us, the highest and the lowest, the richest and the meanest of us, are all equal. The man on whom an empire depends, the man whose name written on a bit of paper can dispose of millions, can decide on the peace of the world and the happiness of nations and the course of history, is as much open to pain in its direst form, is its subject and perhaps its victim, is as absolutely at its mercy, as the weakest and most miserable of his fellow-men. Here all are equal. But when we think of what may be done to ease pain, to arrest disease, to help the sufferers to bear it, oh, brethren and fellow-men, is it not almost terrible to think of the inequalities and contrasts in men's lot? Two men are racked with pain: the one with everything round him which can give the chance of even a moment's relief; with everything that money can buy, or skill devise, or tender affection minister; with everything to amuse him, to soothe him, to console him: the other, starved, and cold, and destitute, with all his power of earning stopped, with all his small possessions, all his small comforts gradually slipping away and disappearing; a prisoner – perhaps a solitary prisoner – through dreary days and sleepless nights, in a close and unwholesome garret. Two young girls are touched by the hand of consumption; for one of them there is a respite, perhaps a cure: she has the chance of a change of scene and climate, of softer air, of the reviving influences of Southern warmth and brightness: the other – she cannot be moved – no one can afford to move her, though that alone can save her – not even to an English hospital; she must stay where she is, and in the cold and damp, the raw mornings and chilly nights she cannot escape from, gasp out her life. These are the inequalities under which men have to meet pain.

Shall we not, we whom God has prospered and perhaps enriched, do what we can to make these inequalities at least a *little* less ? Shall we not, in the name of our great Master, who has made us all fellows in suffering, but put into the hands of some of us the remedies which make suffering tolerable, do what we can to cooperate with his purpose ? *One* was once on earth who came from God, and whom we now recognize as the example and hope of humankind. To him no form of human suffering appealed in vain. Miracle after miracle in his wondrous history tells of his compassion and pity for sickness and pain. To express that never-failing sympathy it is said of him, 'Himself took our infirmities, and bare our sicknesses.' The Lord and Master of pain, quelling it in a moment with his touch, yet for our sakes he made himself subject to it. His fellowship with us would not be complete unless he shared the sufferings he came to cure. He calmed the fever, and cleansed the leprosy, and gave power to the palsied, and sight to the blind, and speech and hearing to the dumb; and then, for us men and for our salvation, he was in agony in the garden, he suffered, and was crucified, and died.

36

WILLIAM THOMSON (1819–90)

WILLIAM THOMSON was born at Whitehaven and, after being Provost of Queen's College, Oxford, (1855), he was consecrated Bishop of Gloucester and Bristol in 1861. Within ten months, however, he was appointed Archbishop of York, where he remained for twenty-eight years. Thomson took a keen interest in social, economic and political questions and was appreciated and trusted by working men. He sought to improve the social conditions of the poor and devoted himself to such problems as sanitary conditions and over-crowding, fever hospitals and unemployment. 'He was among the first of the leaders of the Church,' said the *Hull and Yorkshire Times* (27 December 1890), 'to recognize that the health question is also a momentous moral question.'

LVII

From a sermon entitled 'She is a Sinner', preached at St James, Piccadilly, for the 'St James Home', an institution 'for fallen women of the non-educated class' (no date), on the text: 'Now when the Pharisee which had bidden him saw it, he spake within himself, saying, This man, if he were a prophet, would have known who and what manner of woman this is that toucheth him: for she is a sinner' (Luke vii, 39). *Adultery is as much due to social conditions as to moral weakness: long hours of work for a meagre pittance; callousness in workhouses; the uncharitable attitude of society towards 'the fallen woman'.*

It may be said that society is not answerable for the poverty which is the most frequent cause of sin; I will not dispute this wide question, but whether we have taken every pains to teach poor people to guard against thoughtless habits, whether we have seen that the labour we employ is fairly remunerated, so that none who work for us shall have the dread alternative offered them of sinning or starving; whether the lawful claims of the poor to a maintenance are always fairly met, are questions upon which, to say the least, two opinions might be held. But all that I now argue for is, that if the operation of social rules has in any measure caused sin, we that make and uphold social rules should deal considerately with the sinner. Even if it be an imperfection, and not an inherent wickedness in our social arrangements, that causes them to generate sin, we must not be too ready to visit on the erring, guilt which is only their own in part, guilt which they groan under, and perhaps would fain be delivered from. Imagine a friendless woman in this great city, working from the dawn of one day till the strokes of midnight announced the next, to earn at the week's end a sum that might almost be told in pence; think of the time when, after bearing up long against hunger and weakness, hope gave way, and the fruitless industry was abandoned; think of the misery endured by a mind tutored for better things in eating the bread of sin, whilst it was known that the wages of sin is death. Follow her as she rushes forth some inclement night, clutching to her side her child, the one humanizing influence left to her by a merciful God, determined to turn from sin, and hide herself from besetting temptations in no better sanctuary than a workhouse. See her sink down in the snow at a door, her child's feet frozen to her side, and she fainting from starvation. And when the good Samaritan that lives there has opened the door, and set food before her, and rubbed back the life into the numbed limbs, she shall go on her way and seek entrance at the workhouse door, which would be to her as the outer porch of the gates of heaven, for sin would be shut out behind her; and she shall be rejected, no doubt by rule, for some formality which has not been complied with; and she shall fall back again into the old life of guilt, shame, and sorrow. And the well-dressed passer-by, wearing on his back the labour of her fingers, paid for at the rate of threepence for nineteen continuous hours, avoids her path, and whispers 'She is a sinner.' Did I say *imagine?* It is a true tale, to which not even one particular has been added. She, indeed, escaped at last, for great is the mercy and love of God; but others have suffered and not escaped. And when we are told that not in one case, but in hundreds, this tragedy is being acted over and over again – the incident different, the catastrophe the same – we must, if we are honest, change the Pharisaic formula,

'She is a sinner', for one that is more humane. 'She is a great sufferer, sick in soul; may the Lord take her to the arms of his mercy'!

Now let us give due weight to the other fact, that there is hardly any escape for those who have once entered the path of sin. Where should a woman like this one of my text betake herself for a shelter, when she tastes the bitterness of her degradation, and longs eagerly to escape from it? The door of her home is often shut against her; the home affections that once refreshed her flow no longer towards her. Unblemished character is an indispensable condition for almost any safe employment; and the most sincere and heartfelt repentance would not stand instead of it. We seem to bid her fill up the measure of her sin; we will not help her to escape. '*She is a sinner*'; no one will take her into a blameless home to employ her; no one will visit her and give her counsel. The consciousness that she belongs now to a class of outcasts fills her with shame; and the more that feeling exists, the less likely is she to return into the presence of those who might be able to restore her. Thus does one step in sin utterly destroy one whom God created to serve and praise him. God bids the sinner turn from evil ways; and we will give her no chance of turning. Christ came to turn every one of us from his iniquities; and we interpose against one form of sin. He was sent to bind up the broken-hearted, to proclaim liberty to the captives, and the opening of the prison to them that are bound; and who are we that we should neglect a breaking heart and its agonizing cry, and leave captives groaning in a bondage of sin worse than death? There is not perhaps one point upon which the world of professing Christians has more more strongly resisted the Gospel than this. We tend the sick because our Lord has bidden us; and there is not one large town without its hospital. We teach the poor; we build churches for worship; we set up clubs and charitable institutions for physical wants. But very few have been the Houses of Refuge in which a penitent woman may hide her shame, and find, instead of scorn, some portion of that spirit in which our Saviour said of one like her, that came and shed the tears of repentance upon his feet, and wiped them with the hair she had once been vain of, 'Her sins, which are many, are forgiven, for she loved much: but to whom little is forgiven, the same loveth little.'

37

JOHN HENRY NEWMAN (1801–90)

JOHN HENRY NEWMAN was born in the City of London and was elected Fellow of Oriel College, Oxford, in 1822. Six years later he was appointed Vicar of St Mary's, Oxford. He was one of the foremost leaders of the Oxford Movement, and published a number of *Tracts for the Times*. In 1845 he was received into the Roman Church and was afterwards made a cardinal (1879). In politics he was a Tory and was bitterly opposed to the French Revolution. His sermons had a profound influence because of their deep spirituality. They were lucid, vigorous and beautifully composed, displaying both intellectual and emotional power. Their effect was enhanced by his fine delivery.

LVIII

From a sermon entitled 'The World our Enemy' (no date or place), on the text: 'We know that we are of God, and the whole world lieth in wickedness' *(1 John v, 19). The world is the enemy of Christian growth and we should be detached from it.*

By the world, then, is meant this course of things which we see carried on by means of human agency, with all its duties and pursuits. It is not necessarily a sinful system; rather it is framed, as I have said, by God himself, and therefore cannot be otherwise than good. And yet even thus considering it, we are bid not to love the world: even in this sense the world is an enemy of our souls; and for this reason, because the love of it is dangerous to beings circumstanced as we are – things in themselves good being not good to us sinners. And this state of things which we see, fair and excellent in itself, is very likely (for the very reason that it is seen, and because the spiritual and future world is not seen) to seduce our wayward hearts from our true and eternal good. As the traveller on serious business may be tempted to linger, while he gazes on the beauty of the prospect which opens on his way, so this well-ordered and divinely-governed world, with all its blessings of sense and knowledge, may lead us to neglect those interests which will endure when itself has passed away. In truth, it promises more than it can fulfil. The goods of life and the applause of men have their excellence, and, as far as they go, are really good; but they are short-lived. And hence it is that many pursuits in themselves honest and right, are nevertheless to be engaged in with caution, lest they seduce us; and those perhaps with especial caution, which tend to the well-being of men in this life. The sciences, for instance, of good government, of acquiring wealth, of preventing and relieving want, and the like, are for this reason especially dangerous; for fixing, as they do, our exertions on this world as an end, they go far to persuade us that they have no other end; they accustom us to think too much of success in life and temporal prosperity; nay, they may even teach us to be jealous of religion and its institutions, as if these stood in our way, preventing us from doing so much for the wordly interests of mankind as we might wish.

In this sense it is that St Paul contrasts sight and faith. We see this world; we only believe that there is a world of spirits, we do not see it: and inasmuch as sight has more power over us than belief, and the present than the future, so are the occupations and pleasures of this life injurious to our faith. Yet not, I say, in themselves sinful; as the Jewish system was a temporal system, yet divine, so is the system of nature – this world – divine, though temporal. And as the Jews became carnal-minded even by the influence of their divinely-appointed system, and thereby rejected the Saviour of their souls; in like manner, men of the world are hardened by God's own good world, into a rejection of Christ. In neither case through the fault of the things which are seen, whether miraculous or providential, but accidentally, through the fault of the human heart.

But now, secondly, let us proceed to consider the world, not only as dangerous, but as positively sinful, according to the text – 'the whole world lieth in wickedness'. It was created well in all respects, but even before it as yet had fully grown out into its parts, while as yet the elements of human society did but lie hid in the nature and condition of the first man, Adam fell; and thus the world, with all its social ranks, and aims, and pursuits, and pleasures, and prizes, has ever from its birth been sinful. The infection of sin spread through the whole system, so that although the frame-work is good and divine, the spirit and life within it are evil. Thus, for instance, to be in a high station is the gift of God; but the pride and injustice to which it has given scope is from the devil. To be poor and obscure is also the ordinance of God; but the dishonesty and discontent which are often seen in the poor is from Satan. To cherish and protect wife and family is God's appointment; but the love of gain, and the low ambition, which lead many a man to exert himself, are sinful. Accordingly, it is said in the text, 'The world lieth in wickedness', – it is plunged and steeped, as it were, in a flood of sin, not a part of it remaining as God originally created it, not a part pure from the corruptions with which Satan has disfigured it.

Look into the history of the world, and what do you read there? Revolutions and changes without number, kingdoms rising and falling; and when without crime? States are established by God's ordinance, they have their existence in the necessity of man's nature; but when was one ever established, nay, or maintained, without war and bloodshed? Of all natural instincts, what is more powerful than that which forbids us to shed our fellows' blood? We shrink with natural horror from the thought of a murderer; yet not a government has ever been settled, or a state acknowledged by its neighbours, without war and the loss of life; nay, more than this, not content with unjustifiable bloodshed, the guilt of which must lie somewhere, instead of lamenting it as grievous and humiliating evil, the world has chosen to honour the conqueror with its amplest share of admiration. To become a hero in the eyes of the world, it is almost necessary to break the laws of God and man. Thus the deeds of the world are matched by the opinions and principles of the world: it adopts bad doctrine to defend bad practice; it loves darkness because its deeds are evil.

And as the affairs of nations are thus depraved by our corrupt nature, so are all the appointments and gifts of Providence perverted in like manner. What can be more excellent than the vigorous and patient employment of the intellect; yet in the hands of Satan it gives birth to a proud philosophy. When St Paul preached, the wise men of the world, in God's eyes, were but fools, for they had used their powers of mind in the cause of error; their reasonings even led them to be irreligious and immoral; and they despised the doctrine of a resurrection which they neither loved nor believed. And again, all the more refined arts of life have been disgraced by the vicious tastes of those who excelled in them; often they have been consecrated to the service of idolatry; often they have been made the instruments of sensuality and riot. But it would be endless to recount the manifold and complex corruption which man has introduced into the world which God made good; evil has preoccupied the whole of it, and holds fast its conquest. We know, indeed, that the gracious God revealed himself to his sinful creatures very soon after Adam's fall. He showed his will to mankind again and again, and pleaded with them through many ages; till at length his Son was born into this sinful world in the form of man, and taught us how to please him. Still, hitherto the good work has proceeded slowly: such is his pleasure. Evil had the start of good by many days; it filled the world, it holds it: it has the strength of possession, and it has its strength in the human heart; for though we cannot keep from approving what is right in our conscience, yet we love and encourage what is wrong; so that when evil was once set up in the world, it was secured in its seat by the unwillingness with which our hearts relinquish it.

And now I have described what is meant by the sinful world; that is, the world as corrupted by man, the course of human affairs viewed in its connexion with the principles, opinions, and practices which actually direct it. There is no mistaking these; they are evil; and of these it is that St John says, 'If any man love the world, the love of the Father is not in him. For all that is in the world, the lust of the flesh, and the lust of the eyes, and the pride of life, is not of the Father, but is of the world.'

The world then is the enemy of our souls; first, because, however innocent its pleasures, and praiseworthy its pursuits may be, they are likely to engross us, unless we are on our guard: and secondly, because in all its best pleasures, and noblest pursuits, the seeds of sin have been sown; an enemy hath done this; so that it is most difficult to enjoy the good without partaking of the evil also. As an orderly system of various ranks, with various pursuits and their several rewards, it is to be considered not sinful indeed, but dangerous to us. On the other hand, considered in reference to its principles and actual practices, it is really a sinful world. Accordingly, when we are bid in Scripture to shun the world, it is meant that we must be cautious, lest we love what is good in it too well, and lest we love the bad at all.

38

ROBERT WILLIAM DOLLING (1851–1902)

AFTER ORDINATION in 1883 Robert Dolling worked in Stepney and in 1885 became Head of Winchester College Mission, Portsmouth. He was one of a group of slum ritualists and on this score, and because of his views on purgatory, he resigned in 1896. He was instituted Vicar of St Saviour's, Poplar, in 1898. He was active in Labour politics and assisted the Trades Union Movement. 'He was essentially a parish priest, unafraid of public controversy, but chiefly concerned to minister to the needs of the poor around his church.'*

LIX

From a sermon entitled 'Soldiers and Sailors', preached at St Edmund's, Lombard Street, London, in Lent 1894, on the text: 'I sent you to reap that whereon ye bestowed no labour: other men laboured, and ye are entered into their labours' (John iv, 38). One of a course of sermons in Lent organized for business men by the London Branch of the Christian Social Union. The following extract is given because of the picture it presents of conditions in the armed services.

A man is drawn into the ranks of the army on practically false – I say shamefully false – pretence. Nominally he receives a shilling a day and rations.

What are the facts ? Threepence out of every shilling is stopped to supply extra food necessary for his bodily health, whether he will or no.

A halfpenny is compulsorily stopped for washing; thus his shilling becomes eightpence-halfpenny; but these deductions do not stop here: barrack damages, library, hair-cutting, and often-times other compulsory subscriptions, make a still further re-

* Stephen Mayor, *The Churches and the Labour Movement*, Independent Press, 1967, p. 44.

duction, so that at the end of the week the shilling is seldom more than sevenpence.

Until he gets his shilling per day, and his accounts are simplified, so that he can easily understand the deductions made, you need never expect to enlist efficient and intelligent men. Again, he is supplied with a nominally free kit, but the uniform part, if it does not fit him, which is usually the case, is altered at his expense.

This kit is by Government renewed from time to time, but his under-kit, consisting of three pairs of socks, two shirts, two towels, one little bit of soap, and other things necessary for what is called cleaning, he has to maintain for seven long years.

He has to show his kit monthly, and if he is lacking in any of these articles, or they are not in good repair, he has to pay for new ones, and he is punished as well. From such causes I have often known a soldier driven into a state of practical sullen rebellion, out of heart with his profession, out of heart with his officers, a man most dangerous to himself and especially dangerous to the society in which he lives. This kit question must be settled upon an honourable basis.

Again, the present short service system is a great hindrance to recruiting.

The lodging-houses of England are full of those soldiers in the reserve living on their sixpence a day; seven years, the best of their lives, have been taken, rendering them unfit (according to the testimony of employers of labour) for ordinary work.

The deferred pay – amounting to £21 – is just enough to allow them to revel in a month or two of debauch, not enough to enable them to set up in any useful business. Of course there are very many exceptions to this description, but there are a large number of these men loafing round public houses, a continuous warning to mothers and fathers to prevent their boys from becoming soldiers or sailors.

The pay in the navy is a little in advance of that in the army, but there a man has to buy and keep up all his whole kit.

Very often a new captain demands a new kind of rig, and so men are being constantly put to a practically unnecessary expense.

Even a chief petty officer, who after qualifying in gunnery and torpedoes and diving, becomes gunnery instructor, and then captain of a turret, only receives five shillings and a penny per day. This is a man of such true intelligence and attainment that in civil life he would be receiving a very large salary. It is fair, of course, to add that he has a pension in view, but so few men attain all these qualifications that they hardly affect the question.

But it is not merely a question of pay; it is surely a question of risk as well.

These men carry their lives in their hands for your sakes. It is a noble thing truly to die for one's country, but if you leave wife and children behind to beggary, and worse, surely the country does not fulfil her part of the bargain.

I need not refer to the shameful management of the Patriotic and *Victoria* Funds; but shameful as is the provision made for widows and orphans in the *Victoria* case, happy, you may say, is the woman whose husband happens to die in a crowd; if he had fallen overboard on some stormy night, or been killed pursuing a slaver on the African coast, his wife and children would have got nothing at all.

It is this awful uncertainty about the future of those he loves best that is a continual menace to the peace of mind of the soldier and sailor. One little incident will illustrate the heartlessness and cruelty of the Admiralty.

A man's kit is his own; if he dies on board ship it is auctioned on board amongst his comrades, who always pay a great deal more than its value, and send the money home as a loving present to his friends.

But because the *Victoria* went down, the men who were lost in her had no compensation allowed to their relatives. The men who lived got something inadequately small. It is this red-tape of the Whitehall officials that strangles the loyalty of the bluejacket.

But there are other difficulties which I am bound, though unwillingly, to mention. Practically, marriage is forbidden to the soldier; at least, for the first five years of his service, and then only a few are allowed on the strength of the regiment. God's Apostle says, 'It is better to marry than to burn.' Many of these men marry. Out of their pay of sevenpence per day, what can they give their wives? It means that the wife has no recognized claim for support on her husband at all. Either she tries to follow the regiment at her own expense, with the chance of being sent back by the Government, or drags on a miserable existence – married, yet practically unmarried. It is almost impossible to imagine the lives of these women, as they are spent in Portsmouth and other military centres.

The sailor, on the other hand, is allowed to marry, and a certain portion of his pay he can allot to his wife; but when I tell you that in the case of an ordinary seaman this amounts to £1 per month, and as his rating increases a little more is added, I need hardly do more than ask you to imagine what a wife with little children can do under circumstances like these.

If wrong comes of it, and Jack (who for our sakes has practically surrendered wife and children) receives a wound to his honour which is worse than death, a very stab in his heart, gentlemen, on whom lies the blame?

But there is another side of the question worse than marriage.

Think of those strong, vigorous, well-groomed, fairly-fed men, with all to make their body strong, their passions powerful, think of them living separated altogether from womankind, with the common talk of the barrack-room, or of the lower deck, ever sounding in their ears, centred in such sinks of iniquity as Portsmouth, Plymouth, Chatham, Aldershot, and other garrison towns, where the streets are beyond measure disgraceful.

In Portsmouth, for instance, which I know well, there are to be found on the Hard, at the very Dockyard gates, no less than fourteen buildings constructed and carried on for the sale of intoxicating drinks, twelve being fully-licensed houses, out of a total of twenty-six.

The post-office, where sailors have very frequently to go, stands between a group of seven, five being next door to each other on the one side, and two on the other. Out of the Hard opens Queen Street, the practical thoroughfare of Portsea, with a very large number of public houses in it, and several alleys and courts – you can hardly call them streets – which are practically full of brothels.

Is it any wonder, then – to quote the words of his worship the Mayor of Portsmouth – 'that even in this garrison there were nearly half the men in hospital, owing to the repeal of the C.D. Acts'?

Is it any wonder that the Admiralty and War Office have communicated with Lord Clanwilliam and the general commanding at Portsmouth and other garrison centres, telling them to take steps with the civil authorities to ameliorate these evils?

39

FREDERIC WILLIAM FARRAR (1831–1903)

FREDERIC WILLIAM FARRAR was born in Bombay but was
brought up and educated in England. After ordination in 1854 he
became a master at Marlborough College and in 1871 was appointed Headmaster. While he was there he published his *Life of
Christ*, which earned him a popular reputation. In 1876 he became
Canon of Westminster and Rector of St Margaret's, Westminster,
where he became known as an outstanding preacher. He was
described as a 'Broad Church Evangelical', but in spite of his
unusual views he became Dean of Canterbury in 1895.

LX

*From a sermon entitled 'Legislative Duties', preached at St
Margaret's, Westminster, 1879, at the opening of Parliament, on the
text:*

I exhort therefore, that, first of all, supplications, prayers, intercessions, and giving of thanks, be made for all men;
For kings, and for all that are in authority; that we may lead a quiet
and peaceable life in all godliness and honesty (*1 Tim. ii, 1–2*).

*It describes some of the evils of society, indicates the great blessings of
recent parliamentary legislation and the improvements which have
followed.*

Let none of us, my brethren, be so vulgarly absorbed by our shops
and our families, by our private interests and selfish domesticities,
as to think that Parliaments and laws make small difference to
him. Their functions are so far-reaching that there is not a home
or hearth in England which is not happier or more dismal from
their influence. Not only does the safety of nations, the peace of
churches, the prosperity of commerce depend on them, but even
no little of the security, the order, the happiness of our individual

lives. With them rests the continuance of the loyal affection of our colonies, over realms on which the sun never sets. To them we owe it that the shores

> Of Australasia, lustrated at length,
> Collect no longer the putrescent weed
> Of Europe, flung by senates to infect
> The only unpolluted continent.

When some great social iniquity has entrenched itself in the citadels of power it is theirs to drive the battering-ram against its walls. If men, in greed or ignorance, have infected the sweet rivers of England with filthy stains – if they have neglected the laws of nature by perpetuating the conditions of disease – if they have made cities unhealthy by poisoning the air with sulphurous chemicals and the soil with the relics of the dead – if individual selfishness has ever tried to encroach, in a thousand directions, on universal rights; if deadly poisons are sold with ruinous facility; if national sins are perpetuated by the reckless diffusion of terrible temptations; if scoundrels would deprave with pestilent literature the morals of our sons; if landlords will crowd the poor into tenements scarce fit for swine; if banded unions have striven to persecute opinion and make thought a crime – then theirs is the god-like function to secure dwellings for the honest; to shield the innocence of the young; to diminish the perils of the tempted; to repress the violences of the criminal; to protect the independence of the thinker; to prevent the recklessness of the avaricious; to see that none grow rich on profits drawn from the nation's ruin; to restore its crystal to the river, and its sweetness to the air; by fearless repression of wrong, by wide encouragement of right, by high moral influence, by strong sanitary legislation, it is theirs to secure the righteousness of our land, and the health of our people. The sundial of Lincoln's Inn says, '*Lex anchora Regni*' – Law, the anchor of the realm; and since the majestic principle of that Divine Law, 'whose home is the bosom of God and her voice the harmony of the world', can only be ensured by human laws, it is the function of Parliaments, in the words of a recent statesman, to be able to claim that 'they found law dear and left it cheap; they found it a sealed book, they left it an open letter; they found it the patrimony of the rich, they left it the inheritance of the poor; they found it the two-edged sword of craft and oppression, they left it the staff of honesty and the shield of innocence.' Only the future will be able duly to estimate the full beneficence of the home legislation of the last fifty years. Take but the abolition of the Test Acts, with their tyrannies and hypocrisies, in 1828. Take the abolition of slavery in 1830. Take the Reciprocity of duties, which so vastly increased our shipping in 1829. Take the Reform Bill, which saved the very bases of our constitution in 1832. Take the abolition of the Corn Laws, with the vast relief which it gave to a teeming population, in 1846. Take the Bill for the protection of women and children in mines and collieries in 1842. Take the shortening of the weary hours of factory labour in 1847. Take the large measure for the purification of the Thames in 1858. Take the establishment of a national system of education in 1870. Take the Acts for the protection of life and property in mines, and railroads, and ships, and banks, and companies. Take the defence of even dumb animals from reckless cruelty, and the preservation of the harmless birds of land and wave. There is not one man of us all in England who has not gained by the blessings which flow from measures such as these; and it is due in no small degree to them that population is nearly doubled; wealth vastly increased; crime diminished; longevity extended; our Empire vaster; our people stronger; classes more united; Englishmen better governed, better taught, better housed, better protected, and better fed. And how is it, that – often in the very teeth of the most determined and unscrupulous opposition, these triumphs have been won? Chiefly because God has given us statesmen with the insight to perceive their blessedness, and the courage to enforce their necessity, and Parliaments with whom reason has been stronger than prejudice, and opponents ready to acquiesce with loyalty even in those measures which have subordinated private interests to the public good. When they have passed peacefully into law, victorious over passionate antagonism, men have felt gladly that a great strain was removed. Some here are old enough to remember the passing of the Great Reform Bill in 1832. Passions were then so intensely excited, that, in another country, a throne might well have toppled over into the dust; and even in our own country it seemed at one time as if Revolution sat 'nursing the impatient earthquake'. And yet, by God's blessing, all was done by legal and constitutional processes. A great man who was present at one of the final divisions has told us that it was a scene never to be forgotten, like seeing Caesar stabbed in the senate house, or Cromwell ordering the removal of the mace. From the 608 members present, the Ayes and Noes came like volleys of artillery; with breathless silence the votes were counted; suppressed cries began to break out towards the close, and when it was known that there was a narrow majority of eight in favour of the bill, strong men burst into weeping and laughter, and the stillness of the night was broken by storms of loud huzzahs, which swept far along the dark excited streets.

I have tried, then, to show you why, as English citizens, it is a plain duty for us, as we do, to pray for the Parliament which thus powerfully sways our social legislation.

LXI

From a sermon entitled 'Work in the Groaning Creation', preached in Westminster Abbey (no date), on the texts:

And God saw every thing that he had made, and behold, it was very good. And the evening and the morning were the sixth day (*Gen. i, 31*).

For we know that the whole creation groaneth and travaileth in pain together until now (*Rom. viii, 22*).

And there shall be no more curse: but the throne of God and of the Lamb shall be in it; and his servants shall serve him (*Rev. xxii, 3*).

The blessings and the evils of the age, with special reference to scientific and medical advances and to environmental pollution.

Man has done much to make the world in all senses a worse place for himself, but he has also, thank God, done much to make it better, and he may, to an almost unspeakable extent, remedy for himself and for his race the throes and agonies of the groaning universe. God meant his earth to be a more blest place for us than it is, and in every instance men have made it more blest when they have read the open secrets, by virtue of which, for our excitement, if not for our reward, 'herbs have their healing, stones their preciousness, and stars their times'. Ancient nations have shuddered at the awfulness of the sea. It drowns ship and sailor; but 'trim your sail, and the same wave which drowns the bark is cleft by it, and bears it along like its own foam, a plume and a power.' The lightning shatters tower and temple; but once learn that it is nothing but the luminous all-pervading fluid which you may evolve by rubbing a piece of amber, and brush out of a child's fair hair, and then with no more potent instrument than a boy's kite you may dash harmless to the earth the all-shattering brand which was the terror of antiquity; nay, you may seize it by its wing of fire, and bid it carry your messages around the girdled globe. Zymotic diseases smite down the aged and young, but, when you have learnt that they are caused by myriads of invisible germs which float in the water or the air, you have but to observe the commonest rules of sanitary science, to filter and boil the dangerous water, to insure free currents of air, to breathe as nature meant you to breathe, through the nostrils, and not through the throat, and you rob them of half their deadliness. Why has smallpox been stayed in its loathly ravages, and deprived of its hideous power? Why does the Black Death rage no longer, as it raged among the monks of this Abbey four centuries ago? Why do we not have pestilence, like that great plague of London, which destroyed 7,165 persons in a single week? Why has jail fever disappeared? Why are the cities of Europe horrified no longer by the hideousness of medieval leprosy? Because men live amid cleaner and purer surroundings. Because rushes are no longer strewn over floors which had been suffered to be saturated with the organic refuse of years. Because the simplest laws of nature are better understood. Because, in these respects, men have remedied by God's aid, some of those miseries for which the Saviour sighed.

And this amelioration of man's miseries is a great, and noble, and Christ-like work. Would that there were no other side to the picture! Man, alas! also has done, and may do, infinite mischief to the world he lives in. He may cut down the forests on the hills, and so diminish the necessary rain. He may pluck up the grasses on the shore, and so lay waste whole acres to the devastating sands. He may poison the sweet, pure rivers of his native soil, till their crystal freshness is corrupted into deathful and putrescent slime.

He may herd together, as we suffer our poor to do, in filthy tenements which shall breed every species of disease and vice. He may indulge or acquiesce in senseless fashions and pernicious vanities which shall mean not only wasteful ugliness and grotesque extravagance, but leave shattered health and ruined lives, to the mothers of his race. He may in greed of competition extirpate the game of the forest, the fishes of the sea. He may destroy the exquisite balance of nature, by shooting down or entrapping the sweet birds of the air, till his vines and his harvests are devastated by the insects on which they feed. He may suffer the chimneys of his manufactories to poison the atmosphere with black smoke and sulphurous acid, till his proudest cities are stifled at noonday, as we all have seen in London for these many weeks, with the unclean mirk of midnight fogs. He may suffer noxious gases to be vomited upon the breeze, till the most glorious buildings in his cities corrode and crumble – as the stones of this Abbey are doing – under their influence, till the green woods blacken into leafless wastes, and life is lived at miserable levels of vitality under the filthy reek. There is hardly any limit to the evil, no less than to the good, which man may do to this his earthly environment. Nor is it less deplorable that he may go out of his way to do endless mischief to himself by his misuse or abuse of the properties of things. From the dried capsules of the white poppy he extracts opium, and he grows acres of poppies that with thousands of chests of that opium he may degrade into decrepitude and wretchedness the most populous nations upon earth. Nature gives him the purple grape and the golden grain, and he mashes them and lets them rot and seethe, and assists, and superintends, and retards their decomposition, till he has educed from them a fermented intoxicating liquor; and not content with this luxury, he pours it into Circean cups of degrading excess; not content with even fermentation, he further, by distillation, extracts a transparent, mobile, colourless fluid, which is the distinctive element in ardent spirits, and these, whatever may be their legitimate use in manufacture or in medicine, he has so horribly abused that they have become to mankind, the *spiritus ardentes* indeed, but not of Heaven – fiery spirits of the abyss, which have decimated nations, ruined continents, shortened millions of lives, and turned for millions of God's children, and millions of Christ's little ones, life into an anguish, and earth into a hell. Do not say we can do nothing to soften for man the deadly agencies which are working in the world, for all this mischief, and incalculably more than this, is man's own doing.

But let me ask you to glance for a moment at one of the beneficent secrets which nature has yielded up to man. Have you ever realized, with heartfelt gratitude to God, the priceless boon which he has granted to this generation in the diminution of pain? One of our best surgeons has just told us the strange yet simple story of this discovery, from the first dim intimation of the possibility in 1789, till in 1846 it might almost be said that in Europe we could name the month, before which all operative surgery was agonizing, and after which it was painless. But what an immense, what an enormous boon is this application of anodynes!

Past all counting is the sum of happiness enjoyed by the millions who have, in the last thirty-three years, escaped the pain that was inevitable in surgical operations; pain made more terrible by apprehension; more keen by close attention; sometimes awful in a swift agony; sometimes prolonged beyond even the most patient endurance, and then renewed in memory, and terrible in dreams. This will never be felt again.

And besides this abolition of pain, it would take long to tell how chloroform and ether 'have enlarged the field of useful surgery, making many things easy which were difficult, many safe which were perilous, many practical which were nearly impossible'. But another lesson this eminent man of science draws, which bears directly on our subject, is that while we are profanely decrying nature, discoveries the most blest, boons the most priceless, may lie close to us and yet God leave us to discover them; and that we may endure many needless miseries, falsely accusing nature and even God, only because we have neither hope enough to excite intense desire, nor desire enough to encourage hope. We wonder that for forty years the discovery of anaesthetics was not pursued, tho', after the pregnant hint of Sir H. Davy, it lay but half hidden under so thin a veil. Our successors will wonder at us, as we at those before us, that we were as blind to who can tell how many great truths, which, they will say, were all around us, within reach of any clear and earnest mind. They will wonder at the quietude with which we stupidly acquiesce in, or immorally defend, the causes which perpetuate and intensify our habitual miseries. Our fathers needlessly put up with these miseries 'as we now put up with typhoid fever and sea-sickness; with local floods and droughts; with waste of health and wealth in pollutions of rivers; with hideous noises, and foul smells'; with the curse of alcoholic poisoning, and many other miseries. Our successors, when they have remedied or prevented these, will look back on them with horror, and on us with wonder and contempt, for what they will call our idleness or blindness, or indifference to suffering. Alas! in the physical as in the moral world, we murmur at the evils which surround us, and we do not remove them. We multiply those evils, and make life wretched, and then curse nature because it is wretched, and neglect or fling away the precious gifts and easy remedies which would make it blest. And is it not so in the spiritual world? Nine tenths of our miseries are due to our sins. Yet the remedy of our sins is close at hand. We have a Saviour; we have been commemorating his birth, but we live and act as tho' he were dead; in our own lives and those of others we suffer those miseries to run riot which he came to cure; we talk and live as tho' those remedies were undiscoverable, while from day to day his Word is very nigh us, even in our mouths and in our hearts!

For one sermon you hear about work for the secular amelioration of the suffering world for which Christ sighed, you may (I suppose) hear fifty on passing ecclesiastical controversies and five thousand about individual efforts for personal salvation. And yet one pure, self-sacrificing deed, one word of generosity to an opponent, one kindly act to aid another, may have been better for you in God's sight and far harder for you to do, than to attend in the year the 730 daily services which this Abbey provides. Yes, I am glad that I have preached to you today the duty of what some would call secular work – as tho' secular work were not often the most profoundly religious work! – for the amelioration of the world. And I say, it were better for you to have made but two blades of grass grow where one grew before, than if, with the hollow, hateful, slanderous heart of some false prophets of modern religionism, you were every morning to do whatever modern thing may be analogous to binding your fringes with blue, and broadening your phylacteries – to making the hilltops blaze with your sacrificial fires, building here seven altars, and offering a bullock and a ram on every altar. And so, my brethren, let us leave this Abbey today with conceptions of duty large and more hopeful; with more yearning both after the sympathy of Christ and after his activity; with more faith to see that the world would not be so utter a ruin but for our perversity; with more hope to be convinced that even we can help to redeem its disorders, and restore its pristine perfectness.

40

THOMAS HANCOCK (1832–1903)

THOMAS HANCOCK was ordained in 1863. He held a succession of curacies but, because of his political and social views, he was overlooked by the Church authorities for most of his life and lived from hand to mouth until 1883, when H. C. Shuttleworth made him Lecturer of St Nicholas Cole Abbey in the City. He was a leading figure in the Christian Socialist Movement and was a prominent member of the Guild of St Matthew. He was a brilliant, complex writer, a Church historian and a first-class theologian. He was an uncompromising High Churchman. He preached that the pulpit was the only hope for social salvation because the so-called 'free press' was controlled by Mammon and dared not handle the explosive economic and social issues honestly. Although many of his sermons were complex, they were influential. 'If every preacher in London could have been compelled to hold his tongue and come and learn from Hancock, say, once a month, it would have been well for them and for the Church. ... The Bishops – what might they not have done!' (*Commonwealth*).

LXII

From a sermon entitled 'The Banner of Christ in the Hands of the Socialists', preached at St Nicholas Cole Abbey, 1887, on the text:

In that day there shall be a root of Jesse, which shall stand for an ensign of the people: to it shall the Gentiles seek: and his rest shall be glorious.

And it shall come to pass in that day, that the Lord shall set his hand again the second time to recover the remnant of his people which shall be left ... (*Isa. xi, 10–11*).

The 'masses of the common people' will deliver the Church from the patronage and control of the rich; the Church is on the side of

'Mammon and Caste', of feudal and commercial interests; the Socialists are the true exponents of the life and teaching of Christ.

For fifty years the national bishops and the patron-made clergy – pastors who have been chosen for the 'masses' by Mammon and Caste – have been at their wits' end how to persuade the crowds of the disinherited and oppressed to become, or own themselves to be, members incorporate of Christ's Church. They have spent millions of pounds, they have held thousands upon thousands of anxious discussions for the solution of the pressing question – 'How are we clergy to get the masses?' I can only repeat, what I have perhaps said often enough, that they are beginning at the wrong end: that it is the will of God that the so-called masses should 'get' the clergy. So far as concerns the national bishops, and in a less degree all those clergy who are appointed by the state, commonwealth, or fatherland, they are *indirectly* 'got' by the masses, at least by so many amongst them as are freemen, are citizens, possess votes. By becoming voters they have become, in their place and degree, factors of the Government, electors of the Government; and thus they indirectly, through their Government, nominate to the bishoprics. But the parochial clergy, the pastors of the local communes, do not even possess as legitimate and as Christian a foundation for their position as that which can be claimed by the parish churchwardens. The parish churchwardens are the elect of the people, Church, or congregation: they are the men chosen for office by 'the masses'; they stand on exactly as secure a ground, in point of popular authority, as St Stephen or St Philip did. They have been placed where they are, as St Stephen and St Philip were, by 'the multitude of the disciples'. The rector or vicar, on the contrary, has not been placed where he is by 'the multitude of the disciples' – by 'the masses' as we now talk. He has been placed there by some individual lord of land, some individual owner of money, or by some caucus of trustees who want to confine the Universal Church of all ages and all persons within the narrow bounds of some party which represents the prejudices, ignorances, and negligences of one particular age or class. The assistant clergy – who in really civilized states and parishes are freely elected by 'the masses' – in our semi-civilized England are dismissible wage-servants of the patron-imposed incumbent. Unless they are careful to offend neither Caste nor Mammon – the feudal and the commercial exploiters of the one common Church – they usually find themselves, when they have arrived at middle-age, excluded by these two allied Antichrists from any further exercise of the ministry which they have received of the Lord. No power but that of 'the multitudes of the disciples', nothing but an extension of the so-called 'invasion of the Church by the masses' from the material to the spiritual or social Church – can restore to Jesus Christ the service and ministry of which he is now being robbed by Caste and Mammon. The poor priests of the Lord ought to look to the poor alone, to the masses of the common people, to 'the multitudes of the disciples', to liberate His Church 'from the patronage and control' – not 'of the state' or sacred fatherland, as the plutocratic Liberationists say – but from the patronage and control of anti-Christian Caste and Mammon. 'The mighty' and 'the rich' of the *Magnificat*, by getting the officering of all the local congregations of Christ into the grasp of landlords and money lords have not only despoiled every local people of their highest spiritual rights and obligations, but by substituting 'patronage' for free election they have perverted the very tribune of the people, the local representative of Jesus Christ the Redeemer – the parish priest – into a creature and a representative of class and 'property'.

The 'masses' know, or are beginning now in the Father's good providence to know, not merely what it is to be robbed, but that they have been and are being robbed. They are beginning to learn that they have been thrust off the common land: the 'commons' of the local commonwealths have been perverted into sporting preserves for Caste, or into 'eligible building estates' for Mammon. They are beginning to learn that the free common schools have been appropriated to the sole profit of the same two Antichrists. But they have yet to learn the last and most momentous lesson of all – that Caste 'the mighty' and Mammon 'the rich' have successively expropriated 'the multitude of the disciples', or 'the masses', or 'the common people' of that which is God's appointed witness to their rights in the land and the school. Caste and Mammon have made the Church and its priesthood their own. The mighty and the rich have carried away Sion itself into captivity in Babylon. If 'the masses' – the carpenters, the fishermen, the rate-collectors, the tent-makers – had retained the common Church and her ministry, which the Son of Man entrusted to their keeping, in which his apostles declared them to be rightful freemen or electors, it would have been impossible for them to be robbed of the common land or the common school. If 'the whole multitude of the disciples', the masses, the common people, will but reassert their claims and place in the universal Spiritual Society, in the common Church of all the peoples, then the common land and the common school must infallibly return to that whole humanity to which the Lord gave the one and for which he instituted the other. The Church is his permanent spiritual and social witness – to 'all nations' by the apostolic or episcopal order, to every local parish or commune by its own freely-elected priest – that the earth hath he given to the children of men, and not the caste of *Raubritter* or *Raubadel*, robber-nobles or robber-knights, which in 'the times of ignorance' degraded Christ's freemen into its own slaves or villeins. The bishops and priests of the common Spiritual Society are God's witnesses that 'every man that cometh into the world' is the subject of His own inward enlightening and educating Word, and therefore an inheritor by divine right of the school.

I am quite aware that some will object, 'Do you then call the organized mob of Socialists who thronged into St Paul's Cathedral on Sunday* a "multitude of the disciples?"' I will not stay to indicate in detail the signs of discontent, murmuring, and quarrelling which the apostles saw in those 'masses' in Jerusalem, whom *they* nevertheless included within 'the multitude of the disciples'. A 'disciple', I need scarcely tell you, is a learner. A disciple is one who adopts the maxims and laws of another as the only full and complete expression of his own belief and his own duties. It is very hard indeed to conceive of the minority whom the journalists call 'the respectable churchgoers' – who regard the

* A visit to St Paul's Cathedral for Evensong by an army of Socialists in February 1887 which caused considerable disturbance, both inside and outside the cathedral. It was organized as a protest against the government.

church-going of the Socialists as an invasion of their own private spiritual ecclesiastical preserve, who think that the proper use of St Paul's Cathedral is to provide gratuitous concerts and entertaining sermons for the well-to-do – as 'disciples' of Jesus Christ. The very first lesson which Jesus teaches every 'disciple' who enters into his school is the ungodliness and inhumanity of the attempt to be rich. I need not quote texts. You know them all. Although you will not find them in the publications of the Tract Societies which Caste and Mammon maintain for the 'conversion' of the masses, and although you will never see them exposed upon the walls of a railway station, you can easily find them in a New Testament, or you may read them on the banners of the Socialists.

If some old Athenian philosopher had risen from the dead, or some Mohammedan, ignorant of the words of Christ and his apostles, had come into the streets of London on Sunday and watched the great multitude surging into St Paul's Cathedral, they would naturally have asked, 'Whose disciples are all these men? What leader do they follow? From whom do they derive the axioms and rules which are moving them?'

Have you, my brethren, looked at the banners of this 'mob'? Have you observed 'whose image and superscription' they bear? It is not Caesar's, not Victoria's, not Gladstone's, not Schnadhorst's, not Hyndman's.

You see that they carry banners with mottoes upon them. Who is *the author* of those texts which express the social faith of this huge multitude? From what teacher have they borrowed the dogmas which they call upon all the city to read and to respect, to observe and to obey? On whose authority are these innumerable crowds of the poor and rough doing this unwonted thing? They, or a great many of them, call themselves 'Socialists'. Let us read what is on their banners; let us discover *who* is the ultimate dogmatist of this multitudinous sect.

Christians, as you watch the mighty multitude pass by, you will soon be shaken out of many of your hasty *a priori* conjectures. Do you expect to read upon their banners wild words of their own invention? Do you expect extracts from Babeuf or from Proudhon, or even from Ferdinand Lassalle or Karl Marx? Are not the 'Socialists' their disciples? Ought not the mottoes by which they declare before the world their convictions, their demands, their faith, to be extracted from *Das Kapital* or from the *Arbeiterprogramm*? Oh, come, all ye faithful! Look again and again at these inscriptions. Recognize, while you have time, what they are: see, clergy and laity, out of whose mouth the cries of 'the mob' have come. They are the words of *your* Master. They are the laws of the Eternal Father. They are the lessons which he taught us by his Son. They are the new commandments which you and I were pledged at our baptism to keep. 'Feed *My* lambs!' '*My* house is a house of prayer, but ye (capitalists and landlords) have made it a den of thieves!' '*I* was an hungred, and ye gave *Me* no meat; naked, and ye clothed *Me* not.' It is a small matter to what sect or party this great 'multitude' fancies it belongs, or by what denomination it pleases to call itself. You can see to *whom* they have felt obliged to go in order to find the fullest expression of their faith. 'In the name of our God,' said the crowds of the London poor, as well as the Hebrew psalmist, 'we will set up our banners.' We have not seen in our generation any other such warning, or any other such an acknowledgement, that Jesus Christ the crucified is he whom the Father has exalted to be the Head of Humanity, to lift up an ensign for the peoples, to be the one and only all-sufficient mediator, representative, spokesman, and avenger of 'all that are desolate and oppressed'. This 'sign of the son of Man' is all the more amazing because it is so unintentional.

What is all the after-dinner talk at the tables of Caste and Mammon, or all the unmoral and unsocial wordspinning of Christian Evidence companies, over the possibility of reconciling Darwinism and 'Christianity' compared with that evidence which the Son of Man himself sets before the corrupt and unbelieving Church in the faith and hope, in the hunger and thirst after righteousness, of those who do not even know that He is their teacher and their leader? Can we doubt that it is the Son of Man himself who has come again into his Church in the persons of this rough multitude of his disciples? 'The Son of God goes forth to war.' These, whatever they may call themselves, are bearing his banner; they 'follow in his train'. They are marching 'manfully under his banner', as the office for Holy Baptism puts it, 'against sin, the world, and the devil' – against selfishness, Caste-rule, and

Mammon-rule. May each one of them 'continue Christ's faithful soldier and servant unto his life's end'. May he freely subject himself to the rule of him by whom he sees the world needs to be ruled.

The undogmatic 'socialism' of the desolate and oppressed, when it speaks freely out of its own heart and conscience, falls back upon the words with which the crucified and ascended Head of Humanity has provided his brothers and sisters. It reminds 'Christians' that they are living in rebellion against Christ. It does not articulately name itself 'Christian Socialism'. No: but it declares inarticulately that the thing which economists, politicians, scholars – in hatred or in love – call 'Socialism' is itself 'Christian'.

LXIII

From a sermon entitled 'The Church and the Public House: or Temperance not to be used as a Cloak of Maliciousness', preached on Temperance Sunday, 3rd Sunday after Easter 1888, on the text:

As free, and not using your liberty for a cloak of maliciousness, but as the servants of God.

Honour all men. Love the brotherhood. Fear God. Honour the king (*1 Pet. ii, 16–17*).

In contrast to most preachers, Hancock praises the public house and condemns the temperance movement.

As it is the special temptation of the free man to abuse his liberty to libertinism in thought and conduct, so it is the special temptation of the professional temperance-man to rush into the wildest degrees of tyrannical intemperance. It has become a truism that he exceeds all the rest of mankind in his intoxication. He has to be particularly on guard lest his temperance, like the other's liberty, be used 'as a cloak of maliciousness'. The maliciousness of the temperance man, as the outsiders view it, assumes two forms – firstly, a most unreasonable social or rather anti-social economy, which preaches against the public house, as if it were the very Babylon of the Apocalypse, and as if the shortest and surest way of founding Sion in the earth would be the burning down of all inns, ale houses, and hotels; and secondly, a most uncharitable indication of the landlords of inns as the chief agents of Satan and the most hurtful of all the foes of individual and social morality. A popular Independent preacher said a few days ago to a crowded audience, '*I* could make a garden of Eden down in the East End in three months if I had *my* way.' If he might 'use his liberty', as St Peter puts it, what would be his use of his liberty? 'My way,' he continued, 'would be a rough one at the first. I should do nothing but burn down all the breweries, and shut up all the public houses. That is the way back to Paradise.'

Is it? Paradise is the home of undivided religious unity as well as sobriety, and if we began by burning all the public houses to secure national sobriety we should end by burning all the churches, or all the dissenting chapels, or all the secular halls to secure national religious unity. That 'rough' method has been tried as the infallible way to national religious unity, and it has failed. Its failure would be equally conspicuous as the way to national sobriety. Men are not drunkards because there are breweries, but because they get from breweries what if there were no breweries they would get elsewhere. In 'the Garden of Eden', according to the tradition, there seems to have been neither a brewery nor a public house. Nevertheless, the tempter found his way into the Garden of Eden, and brought ruin upon all its inhabitants, who were all strict teetotallers. Neither, according to the tradition, did Cain come out of an inn when he murdered Abel, although it is the habit of our intemperate temperance-men to trace every modern murder directly or indirectly to 'the bottle'. But Cain was certainly a teetotaller.

A public house is ideally a very noble, humane, and social institution. It is much more democratic than the modern club. The club is too often the centre of a caste, a class, or a party; it is exclusive, pharisaic, and anti-social. One club shuts out all who are not 'gentlemen', another all who are not working men. One club excommunicates Tories, another puts its ban upon Radicals. But the public house or inn, according to its name, belongs to everybody, whatever his class, whatever his party. A man used to be welcome there, as in the Church of God, because he was human, and not because he was a sectary who could proffer some pharisaic or aristocratic differentiation between himself and the rest of the parish. The ancient relations between the parish church and the parish inn, as the spiritual and secular 'public houses' of the local republic, had a very wholesome side. The keen dialectic Archdeacon Paley chose an inn to write in. The saintly Archbishop Leighton said that he should like to die in an inn. Charles Kingsley, whom the greatest of modern theologians called 'the best of modern parish priests', would smoke his pipe in the village public house, and drink out of the same pot as his poor parishioners. St Francis de Sales, the most sensitive and refined of prelates, advised all his parochial clergy to begin by making a friend of the village innkeeper. That most terrible mischief is done in public houses – as well as in churches and dissenting chapels – is too evident for anybody to deny. But nothing is so intemperate or fanatical as to sweep away an institution with a fine ideal, and still capable of being redeemed to excellent social service, because that ideal is now blurred and those services are not now rendered. The reasons why the public inn is degraded and mischievous lie far deeper than the intemperate 'temperance-men' dare to look.

It would much help us to grow in temperance if we would recollect that when Christ's holy apostle beseeches the Church to 'honour all men' he does not add 'except inn keepers'. Those Christian bishops and priests, whom I have just cited, honoured the 'man' in the innkeeper, and that was the true way of awakening in him the consciousness of the honourable function entrusted to him in the parish and the commonwealth, to which the ancient title of 'host' bears witness. Samuel Fisher, the Quaker, in his answer to the attacks of the famous Independent, John Owen, protested against the Calvinist's denunciation of alehouse keepers. 'The calling is as honest in itself,' said the sturdy Quaker, 'as that of Gaius, the Church's host, or any other innkeeper, though it be often much abused. What trade is not, when evil men manage it?'

I have but skimmed hastily the surface of an important subject, which I could not pretend to handle satisfactorily in so short a time. We cannot grow in the inward liberty, which is true temperance, if we pervert our liberty or our temperance into a 'cloak of maliciousness'. We do not change the ungodly character of such abuse by giving it the specious name of 'Liberalism'. To free our commonwealth from the gross sin of drunkenness, and from the miseries which follow it, is a noble and Christian object. But we shall help little towards that liberation if we are ourselves in bondage to the intemperate superstition that inns are the cause of drunkenness, or if we indulge the least degree of an intemperate and pharisaic spitefulness towards the innkeeper. Rather 'honour all men' – honour the man in the wretched slave of drink, as the Saviour honours the man under that and every other form and variety of sinner. Honour the man in the innkeeper, whom our manifold social apostasies from Christ's Law, which I cannot here specialize, has degraded from the 'host' which he ought to be, into a seducer of the poor and a tool of the capitalist fortune-hunter, which he ought not to be. The public house does evil for the same reason that every other social institution does evil, because we have come to regard Mammon and not God as its proper ruler, as the supreme inn keeper. It may be in part the fault of Christ's bishops and priests that the landlords of inns are so often apostates from their calling, and expropriate as their 'customers' those whom they ought to honour as their 'guests'. But here in England, and in parts of the world, there are still hosts who care for the health and soberness of their guests, and who set their fellow Christians an example of walking worthy of the vocation wherewith they are called.

41

HENRY SCOTT HOLLAND (1847–1918)

HENRY SCOTT HOLLAND was born in 1847, became Student of Christ Church, Oxford, in 1870 and, in 1884, was appointed Canon of St Paul's Cathedral. Finally, in 1910 he became Regius Professor of Divinity in the University of Oxford. He was an accomplished theologian and preacher, and was particularly concerned to relate Christian principles to social and economic problems. He was a Socialist and the first Chairman of the Committee of the Christian Social Union.

LXIV

From a sermon entitled 'National Penitence', preached at St Edmund's, Lombard Street, London, 1884, on the text: 'Cursed be he that removeth his neighbour's landmark. And all the people shall say, Amen' (*Deut. xxvii, 17*). *The first in a series of Lent sermons on social subjects arranged by the London Branch of the Christian Social Union. The evasion of responsibility by organized commerce for the sufferings of the workers; the evils of commercial speculation; the Church's failure to witness against evils in the social system.*

Let us take [irresponsibility] in the case of a company or a board. We know how easily it all happens. The responsibility for the action taken finds no lodgement anywhere, has no seat of judgement, no Court of Appeal. No one knows with whom exactly the responsibility lies. It is shifted from shoulder to shoulder, until the last man, finding no other to whom he can pass it on, drops it quietly off into some ditch. And it is no one's business to note its disappearance. There is no audit on the side of conscience, no annual report in the company's books how it fares. Everybody supposes that somebody else is looking out to see that nothing is wrong; or else they may have settled down to a practical belief that morality is not the affair of a company, of an industry, or of a corporation; in the familiar and most wicked phrase, 'A company has no conscience'. Such societies must seek their own interests; they cannot spend their time in inquiring how their neighbours would be affected by their action. They have enough on their hands already in determining the conditions of their own success, which is their proper business. How can a railway company or a joint stock bank have moral obligations beyond those elementary principles of honesty without which trade itself could not exist? How can they be saddled with duties to their neighbours as well as to themselves? So we all murmur palliative phrases to choke down the sense of discomfort with which we now and again find that we ourselves have reaped profit from some course of action which has sweated down some miserable workers into infamous conditions of toil and life; or has made home for them unknown and impossible through the long hours that we have mercilessly imposed upon them; or has given them over to heartless death under chemical poisons, through sinful neglect of the precautions which one touch of human nature would have made imperative; or we have been dependent for our dividends upon casual and disorganized labour, which was inevitably bound to demoralize all who were concerned in it; or have got rents from slums which were a sanitary disgrace and a moral degradation; or from public houses which fatten on the hideous drunkenness which their blazing gas and roaring heat fanned nightly into fever.

Ah! is there no room here for a plain, straight curse upon the sins that are open, on the sins that are reckless, on the sins that are savage? And yet they are sins which we in some corporate capacity too often aid and abet. As we review the ugly work of wrong, let us seriously ask ourselves, Is it against others only, and in no way against our own shamefaced selves, that we today pronounce, 'Cursed are they that make the blind to go out of his way, or taketh reward to slay the innocent? Cursed are the unmerciful, fornicators, and adulterers, covetous persons, idolaters, slanderers, drunkards, and extortioners. Cursed is he that putteth his trust in man, and taketh man for his defence, and in his heart goeth from the Lord.'

We may sin but too easily, through the irresponsibility of companies; or, again, we sin through becoming the tools of a system.

We all know how heartless, how mechanical, a system can become. Take commercial speculation. Take the money market. The men engaged in it are honest, kindly, and excellent. They propose to themselves nothing that is not legitimate, according to the rules of business. Yet the system itself that is created by their concerted efforts – what of it ? What of its effects ? How blind, how regardless, how inhuman may its workings be! How far it may carry us from all conceivable relations to moral responsibilities! As a system it is but too apt to take advantage of others' ignorance, of others' stupidity, of others' infirmities; it reaps its gain by others' vanity and greed; its normal work tends to exaggerate all fluctuations and uncertainties and disturbances of the money market, driving them into unnatural excess in order that the rapidity and extravagance of the variations may heighten the possibility of profits. As a system, it stamps down that which shows some signs of weakness, however temporary and accidental these may be, so that recovery is made impossible; it runs up anything that promises well into some unhealthy and inflated pre-eminence, and then hastily deserts it, before the terrible recoil follows which its own exertions have made inevitable, leaving the disaster to break on the foolish and ignorant, who had not wit enough to understand that they were following leaders who would be found to have withdrawn before the crisis came. My brothers, as we look round the English money market today, dare we say that there is no meaning for us in the curse on him who removeth his neighbour's landmark; on him who is unmerciful; on him who maketh the blind to go out of his way ?

And classes, interests, professions – these all can commit gross sins from which any individual member of these would instinctively shrink. There is a horrible momentum which a vast profession or class may acquire – a momentum of accumulated self-interest. Always a profession makes in the mass for what is best for itself. It sustains an unceasing pressure in the one direction; it pushes its own way forward with the blind weight of a tide. Year by year, and bit by bit, it will go on piling up its resources; it never loses a step once gained, and never misses an opportunity for secret and solid advance. It thrusts aside by sheer pressure what obstructs; it beats under what is weaker than itself. It all happens by the sheer force of the situation. No one person in the profession or class exactly intends it; only each will tolerate on behalf of his class what he would never dream of doing on behalf of himself; and the volume of united selfishness is therefore ever moving on. And so it has come about that a great and honourable profession, such as that of the law or of the clergy, has, before now, found itself, to its own surprise, convicted, by the outraged conscience of its fellows, of injustice, harshness, greed, ambition. So a propertied class has before now come to build up its stability on some unhappy oppression; it has tolerated criminal miseries at its very doors without seeming to see that they existed. It has acquiesced in a condition which its own supremacy has made to seem familiar and natural, yet which every human-hearted member in the class would condemn with indignation if it was his *own* benefit which was bought at such a price. A class, an institution, has no eyes to see what its own prosperity costs to others. Thus it is that those social crimes have been committed which have been blotted out in revolution and in blood. Thus it is that the Church of Jesus Christ, founded in mercy and pity and loving-kindness, knit together in the love of the brotherhood, in the unity of the Spirit, in the bond of peace, has, as an organization, as a national institution, yielded so often in the past to the impulsion of its own self-interest, and has suffered itself to arrive at a position which has made it become the very by-word for arrogance and merciless ambition. All this has happened – we know it but too well; history records it over and over again with an iron pen graven upon rock for our warning.

And can it be that this old story should, in any degree, be repeating itself before our eyes today in England? There is, at least, evidence enough to make us suspect ourselves. We all feel so innocent, so well-intentioned, so right-minded. Why, then, this cry of sullen hate which rises into our ears from those who suffer? Why should the cloud of dismay hang so heavy over England, our fair motherland, the home of freedom, set as a jewel in the midst of the seas? Why do we fear to look our brethren in the face as the fierce war of competition clangs on and on in ruthless disregard;

and the weak are crushed; and the old are forsaken; and the bitterness of misunderstanding sharpens our divisions? Why is it that this Church of ours, this Church of England, so dear to us, so rich in her catholic inheritance, so interwoven into England's story, so tingling with English blood; a Church, too, so teeming with activity, so fervent, so alive with prayer and worship – why is it that nevertheless she should somehow appear to the masses of English workers in country and in town, now at the very crisis of their fate, as if she stood aloof from their life, and was cold to their aspirations, and suspicious of their aims, and helpless in their needs; why should she wear the aspect to them of something privileged and propertied, jealous and timid, and carry with her so little of the likeness of Christ? Surely there is wrong here, wrong deep and large and gross, such wrong as may fall under a curse.

We can find no such wrong in ourselves. No; but we are members of the society which is thus at enmity with itself; members of a nation which is embittered by these heart-burnings; members of this Church which so fails to interpret and justify to the democracy the goodness of God the Father, the compassion and joy and strength of Christ our King. Look away today over the nation at large, and behold there the evil to which our selfishness contributes, the sorrow and the hate for which we must share the responsibility. It is our public burdens that we are summoned to assume. That which dishonours England is our personal dishonour. That which puts Christ to shame lies heavy on our souls. Let today be a day of national humiliation for presenting to God so disheartening a result of Christian civilization as that on which our eyes so sadly fall. Let us ask ourselves why we, as a nation, have lost so much of our national peace – our national confidence in the name of Jesus. Why has the curse fallen upon us, the curse of a divided house, and of paralysed judgement, and of wounds that will not heal? Into each separate soul these questions must pierce like barbed arrows that cannot be withdrawn. Only according to the measure with which each solitary conscience takes home these things as matter of private personal concern, will the day of remedy dawn. True, it is not all wrong, not all black. There is earnestness in all classes, and patience, and moral soundness, and charitable zeal. There is a spirit of Christ-like devotion at work in the Church, that impels thousands of men and women into lives of mercy, that make for goodness and for peace. These are the salt that saves society from corruption. These keep alive the fire of sacrifice, and therefore of hope. But nothing of this should blind us to the terrible things still left undone, or should bribe us into murmuring 'peace' where peace has not yet been won.

LXV

From a sermon entitled 'A Social Conscience', preached at St Edmund's, Lombard Street, London, 1895, on the text:

Blow the trumpet in Zion, sanctify a fast, call a solemn assembly:
Gather the people, sanctify the congregation, assemble the elders, gather the children, and those that suck the breasts: let the bride-groom go forth of his chamber, and the bride out of her closet.
Let the priests, the ministers of the Lord, weep between the porch and the altar, and let them say, Spare thy people, O Lord, and give not thine heritage to reproach, that the heathen should rule over them: wherefore should they say among the people, Where is their God? (*Joel ii, 15–17*).

Another in the series of Lent sermons arranged by the London Branch of the Christian Social Union. Man ought to have a social, as well as an individual, conscience; social conditions witness to the value set by society upon human personality.

Round and about a nation's positive law lies the immense ring of its public customs. These are the richest and most delicate evidence of its social conscience. In these is fixed the indelible record by which we can tell exactly what is the value it sets on the human brotherhood, on women, on children, on labour, on service. We see precisely what, as a body corporate, it honours and what it despises; what it prizes and what it neglects; what are its public ideals and what its public fears. And this, not accidentally, not according to individual temperament, but according to the recognized moral instincts, which are the common property of the nation at large, and which are realized in their permanent body of custom.

English law, English custom – by these, then, this social conscience here in England puts itself in evidence. By these, it submits to judgement. These are not merely protective defences to shield us from dangerous incursions, or to prevent us from hitting one another over the head. They are the positive expression of our belief that England, as a whole, is responsible for the character and fashion of English life; that she has her own peculiar methods and principles, by which she controls and directs her own development, and shapes it to a worthy fulfilment. Here, in law and custom, all may see and know how England understands her own work, as compared with France, Germany, Russia; how Englishmen undertake their public responsibilities; what an Englishman understands by an English civilization.

Well, what is it? How does he understand it? What is this scene to which he would invite a foreigner, saying 'Look! there is what we Englishmen have made of England! There is the genuine sample of our free, self-governing community! Look! there is a city such as we English build. There is the existence which, by law and by custom, we free Englishmen have laboriously contrived. Let the historian come and note it all down, as the sample of what Englishmen can do to make human society fair and honourable and pure.'

Ah! the bitter irony of such a proposal as we look out of railway windows, in our passage to and fro from city to suburb, at that dismal sight, which can never, surely, lose its amazement and its terror. That sordid monotony of hideous streets into which we look as we hurry through! Those dingy, dismal, contemptible courts! The huddled filth of the back yards! How did it all come about? How was it that we, by our united efforts, arrived at such a result as that? What temper was it, what belief, what moral code, that went to the making of it? What public standard was there at work in the minds of all those who brought it to pass, as to the value of human life; as to its proper and natural environment; as to the type of dwelling that was fit for men and women to live in, for children to be born and bred in? How was it that builders considered these houses adequate for their purpose; that municipal inspectors were satisfied that they could not require anything better? How did it come to pass that anyone had the face to take a rent for them – and a high rent, too? How is it that a civilized

Christian society has failed, by the weight of its moral judgement, to make such things inconceivable, intolerable? Are not these the questions that storm again at the heart's doors, as we rush along, for instance, in some express through the heart of the Black Midlands? A train gives us so valuable an outlook, because it shows us exactly what our life would appear to a spectator carried through it, carried close to it, yet so far a stranger that he can retain a free judgement, unswayed by daily familiarity or local prejudice. And as we fly past those degraded ash-heaps, to which men are not ashamed to give names, as if they were human towns; as we catch sight of the few dirty, rackety boards, loosely nailed together, which are called stations; as we see the sodden, naked wastes of rubble where alone the children have space to play and breathe; as we note the slimy foulness of the canals where the poor boys are struggling to bathe; as our souls sink under all the wilful infamy of the smoke-burdened skies; we learn to gauge the contempt for human life of which all this baseness is the embodiment. Contempt! Public social contempt for human beings! This alone can explain why it was not thought worthwhile to meet the common human needs with a little more attention, a little more honour. No one who valued the body and soul of a man could hath given him such homes to house in. No one who loved a child could ever have had the heart to say, 'There! that black heap of refuse from a coal-pit is all we can afford you for a play-ground.' Yet we English people do love our own children, and in our own homes cherish reverence and affection for one another. Yes! it is not the private standard that is deficient. Privately, we do not despise human instincts and human charities. The English love of hearth and family survives in its traditional strength. But all this kindly moral impulse is arrested, somehow, at the house door. Outside – in the ordaining of the public life, in the framing of our towns – there is no public conscience that carries into general action the inner mind of the English home, and demands that, in the city as in the house, humanity shall be handled with respect, with reverence, with tenderness, with some touch of delicate affection. Therefore it is that we have suffered these horrible growths to defile the face of fair England, because the social conscience pitches its demands at so terribly low a level.

It enforces so pitiful an estimate of what humanity needs for a dwelling-place. It uplifts no fixed standard to which honourable men recognize their obligation to conform. It carries with it so little of rebuke, to shame and to confound those who, in the pursuit of their private interests, have created, or profited by, so ignominious a scandal.

Positive law is, indeed, beginning to insist on some rudimentary decency and fitness in buildings intended for man to live in. But law, unsupported, toils in vain against ingrained custom. Nothing but the pressure of the public conscience can avail to lift our corporate life to a better level. It alone can stem the multitudinous force of private greeds, in face of which we, for all our regrets, find ourselves so impotent. For are we not impotent ? Individually, we, each one of us, bewails what our cities have already become ; and yet we still sit by and permit the same rush of private speculation to reproduce the old intolerable conditions wherever populations are now spreading for the first time. Private regrets have proved powerless to prevent these things.

42

JAMES EDWARD WELLDON (1854–1937)

JAMES WELLDON was born at Tonbridge in 1854. He was ordained in 1883, became Master of Dulwich College and in 1885 was appointed Headmaster of Harrow, where he established his fame as a great schoolmaster. In 1898 he was consecrated Bishop of Calcutta, but he resigned in 1902 because of ill-health and disagreement with the Viceroy on missionary questions. After a period as Canon of Westminster, he was appointed Dean of Manchester in 1906, where he made the Cathedral a centre of spiritual and civic influence. Finally in 1918 he became Dean of Durham. Possessed of great personality he was a brilliant scholar and impressive preacher. He was sympathetic to Socialism, but was well aware of its dangers.

LXVI

From 'A New Year's Sermon', preached in Manchester Cathedral (no date), on the text: 'And he that sat upon the throne said, Behold, I make all things new' *(Rev. xxi, 5). Socialism is not un-Christian, but it expects far too much from a change in social conditions and dwells too little on 'the conversion of human hearts'.*

If I may speak of Socialism as I know it in the north of England, the Socialists – or many of them – seem to be so deeply impressed by existing social evils that they are ready to adopt almost any nostrum as a remedy for them. They declaim long and loudly, not indeed without some reason, against property and privilege. But I have never yet succeeded in bringing them to the sober, prosaic office of working out the social problem upon their own hypothesis of human rights and human duties. In a word, they anticipate far too much from a change of social conditions; they dwell far too little upon the conversion of human hearts. May I then remind them that high hopes of human regeneration have not seldom been dashed to the ground? Students of economical science are well aware that in the early days of cooperation, Robert Owen, in the fresh thrill of his enthusiasm for a movement which was destined, as he thought, to abolish the anti-social competitive instincts of mankind, inscribed on the facade of Tytherly Hall the mysterious letters 'c.m.', signifying the 'Commencement of the Millennium'. But, as the historian of cooperation, the late George Jacob Holyoake, shrewdly observes, 'The obstinate millennium declined to begin its career there.'

The Socialists of today see so clearly the evils of the present that they fail to see the possible evils of the future. They are so deeply impressed by the poverty and misery and inequality of the world that, rather than 'bear those ills they have', they are ready to 'fly to others that they know not of'. It is a just complaint against them that they indulge in rhetoric at the expense of reason; they declaim against the existing social order, and they have not thought out how a new social order is to be created.

It is no part of my purpose in this sermon to enter upon an elaborate examination of Socialism. For me, at least, it is impossible to look upon Socialism as being intrinsically irreligious or immoral; I cannot forget that the earliest Christians were Socialists. Yet that Christian Socialism, voluntary as it was, dependent on an elevated morality and practised for a brief while only on a small social scale, can scarcely be regarded as affording a guarantee for the success of a complete Socialistic reconstruction of civilized human life.

There are, I think, three mistakes which the Socialists of today almost uniformly make:

1. They underrate the magnitude of the change involved in Socialism. It has been found practicable to nationalize or municipalize the control of gas and electricity, of the tramways, and even of the railways. But the nationalization of all the means of communication, of all the supplies of coal and food, of all banks and factories, and of all the land as well, would involve the re-building of human society from the foundation. Yet in the catechism published by the Executive Council of the Social Democratic Federation there is this explicit statement: 'Instruct your delegates to proclaim that private property in railways, shipping,

factories, mines, and land must cease to be.' How is a change so revolutionary to be effected? If by compensation, it means national bankruptcy; if by confiscation, it means national immorality; at the best it may involve a complete loss of national credit, and with it the loss of national honour and dignity.

2. Again the Socialists seek to lay upon the state a burden which the state is wholly impotent to bear. Already the state is charged with so many duties that it proves unequal to its responsibilities. There have been instances enough of municipal incompetence, of municipal dishonesty. To overtax administration is to render administration inefficient. Yet 'the Socialist', as a modern writer says, 'would completely change the function of the government. Instead of continuing it as the ruler over persons, he would make it the organizer and distributor of the material things in our life.' In the Socialistic state the Government will become over-powerful; the operatives will be employees of the government, and it will be in their power to use their votes as menaces to their employer; nor will the government itself be reinforced by individual originality or enterprise.

3. The Socialists of today misread human nature. They think at once too well of it and too ill. In their contempt for the self-regarding impulses of mankind, they forget that it is enlightened self-interest which is frequently the motive to improvement; they forget that, if all men are reduced to an equality, that equality must be the level of the least competent. Yet at the same time Socialists lay an undue stress upon the material conditions of life. It is wealth and wealth alone which fills their thoughts; they forget that 'Man shall not live by bread alone.' But, necessary as bread is, there is nothing which lowers human nature so irreparably as the concentration of human thoughts and human efforts upon the accumulation of wealth and the advancement of material interests alone.

Brethren, the millennium, if it comes at all, will not begin in any Hall of Science or Socialism; it will begin and can only begin in regenerate human hearts. 'The Kingdom of God,' says the Saviour, 'is within you.'

Men need reform, but the most needed of all reforms is self-reform. The poverty and the misery of the world are solemn facts, and when all that can be said is said against the faults and the follies of parents, it remains true that the children, crying for food in the slums of great cities, make an appeal which touches the heart of humanity; they at least are innocent and helpless, they are not bearing the penalty of their own sins. Yet who doubts that the greater part of the sufferings and privations which fall upon the poor are the inevitable results of their own conduct? If it were only possible that they should obey the simple and severe laws of thrift and temperance and purity, there would be no need for a Socialistic regeneration of English life.

With all my heart I believe in the amelioration of social environment; I believe in it as giving free play to the best elements of human nature. But not science nor education nor civilization will provide a panacea for the evils of society, apart from the reformation of human characters and human lives.

The new heaven and the new earth will be realized, so far as they are possible upon earth, only when Jesus Christ has become Lord over the hearts and consciences of men. It is he who sits upon the throne; it is he who says, 'Behold, I make all things new.'

LXVII

From a sermon entitled 'The Problem of Unemployment', preached in Manchester Cathedral (no date), on the text:

And said unto them; Go ye also into the vineyard, and whatsoever is right I will give you. And they went their way.

Again he went out about the sixth and ninth hour, and did likewise.

And about the eleventh hour he went out, and found others standing idle, and saith unto them, Why stand ye here all the day idle?

They say unto him, Because no man hath hired us. He saith unto them, Go ye also into the vineyard; and whatsoever is right, that shall ye receive (*Matt. xx, 4–7*).

Violence by the unemployed cannot be tolerated; relief should be available for the genuinely unemployed; a description of what is being done nationally and locally; indiscriminate charity is wrong.

I should perhaps be doing them* less or more than justice, if I

* i.e. the labourers in Christ's parable of the Labourers in the Vineyard, referred to in the preacher's text.

were to assume that they were particularly anxious to find work. They had not apparently troubled themselves to look for it; they stood in the market-place, waiting on the chance of its coming to them. They were idle; but as the sequel shows they were not unwilling to work, if work were put in their way. It may be observed, however, that although they were unemployed, they were not disturbers of the public peace. They did not interrupt traffic in the streets; they did not destroy or injure property; they did not come into collision with the police. So far, then, their self-restraint entitled them to sympathy. For it is impossible to urge too strongly that the unemployed men who commit breaches of order are the enemies of their own body; they alienate public sympathy, they excite bitter feeling between class and class. I say so here, and I have said so to them when a deputation of the unemployed waited upon me shortly after the night of 25 September,* and I told them that I sympathized with their position (it was a pleasure to me that they interjected, 'Yes, sir, we know that'), but that they would forfeit the sympathy of Manchester, if they did not behave as respectable, law-abiding citizens. It is only just to them to admit that the misconduct at which I hinted was confined to a few persons, and was short-lived.

The preservation of public order is the primary duty of a civilized community. It is the distinction between civilization and barbarism. However much it is right to feel for the hungry, suffering members of society, I should be prepared to take the strongest possible measures, if they seemed to be necessary, for the maintenance of order in the streets. Nor do I believe that the police of this city have used more than the minimum of force, which was indispensable on a certain critical occasion to the public weal.

But let me come back to the parable. The remedy for unemployment is work – not charity, but work. 'Go ye also into the vineyard.' The Master does not say, as it were, 'Here, take this money, and spend it as you will.' He says, 'Go, work for it, earn it, let it be your own wage.' That is the true Christian political economy. If a man will not work, he shall not eat; but, if he has not got enough to eat, then give him work.

* The night on which a conflict between the police and the unemployed took place in Manchester.

334

There can be no greater social error than indiscriminate alms-giving. It perpetuates and aggravates the evil which it purports to relieve. It clothes what is really a selfish spirit in the garb of un-selfishness. Yet a Christian community can scarcely be said to be performing its duty, if it leaves the labour question to the mere rigid law of supply and demand; if it says to its own deserving but unfortunate members, 'There is no home for you but the Union.'* It seems to me that in periods of acute social distress civic authori-ties are justified, and more than justified, in taking exceptional measures to provide employment for deserving men and women. The idle, the thriftless, the wastrels, the drunkards, the ne'er-do-wells possess no title to consideration, or they deserve it only in so far as their innocent wives and children are the victims of their evil ways; but the honourable toilers, who are out of work through no fault of their own, may fairly claim consideration and com-passionate treatment. 'Go ye also into the vineyard,' is the Divine command. The master gives them work. He gives them also a just wage for the work which they do – 'Whatsoever is right, that shall ye receive.' . . .

There are persons, whether many or few, who can do but little work, or who cannot find such work as they might do – the sick, the aged, the infirm, the crippled, the afflicted – it is they who make an irresistible appeal to human sympathy. Their necessity is no fault of their own. It may be the direct result of hard industrial conditions. Even an act so charitable in its purpose as the Em-ployers' Liability Act or the Workmen's Compensation Act has rather augmented than lessened the difficulty which the in-effective members of society experience in obtaining employ-ment; for it has deterred employers from engaging servants whose physical weakness would render them especially liable to such accidents as might create a title to pecuniary compensation. Yet neither Christ nor his Church may leave these ineffective members of society in the lurch. Still, as of old, he inspires the temper of charity – not less generous, but more scientifically organized charity – for the problem of relieving distress was comparatively simple when he was upon earth, but in the complicated state of modern society it demands perpetual thoughtfulness, lest the

* i.e. Poor Law Institution.

almsgiving, which is itself the fruit of his Spirit, should do more harm than good to the community. There is need of thought, there is need of painstaking. It is necessary not only to relieve cases which meet the eye, but to seek out cases which languish in obscurity; for not a few of the sufferers whose lot is saddest and harshest endure hunger, and, it may be, die in silence.

Thus the wise administration of the Lord Mayor's Fund for the relief of distress has done and is doing noble service. If I may offer a word of counsel to the citizens of Manchester, I would beg them to refrain from indiscriminate charity; I would beg them to concentrate their sympathy upon the support of a Fund administered in accordance with sound economical principles by men who are experts in the cause of philanthropy. Thus, too, it is that the City League of Help affords all citizens the means of learning where genuine stress exists, and of relieving it quietly and wisely, not without that sacred touch of personal sympathy which gives charity half its blessing and its value.

The civic duty, then, of today, so far as it touches the problem of unemployment, a duty which falls in larger or less degree upon us all, as we are 'members one of another', is:

Firstly, to maintain the public order which is at once the sign and the safeguard of civilization.

Secondly, to provide work as far as possible for all citizens who are willing to perform it – such work as it may be within their power to do – and to pay them for doing it.

Thirdly, to dispense scientific charity to the citizens who cannot help themselves, the victims of modern social and economic conditions, the fallen and wounded soldiers in the battle of human life.

It is impossible, therefore, to help recognizing the Christian value of such provisions as the old age pensions, which will do much to maintain the blessing of home life for humble citizens who can no longer earn their living, or the free meals given with all due caution to the children who would otherwise be unfit to receive teaching in elementary schools, and who, as suffering hunger from no fault of their own, must touch the heart of even the coldest student of modern social life.

43

WILLIAM TEMPLE (1881–1944)

WILLIAM TEMPLE, born in 1881, was the son of Frederick Temple, Archbishop of Canterbury. He became Fellow of Queen's College, Oxford in 1904 and Headmaster of Repton in 1910. After a period as Rector of St James's, Piccadilly, he became Canon of Westminster in 1919, where he devoted his time and energy to the Life and Liberty Movement, which aimed at achieving greater self-government for the Church of England. In 1921 Temple was consecrated Bishop of Manchester and eight years later was appointed Archbishop of York. From there he was translated to Canterbury in 1942 and died two years later. Throughout his life Temple was deeply concerned with social and economic questions and was one of the outstanding leaders on social thinking in the Church of England. He was an able theologian and philosopher and an outstanding preacher. Most of his social thinking is to be found in his speeches and writings rather in his sermons.

LXVIII

From a sermon entitled 'Unity and Peace', preached in Repton School Chapel, 1 October 1911, on the texts:

Now the works of the flesh are manifest, which are these; Adultery, fornication, uncleanness, lasciviousness . . .

But the fruit of the Spirit is love, joy, peace, longsuffering, gentleness, goodness, faith . . . (*Gal. v, 19, 22*).

For he is our peace, who hath made both one, and hath broken down the middle wall of partition between us;

Having abolished in his flesh the enmity, even the law of commandments contained in ordinances; for to make in himself of twain one new man, so making peace (*Eph. ii, 14–15*).

The Christian responsibility for social evils. This early sermon enunciates such principles as the proper provision of education, leisure and just wages for the workers, for which Temple was to fight throughout his life.

Most of us, I expect, were a good deal startled during the holidays by the manifestation of unrest and discontent among those of our fellow-citizens who work for wages; we had been content to ignore the long history which was surely and inevitably leading up to that crisis; but when our own personal convenience seemed likely to be affected by the strike on the railways we suddenly awoke to the fact that all is not well with our national life. There can be no doubt that the country has had a fright. We are not here concerned with the matter in dispute; but as people engaged in the effort to understand the world, so that we may spend our lives in it most serviceably, we are very much concerned with the fact that such a dispute has arisen and has forced itself upon our notice. Such an occurrence is a direct call from God to every educated man to consider his duty and responsibility afresh. Merely to take one side or the other according as the general habit of our mind or the custom of our friends may suggest, is to shirk responsibility. We are not called upon to decide who is right or who is wrong; our duty is something much less habitual – our duty is to think.

And above all our duty is to think out the relation of our religious belief to such occurrences as this. And that relation is singularly close. St Paul is quite clear that strife, jealousies, wraths, factions, divisions are the works of the flesh, of that part of our nature which resists the Holy Spirit, whereas the fruits of the Spirit are love and joy and peace. If this is true, the only real solution for our social and industrial chaos is to be found in the power of God's Holy Spirit. But that is the last source to which most of us would apply for guidance.

I want to impress upon you if I can that the troubles we have been witnessing are not only a challenge to our faith for the future but are a proof of the hollowness of our religion in the past. If the spirit of Christ were in our nation, the fruits of the Spirit, which are love and joy and peace, would mark our national life. But it is now marked by strife, jealousies, wraths, factions and divisions, which spring from the selfish side of man's nature, from all in us that is opposite to the Divine.

The bitterness of class feeling, and the oppression which still undoubtedly exists, do not spring from the peculiar wickedness of separate individuals or groups of individuals. They are the inevitable result of our lack of true Christianity. If you take a large number of people, with varying abilities, but not varying selfishness, and put them to live together for generations, the result will be the accumulation of wealth in comparatively few hands, and consequently oppression, neither deliberate nor even conscious, of the great majority. There are some who say that our social problem is entirely due to the conditions in which the poor are compelled to live; and that, no doubt, is more true than to put it all down to weakness of character in the poor themselves, for that weakness, where it exists, is produced by those conditions. But if we want to go to the root of the matter we must go further than this. What we call the social problem – which means class hatred, oppression, ignorance and vice – exists really because people generally are as good as we are and no better. The first effect of the recent disturbances upon us ought to be a shock to our self-complacency. The sort of character that we have been content with is the sort of character that issues in enmities, strife, jealousies, wraths, factions, divisions – with all their inevitable consequence of hunger and distress for the poor . . .

There is no way by which we may be sure of bringing men into harmony with one another except by bringing both into allegiance to the will of God. The Purpose of God includes the welfare of all, and nothing else does that; and therefore it is only in obedience to that Purpose that we all find ourselves united and harmonious. And we are won to that allegiance because the appeal of the Love of God is irresistible when once we understand it. As we make our intercourse with God and Christ more constant and sincere, we find ourselves taken hold of by a power stronger than our passions; as the image of the Cross fastens on our minds we are conquered by the appeal of God's self-sacrifice.

Do you think it is fantastic to appeal to the Crucifixion of Christ as the solution of our labour troubles or of the railway strike? Then read the story of Bishop Westcott's intervention in the

Durham coal strike.* He knew little of the points in dispute. But he invited the two Committees of Masters and Men to Bishop Auckland, and urged upon each the necessity of seeing the matter from the other's point of view; and all the time when he was not with them he was praying in the Chapel. A settlement was reached and the settlement proved sound.

The responsibility for our social troubles lies very near ourselves. We cannot escape it. Let me remind you of a few perfectly familiar facts. While you are here, passing by slow stages from childhood to manhood, with gradually increasing freedom and responsibility, most of your fellow-citizens of the same age are out in the world, already at work to earn their living. Naturally they tend to take up whatever work is best paid at the moment, and as a rule that is work of a kind that gives no real training, so that when they reach manhood and need a man's wage they are turned out upon the streets knowing no useful trade; and so they drift into the casual labour market, picking up jobs as best they may, always the first to be out of work in times of depression – and we grumble because they are liable to be led astray by any noisy demagogue. But it is all our fault. We have allowed them to be taken away from school while their faculties are still undeveloped, before they have had the training which enables men to distinguish sense from nonsense. I was in Glasgow some time back when there was much unemployment on the Clyde, and there was a little rioting. A worthy lady said to me one day – 'Of course those people who riot are not the real unemployed, they are only the unemployables.' Only unemployable! And by whose fault are they unemployable?

Again, we all know the havoc that is wrought by and yet we are content that the great majority of our fellow-citizens should have no opportunity for the social recreation and merriment which are the birth-right of all God's children, except where the influence of alcohol is supreme. Why are not other places provided? I suppose because it would cost money. And are we going to withhold so far as we can salvation from all these for fear of spending a little money, and then have the impertinent

*1892. See A. Westcott, *Life and Letters of Brooke Foss Westcott*, 1903, II, pp. 115ff.

audacity to claim our own redemption by the Cross of Christ?

Or, once more, we may remember that there are women employed at such low wages that, human nature being what it is, some of them are quite certain to eke out their livelihood at the cost of their honour. And the goods so made enter in the open market into competition with other goods and lower prices. So it is literally true that every shilling I possess buys more because of that traffic in sin. We are told to use only clean money; but the purchasing power of all money is tainted. We must use the cleanest money we can find, and we must at least earn our money in a clean way. But we cannot use only clean money; there is no clean money.

The responsibility comes right home. And we know that all this horror arises simply because men generally are as good as we are and no better. No one ever deliberately planned the state of society which now exists in England. The criminal capable of that has not yet been born. It is the working out of just our own character – our own selfishness and contempt for humility, our own un-Christ-likeness.

LXIX

From a sermon entitled 'Inasmuch', preached in Westminster Abbey, 17 August 1919, on the text: ' Inasmuch as ye have done it unto one of the least of these my brethren, ye have done it unto me ' (*Matt. ₃, 40*). *Christian worship must issue in love for the oppressed; when we help the poor and oppressed, it is the Christ in them to whom we minister.*

If we really believe that the Christ whom we adore, in whose name we present our prayers, and whom we receive in his own sacrament that he may become the very life of our souls, is waiting in the souls of those whom we neglect or despise for the word of kindness or the helping hand that we can offer if we will. Of what avail is it that I glorify him in his sanctuary or adore him in the Blessed Sacrament, if when I meet him in the street I turn away from him, or if I leave him to languish uncared for in the prison? Because he is perfect Love, he is perfectly united in the bonds of love with all who in virtue of his incarnation are his fellow-men. As we serve them we serve him. When we neglect or ignore them, we are ignoring or neglecting him. What wonder then if worship becomes cold and dead while this continues. But what power there is in any worship, that is still real and sincere, to drive men forth to service and thereby to the rekindling also of their devotional ardour.

The services spoken of are simple, and in the simplest service of those who lack, service is given to Christ. But it is not always in simple fashion that service can be rendered. We have all learnt, for instance, that only seldom can real good be done by giving to beggars. Something more than perfunctory giving of our super-fluities is wanted. The man who asks for money may really be needing trust and the sense that someone cares for him enough to want to see him living a useful life. Very often the giving of money is a purely selfish indulgence of feelings that are stirred or torn by the appearance of misery or of personal charm combined with want. We give; so we satisfy our feelings; and we think no more. Is that our love and worship for the Christ who suffers before us in his little ones? It is true that we cannot always, or indeed often, give the time that is needed to offer ourselves the service that will really help. But then we ought to support to the utmost those who are giving that service and spend our lives in giving it. And in the modern world we should use our influence as citizens to secure that the state, which is just our united strength organized for action, effectively remedies the conditions which cause misery, and effectively helps those who bring misery on themselves. How many of us have ever reflected, for example, that we as Christian citizens are responsible for the conditions to which our citizens who are condemned to imprisonment are subjected. We cannot all be visitors in gaols; but we can all insist that the conditions in gaols should be such as may encourage reformation instead of such as are bound to be degrading. And probably that is the way by which most of us could most surely win the greeting: 'I was in prison and ye came unto me.'

That is a single illustration; but it serves to represent the principle applying to all the various spheres. And it leads to the other side of the matter. When the state takes charge of people's welfare, whether by way of discipline or in other ways, or when benevolence is scientifically organized, there is a great danger of hardness and unsympathetic treatment. We all know of men and women who work with great self-sacrifice in the cause of social welfare and yet seem hard and unsympathetic. They give their goods to feed the poor; they are quite ready to give their bodies to be burned; but they have not love. And we feel that, if untutored impulse can only do harm when it seeks to be charitable, there is equally little hope that this laborious conscientiousness can do any real good. We sum up our objection to it in the familiar phrase 'red tape'. It appears whenever individual men and women are treated as merely 'cases'. At its root the trouble is simply lack of love . . .

It is Christ who pines when the poor are hungry; it is Christ who is repulsed when strangers are not welcome; it is Christ who suffers when rags fail to keep out the cold; it is Christ who is in anguish in the long-drawn illness; it is Christ who waits behind the prison doors. You come upon one of those who have been broken by the tempests of life, and if you look with eyes of Christian faith and love, he will lift a brow 'luminous and imperial from the rags' and you will know that you are standing before the King of Kings, the Lord of Lords.

Christ brought to the world a new conception of royalty. He rules by love and not by force. That, as he expressly said, is the difference between his Kingdom and the kingdoms of this world. His most regal act was the supreme self-sacrifice whereby he would draw all men to himself and make them willingly obedient to him for ever. In full harmony with this, he never speaks of himself as King except on one occasion only. He accepts from others the title of Messiah with its kingly connotation, but the only time when he speaks of himself as King is when, in this parable of the sheep and the goats, he identifies himself with the failures of the world and the outcasts of society. 'Then shall the King say unto them on his right hand. . . . I was an hungered and ye gave me meat; I was a stranger and ye took me in; naked and ye clothed me; I was sick and ye visited me; I was in prison, and ye came unto me.'

Civilization, as we know it, produces much human refuse.

Slum-dwellings, long hours of work, underpayment, child labour, lack of education, prostitution; all these evils are responsible for stunting and warping the development of souls. Things are improving, we hope. But unless we are exerting all the strength that Christ gives us in ending these bad conditions, then the responsibility for wasted lives lies at our door, and from the streets of cities or the lanes of country sides the cry goes up through the lips of their Saviour and our Judge: 'Inasmuch as ye did it not unto one of these least, ye did it not unto me.'

44

EDWARD LYTTLETON (1855–1942)

EDWARD LYTTLETON became Master of Haileybury in 1890, Headmaster of Eton in 1905 and Rector of Sidestrand, Norfolk, in 1918.

LXX

From a sermon entitled 'Recreation', preached at St Edmund's, Lombard Street, London, 1894, on the text: 'Whether therefore ye eat, or drink, or whatsoever ye do, do all to the glory of God' *(1 Cor. x, 31). Part of a course of Lent sermons arranged by the London Branch of the Christian Social Union. A criticism of commercialism in sport and in the press.*

To make clear what I mean by degeneracy, let us contrast the two following pictures. The first refers to cricket as it was played in many parts of the country some twenty-five or thirty years ago. A club was formed, including men of all classes of society – the sons of the squire, the parson, the local gentry, the shopkeepers, the clerks in the village, the gardeners and men-servants from the wealthier houses. On most evenings in the week there was practice on the ground in the squire's park, where in all friendliness these different members of society gathered together in thoroughly healthy play; and their unity was still further cemented by the good spirit evoked in the weekly matches. Keen rivalry without bitterness, honest effort, unselfishness, manly endurance of failure, insight into others' claims – all these qualities were directly encouraged by such recreation as this; and I doubt if any amusement so thoroughly beneficial to all concerned could be found in any form of recreation known to the civilized world. Now, this has not wholly died out yet. But let us contrast it with the other picture, representing an Association football match in the north of

England. A club has been formed in a big town. How ? Not by local energy and love of the native country district, but by a company with a keen eye to profit. Everything depends, therefore, on the gate-money, as it is known that with sufficient inducements 20,000 or 30,000 people can be gathered together and pay so much a head to see an exciting football match. But to make it exciting the play must be first-rate, and what matter if the players have no connexion whatever with the locality ? The players are only important as bearing on the question of spectators. So agents are sent far and wide, mostly into Scotland, to secure recruits to supplement the local talent if there is any. Sometimes, it appears, every single man in the team is an importation. From eighteen to twenty-eight years of age, these young fellows are paid enormous wages; if successful, they can command their own price, and, so far from having any interest in the particular district to which they have been allured, their chief anxiety is to let it be known that they are willing to transfer themselves to any other club or company that will offer higher wages than they are now receiving. This goes on till the prime of their youth is past, and they are turned out into the world unfit to learn any trade, and almost certain to be burdens on their country as long as they live. And among the spectators – so far has the English instinct for fair play suffered in the prevailing frenzy – it has, I am told, again and again happened that the life of a referee at the end of a match is hardly safe from the mob of disappointed loafers who have put their money on the losing side, and are ready for any violence against him, though they know he has only done his duty.

This is a sad and sorry sight, my friends; and yet even Association football was for a few years, between 1870 and 1880, played in much the same spirit and with the same good effects as village cricket. Its name has not always been the mockery that it now is.

Now, what are the chief characteristics of these two forms of so-called recreation ? The first did good in many ways, but its chief and most admirable characteristic was the spirit of *brotherliness*.

And the other ? The other does harm in many ways, but its chief characteristic is the spirit of *estrangement*. There is no evoking of local patriotism; there is no concord between the managers and the rank and file; there is suspicion, born of greed, and smouldering animosities, because everybody who is connected with the arrangements and the play is bent on making money.

But we must consider come collateral and less direct effects of this state of things. So vast and widespread an organization is certain to tell in many subtle ways on the tone of society. First, there is the mischief that looking-on is substituted for bodily exercise. We have no right to talk of national games unless we mean games that are played by the people of the nation; but we are drifting to a state of things when the games will only be national because Englishmen look at them, and those who play them are paid £200 or £300 a year for doing so. Paid players and vast hordes of idle spectators – these were symptoms of the decline of Rome; but we have a feature to add peculiar to ourselves – our spectators come together by the thousand for betting. And then I would have you remember that the unhealthy excitement caused by these public displays goes far to corrupt the tone wherever football is played. Such a glamour is thrown round it that it has become a doubtful question among some energetic young town clergy whether they ought to encourage their lads to form a club among themselves, the truth being that as soon as they give themselves to a game so infected with spurious excitement and feverish rivalry, they can think and talk of nothing else. This means that the mischief spreads from the centres of excitement and corrupts the outlying districts, where there was, at least, a hope that the game might be played in its primitive simplicity.

But there is one baneful effect of this state of things less obvious than those I have mentioned, but well worth considering – I mean its effect on the tone of the public press. Consider the problem set before newspaper editors. To make a living for them, the paper must sell, and, in presence of fierce competition, it soon becomes recognized that pence must flow in without too much attention being paid as to the quarter whence they come. What the average mass of people require, that they must have, or the sale dwindles. Now, what do average people require ? We will think of the way a working man spends his leisure. In the afternoon he witnesses an exciting football match; in the evening, if he has the chance, he goes to a political meeting – all the more readily he thinks the speaking will be of the vituperative kind. The following morning he buys a daily paper which professes to discuss all sorts of difficult and complex questions relating to public affairs. Is it not certain that his appetite by this time has been quickened and stimulated in the direction of a craving for excitement, so that if by chance he comes across some impartial and well-balanced decisions in the paper he finds them intolerably dull? He is learning, not only to feed himself on excitement, but on that special form of excitement which comes from being a spectator of a conflict; and his natural propensity to be a partisan has been so much encouraged that life without conflict is to him a poor and tame affair.

Hence the peculiarly modern development of abusiveness in politics and abusiveness in the public press. A newspaper must not only take a side, but must take it violently; and to anyone who knows anything of the atmosphere that surrounds football matches, especially in the North of England, it will not appear a fanciful or far-fetched inference to say that this woeful eagerness to witness sharp conflict is materially quickened by the prevalence of these violent athletic contests in which a score of paid men play and 20,000 look on, imbibing, surely, all the mischief and none of the benefits that belong to modern athleticism. If there are any here who think that acute party spirit, and the desire to treat politics as if they were a game between two sides, are favourable symptoms of modern social life, they may be content to acquiesce in modern developments of football. But those who do not may surely trust that some healing influence is at hand to save the tone of English public life, and with it a grand English game.

I do not deny that there would be some justification for calling this a needlessly sombre picture. But the gloom of it is relieved by enough light to let us perceive one great and encouraging fact – the presence of law. It is a violation of the law of brotherliness which has wrought the sad effects we know so well in the commercial world; and the same violation of the same law is producing the same effects in athletics. Let us take heart in the thought that this lesson is one which it is not yet too late for us to learn. We need discipline before we can grasp large and unfamiliar truths, and now is the time for us to take note that the time of discipline is at hand – 'the axe is being laid at the root of the trees'. Is there anything, then, that we can do?

First, we can give a hearty support to the managers of the Rugby Union, who are doing their utmost to stem the rising tide of professionalism – not as men who are merely consulting a passing convenience, but as those who in a gallant and unpretending way are doing something to keep alive the true idea of recreation. That is one thing. But as regards the whole question, it is painfully and abundantly evident that we have here a disquieting symptom of a deep-seated social evil.

To lop off a dead branch from a precious tree is better than nothing, but it is not the same thing as curing a disease at the roots. Covetousness is at the root of this decaying branch of our English oak; and to cure a deep-seated evil your remedies must go deep and begin early. Men of business can, if they choose, train up their sons to look upon money as a trust, and not as a possession, because the first condition of brotherliness is that those who have should know themselves as stewards. And if you choose, you can do more than this; you can inspire them by your own example with a true view of the meaning of life and of the recreation of spent energies. God has placed us here not to become wholly absorbed in a complex commercial machine of our own fabrication, nor to give all we have to the building up of a muscular body, but to learn the great mystery that bodies are the temples of mind and spirit, and not only are as wonderful in structure, but are also immortal in their destiny; and for those reasons, and those only, are they to be jealously guarded, harmoniously developed, and lovingly adapted to the spiritual service of our Incarnate Master, Jesus Christ.

45

HERBERT HENSLEY HENSON (1863–1947)

HENSLEY HENSON was born in 1863 and in 1888 became Vicar of Barking. After a period as Chaplain of St Mary's Hospital, Ilford, he was appointed Canon of Westminster and Rector of St Margaret's, Westminster, in 1900. Twelve years later he became Dean of Durham. In 1918 he was consecrated Bishop of Hereford and was translated to Durham in 1920. Henson was an individualist whose liberal theological views gained him considerable criticism. He was one of the most outspoken bishops on the bench. Stephen Mayor describes him as 'the most formidable opponent of Christian Socialist tendencies'*.

LXXI

From a sermon entitled 'Christ's Mission in the Church', preached in Westminster Abbey, 10 November 1901, on behalf of the East London Church Fund, on the texts:

And Jesus went about all the cities and villages, teaching in their synagogues, and preaching the gospel of the kingdom, and healing every sickness and every disease among the people (*Matt. ix. 35*).

And when he had called unto him his twelve disciples he gave them power against unclean spirits to cast them out, and to heal all manner of sickness and all manner of disease (*Matt. x, 1*).

A description of conditions in East London, for the alleviation of which the Church is needed.

East London, as we use the term in the pulpit, is less a geographical than an ethical and social term. It includes all that mass of congregated city folk who live, broadly, under the same conditions;

* Stephen Mayor, *The Churches and the Labour Movement*, Independent Press, 1967, p. 222.

who are manual workers, skilled or unskilled; who are separated by a wide and, I fear a widening gulf from the comfortable and cultivated sections of the people; who live in chronic anxiety lest by some economic crisis their employment shall suddenly fail, and with it their means of living and the securities of their civic self-respect; who are, in many cases, exposed to grave risks of life and limb, and whose normal length of years is considerably less than that of the classes above them in the order of society. This vast multitude of people, numbering, perhaps, if we include, as for my argument we are bound to do, the inhabitants of South London, and of London over the border, as well as those of East London – some three millions of souls – is for the most part a very recent and a very artificial aggregation. Seen from the outside by a super-ficial observer, it has an aspect of depressing sameness: every-thing seems to proceed on a dead-level of monotonous and rather squalid activity; but seen from within, the effect on the observer is rather that of an astonishing and, so to say, wilful variety. The law of social aggregation which accumulates these vast multitudes works together with a law of social segregation which isolates class from class, trade from trade, interest from interest, nationality from nationality, creed from creed. There is a principle of caste which penetrates society from one end to the other, neutralizing the kindly influences of neighbourhood, and stereotyping the prejudices of men. At the bottom of society there is a lamentable collection of human wreckage, the 'jetsam and flotsam' of the social sea, carried by its winds and tides to the harbourage of the great city. One of the most cautious and careful of our social students, Mr Charles Booth, to whose patient and devoted labour we are all greatly indebted, has described this bottom-most class in the hierarchy of London life*:

Their life is the life of savages, the vicissitudes of extreme hardship and occasional excess. . . . From these come the battered figures who slouch through the street, and play the beggar or the bully, or help to foul the record of the unemployed; these are the worst class of corner men, who hang round the doors of public-houses; the young men who spring forward on any chance to earn a copper; the ready materials for disorder when occasion serves. They render no useful service; they

* Charles Booth, *Life and Labour of the People of London*, 1902.

create no wealth; more often they destroy it. They degrade whatever they touch, and as individuals are perhaps incapable of improvement. They may be to some extent a necessary evil in every large city; but their numbers will be affected by the economical condition of the classes above them, and the discretion of 'the charitable world'; their way of life by the pressure of police supervision.

This class of hereditary outcasts is continually fed from above. Every variety of failure in the superior classes of society tends to find its way to this Alsatia of the worthless. Drink, vice, misfortune, crime, are the recruiting sergeants of that doomed host. The only effectual way of dealing with this scandal and problem of our irreformable class is by arresting the stream of recruits from the classes above it. East London needs an arrestive agency, ubiquitous, ever-active, resourceful, which shall come between drink, vice, misfortune, crime, and the social abyss towards which their victims are inexorably carried. The higher you go in the hierarchy of life the more the individual counts for, the more amenable he is to agencies of reformation. You are not neglecting the criminal residuum when you bend your principal efforts to the rescue of those who are drifting into it.

East London, as every great aggregation of men, contains within it a multitude of morally broken folk, men and women who have lost heart and lost character, and who, if they are to escape an utter bankruptcy of their lives, need some regenerating, re-creating force which shall quicken and recover them. East London, when all is said, is an unkindly soil for the best things to grow in. Life is dull, toilsome, prosaic, even squalid. It is not favourable to the development of character; it is bad for the upbringing of children. I notice that even our devoted clergy, who will certainly endure any personal hardships which their duty demands, eagerly seize the opportunity to desert the East End when their children begin to grow up. There is urgent need, then, of some inspiring, elevating influence which shall encourage men to resist the impressions of their environment, to rise above the traditions of society, and to move morally and spiritually towards worthier ideals than any native to their neighbourhood. East London wants discipline and unity. Into its bewildering movement there come continually, not in hundreds but in thousands, the immigrants from the country. They are drawn to the great city by many forces, some known, some but dimly suspected. They come in the ardour of youthful hope, with youth's keen curiosity and fierce thirst for pleasure, and, we must add, with youth's perilous self-confidence and inevitable ignorance. They leave behind them in their ancestral villages the normal disciplines of life – home, and the kindly interest of neighbours, and the salutary deference for social superiors. At an age when these protective disciplines are most needed they are suddenly withdrawn. In this terrible city these exiles from home are amid strangers; they must make for themselves some substitute for all they have lost. Is it any marvel that in multitudes of cases they fall under the novel and exigent strain of their circumstances ? I am speaking to those who can fill in the outlines of my speech from the resources of their own knowledge. You know how many a bright lad, many a pure maiden, the hope and pride of some simple rustic home, for whom parental prayers rise daily to the Eternal Father, about whom are gathered the tenderest love of mothers' hearts, are brought to destruction here. Caught up by the eager, multitudinous life of London, carried along by its depraved fashions, deluded by its base sophistries, deserted by its cynical indifference, what hope is there for them if there be not present and active in the scenes of peril an energy of discipline, of restoration, and of hope ? East London, I said, is inwardly divided. Those multitudes are gathered into sections and parties, which are mutually ignorant, and therefore suspicious and hostile. There is no cohesion, because there is no confidence; and there is no confidence because there is no common enthusiasm, no common sympathy. The social reformer laments, as the rock on which his benevolent projects are broken, this inveterate incoherence of our poorer people. There is need of some strong, patient, persistent force which shall make war against ignoránce, which shall create confidence, which shall make cohesion possible, and thus provide the conditions of social regeneration.

Consider, I pray you, these grave and apparent necessities of city life. Arrestive agencies to intercept the falling; regenerating agencies to rescue and renew the fallen; disciplinary agencies to protect and order the incoming strangers; inspiring agencies to move men to break through the iron restraints of routine and rise above the demoralizing dullness of uncultured society; unifying agencies to discover some latent principle of common action, and to bind together the segregated sections of the community – where shall these blessed powers be found ? At least we can be in no doubt where we, as disciples of Jesus Christ, were directed to find them. We turn to the Gospel and contemplate the Son of God as he reviews the mingled life of sin-stricken humanity, and takes action to redeem it. 'When he saw the multitudes, he was moved with compassion for them, because they were distressed and scattered, as sheep not having a shepherd.' Is not that a just and pathetic description of our modern society? Would not Christ speak thus of our great city ? Mark, then, his action. From the eloquent spectacle of human disorder and distress, he turns to his disciples, and constitutes them a commissioned Church. 'Then saith he unto his disciples, The harvest truly is plenteous, but the labourers are few. Pray ye, therefore, the Lord of the harvest, that he send forth labourers unto his harvest.' Immediately the evangelist records that solemn and momentous act from which the Christian Church has proceeded: 'He called unto him his twelve disciples, and gave them authority over unclean spirits, to cast them out, and to heal all manner of disease and all manner of sickness.' East London needs the Church of Christ.

LIST OF SOURCES

Hugh Latimer:
I   *Sermons*, Parker Society, Cambridge University Press, 1844, pp. 63 ff.
II   ibid., pp. 98 ff.
III   ibid., pp. 189 ff.
IV   ibid., pp. 249, 252 f., 279.
V   ibid., pp. 398 f., 410 f.

Roger Edgeworth:
VI   *Sermons*, London, 1557, Fol. clxxxxviii^v – ccii.

The Book of Homilies:
VII   Society for Promoting Christian Knowledge, 1851, pp. 609 ff.
VIII   ibid., pp. 327 ff.
IX   ibid., pp. 553 ff.

Thomas Lever:
X   *Sermons*, edited E. Arber, English Reprints, London, 1870, pp. 120 ff.

Edwyn Sandys:
XI   *Sermons*, Parker Society, Cambridge University Press, 1842, pp. 47 ff.
XII   ibid., pp. 392 ff.

Henry Smith:
XIII   *The Sermons of Mr Henry Smith*, London, 1675, pp. 78 ff.
XIV   ibid., pp. 430 ff.

John Stockwood:
XV   *A Sermon Preached at Paul's Cross, 24th August 1578*, London, 1578, pp. 23 ff., 50 ff., 85 ff., 133 ff.

Thomas White:
XVI   *A Sermon Preached at Paul's Cross, 3rd November 1577 in the time of The Plague*, London, 1578, pp. 42 ff.

John Hoskins:
XVII   *Sermons Preached at Paul's Cross and Elsewhere*, London, 1615, pp. 28 ff.

John Donne:
XVIII   *The Sermons of John Donne,* edited G. R. Potter and
             E. M. Simpson, University of California, 1959, IV,
             pp. 313 ff.

Thomas Adams:
XIX   *Works,* James Nichol, Edinburgh, 1861, I, pp. 318 ff.
XX   ibid., II, pp. 228 ff.

Robert Sanderson:
XXI   *Works,* London, 1884, III, pp. 108 ff.
XXII   ibid., II, pp. 356 ff.

Jeremy Taylor:
XXIII   *Works,* London, 1850, IV, pp. 204 ff.

Isaac Barrow:
XXIV   *Theological Works,* Oxford, 1818, III, pp. 54 ff.
XXV   ibid., I, pp. 465 ff.

John Tillotson:
XXVI   *Works,* Richard Priestly, 1820, X, pp. 180 ff.
XXVII,   ibid., III, pp. 183 ff.
XXVIII   ibid., pp. 495 ff.

William Beveridge:
XXIX   *Works,* Library of Anglo-Catholic Theology, Parker
             & Son, Oxford, 1845, VI, pp. 134 ff.

Francis Atterbury:
XXX   *Sermons and Discourses on Several Subjects and
             Occasions,* London, 1776, II, pp. 237 ff.

Jonathan Swift:
XXXI   *Irish Tracts and Sermons,* edited H. Davis, Blackwell,
             1963, pp. 190 ff.

Joseph Butler:
XXXII   *Works,* Macmillan, 1900, I, pp. 220 ff.
XXXIII   ibid., pp. 272 ff.

Thomas Wilson:
XXXIV   *Works,* Library of Anglo-Catholic Theology, Parker,
             Oxford, 1847, III, pp. 330 ff.

Thomas Sherlock:
XXXV   *Discourses Preached on Several Occasions,* J. Whiston,
             London, 1776, V, pp. 227 ff.

John Wesley:
    XXXVI   *Sermons on Several Occasions*, Wesleyian Conference Office, London, 1869, II, pp. 142 ff.
    XXXVII   ibid., pp. 119 ff.

Samuel Horsley:
    XXXVIII *Sermons*, London, 1824, II, pp. 420 ff.
    XXXIX   ibid., I, pp. 223 ff.

Thomas Whitaker:
    XL   *A Sermon Preached at the Consecration of the Chapel of Salesbury in Lancashire*, London, 1807, pp. 2 ff.

Thomas Arnold:
    XLI   *Sermons*, Fellowes Ltd, London, 1832, II, pp. 371 ff.
    XLII   ibid., pp. 403 ff.

Sydney Smith:
    XLIII   *Sermons Preached at St Paul's Cathedral*, etc. Longmans, 1846, pp. 187 ff.
    XLIV   ibid., pp. 367 ff.

Frederick Robertson:
    XLV   *Sermons on Religion and Life*, Everyman Library, J. M. Dent & Co., 1906, pp. 37 ff.

John Whittaker:
    XLVI   *A Sermon Preached at the Parish Church, Blackburn*, Blackburn, 1839, pp. 13 ff.

Frederick Maurice:
    XLVII *Sermons in Lincoln's Inn*, Macmillan, 1891, III, pp. 220 ff.

Samuel Wilberforce:
    XLVIII *Sermons*, Parker, Oxford, 1854, pp. 265 ff.

Charles Kingsley:
    XLIX   *The Message of Christ to Labouring Men*, London, 1851, pp. 13 ff.
    L   *The Water of Life*, Macmillan, 1876, pp. 190 ff.
    LI   *All Saints Day and Other Sermons*, Kegan Paul, 1878, pp. 302 ff.
    LII   ibid., pp. 57 ff.

Edward B. Pusey:
    LIII   *University Sermons*, Parker & Rivington, 1872, pp. 377 ff.

Joseph B. Lightfoot:

LIV   *Sermons Preached on Special Occasions*, Macmillan, 1891, pp. 28ff.

Henry P. Liddon:

LV   *University Sermons*, 2nd Series, Rivington, 1880, pp. 286ff.

Richard Church:

LVI   *Pascall and Other Sermons*, Macmillan, 1895, pp. 233ff.

William Thomson:

LVII   *Lincoln's Inn Sermons*, 1861, pp. 378ff.

John H. Newman:

LVIII   *Parochial and Plain Sermons*, Rivington, 1878, VII, pp. 29ff.

Robert W. Dolling:

LIX   *Lombard Street in Lent*, Stock, London, 1894, pp. 114ff.

Frederick W. Farrar:

LX   *Ephphata*, Macmillan, 1880, pp. 275ff.
LXI   *The World's Great Sermons*, compiled G. Kleiser, Funk & Wagnalls, 1909, VII, pp. 234ff.

Thomas Hancock:

LXII   *The Pulpit and the Press and Other Sermons*, Brown, Langham & Co., 1904, pp. 34ff.
LXIII   ibid., pp. 78ff.

Henry S. Holland:

LXIV   *Lombard Street in Lent*, Stock, London, 1894, pp. 5ff.
LXV   ibid., 1895, pp. 175ff.

James E. Welldon:

LXVI   *The Gospel in a Great City*, Smith, Elder & Co., 1910, pp. 29ff.
LXVII   ibid., pp. 40ff.

William Temple:

LXVIII   *Repton School Sermons*, Macmillan, 1913, pp. 169ff.
LXIX   *Fellowship with God*, Macmillan, 1920, pp. 37ff.

Edward Lyttleton:

LXX   *Lombard Street in Lent*, Stock, London, 1894, pp. 158ff.

H. Hensley Henson:

LXXI   *Godly Union and Concord*, Murray, 1902, pp. 169ff.

ACKNOWLEDGEMENTS

For permission to reprint copyright matter the following acknowledgements are made: for extracts from *Godly Union and Concord* by H. Hensley Henson and *The Gospel in a Great City* by James E. Welldon to John Murray (Publishers) Ltd; for extracts from *Repton School Sermons* and *Fellowship with God* by William Temple to Macmillan & Co. Ltd.

BIBLIOGRAPHY

General

BINYON, G. C., *The Christian Socialist Movement in England*, Society for Promoting Christian Knowledge, 1931.

BLENCH, J. W., *Preaching in England in the late 15th and 16th Centuries*, Blackwell, 1964.

BROWN, FORD K., *Fathers of the Victorians: The Age of Wilberforce*, Cambridge University Press, 1961.

DAVIES, G., 'English Political Sermons, 1603–1640', *Huntingdon Library Quarterly*, III.

EVANS, STANLEY G., *The Social Hope of the Christian Church*, Hodder & Stoughton, 1965.

FAULKNER, H. U., *Chartism and the Churches*, New York, 1916.

GLOYN, C. K., *The Church in the Social Order*, Pacific University, Oregon, 1942.

GREENSLADE, S. L., *The Church and Social Order*, Student Christian Movement Press, 1948.

HAWEIS, J. O. W., *Sketches of the Reformation and Elizabethan Age, taken from the Contemporary Pulpit*, London, 1844.

HEASMAN, K., *Evangelicals in Action*, Bles, 1962.

HERR, A. F., *The Elizabeth Sermon*, Philadelphia, 1940.

HILL, C., *Puritanism and Revolution*, Secker & Warburg, 1958.
   Society and Puritanism in Pre-Revolutionary England, Secker & Warburg, 1964.
   Reformation to Industrial Revolution, Weidenfeld and Nicolson, 1967.

HOWSE, E. M., *Saints in Politics*, University of Toronto Press, 1952.

INGLIS, K. S., *Churches and the Working Classes in Victorian England*, Routledge and Kegan Paul, 1963.

JONES, M. G., *The Charity School Movement*, Cambridge University Press, 1938.

JONES, P. D'A., *The Christian Socialist Revival, 1877–1914*, Oxford University Press, 1968.

JORDAN, W. K., *Philanthropy in England, 1480–1660*, Allen & Unwin, 1959.

LASLETT, P., *The World We Have Lost*, Methuen, 1965.

BIBLIOGRAPHY

LONGMATE, N., *King Cholera: the Biography of a Disease*, Hamish Hamilton, 1966.

MACLURE, M., *St Paul's Cross Sermons, 1534–1632*, Oxford University Press, 1958.

MAYOR, S., *The Churches and the Labour Movement*, Independent Press, 1967.

MORGAN, I., *Godly Preachers of the Elizabethan Church*, Epworth Press, 1965.

OLIVER, J., *The Church and Social Order: Social Thought in the Church of England, 1918–1939*, Mowbray, 1968.

OWEN, H. G., 'Paul's Cross: The Broadcasting House of Elizabethan London', *History Today*, Dec. 1962.

PECK, W. G., *Social Implications of the Oxford Movement*, New York, 1933.

RECKITT, M. B., *Maurice to Temple: A Century of the Social Movement in the Church of England*, Faber, 1947.
> *For Christ and the People: Studies of Four Socialist Priests and Prophets of the Church of England between 1870 and 1930*, Society for Promoting Christian Knowledge, 1968.

SCHLATTER, R. B., *The Social Ideas of Religious Leaders, 1660–1688*, Oxford University Press, 1940.

SOLOWAY, R. A., *Prelates and People. . . . 1783–1852*, Routledge and Kegan Paul, 1968.

TAWNEY, R. H., *Religion and the Rise of Capitalism*, J. Murray, 1926; Pelican Edition, 1938.

WAGNER, D. O., *The Church of England and Social Reform since 1854*, Columbia University Press, 1930.

WARD, J. T., *The Factory Movement*, Macmillan, 1962.

Biographical

Arnold, T.: BAMFORD, T. W., *Thomas Arnold*, Cresset Press, 1960.

Barrow, I.: OSMOND, P. H., *Isaac Barrow, His Life and Times*, Society for Promoting Christian Knowledge, 1944.

Butler, J.: MOSSNER, E. C., *Bishop Butler and the Age of Reason*, Macmillan, 1936.

Church, R.: SMITH, B. A., *Dean Church*, Oxford University Press, 1958.

Dolling, R. W.: OSBORNE, C. E., *Life of Dolling*, Edward Arnold, London, 1903.

Donne, J.: MUELLER, W. R., *John Donne: Preacher*, Oxford University Press, 1962.

Farrar, F. W.: FARRAR, R., *Life of Dean Farrar*, Nisbet, 1904.

Holland, H. S.: PAGET, S., *Henry Scott Holland*, John Murray, 1921.

Kingsley, C.: POPE-HENNESSY, U., *Canon Charles Kingsley*, Chatto and Windus, 1948.

Latimer, H.: DARBY, H. S., *Hugh Latimer*, Epworth Press, 1953.

Liddon, H. P.: JOHNSTON, J. O., *Life and Letters of Henry Parry Liddon*, Longmans, 1904.

Lightfoot, J. B.: ed. EDEN, G. R. and MACDONALD, F. C., *Lightfoot of Durham*, Cambridge University Press, 1932.

Maurice, F. D.: HIGHAM, FLORENCE, *Frederick Denison Maurice*, Student Christian Movement Press, 1947.

Newman, J. H.: ROBBINS, W., *The Newman Brothers*, Heinemann, 1966.

Pusey, E. B.: PRESTIGE, G. L., *Life of Pusey*, Philip Allan, London, 1933.

Robertson, F.: HENSON, H. H., *Robertson of Brighton, 1816–1853*, Smith Elder, London, 1916.

Sherlock, T.: CARPENTER, E. F., *Thomas Sherlock*, Society for Promoting Christian Knowledge, 1936.

Smith, S.: PEARSON, HESKETH, *The Smith of Smiths*, Hamish Hamilton, 1934; Penguin Books, 1948.

Swift, J.: JACKSON, R. W., *Swift, Dean and Pastor*, Society for Promoting Christian Knowledge, 1939.

Taylor, J.: STRANKS, C. J., *The Life and Writings of Jeremy Taylor*, Society for Promoting Christian Knowledge, 1952.

Temple, W.: IREMONGER, F. A., *William Temple*, Oxford University Press, 1948.

Thomson, W.: KIRK-SMITH, H., *William Thomson*, Society for Promoting Christian Knowledge, 1958.

Tillotson, J.: LOCKE, L. G., *Tillotson*, Copenhagen, 1954.

Wesley, J.: VULLIAMY, C. E., Epworth Press, 1954.

  DOUGHTY, W. L., *John Wesley, Preacher*, Epworth Press, 1955.

Wilberforce, S.: NEWSOME, D., *The Parting of Friends*, Murray, 1966.

INDEX

MORE ABOUT PENGUINS
AND PELICANS

Penguinews, which appears every month, contains details of all the new books issued by Penguins as they are published. From time to time it is supplemented by *Penguins in Print*, which is a complete list of all books published by Penguins which are in print. (There are well over three thousand of these.)

A specimen copy of *Penguinews* will be sent to you free on request, and you can become a subscriber for the price of the postage. For a year's issues (including the complete lists) please send 4s. if you live in the United Kingdom, or 8s. if you live elsewhere. Just write to Dept EP, Penguin Books Ltd, Harmondsworth, Middlesex, enclosing a cheque or postal order, and your name will be added to the mailing list.

Other books published by Penguins are described on the following pages.

Note: *Penguinews* and *Penguins in Print* are not available in the U.S.A. or Canada

ROMAN CATHOLICISM

Sebastian Bullough

The Roman Catholic Church is one of the two oldest and the largest communion of Christian believers.

In this new book Father Bullough, who is a Dominican and a member of that order's house at Cambridge, outlines the faith and practice of the Roman Catholic Church for the non-theologian – Catholic, Anglican, Protestant, Orthodox, or agnostic. He shows how the Christian vocation is fulfilled in Christian faith, is worked out in the life of the Church, bears fruit in the holy life, and has its effects in the world. But, above all, he shows that the main tenets of Catholicism are both reasonable and consistent.

At a time when Christians are drawing closer together and facts are vital to mutual understanding, this book must be of great interest to all believing Christians of whatever denomination.

Also available

METHODISM

THE ORTHODOX CHURCH

Timothy Ware

This book is a clear, detailed introduction to the Orthodox Church, written for the non-orthodox, as well as for Orthodox Christians who wish to know more about their own tradition. Part One describes the history of the Eastern Church over the last 2,000 years and particularly its problems in twentieth-century Russia. Part Two explains the beliefs and worship of the Orthodox today. Finally the author considers the possibilities of reunion between East and West.

During the last few years the interest of western Christians in the Orthodox Church has increased in a way that is altogether astonishing. Timothy Ware believes that an understanding of Orthodoxy is necessary before the Roman Catholic and Protestant Churches can be reunited, and here he explains the Orthodox views on such widely ranging matters as Ecumenical Councils, Sacraments, Freewill, Purgatory, Icons, the Papacy, Protestantism, and the relation between the different Orthodox Churches.

More than ten per cent of Russia's 208,000,000 people attend church regularly, even after fifty years of active hostility and persecution by the state. This book answers the questions most often asked about their faith.